Political Elites in Arab North Africa

Morocco, Algeria, Tunisia, Libya, and Egypt

I. William Zartman
Mark A. Tessler
John P. Entelis
Russell A. Stone
Raymond A. Hinnebusch
Shahrough Akhavi

Longman

New York & London

POLITICAL ELITES IN ARAB NORTH AFRICA
Morocco, Algeria, Tunisia, Libya, and Egypt

Longman Inc., 19 West 44th Street, New York, N.Y. 10036
Associated companies, branches, and representatives
throughout the world.

Copyright © 1982 by Longman Inc.

All rights reserved. No part of this publication may be
reproduced, stored in a retrieval system, or transmitted
in any form or by any means, electronic, mechanical,
photocopying, recording, or otherwise, without the prior
permission of the publisher.

Developmental Editor: Irving E. Rockwood
Editorial and Design Supervisor: Diane Perlmuth
Manufacturing and Production Supervisor: Robin B. Besofsky
Printing and Binding: BookCrafters, Inc.

Library of Congress Cataloging in Publication Data
Main entry under title:
Political elites in Arab North Africa.
Includes bibliographies and index.
1. Africa, North — Politics and government.
2. Elite (Social sciences) — Africa, North.
I. Zartman, I. William.
DT176.P6   306'.2'096   81-145
ISBN 0-582-28251-9 AACR2

Manufactured in the United States of America
9 8 7 6 5 4 3 2 1

to
RLW
and
RBW,
political elites

Acknowledgments

This study was made possible by a grant from the United States International Communications Agency's Office of Research· It should be noted, however, that the inclusion of material on Libya was outside the scope of the original USICA grant. In particular the project benefitted greatly from the professional guidance and assistance of Mr. Ralph Greenhouse of the Research Office. In expressing our appreciation for this support, we must also point out that USICA does not endorse the conclusions of this work nor do the contents reflect official U.S. Government opinion or policy.

In addition to this grant, this project also received support from the National Endowment for the Humanities through the American Research Center in Egypt, which is also most gratefully acknowledged.

During the preparation of the chapters, a review conference was held, involving the participation of the authors and James Allman of Battelle Institute, Abdelmalik Aouda of the University of Cairo, Charles Butterworth of the University of Maryland, Carleton Coon of the Department of State, David Gibson and Ralph Greenhouse of the USICA, Iliya Harik of Indiana University, Farhad Kazemi of New York University, Robert Mortimer of Haverford College, Fareed Trabulsi of the American Embassy in Algiers, Ahmed Rhazaoui of the University Mohammed V, and Abdelkader Zghal of the University of Tunis. Their contribution is also gratefully acknowledged.

Contents

About the Authors

I. William Zartman, Director of the African Studies Program at the School for Advanced International Studies of The Johns Hopkins University, is well-known among students of comparative politics for his extensive publications on Africa and the Middle East. His articles have appeared in such journals as *Journal of Conflict Resolution, Etudes Internationales, Foreign Affairs, International Journal of Middle East Studies, Journal of International Affairs, World Politics, Africa Report, Middle East Journal*, and *International Organization*. He has written, edited, or contributed to more than 40 books, and his most recent publications include *Elites in The Middle East* (Praeger, 1980) and *Africa in the 1980s: A Continent in Crisis* (McGraw Hill, 1979).

Mark A. Tessler, Professor of Political Science at University of Wisconsin-Milwaukee, has conducted extensive field research in Africa and the Middle East under the auspices of the Social Science Research Council, the American Philosophical Society and the American Universities Field Staff. He has also received two Fulbright Lectureship awards. His articles have appeared in *International Journal of Middle East Studies, The Maghreb Review, Western Political Quarterly, Middle East Journal, Social Science Quarterly, The New Republic*, and *Comparative Political Studies*. He has contributed chapters to nearly a dozen books, including three that he edited, and is the coauthor of *Tradition and Identity in Changing Africa* (Harper and Row, 1973).

John P. Entelis, Professor of Political Science at Fordham University, is a long-term student of politics in North Africa and the Middle East. His published articles have appeared in such journals as *International Studies Quarterly, Arab Journal, International Journal of Middle East Studies, The Journal of Modern African Studies, Orbis*, and *Polity*. He is the author of *Comparative Politics of North Africa* (Syracuse University Press, 1980) and a coauthor of *The Government and Politics of The Middle East and North Africa* (Westview, 1980).

Russell A. Stone, Associate Professor of Sociology at State University of New York at Buffalo, is a specialist in the culture of the Middle East and Arab North Africa. He has published articles in such journals as *International Journal of Middle East Studies, International Review of History and Political Science*, and *Africa Report*. He has contributed chapters to several books and has edited or coedited two others, *Change in Tunisia: Studies in the Social Sciences* (State University of New York Press, 1976), and *OPEC and The Middle East: The Impact of Oil on Societal Development* (Praeger, 1977). His current research activities include a study of Israeli public opinion and further work on Tunisian elites.

Raymond A. Hinnebusch is Assistant Professor of Political Science at the College of St. Catherine in St. Paul, Minnesota. Previously he was a member of the Political Science faculty at the American University in Cairo. His published work includes several studies of party organization, rural policy and political recruitment in Syria published by AUC and in the *Middle East Journal* and *International Journal of Middle East Studies* and forthcoming articles on political change in Egypt and on the Islamic movement in Syria.

Shahrough Akhavi, Associate Professor of Government and International Studies at University of South Carolina, is a specialist in Egyptian and Iranian politics. He has contributed chapters and articles to several books and journals on these subjects and recently published *Religion and Politics in Contemporary Iran* (State University of New York Press, 1980). His current research interests include the political economy of the Middle East peace and the political culture of Egyptian workers. He conducted field research in Iran in 1975 on a Ford Foundation grant and in Egypt in (1980–1981) under a grant from NEH and ARCE.

1

Political Elites in Arab North Africa:
Origins, Behavior and Prospects

I. William Zartman

Politics can best be understood through a study of those who exercise power—those who make the decisions and rules that run society. Although the institutions through which they act or the issues that challenge and constrain them are important, it is the elites of politics who operate the political system. Elites are known through their origins, their behavior, their relation to the rest of society, and their ways of entrance and exit. Used separately, these elements provide a comprehensive portrait of those in power; combined, they constitute a dynamic of their own that impels society in explicable directions. Developing countries have fewer elites than developed countries, but the importance of the elites is predominant in both. Arab North Africa — Morocco, Algeria, Tunisia, Libya, and Egypt — is no exception.

But what is an "elite"? One notion of "elite" that is both real and useful refers to those few individuals who occupy the top political positions — ministers and top military and party leaders, varying according to the particular national institutions of power — plus any other individuals with an equivalent role in decision making. These people can be called the "core elite", but such a restrictive definition does not cover all the meanings of relevance.

A larger category may be termed the "general elite(s)", referring to those, in whatever institutional position, who are regularly in political contact with the core elite and therefore in a position to provide policy input on a regular basis. The term can be in the plural because different parts of the general elite may be operative only on specific policies or policy areas, a differentiation that may be useful to specify during parts of the discussion. When used alone, "elite" here will refer to both categories, the general elite including within it the core elite.

Elites, however, do not work in a vacuum, and it is one of the mistaken implications of some elite studies to suggest that they do. In any society, they are related in some way to the masses or the nonelites — those who wield a disproportionately small amount of power or none at all. The way in which they are related, the degree of disproportion, and the nature of the gap between the two are all empirical questions to be addressed to individual polities. Elites make their careers on the backs of the population, whose feelings do not become movements, demands, or programs until they find a leader and spokesman. Even in polities such as those of northern Africa, where neither power nor the choice of those who do exercise it is in the hands of the people, political elites are linked to the population both directly and through various kinds of intermediates.

The latter, the subelites, fill a number of functions. Opinion makers are the purveyors of publicly available information and ideas, through press and radio, books, movies, and speeches, as well as educational lectures and religious sermons. Their audience includes both the public and the elite, and they may be independent of, inspired or controlled by the elite. Mediators carry messages, questions and answers and supplies and demands up and down between elite and people. They are "tax farmers in power," drawing off some of the commodity in which they deal to establish and enhance their own position. Administrators benefit in the same way but operate only in one direction. Their power is considerable in small areas, and under the guise of executing they too make decisions. A number of other categories could be added, although it should be clear that reality is not as neatly divisible as separate names might suggest.

Elites are political in that the term refers to those who wield a disproportionately large amount of power or participate in making nationally authoritative decisions. There are also social elites (who have a disproportionate amount of social value or prestige) and economic elites (who have a disproportionate amount of economic value or money), but the term "elite" is used here without an adjective when referring to political elites simply to lighten the language. It is an empirical question, to be decided country by country, whether there are separate political, economic, and social pyramids. In other words, elites with prestige and/or money may also have power to participate in making nationally authoritative decisions but do not necessarily do so by definition.

In Arab North Africa, the general (political) elite covers most of the economic elite and much of the social elite. Some individuals with wealth avoid or are unable to obtain regular contact with the core elite (more in Egypt than elsewhere because of sheer numbers), primarily because of the old Middle Eastern notion that politics and economics are best kept separate and that economic activities are more likely to suffer from discovery than to benefit from protection. A larger segment of those with prestige do not cultivate regular contact with the core elite because their prestige comes from intellectual or religious activity that does not require government concern; but the more successful this segment becomes, the harder it is to avoid government surveillance. In general, however, political activity tends to confer wealth and prestige, and wealth and prestige frequently require political involvement and power or invite political control. A few former core-elite members are poor, but not many, and most retain some prestige. In fact, retired core-elite members, even from the opposition, often continue to draw their salaries in unemployment.

Although political elites are usually those who occupy top institutional positions, the term "political" does not restrict them to institutions alone; even core elites may include individuals who are powerful — in the above sense — without holding a regular state job. Whether or not they do is also an empirical question, to be established state by state. In Arab North Africa, the core elites tend to be those in top positions. Position confers authority, and if individuals should rise in political importance outside of office, they tend to be rewarded by appointment to formalize their authority. The middle elite does include some people outside the public sector, although they constitute a small minority of the general elite because the private sector is generally small. ("Public" includes party and national organizations.) Where they do exist — above all in Morocco, Tunisia, and Egypt — such nonstate members of the middle elite include big businessmen (particularly those with international connections), doctors, journalists, lawyers, engineers, and large landowners.

Understanding a polity requires an understanding of its elites — who they are and what they do. But there are no shortcuts: Understanding who they are alone is not enough to explain what they do. Such an intellectual leap has been promised by the Marxists, but it is invalid. Of course, one thing elites will usually do (but not always) is defend their position, for they cannot do whatever else they want to do without hanging on to the means — the power their position carries — to do it. Again, how much time they spend in position politics and how much in program politics is an empirical question, although one that is difficult to interpret. Just as difficult is the question about individual motivational mixes, between the desire to enjoy the position oneself and the desire to carry out programs benefiting others. Beyond that, repeated research attempts have been unable to establish any unique and direct correlations between elite characteristics and elite behavior. This is not to deny relationships between the two but to point out that such relationships are ambiguous and mediated by other variables, such as attitudes or structure. Interestingly, the roots and reasons of an action may well be found in the characteristics of the actor, but those same characteristics may also underlie other, and even opposite, actions.

Yet characteristics are important because they relate to position politics more than to program politics. If elites circulate freely in terms of age, socioeconomic backgrounds, regional origins, or even programatic orientations, their politics will be different toward their position and their competitors and aspirant successors than if incumbents hold on to their positions. Entrenchment, along any dimension, tends to create resentment and rebellion on the part of those excluded. Comprehensive core elites — broadly representative along a number of dimensions — are generally associated with times of power consolidation; cohesive elites, characteristically homogeneous, are often associated with times of programatic innovation. Institutional channels will be used during routine operations; informal networks will be relied on in times of crisis.

Such questions and hypotheses will be important in forming the following inquiry into northern African elites. First, in this initial chapter, the general characteristics of the elites in the five countries at the beginning of the 1980s will be presented, collectively where similarities exist and individually where the polities differ. Second, the elites so characterized will be placed within more dynamic concerns and patterns, related to generations, values, issues, and policies, in order to portray the past circulation of elites in Arab North Africa over the preceding two decades and then, third, to prepare for understanding new evolutions in the 1980s.

CHARACTERISTICS

Elites in all five countries are concentrated in and around executive institutions of national government. Anyone outside this institutional location who has influence on the national decision-making process is a personal exception; he may be individually important but his case is numerically rare. Important members of the elite may be rewarded with nonexecutive positions (for example, nomination to the national assembly) or with ad hoc executive positions (for example, advisor to the president), so even in these cases there is still an effort to institutionalize personal influence.

The only temporary exception to a clear executive pyramid occurs after a shift in leadership (for example, the successions of Benjedid in Algeria, Sadat in Egypt and a future figure in Tunisia) where the hierarchy of personal roles needs about a year to be worked out to fit the formal presidential system; there, the newcomer does not stand as high above his peers as did his predecessor, but restoration of clear presidential supremacy is only a matter of time.

The main category of influentials outside institutional positions can be called the "fixers." These individuals, with personal contacts within the general elite born of past experiences together or of family ties, facilitate arrangements and contacts, frequently of a commercial nature but occasionally also political. They are not decision-makers, and the integrity of their role is maintained by keeping it procedural rather than substantive.

Fixers form a new, growing, and very large group of people in Egypt, ranging from subcontractors to black marketeers, who operate in the interstices between the state and the private sectors. In Morocco, Libya, Tunisia, and Algeria, a similar situation exists. But the group of fixers is small in Morocco and Libya, still smaller in Tunisia, and smaller still although not unimportant in Algeria. This category may also include former political figures (formal position holders) who have retired or fallen from favor. The function is characteristic of the region; only its size varies by country.

In Arab North Africa in the 1980s, higher education is the most common characteristic and hence the most important predictor of membership in the general elite, after male sex. Higher education is necessary for core elite membership in Egypt, and it is only slightly less important in Morocco, Algeria, and Tunisia. But in Libya, higher education is the most common characteristic of the general elite rather than of the present core elite. Age is not very important; while the members of the core elite are oldest in Egypt and Tunisia and youngest in Libya, the average age is still the late 40s, and the general elite has a fairly wide spread of ages.

The core elites in Egypt, Algeria, and Tunisia tend to come from small towns with an important admixture from the major city (Tunisia and Egypt) or cities (Algeria). The reverse is true in Morocco, where the core elite is Fassi in origin, with additions from other towns and cities. In Libya, the core is rural. General-elite members benefit from easier access and promotion when they have common origins with core-elite members, but general elites also come from elsewhere in the country.

No matter where they come from, general elites are likely to be concentrated in the capital city, with some allowance being made for more complex urban structures in Algeria and Morocco. The capital is the concentrated center of decision making, and the capital culture is predominant. Other areas, including other large cities, tend to be "the provinces," except in Morocco. Assignment to a provincial center may afford a certain autonomy to an elite member and even the ability to build a local political clientele, but his national influence must generally be exercised in the capital. This does not mean that provincial assignment is exile, however; an important position in a provincial center may be a good springboard to a higher position in the capital (for example, Benjedid in Oran over Bouteflika and Yahiaoui).

The antidote to the pervasiveness of the capital culture is the continued maintenance of ties back home. For example, Fassis go home to Fez for their weddings and family gatherings and Algerois visit their family members that remained home in their native town; Bourguiba made his hometown of Monastir the showplace of the Sahel, and Sadat chose his village of Mit Abu Kom as his year-round retreat. In another generation, ties to the village will be under greater strain, but for the moment elites are in part delegates from their hometown or region to the capital and the capital is only the agglomeration of regional representatives: a Washington rather than a Paris. Predictably, this will change as the region loses power and the elites find that their interest ties up with the capital. This change has already begun in Tunisia and Egypt, more than in the other three countries of Arab North Africa.

Elites in Arab North Africa are the products of significant social promotion (upward mobility) over the past quarter century. Judged by the professions of their fathers, elites tend to have middle- and lower-middle-class socioeconomic origins. This is predominantly so in Algeria, Libya, and Tunisia and importantly so, with some upper-middle- and upper-class origins as well, in Egypt and Morocco. Across the area, middle- and even lower-middle-class elites came to power through violent overthrow and revolution against the colonial or monarchial regime that had kept them out, and they opened the way for broadened social promotion. The "class average" and spread of core elites vary from country to country, but in all five countries both rural and lower-class urban origins are widespread in the general elites. In all five countries, tribe and sect are insignificant as criteria for elite membership. In Morocco and Algeria, however, some ethnic (Berber) and regional balance are required for core-elite membership.

Interests are organized by and in support of the party-government elites in Arab North Africa, and interest-group leaders are allowed to press their own demands as long as this support remains. Constraints on such expression are loosest in Morocco and Egypt and tightest in Libya; organized interests are under considerable tension between demands from below and controls from above in Algeria and Tunisia. Interest-group leaders are certainly members of the general elite, but they rarely find their way into the core elite in any country in the area. The only prominent exception is constituted by elite members who rise through the student union or party youth wing, but this is an age phase rather than a function of interest representation. The other singular exception is the head of the labor union in Tunisia, who is generally part of the party political bureau and hence part of the core elite; elsewhere the position is one of sectorial control rather than of core-elite membership. Rather than coopt business, labor, or farm elites into their midst, the core elite coopt the demands of these groups and manage their spokesmen, bringing them into the general elite but replacing them with more manageable spokesmen if the occasion requires.

Besides the military (in Algeria, Libya, and Egypt), the professional origins of core elites are most frequently found in teaching (in all five countries) and engineering (especially in Egypt and Tunisia) and secondarily in administration and law. "Professional origins" refer to the individual's first job or the job for which he was trained. In all five countries, general elites come increasingly from business and administration schools and faculties and from technical faculties, notably engineering. Liberal professions (medicine and law) are major sources of general elites only in Tunisia and Morocco, as they were to the *ancien regime* (and are suddenly reappearing) in Egypt. To a large extent, core and many general elites in the five countries are now and will increasingly be trained directly for government service and rise to core-elite positions from within the civilian and military bureaucracy, rather than from outside; their education is in administrative law, management, or engineering. Even where elections come to constitute a means of recruitment from the private sector into legislative and then executive positions, the same professional background predominates: education, management, engineering, plus public-sector employment in the same professional areas. Farming, labor, and small business are not and are not likely to be sources of general or core elites.

Unlike many of the other components of the elite, the military plays very different roles in each of the five countries. In Algeria, the top officer corps is the guardian of the institutionalized state, the largest interest group within the elite, and the source of important position-holders in the cabinet and some other political institutions as well as in the military regions and other military bodies. In Egypt, the military is in much the same position, only less prominent in civilian positions. In Morocco, the military is still reeling from its decimation by king and mutineers alike in the early 1970s and has been removed from an earlier involvement in civilian positions of government. But it is still the most powerful interest group in society and one that may again turn against the throne if humiliated in the Saharan affair. In Tunisia, the military is a tightly organized and controlled interest group, allowed involvement only in security affairs but still able to intervene in political affairs if the succession crisis were to turn sharply worse after Bourguiba's death. In Libya, the army is in a similar position, despite many other differences; former senior officers have been retired, and those promoted in their places are held outside of politics by the core elite of Free Officers.

In all five countries, religious figures are absent from the core elite and are minor members of the general elite. Leading *'ulama* (theologians) have access to the core elite but do not provide a major influence on matters of political decision. The equivalent of the clergy in Sunni Islam — sheikhs of sects, ordinary *imams* and most of the *'ulama* — do not fall within the definition of the general elite in Arab North Africa. Secular members of the elite have their own religious views, and core elites frequently include a member with more fundamentalist religious views than the rest. Such a member tends to be a representative of his viewpoint rather than a representative of a sector of activity, protecting it from secular encroachments. General religious concerns and sensitivity to Muslim symbols are matters of political culture in all five countries, but the elite do not govern according to specific religious principles. The apparent exception is Libya, although the neo-Islamic *Green Book* of

Qaddafi is the guide, not the Quran itself. Elites will use Muslim references and signs of identity in their discourse, but this does not mean that they are about to rule according to the Quran.

The most important prediction of elite membership after higher education and male sex is shared experience with incumbent members of the core elite, although its form may be very diverse. Shared experiences may take the form of common education (Morocco, Algeria, Tunisia, and Egypt); common regional origin (Morocco, Egypt, but especially Algeria); common nationalist experience (Algeria); common occupational experience (Morocco, Algeria, Tunisia, Libya, and Egypt); or family connections by blood or friendship.

In each country there is an informal structure or group of individuals in positions of power around the president, comprising about six to eight people whose ties include a history of experience together plus some family or regional ties. These groups are continuing but are somewhat flexible, as members fall out of favor and return or individuals in new institutional positions rise to the attention of the head of state and find favor. As informal networks, they are important sources of recruitment, communication, and interests within the general elite of all five countries. But they operate within the framework of government institutions and positions, not outside, and they are frequently established on the basis of modern criteria and experiences. On the other hand, their specific nature is different in each country.

In Algeria, patron-client networks are the basis of politics. Junior members seek to attach themselves to a member of the core elite in a relationship that is durable but not permanent and that can be rearranged by shifts in political fortunes or new experiences. The basis of the relationship is found in some element of commonality — region, wartime experience, political experience, common education and, rarely, ideological compatibility. In Tunisia, factional groups tend to have greater ideological homogeneity, and they contain a number of political leaders (core-elite members or former members) and their followers rather than comprising the clients of a single individual. In Morocco, family ties of blood or marriage are the primary characteristic, and ideological affinities are much less important. Such ties in Morocco constitute networks rather than groups and are modernized versions of the segmentary system, in which each family unit maintained ties to both sides of every major political divide. In Egypt, individuals are members of many groups (*shillas*), by school, region or profession, providing a choice of communications channels and affinities. Such groups may also constitute political groups of friends devoted to watching out for their common interests and promotions. Although the existence of the small core elite as a cohesive group (*shilla*) in Libya appears on many occasions, the nature of members' links with followers is unclear. Thus, each network takes a specifically national form, with the common characteristic that each provides effective channels to bypass and link together formal political structures.

Three networks operate in all the countries to hold the core — and beyond it, the general — elite together. One is the network of official lines of authority and communications about the position the individual occupies. The bureaucratic structure of the five governments means that such vertical institutional channels are primary. The second is the network of groups and personal ties, sometimes merely old-boy networks and sometimes clearly patron-client chains, that cuts across institutional structures. The conspiratorial origins of all five governments (in national movements or military coups) in their recent past, as well as the still-personal nature of politics, means that such "diagonal" channels are important. The third is the grapevine of communications that keeps elite members overinformed about the goings-on of other elite members, usually with enough error and exaggeration that it becomes important to reinforce rather than reduce it.

Muslim societies of northern Africa operate within a traditional view of politics that considers power to be the legitimate arena of the political elite. As a result, individuals doing lesser things (citizens) or other things (businessmen, *'ulama*) do best to keep clear of politics and elites. On the other side of the coin, such attitudes form a ready basis for charismatic leadership or for a sharply representative notion of government, according to which a specific minority does the business of governing for the rest. Such attitudes also lead citizen-observers to disassociate themselves from internecine conflicts and to follow the winner, rather than taking sides "The sharks are at it again," is a common expression. This does not mean that democratic notions of government are absent but merely that they are rare, new, and imported and to become widely adopted, they face an uphill struggle against both traditional views and modern incumbents.

One of many offshoots of this traditional approach to elite power is that it prepares both the mediating and the bureaucratic function. Mediation, both in the form of upward supplication and in the form of easing the downward burden of power on the subjects, is an important traditional concept of politics that has carried over into modern life, coloring — for example — the idea of representation when candidates are elected to office. Bureaucracy also takes on a special function, as a modern extension of the group of people exercising power and giving them great prestige as defenders of regulations, but not admitting them into an inner elite who make decisions (cf. Weinbaum in Zartman 1980).

Little is known, in either the theoretical or the applied sense, about the relationship between who elites are and what they do. In general, each regime has an image that corresponds to a number of decisions it makes and that relates the nature of the elite to the use of power. Nothing guarantees that these images correspond to any individual member of the elite, however. In Morocco and Egypt, the elite follows policies that seek to increase the size and satisfaction of the upper and middle classes, which are the basis of its power. In Tunisia, the elite uses its power to favor the middle classes; in Algeria, the middle and urban-lower classes; and in Libya, the urban and rural lower-levels of the population. Such aims change relatively rapidly: Under Nasser, the Egyptian elites disfavored the upper classes and favored the promotion of lower-class elements into the middle class, while under Boumediene Algerian programs sought to improve the lot of the rural lower-classes.

Elites always pursue some mixture of two goals: using power to maintain positions and to resolve problems. In the first category, elites in all five countries control and repress their opposition: While opposition parties are banned in Algeria, they are selectively licensed in Tunisia and Egypt, and are permitted in Morocco if not opposed to the monarchial system. Opponents are assassinated in Libya, jailed as political prisoners and then amnestied in Morocco and Tunisia, harassed bureaucratically and exiled in Egypt, and controlled or exiled in Algeria. More broadly, the core elite's strategy of power in Morocco is to rally all political forces about the Saharan issue and to take the edge off problems as they arise. In Tunisia, the core elite seeks to build support within a unitary political system by developing broad agreements with interest groups and socioeconomic sectors, giving them enough socioeconomic security for them to see their interests assured through the continuance of the existing system. In Algeria, the core elite seeks to organize all political forces under the framework of the party-state and then to mobilize them for increased productivity and improved services. In Egypt, the current position-power strategy hangs largely on maintaining movement and initiative in foreign affairs while harnessing political forces in productive competition in politics and economics. In Libya, the revolutionary elite seeks to transform society by mobilizing followers and eliminating opponents, while using the revenues of petroleum production to improve living standards.

In all five countries, organization is the most important source of power, given the high degree of centralization within the political system. Private benefits are achieved above all through access to government, and government provides such benefits by monopolizing the employment of technical skills. Thus the very primacy of organization brings in skills and access as additional sources of power. Access, in Tunisia, is used to reinforce the power of an auxiliary organization, the party, whereas in Morocco and Egypt access is increasingly in the hands of the fixers; access, however, as noted above, is by definition a secondary, not a decision-making, power. Because of the primacy of organization, political reliability is more important than skills as a source of power and a criterion for selection and promotion of elites.

On the basis of the little information available, the major characteristic of sectorial power is that, outside of the presidency or monarchy, it is channeled along lines of institutional competence (for example, educational policy is made by the ministry of education with related interest organizations — youth organization, teachers' union, education section of the party, and so on—providing inputs). This characteristic seems to hold for all five countries, although there is little evidence on which to base a comprehensive conclusion and therefore to judge any changes. (Studies on sectorial decision making are far out of date because they are drawn from a past era when scholarly access to government machinery was more liberally open; cf. Moore 1965, Zartman 1964. Current studies of sectorial policy do not focus on power and decision making; cf. Baker 1978.)

Innovation and change seem to come more from individuals and from situations than from identifiable elite elements. However, sources of change appear most clearly in structural terms. Pressure for change in all five countries comes from the parties or from organized or anomic opposition, in threat if not in practice, rather than from within the core elite, showing the importance of pluralism in a political system even if the system does not encourage it. In the early years of independence or re-gime change (in Egypt), change and innovation came from within the new government, which was the opposition newly arrived in power. As time has passed, the incumbent elites have come to appear to excell most in management of "things as they are." Pressures for change as well as in-novative ideas have come from within the political parties—particularly the loyal opposition—trying to carve out a place in the political system (in Morocco); from the political factions and the labor union speaking from their program or their position of interest (in Tunisia); and from a preemptive response to popular dissatisfaction expressed by ad hoc groups (in Algeria and Egypt). To draw back another step and state a broader conclusion in different terms, pressure for change comes from spokesmen for lower socioeconomic groups or parts of society seeking better conditions in comparison with the urban bourgeoisie because that is the group in power. In Egypt and Tunisia, the disfavored groups are the urban workers and unemployed intellectuals (including students); in Morocco, the peasantry also qualifies as a disfavored group, in Libya, the urban middle-classes are the ones whose expectations are least well met; in Algeria, the sources of dissatisfaction are more diffused and less well identified.

Most of the core and general elites in the five countries were trained in their leading national university—Mohammed V (Rabat), Algiers, Tunis, and Cairo. A second and smaller group of the core and general elites received their university education in the leading universities of the former metropole—France in the Maghreb and England in Egypt—with no particular concentration within the metropolitan university systems. This second group is largest in Morocco and slightly smaller in Tunisia and Algeria. A third group were trained in the United States—nearly as many as in English universities for Egypt, a smaller percentage than in the metropole in the Maghreb—with no particular concentration in any university in the United States. The rest were trained at different educational institutions — other Arab universities or other European universities and a few have no university training at all.

In university training, the prestige of the university is extremely important — Harvard, Sorbonne, Oxford, and the leading national universities are more impressive than Colorado, Rennes, Manchester, or the lesser national universities. But this said, like prestige itself, its importance can be exaggerated and must be tempered by many other elements. There are elite members from Colorado, Rennes, and so on, and a degree from Harvard or Oxford alone is not trumps; skills and connections (informal networks) are. Scientific education, tends to be most prestigious, but there are few scientists in the general or core elites. Education, management/administration, engineering and even law — that is, fields that train people for the work of politics and government — are and will remain dominant.

"Traditional" patterns of elite circulation — that is, those based on tribe, land, and religion and separate from secular education — are irrelevant in all five countries. Even wealth per se is unlikely to bring individuals into the core elite, although to the extent that a wealthy man needs official contacts, he will enter into the general elite. Since there is now in Egypt and still in Morocco a greater chance than in Tunisia and Algeria of becoming wealthy independent of official position and also a greater chance than in Libya of becoming wealthy at all, wealth in Morocco and Egypt can lead to official position.

Recruitment and circulation in all five countries are essentially a "modern" process, little different from the process in Washington or Paris, with two exceptions: The role of "good schools" is probably less important in Arab North Africa because the range of higher education institutions is smaller and selection processes are more random; and the role of informal networks is probably more important because there are not very many institutionalized (civil service) processes that are as developed. The ingredients of recruitment and promotion are (1) performance and (2) "coming to the attention" of a higher appointive authority. The ingredients of the latter involve a patron or intercessor (informal networks) and a position of some independent responsibility and authority where the candidate can perform visibly and effectively. Thus, an ambitious college graduate would seek an initial position of assistant to a high figure and, for his second position, a post of independent authority, probably not much differently than he would do in the West.

In Algeria, this means that an individual begins to achieve visibility as a young chief of a *daira* (local administrative district), as a director of an administrative unit in a ministry, as a staff officer in a military region, or as military director of an administrative (not military) unit; a subsequent step would be *wali* (governor), ambassador, or secretary-general of a ministry. More is known about Algeria than about the other four countries in these terms, but this description is probably generally applicable.

Since the parliamentary experiment (in its present form) is new in all countries but Tunisia, it is not yet clear where parliament fits into such career patterns. In Tunisia and probably in the other four countries, parliament seems to be a holding pool, where elite members can be rewarded and held in readiness—"laterally promoted"—until a better opportunity appears. In Egypt, Algeria, and Tunisia, at least, keeping present and visible for a decade until the next opportunity appears is as important as making the next jump itself.

DYNAMICS

So seem the elites of Arab North Africa at the beginning of the 1980s. But they have changed over the past decades, and in another decade or two they will be different in a number of ways. The elites of the past have been described in studies, but such successive snapshots still do not tell how elites evolve from past to present. Potential elites of the future have been less frequently studied (see Ashford 1964, Waterbury 1970, Entelis 1974), so events of the coming decades are bound to arrive as a surprise unless there is a sense of likely evolutions from now until then.

There is no lack of proposals on the way to comprehend such evolutions. The handles that have been advanced range from modernization, class formation, group formation, and role specification to secularization and revolution. Some authors describe rather broad trends—indisputable in their sweep, but without a sense of when or how. Others focus on one important phenomenon but make it the only explanatory viariable for a whole field of effects. Still others, of course, fix on an evolution that is closer to their likes than to likelihood or confuse what must happen with what will happen. The challenge of identifying trends and forces that tie past to present and lead into future is one of accuracy, but it is also one of combining specificity and comprehensiveness. One variable alone is insufficient to encompass the flow of events, and broadening it to cover all destroys its discriminating capabilities. The problem then becomes one of identifying several variables and trends and combining then.

A number of trends and forces govern the circulation of elites in Arab North Africa. Some are universal while some are area-specific; or, otherwise stated, some can be applied deductively while some appear from past performance and seem to have imposed their rhythm by that fact. Most trends and cycles cannot escape human control: If an event meets a response that is satisfying to its consumers, a predictable time span is likely to occur before a new challenge appears, but if the response does not work out or if it is upset by exogenous events such as death or war or the overwhelming effect of an interfering trend, the expected cycle will be cut short and begun again. With this kind of conceptual flexibility, it may sound as if all that can be understood is the idiosyncrasy of the past and the uncertainty of the future. Yet more general results can be effected in both directions.

The basic variable is the experiential cohort or political generation. Because of the nature of socialization in response to the different historical experiences of their countries and because of the shifts that occur with time in the nature of issues facing them, elites can be seen as bunches of individuals with similar experiences and attitudes coming to power, hanging on for a while, and then being replaced in a smooth or not-so-smooth transfer to a new generation. Because rules for succession are unclear and uninstitutionalized, alternance among different groups and policy options within the same elite generation is much less characteristic of Arab North Africa (and perhaps of other areas of the developing world as well) than is generational incumbency and succession. Generations of elites are best described in terms of formative characteristics and resultant attitudes. Experience and attitudes toward government, culture, and economics are three identifying aspects of each generation that change as one experiential cohort reacts to and replaces another. These dimensions cannot be combined in any simple, additive way, and their cycles are not necessarily coincident. Instead, they provide component and often competing pressures in the elite's attitudes and actions — sometimes producing indecisive and undistinguished results and sometimes creating elites with strong and salient orientations, actions, and solutions, all according to the way in which the particular characteristics fit together.

Rising elites have their attitudes shaped at a number of times during their careers, but primarily during their "formative years" that is, late teens and early 20s and secondarily on the job. The primary round of socialization forms general attitudes toward the political system, shaping them as a function of the issues through which the person has lived and of his experience — negative or positive — with government in general. Successive elite generations in Arab North Africa have been socialized negatively by their experiences toward government. This means that they form their attitudes in rejection of the current form of government because of its perceived insufficiencies, turning against colonial government, party government, and military government as a result. Consequently, elites in the five countries are on a double search: for a modernizing ideology to replace the political functions of prescription and solidarity originally provided by Islam and then, in the minds of a few, by Western ideas of modernity, and for a form of government to replace each of those three successive experiments — colonial, party and military — in law and order and interest aggregation (that is, the assembling of component public interests into a national program).

In regard to ideology, the cultural history of the Arab world over the past century has been one of a dialectical search for an acceptable combination of modernity and authenticity (cf Khadduri 1970, CEMAM 1980, Laroui 1967, Laroui 1974). Again and again, faced with a culture that is national but traditional, a small group of secular intellectuals have arisen to advocate a culture that is modern, even though it is also foreign. After a time of conflict, a synthesis between national-traditional and foreign-modern is made, in which the negative characteristics — traditionalism, foreignness — are removed and a national, modern combination is achieved. In time (usually the time of a generation) this amalgam is again challenged as being too foreign and alien, and a new attempt to find a national identity in terms relevant to the contemporary world is made. Eventually, a new synthesis results. Sometimes it crystallizes about a striking elite figure. Before independence, this synthesis was produced by the nationalist movement, which combined Westernized leaders of reform groups with more traditional masses. One example among many is that of the Young Tunisians and the old Destour producing the Neo-Destour of Bourguiba; half a century after the party's creation, Bourguiba is rejected by many younger Tunisians as being too Western. In Arab North Africa, reactions to the West in a broad cultural context, outside of momentary political swings, must be placed within this dialetic — the constant element of which is a search for identity, values, and ways that are both modern and national. Hence there is always a degree of emulation of the form for its content, and there is always a degree of rejection of the content for its form.

One current version of the antithesis to Westernistic modernization is radical rightist or neotraditionalist — a response to the needs for values, progress, and identity, but one that finds its answers in modernizing tradition rather than in nationalizing modernity. It is important to understand this neotraditionalist movement as part of the drive for answers to the same questions, rather than as a rejection of all modernity. Neotraditionalism in Arab North Africa is often strikingly open and "modern," rather than merely a return to an unaltered past doctrine. Psychology courses at al-Azhar University in Egypt and Islamic Socialism in the doctrine of the Istiqlal party in Morocco are examples of something more than just "old time religion," something that is non-Western but not unapproachable.

Another way of being both modernist and anti- Western is to be radical leftist or Marxist-Leninist, a specific version of modernism that is universalist rather than nationalist. The attraction of Marxism-Leninism is great to a society that is breaking away from a religious type of ideology but is still seeking an ideological response to the need for values and identity, although in nonreligious terms. There are plenty of reasons to find solace in Marxist-Leninist ideology in contemporary Arab societies: ruling class corruption, lower-class poverty, growing awareness of class distinctions, social uprootedness of former peasants and new urban dwellers, lack of progress in development, continued and pervasive Western presence, and so on. An ideology that finds a common explanation for these evils of "growing up modern" and that prescribes the way to the glorious future, no matter how unreal in the present, is an attractive opiate, particularly when opposing notions are far less certain of where they are going. Marxism is the official language of much college teaching in Algeria and to some extent in Tunisia, and it is the language of students if not of teachers in Morocco and Egypt.

Analytically and operationally, the "modernized traditional" and the "international modern" school of thought are separate in content and origins, although both are a response to the same need for values, progress, and identity and on occasion the two ally or intermingle. It is important to Western observers to recognize the dialetic from which they spring. The incumbent elites themselves and their eventual successors, however, are usually elements of synthesis in the dialectic. This is why Libya is exceptional: Although precise identifications are hard to achieve, it appears that it was the antithesis that took over; contrast this with the more typical case of Egypt, where, between the monarchy and the Muslim Brotherhood, an army interested in both law and order and redistribution—both national and modern—took power. As in both Libya and Egypt, new elites in Arab North Africa are progressively more national-modern.

In regard to political forms, the Arab world has also been searching (for a century) for appropriate structures of order and change that correspond to accepted notions of authority and permit new ideas of participation. The participatory base of Islamic institutions was at best assumed and almost never implemented, and participation in government under colonial rule was refused by the very nature of colonialism while being encouraged among the colonizing populations. Both types of government were governments of order and authority, and any change came from above, imposed on the would-be participants. All the states of Arab North Africa were monarchies at the time of colonization, and all but Algeria became independent as monarchies; indeed, Morocco, Tunisia, and Egypt were protectorate kingdoms, not outright colonies, and Libya was made independent united under a monarchy constructed for the occasion.

New nationalist elites were raised in opposition to the colonial government, but also in suspicion of the monarchial government whose nature denied the element of participation that they embodied. Their rejection of colonialism led them to feel that order could only come about through participation, and therefore that institutions were appropriate only when they provided both authority and participation. The answer was the nationalist movement turned political party, which would dominate the government bodies of the colonialists. Parliaments were not even considered very important because the party so incarnated the heartbeat of the nation that an intermediate assembly was superfluous, a Western symbol that invited factional divisiveness rather than enforcing nationalist party unity. While all countries set up a parliament and filled it with party members, in none did it function very well except in Egypt, where it rapidly clashed with the monarchy; in Egypt, at the time when other countries of Arab North Africa became newly independent, Nasser's party actually became the parliament since both the National Union and its more vigorous successor the Arab Socialist Union replaced the national assembly. Nasser's emulator, Qaddafi, followed the same institutional innovation in revolutionary Libya.

Nationalist parties legitimized themselves through the nationalist monarchy in Morocco, although there was a good deal of suspicion of the arrangement and an understanding among many — notably Medhi ben Barka — that party as an institution of participation could only be subordinate under a monarchy. However, in Tunisia and Egypt, where the monarchy was neither national nor nationalist, opposition to the leftover Ottoman institution soon arose in the party. In Tunisia, the party abolished the monarchy in the original 1957 constitution. In Egypt during the previous generation, the monarchy eventually defeated the party by dividing it and buying off the pieces, leaving the military the job of removing the monarchy and the party at the same time. As in Egypt in 1952, the revolution in Libya in 1969 was against the monarchy first, as the means of eliminating the last vestiges of the colonizer.

Yet those elites who grew up under party government learned more of its shortcomings than its successes, and so the search for appropriate institutions continued. The loss of faith and nerve on the part of party and monarchy alike in Egypt meant that there was not much credibility in the institutions of order and participation after World War II; order was breaking down, and participation was being taken over by the Muslim Brotherhood because it had been refused by the parties. Nasser's coup restored order, not participation, and brought in, as the new form of government, the collective leadership of a small conspiratorial band known as the Revolutionary Command Council. The same institution was adopted by Algeria in 1962 and again in 1965; Libya followed the lead in 1969. But this too did not provide a satisfying answer, primarily because it denied the very quality that new elites were looking for — participation. In all cases, the Revolutionary Command Council has had to return to one of the earlier institutions to meet the pressures for participation and has revived either party or parliament under tight controls. Under Sadat, both government and opposition parties have had a hard time finding a meaningful role in political life, whereas the Peoples Assembly has at least been outspoken, even if not very effective. In Algeria, the party has never come alive, despite regular attempts at resuscitation, because new elites looking for political power go into government, not the National Liberation Front. However, here too the new elected institutions have begun to provide better channels of recruitment and participation for aspirant elites; and hence they are an active part of the political order. In Libya, the search for institutions of order and participation continues with the greatest imagination and disarray. On a number of occasions, the regime has reinvented and renewed both the elected Peoples Committees or local-level cells or soviets, which are the basic institutions of government, and the appointed Revolutionary Committees—"watchdogs of the revolution," which are to "agitate the people to take revolutionary decisions in the Peoples Committees."

The current rising generation in all five countries, born in the 1950s and socialized in the 1970s, appears to be closer to the masses and to notions of participation than their predecessors—either through a reversion to a neotraditionalism after the collapse of inflated hopes in the modernizing order or through a return to a democratic legitimization after the inadequacies of pure technocracy. Where there is a growing gap between current *arriviste* elites and the neglected mass, a reaction of conscience, cohesion, and productivity may seek to narrow that gap through new governmental forms that provide greater accountability than the Revolutionary Council but greater authority than the single party. The major question for an orderly and productive generational succession will be whether the modernized elites who have a sense of the technical requirements needed for economic development will be able to bridge the growing gap to their own people rather than drift away into the type of denationalized, Westernized status described by the dependency theorists (who claim that the world capitalist economy is splitting the developing countries into an alienated mass and a coopted leadership). (See Amin 1975, Hussein 1975, Toumi 1978, Mourad 1972). If the modernized elites do not find governmental forms that integrate as well as develop, others of the same generation also negatively socialized by their experience with government will push them out in the name of the masses and establish an inward-looking, xenophobic, neotraditionalist regime.

Religion as an organized political force is growing but dispersed in Morocco, Algeria, and Tunisia; in Egypt, it is somewhat stronger. Unlike Shi'i Iran, Sunni Islam in Arab North Africa does not provide an organization of *mullahs*. Their counterparts, the *'ulama*, continue to operate in all five countries under government control and without any training or demonstrated capacity for political mobilization. When they did play a political role, during the nationalist movement, they operated in conjunction with Muslim nationalist leaders. When they opposed occasional policies of independent governments, as in Tunisia on the Ramadan issue or Algeria on birth control, they were quickly brought to heel. The *'ulama* are organized into national associations and headed by a *mufti* (or sheikh al-Azhar in Egypt), but are not organized to act as an independent political body. In addition, in Morocco the king is the head of the Muslim community.

The only other organization based on religion is the Sufi sect, a number of which are present in all five countries with an important part of the male population as members. The sects frequently fill the function of a religious-social club as well a mystical rite of worship. They are nonpolitical, hostile to each other, and represent withdrawal from the world rather than mobilization for action in it. They are not effective political expressions of religious revival.

As a result, any Islamic revival that occurs in the five countries is likely to take the form represented by Qaddafi rather than Khomeini — that is, led by a secular leader who wants to use Islam as a modernizing ideology rather than by a religious leader who wants to save his people from the modern world. Islam as a current of thought and a body of symbols is important to politics in all five Muslim countries and plays a greater role in official discourse than religious symbols do in the West. Under appropriate conditions, such thought and symbols can constitute the language of opposition as well as of government. They are particularly appropriate for this purpose since they provide a ready ideology, tailor-made for ideological functions: They provide identity, offer explanations for failure and prescriptions for success, and separate friend from enemy. Thus they are particularly useful in times of prolonged crisis and hardship — in the presence of recession and the absence of government leadership. They have been used most effectively this way by the Muslim Brotherhood in Egypt, which was able to turn instability and indecision into anarchy and disorder in the last years of Faruq's reign, and which is gaining membership again and appearing in the open through its press and its members. Such fundamentalist protest is again on the rise throughout North Africa, among distressed and bewildered members of the lower-middle class and "lumpenbourgeoisie" and notably among their younger elements — high school and college students. Their numbers are small, although larger in Egypt than elsewhere and perhaps larger in Morocco and Tunisia than in Algeria. They are far from power and far from effectively organized political protest. In addition to needing political factors of organization, what they would also require for an increased role is a prolonged economic recession and a corrupt and indecisive government; these elements are not totally absent, notably in Morocco and Egypt, but are still far from a critical point.

In addition to politics and culture, elites are also shaped by the economic context of their experience. Any generational succession tends to go through cycles of growth and absorption, as observers of very divergent areas have noticed. Elites seek to create a greater pie in some sense, and once it is created they are pressed to change their focus from growth to distribution of that growth to a larger number of beneficiaries; the intensity varies according to the degree of concentration in the preceding phase and the means of the potential new beneficiaries to put pressure on the incumbents for a share in the pie. This liberal or radical phase then tends to be followed by a more conservative phase of absorption. Afterward, the cycle starts again as attentions are focused on providing better conditions through another increase in the pie. A smooth cycle assumes success at each of three phases: first in actually providing growth, then in meeting demands for redistribution, and thereafter maintaining it while absorption takes place. A shortfall in any stage, defined primarily in terms of expectations, can create heightened pressures on the incumbent elite and efforts to replace them.

Nationalist revolt itself can be understood in this light, as a distributionalist reaction against the concentrated enjoyment of growth in a given historical period. Whether it refers to the post-World War I nationalist revolt of Egypt or the post-Korean war nationalist revolt of the Maghreb, the nationalist movement of Arab North Africa reached its peak as a national demand for controlling participation in the current economic boom, in a situation where it became plain to the rising elites that participation could never be accomplished with assurance and justice under the colonial system and hence in the absence of political control — or independence. A period of redistribution followed independence, and then a more conservative turn of absorption.

The interwar evolution of Egypt is illustrative of problems. Instead of the three phases of the cycle proceeding to the satisfaction of the body politic, these phases operated in a sort of superficial caricature, for they concerned only the elites and did not reach down much deeper into society. Growth led to distribution, but the beneficiaries narrowed in number in the 1930s and their increasingly conservative mood referred to their own absorption of the body politic in general. As a result, counter-elites arose to undermine the political order, and when the military intervened at the end of the postwar boom after World War II, it was both to restore order and to respond to a demand for redistribution of overly-concentrated benefits of war and independence. In the postwar period, times of absorption are clearly evident in the early Sadat and Benjedid periods of Egypt and Algeria. And times of distribution are evident in the Mohammed V period in Morocco, the 1960s of Bourguiba (and ben Salah) in Tunisia, and the ben Bella and parts of the Boumedienne period of Algeria. Conflicting pressures in these directions can also be the basis of political dynamics; the early Boumedienne years marked a clash between the consumptionist ethic of redistribution and the productionist ethic of growth, as expressed by the *mujahidin* (guerrilla) and the technicians, respectively, until the latter won out.

These divisions also corresponds to political roles that have been used to analyse elite alternance. Elites are identified as either technicians or politicians, experts in outputs and inputs respectively, or in more commonplace terms, those who know the countries' problems and put their skills to resolving them versus those who put their skills to articulating and aggregating demands with less concern for the technicalities of their resolution. Technicians are the experts of growth and problem-solving and politicians of redistribution and solidarity-making. Fully developed politics requires both; developing polities frequently leave the first to the government and the second to the opposition (tolerated or clandestine), which is a contradiction in itself.

These factors work differently in the five countries. Morocco and Tunisia are just emerging from an era when parties or a single party were the major channel of recruitment into politics, whereas Egypt and Algeria may be reentering such an era and Libya has yet to enter it at all. More broadly, all three Maghreb countries have graduated from the era when the politicians' skill were the primary requirement for entry into politics, whereas Egypt is a whole generation away from that era and might be returning toward it again and Libya never knew it. On the other hand, increased education is producing increasing numbers of technicians in all five countries — not only people with college degrees but also people with degrees in technical rather than liberal arts subjects. To some extent, the supply creates the demand, and there is a growing market for well-trained elites.

In the absence of a fundamentalist revolt, elites in all five countries are and will be better educated than their predecessors, and increasingly they will be educated at national universities. Also, in all five countries, the proportion of noncollege graduates will diminish. In the absence of a violent overthrow of the regime, core elites will tend to grow older in office (higher average age), making room for younger members at lower ranks only by expanding and diffusing the bureaucracy. Elites tend to have increasingly urban origins, where better educational opportunities are to be found. However, there is an increasing tendency to overproduction of potential elites and a gradual saturation of the state sector's absorption capabilities. This point has arrived in Egypt and is close in Tunisia; it is only slightly further away in Morocco because of the expansion potentialities of the private sector, and it is conceivable in Algeria. When it occurs, it will either produce mounting pressure for elite change (organized counter-elites and rebellion) or will spill over into a newly reactivated private sector where competition in economics and politics can handle larger numbers of elites. This moment marks an important change in the nature of the political system; it has already occurred as the social basis of Sadat's regime in Egypt, and it will prevail with the arrival of multipartism in Tunisia.

Although there are no precise studies on the interesting question of the type of education that will fit best into these circulation patterns, it is likely that Maghrebi and Egyptian students are no different from others in that political and technical skills are dominant but not exclusive. Political reliability is more important than technical knowledge in appointment to elite positions in all five countries. In Morocco, Algeria, and Tunisia, leaders of student organizations appear later among the higher general elite and even in the core elite, provided that their organizations were not later banned and that they were party-affiliated. At the same time, top students in each discipline do well in later life, particularly those in the elite-training disciplines (education, management, engineering, and sometimes law) and the military. To these two characteristics of leadership, all the others plus chance would have to be added; no one element is so significant that it outweighs all others and provides a single identifying characteristic. In any case, promotion possibilities are now so slim that current graduates in Arab North Africa look for a good position defined in terms of long-term security rather than in terms of acess to better positions.

The few attitude studies of North African elites and aspirant elites indicate that the recent generation (graduates of the classes of the 1970s) is a generation of technicians, interested in efficiency, effectiveness, good government in the sense of technically correct outputs, some popular expression and participation in legitimizing government, self-reliance, increasing autonomy from the West, and an increase in the benefits of modernization to the entire country (development as well as growth). There are no similar studies in Egypt, but current information would suggest that these attitudes might have best fit the preceding generation and those recently rising might be more interested in consumption than production and growth rather than distribution.

Students (from secondary and higher education) tend currently to be less radical, less oppositional, and more job-oriented than their counterparts of a decade ago. They may also be less international-modernist and more nationalist and neotraditionalist. If they enter unimpeded into the general elite, they may provide a productive, committed, and motivated group with more realistic expectations; if they run into restrictions in recruitment because of diminishing resources, they may turn out to be even more frustrated and rebellious at an age when they should normally have settled down. In Morocco, the typical "Frontist"—a member of the small extremist antimonarchial groups left of the Communists—is a man born in the 40s who was a member of the now-outlawed student union or the Communist party in his youth (the 60s). The same type of person appears in Algeria, Libya, and Tunisia; in Egypt, he is younger, and his hopes and beliefs were formed under Nasser. These counter-elites are few and attract no national following, but they form a tight, committed opposition.

Egypt (along with Sudan and a few others outside of North Africa) provides the example of polarized student activism, where organizations from the extreme left and the neotraditionalist right both shape student attitudes. Student organizations (legal or not) are still predominantly left-oriented in Morocco, Algeria, and Tunisia, although religious fundamentalism is growing. Student political organization is spreading among secondary students, whereas a decade ago it was limited to university students.

Algeria has been more successful than the other countries in adopting a policy stance that coincides with student attitudes and therefore has been able to undercut student contestation of the regime. Morocco, Tunisia, and Egypt have been successful in coopting students into the regime and in controlling student organizations, but basic student attitudes still remain in contestation of the regime.

The process of dealing with such newly emerging elites is complex, but it is similar in all five countries. Aspirant elites coming out of school know "what is expected of them" and are further socialized on the job; if either of these socializing activities is offensive, the process of integrating may work in reverse and push students into opposition. "What is expected of them" is not only competence in useful skills but also conformity to the existing system — respect for the monarchy and its episodic ways of doing things in Morocco, support of the institutionalized revolution and its infighting in Algeria, obeisance to the presidential monarch and his courtiers in Tunisia, fervor behind the *mahdi* and his austere revolution in Libya, and adherence to the idiosyncratic leader and the immovable bureaucracy in Egypt. Some of the best elite members sit on the sidelines in a routine private, or even international, job and from time to time try to jump in the saddle and tame a position of responsibility within the system. If they can hang on, they have combined their own sense of values with an ability to work within the established order. If they cannot hang on, they may retire to the sidelines to try again, or at some point they may throw their lot with the counter-elites (for example, Mehdi Elmandjra in Morocco; Ismail-Sabri Abdalla in Egypt, respectively).

On the other side of the divide are a group that form the residual counter-elites: former radical student leaders, dissident military, and disloyal opposition-party leaders — those who at some point (usually early) in their career made a decision not to sit on the sidelines but rather to adopt a position that permanently disqualified them from being coopted into the system.

It is not easy to say where to look for future counter-elites; if we knew, the government would know, too, and they would be eliminated as counter-elites. Three areas to watch for "swing members" who can go either way depending on the impact of the socialization stages are the student union activists, the younger nationalist businessmen, and the members of unusual military classes (for example, the first after independence — Mohammed V class of 1956 in Morocco; the class whose first baptism of fire is against their own citizens — the class of 1977 in Tunisia — or against a winning enemy).

PERSPECTIVES

On the basis of these concepts and trends, a moving picture can be presented of generational elite circulation in Arab North Africa. In this approach, the end of the monarchial era in Egypt can be equated with the end of the colonial era in the Maghreb, not merely because the date is close to their dates of independence but above all because the republican era marks the Egyptianization of elites (just as the independent era marks the nationalization of elites in Morocco, Algeria, and Tunisia). However, beyond this comparability, there are important differences between the national experiences because of the differences in national history in the preceding periods, and therefore a production of different elites to contest and occupy positions of power in the next period.

In the Mohammed V, ben Bella and early Boumediene (until 1968), Idris I, and at least early Bourguiba periods of Moroccan, Algerian, Libyan, and Tunisian history, the independence generation was in place. Its attitudes included some notions of democracy, a consumptionist or distributionist ethic favoring the enjoyment of the fruits of growth and independence that were due to the nationalist elites after the struggle against colonialism, and a sense of both victory and vigilance against the colonialist enemy. In Egypt, the 1950s were covered by a nationalist generation reacting against the excesses of multipartism, the heldover colonial interference, and Israeli aggressiveness; the 1960s marked a shift of policy toward social change and a broadened technicians' role, but this change was accomplished by an opening of the elite to include younger technicians rather than by an actual succession of generations.

In Algeria, in the mid-1960s, the Boumediene and abortive Zbiri coups brought in a younger generation of technicians much like the Nasserites of the 1960s — those with no concern for democratic directives or for parties and politicians under which they had grown up but with a concern for technocratic efficiency and growth for redistribution. In Morocco, Hassan II first sought to work with his father's generation, but after 1965 he gradually began to bring in a new generation of technicians to replace the independence generation, only starting to succeed with the reestablishment of constitutional government in the mid-1970s. In Tunisia, this same technocratic generation has been kept in the wings, either outside the system or held down in lower government posts; it clustered about the reforms of ben Salah in the late 1960s particularly and in large part went with him into opposition, although not into exile. In Libya, technicians came to the fore in the 1970s under Qaddafi, who needed them to spend his oil money wisely. In Egypt, the reaction against the insufficiencies of the Nasser regime — both to its inability to meet its own ideological prescriptions and to its restraints on individual enrichment — has meant that the generation entering into the elite in the 1970s tends to be conservative, individualistic, and technocratic.

In this evolution, there are occasionally clear moments of generational shift, associated with major political and policy events and realignments of issues and attitudes. Some of these even appear in a simple graphic presentation of basic elite characteristics, as portrayed in the accompanying tables.* The basic generational shift occurred in the early to mid-1950s as revolution and independence came across the top of Africa. Libya in 1951, Egypt in 1952–1954, and Morocco and Tunisia in 1955 –1956, brought in a new nationalist generation; only Algeria awaited the

---

*Major changes in any dimension are signaled by a slash on the chart.

TABLE 1.1 Dimensions of Moroccan Elites*

Year	1956	1958	1958	1960	1961	1963	1965	1969	1971	1972	1974	1977	1979
N	22	19	15	16	18	21	25	33	20	23	29	35	38
Carry-overs (%)	—	47 /	33	50 /	33	55 /	37	52	63	52 /	41	43	63
A. Age													
Average	42	38	37	40	44	42	44	45	45	44	42	45	47
Standard Deviation	9.4	8.8	5.7	7.6	7.9	8.1	10.3	9.6	10.4	7.4	5.8	6.2	7.8
B. Geographic Origins													
Fes (%)	45	42 /	27	38	28	40	44	33	30	18 /	10	26	19
Rabat (%)	22	26	20	25	22	15	10	15	15	9	4	9	5
Casa. (%)	5	0	7	0	0	10	10	3	10	4	7	9	3
Marra. (%)	5	15	14	13	17	10 /	0	0	0	8	4	6	8
Rural (%)	18 /	5	7	13	11	10	20	15	20	21	17	15	19
C. Education													
Modern	82	100	100	100	88	91	92	91	95	96	97	100	97
D. Professions													
Labor	0	0	0	0	0	0	0	0	5	4	0	0	3
Business	5	5	0	0	0	0	8	0	5	0	0	0	0
Medicine	9	5	7	12	17	20	8	12	5	13	10	11	8
Party	5	0	7	6	6	5	4	3	0	0	0	0	0
Lawyer	22	15	34	25	17	20	16	18	25	22	20	25	21
Teacher	18	10	14	6	11	15	16	15	20	18	20	20	11
Military	9	0	7	6	6	5	12	6	10 /	4	4	3	3
Engineer	5	5	0	12	17	5	8	6	10	4	10	14	14
Ag-engineer	9	15	7	0	0	0	0	3	0	4	0	6	5
Administration	0	15	20	25	17	25	24	24	20	22 /	38	20	14
Unknown	22	25	14	0	11	5	0	9	5	4	4	0	19

*Council of Ministers, Royal Cabinet, National Security Council

TABLE 1.2.   Dimensions of Algerian Elites*

Year	1962	1963	1964	1965	1968	1970	1977	1979	1980
N	21	16	30	40	21	24	28	42	33
Carry-overs (%)	—	63	40	40 /	95	69	50	55 /	81
A. Age									
Average	41	42 /	39	38	40	40	49	49	49
Standard Deviation	9.9	8.2	7.1	6	4.2	4.6	5.3	5.3	5.7
B. Geographic Origins									
Oranais (%)	28	25	26	22	30 /	16	22		
Algerois (%)	24	50	43 /	27	25	31	25		
Constantinois (%)	38	12	20	40	30	33	30		
C. Societal Origins									
City (A,O,C) (%)	25	25	16	10	9	4	7		
Town (>20,000) (%)	20	25	26	25	45	33	22		
Village (commune, not douar) (%)	45	37	26	40	35	40	32		
D. Education									
Modern higher (%)	43	50	44	50	78	70	82		
E. Professions									
Labor (%)	14	13	13	10 /	5	8	0	2	3
Labor/civil-serv. (%)	10	13	7 /	0	0	4	0	0	0
Artisan, trad. bus. (%)	5	6	7	10	5	4	3	0	0
Business (%)	5	0	0	0	0	0	0	0	0
Medicine (%)	14	7	10	10	19	13	10	7	6
Party (%)	5	13	10	15	15	13	7 /	21	18
Lawyer (%)	14	6	7	5	10	0	0	0	0
Teacher (%)	19	25	10	15	19	17	22	10	9
Military (%)	5	0	7	15	5	4 /	18	31	24
Engineer (%)	5	6	7	3	5	8	7	10	9
Administration (%)	0	0	0	0	5 /	13	18	15	9
Unknown (%)	5	13	20	18	15	17	7	0	18

*Council of the Revolution (from 1965), Council of Ministers (from 1962), FLN Politburo

beginning of the following decade, in 1962. Of less-common knowledge is the subsequent generational shift that occurred around 1970 in nearly all the countries of the same region.

The weakness of the new Algerian regime and the need to eliminate the *mujahidin*, or guerrilla, leadership from the incumbent elite — a problem not faced with the same acuity in other countries where guerrillas did not have the same predominate role in the struggle for independence — made Algeria "catch up" with the prevailing chronology of the region. The Boumediene regime came to power in 1965, but not until 1968 was it able to force out the *mujahidin* elite and regroup as a coherent new generational elite. Libya followed suit in 1969 because the military coup

TABLE 1.3   Dimensions of Tunisian Elites*

Measure	1956	1959	1964		1970	1971	1974	1980
N	21	20	25		28	30	32	36
Carry-overs (%)	—	65	60	/	47	66	60	61
A. Age								
Average	41	44	45		45	48	48	53
Standard Deviation	7.2	5.9	7.1		7.0	7.7	7.9	6.3
B. Geographic Origins								
Tunis (%)	45	45	40	/	25	13	25	25
Sahel (%)	20	35	36	/	54	50	48	44
Other (%)	25	16	24		18	37	25	18
C. Education								
T. mod. secon. (%)	24	25	16		11	10	10	0
Fr. univ. (%)	62	75	76		70	89	80	70
T. univ. (%)	5	0	8		14	0	10	15
Other (%)	0	0	0		4	0	0	3
D. Profession								
Labor (%)	0	5	8		4	3	3	0
Labor/civil-serv. (%)	15	10	8		7	3	3	0
Business (%)	15	10	/ 0		4	0	0	3
Medicine (%)	10	5	4		4	3	6	6
Party (%)	15	15	8		4	10	13	6
Lawyer (%)	20	30	36		14	24	16	15
Teacher (%)	25	20	24		14	27	23	25
Engineer (%)	5	5	0	/	18	10	20	6
Administrator (%)	0	0	/ 12		21	10	10	24
Ag-engineer (%)	0	0	0		7	7	6	6
Unknown (%)	0	0	0		4	3	3	19

*Council of Ministers, Party Political Bureau

brought a sharper break with the past and the dramatic appearance of a generation, that had different origins and attitudes and different experiences and policies from its predecessor.

Tunisia and Egypt brought in a different type of generational change in 1970. For Egypt, the change of *rais* (president) meant the gradual change of the core and general elites but without any of the sudden shifts marked by military coups. Although Sadat was of Nasser's generation and the average age of his core elite was older — about 53–54 years old — than in neighboring countries, the fact that that age remained constant over the decade of the 1970s shows a gradual incorporation of younger members, including people whose only adult experience was under revolutionary Egypt. Tunisia is more complex. It has been dominated by conflicts within the independence generation, while new younger members were being coopted into the political elite after 1964. In 1970, the return to liberal leadership after the eviction of ben Salah occurred, but the core-elite recruitment remained open to diverse younger elements the following

TABLE 1.4a   Dimensions of Egyptian Elites

Year	1952	1953	1953	1954	1954	1956	1958	1958	1961	1962	1964	1965	1966	1967	1968
Month	Sept	Jun	Oct	Apr	Sept	Jun	Mar	Oct	Aug	Sept	Mar	Oct	Sept	Jun	Mar
N	16	19	22	24	23	22	21	33	31	36	44	41	38	29	33
A. Age															
Average	50	45	43	41	43	43	44	45	48	48	50	51	51	50	50
C. Education															
Modern higher (%)	88	100	100	100	100	100	100	97	100	97	98	98	97	100	100
D. Professions															
Labor (%)	—	—	—	—	—	—	—	—	—	—	—	—	—	—	—
Business (%)	19	5	9	8	4	9	10	6	7	6	5	2	2	7	6
Medicine (%)	6	5	5	4	4	5	5	6	3	6	5	2	3	4	3
Lawyer (%)	25	26	18	17	7	8	14	6	3	3	7	5	5	4	6
Teacher (%)	19	16	14	13	9	14	19	21	16	19	23	17	8	14	27
Military (%)	6	26	41	46	52	36	38	49	52	47	36	46	55	65	40
Engineer (%)	0	11	9	8	9	14	14	12	16	11	21	20	18	7	12
Ag.-engineering (%)	—	—	—	—	—	—	—	—	—	—	—	—	—	—	—
Administrator (%)	18	11	5	4	4	5	0	3	3	8	5	5	5	0	6
Unknown (%)	0	0	0	0	0	0	0	0	0	0	0	0	0	0	0

*Council of Ministers, source: Dekmejian 1975

TABLE 1.4.b Dimensions of Egyptian Elites

	1970 Nov	1971 May	1972 Jan	1973 Mar	1974 Apr	1975 Apr	1976 Nov	1977 Feb	1977 Oct	1978 May	1978 Oct	1979 Jun	1980 May
N	33	34	34	38	37 /	36	33	34	31	32	33	33	25
Carry-overs (%)	69	53 /	35	50	67	44	72	77	84	70 /	36	75	76
A. Age													
N known	26	26	29	35	32	35	24	27	23	25	24	26	24
Average	52	52	54	54	54	55	55	55	56	55	55	53	54
Standard Deviation	6.3	5.3	6.9	6.2	6.8 /	5.1	5.6	6.0	6.0	5.2	7.7	7.1	5.3
B. Geographic Origins													
N known	15	17	21	22	19	18	15	15	12	14	16	15	19
Cairo (%)	40	29	33	32	30	28	33	26	25	20	13	13	25
Upper E. (%)	7	12	10	10	11	6	7	0	0	0 /	33	33	25
C. Education													
N known	97	97	97	97	97	100	100	100	100	100	100	100	100
Modern Higher (%)	97	97	97	97	97	100	100	100	100	100	100	100	100
D. Professions													
Labor (%)	3	3	3	3	3	3	3	3	0	0	0	0	0
Business (%)	3	6	0	0	0	3	0	0	0	3	3	3	8
Medicine (%)	9	8	6	3	0	0	0	0	0	0	0	0	4
Lawyer (%)	9	8	9	3	3	8	9	6	6	6	6	12	20
Teacher (%)	30*	41	41	39	46	22	24	21	32	28	33	30	16
Military (%)	33	32	24	18	14	25	15	15	16	13	12	12	16
Engineer (%)	9	9	12	13	19	17	15	18	13	22	24	21	28
Ag.-engineer (%)	0	0	0	0	3	0	0	0	0	3	6	9	4
Administration (%)	9	3	12	16	5	11	12	9	3	9	6	6	4
Unknown (%)	0	0	9	5	8	8	24	21	23	13	9	6	0

*Change in criteria. Data were gathered and organized by Moushira al-Geziri and Liane Dorsey

year. In terms of age, origins, and professions, 1970 shows up as the year of change, as younger Sahelis, primarily engineers and administrators, replaced older Tunisois, primarily lawyers. In 1974, the political trend was reversed, to the exclusion of the liberals, but their replacements were drawn from the same generation as the liberals. This fact, as much as the continuing leadership of Bourguiba, indicates how the regime could hold on, despite contrary appearances of aging in power.

Morocco was the last to join the shift of generations. It was only in the early 1970s, between 1972 and 1974, after two abortive military coups had underlined the need for an end to the state of emergency (rather than the reverse, the imposition of more stringent controls), that a new generation was able to make its way into the core elite, finally squeezing out the old politicians of the independence generation. Thus around 1970 or very soon thereafter, a generational shift occurred in all Arab North Africa, sometimes dramatically but frequently unnoticed because unheralded, replacing an independence generation that had been in power for about a decade and a half.

The nature and behavior of this generation have been discussed in the preceding sections and are described in greater detail in the following chapters, but what about the next round of change? The simple mechanics of the process suggest that a new shift should appear around 1985, about 15 years after the last shift around 1970, with some variations according to individual country chronologies. In some polities, the change may appear gradually, as new elites become absorbed. In others, the shift will be sudden. However, given the relatively small numbers available, even sudden change at the core will involve only a more gradual replacement and a number of holdovers as one looks down into the general elite. In Algeria, a change had already begun to be prepared, according to the Algerian pattern of administrative behavior, in 1978 before the death of Boumediene; it will be consummated when the final consolidation of Benjedid is completed. In Tunisia, where the established pattern of cooptation was undone in the mid-1970s, pressure is growing for a shift in the 1980s. It is certain to be associated with the succession of Bourguiba but may already have begun with the accession of Mzali to the premiership. The remaining three countries, however, have no evident succession in sight in the mid-1980s, unless the present regime be overthrown. Libya has been following its own unique evolution, but both Morocco and Egypt have been essentially stable regimes whose generational shift of the early 1970s was gradual and cooptive. The same pattern is likely to obtain a decade and a half later.

Any opposition takes some of its characteristics from the regime it opposes, and any generational succession and issue realignment is at least a partial reaction to incumbent groups and current emphases. Such dialectic reactions, like the dates of generational shifts, take on the specific characteristics of each country, notably a rejection of the autocratic paternalism of Bourguiba in Tunisia or a swing away from the centralized and industrializing political economy of Boumediene's Algeria. But beyond these national idiosyncracies are some characteristics as common to the region as the projected date of the mid-1980s.

One characteristic is the rise of competetive elites. In Arab North Africa, the production of aspirant elites, through education, political and administrative experience, and social promotion, is reaching the point where alternative groups are forced to form; factions are turning into parties with competing programs; and the public sector is facing private competition. In part, this is a result of development and in part a reaction to overly centralized leadership and monopoly of political functions. There is an oversupply of aspirant elites, and the economy and polity need to — indeed, will be forced to — develop alternative institutions to absorb them. This is the function of competetively elected assemblies, of multiple party councils, and of competing companies because the growth of monolithic institutions, above all state bureaucracies, is approaching its limits.

A second characteristic is the rise of solidarity-making functions, in new directions. Previous analysis has opposed politicians to technicians as the agents of problem-solving versus solidarity-making. The reaction to the dominant role of the technicians in the 1970s, however, is not likely to be the rise of politicians again, but the rise of Islamic leadership to reflect a growing need for authenticism and national solidarity. The reaction refers to attitudes, not necessarily origins, of succeeding elites: They are unlikely to be religious figures, and they need not be primarily concerned with religious law and reform, but they are certain to be more attuned to religious appeals and concerns.

Third, the economic projections for the decade foresee a time for absorption, in which attention turns to consumption and the digestion of growth rather than on growth itself, as was seen in the 1970s. Arab North African economies have shown a positive per capita GDP growth rate in the 1970s, sometimes of a sizeable nature (Egypt 5.4%, Tunisia 5.9%) and sometimes merely relatively impressive considering the challenge (Morocco 3.2%, Algeria 1.9%) (World Bank 1980, figures for 1970–78). Exceptionally, Libya's negative rate (−2.5) shows that it is already into the phase of redistribution and absorption. Economic benefits are needed to assure the loyalty of newly produced elites, particularly in cooptive payoff systems as found everywhere in the region. So used, the system begins to arouse the resentment of those left out, either because they are not among the elites or because they are counter-elites not bought off. This is another reason why solidarity-making politics is on the rise — the competition for economic benefits is straining the social fabric. The new elites of the mid-1980s are facing an increasingly clear challenge: to perpetuate the systems of cooptation and control that are guaranteed to overtax the resources of the country and create a reaction in the coming period or to reorient elite activities toward more productive and distributive activities and expectations, if only preemptively.

Finally, to some extent the new elites have run out of governmental types to reject and political institutions to experiment with. Reactions can therefore be less comprehensive, and the nature of the continuing search for appropriate institutions of government can face the complexities of improving on established forms within a national framework rather than sweeping away all precedents. But if the range of potential forms and experiences is exhausted, the prospects for change can also be seen as less encouraging, leaving counter-elites only the option of taking their turn at the public till rather than of actually improving the way it is run. Again, the challenge is posed to the newly rising elites: to capitalize on the absence of realistic extremes and work on established institutions to produce better results or to embark nonetheless on a fruitless search for new alternatives, with the elements of control, ideologically true belief, and narrowed promotion and participation that that attempt brings.

Arab North Africa, as a region that has done better than most of the developing world in search of the meaning of modernization, stands at the edge of a major challenge of elite circulation. Coming out of an era of political full employment, it is entering a period of overproduction of aspirant elites, while still retaining aspects of underdevelopment for the bulk of society—those who are not only powerless but also lack status and even the minimal resources for basic needs. If the coming incumbents broaden their own coalitions among the elites, strengthen their responsiveness to society's needs, and provide channels of alternance and competition, the system can bump along toward greater satisfaction of aspirations at all levels. If not, and a polarized consumptionist winner-take-all ethic prevails, the bumps will become characteristic and rather than the broadening circulation of elites, Arab North Africa will have established a conflict system of elite politics.

REFERENCES

Abramson, Paul (1974) "Generational Change in American Electoral Behavior," *American Political Science Review*, DXVIII, 1, pp. 93–105.
_____ (1975) *Generational Change in American Politics*. Lexington: Heath.
Amin Samir (1970) *The Maghreb in the Modern World*. Baltimore: Penguin.
Ashford, Douglas (1964) *Second and third Generation Elites in the Maghreb*. Washington: Department of State.
Baker, Raymond. (1978) *Egypt's Uncertain Revolution Under Nasser and Sadat*. Cambridge: Harvard.
Broder, David S. (1980) *Changing the Guard*. New York: Simon and Schuster.
Burns, James MacGregor. (1966) *Presidential Government*. Boston: Houghton, Mifflin.

CEMAM, St. Joseph's University, Beirut (1980) *Thematic Content Analysis of Arab Writings on Acculturation*, mimeographed report.

Dekmejian, Richard H. (1971) *Egypt under Nasir: A Study in Political Dynamics.* Albany: State University of New York Press.

—— (1975) *Patterns of Political Leadership: Lebanon, Israel Egypt.* Albany: State University of New York Press.

Dessouki, Ali E. Hillal, ed. (1978) *Democracy in Egypt.* Cairo: American University in Cairo, Papers in Social Science 2.

Drew, Elizabeth (1973) "Conversation with a Citizen," *New* Yorker, July 23.

Duchac, Réné et al. (1973) *La formation des élites politiques maghrébines.* Paris: Librairie générale de droit et de jurisprudence.

Entelis, John (1974) "Ideological Change and an Emerging Counter-Culture in Tunisian Politics," *Journal of Modern African Studies* 12, 4:543–68.

Eulau, Heinz and M. Czudnowski (1976) *Elite Recruitment in Democratic Politics.* New York: Wiley-Halstead.

Gaxie, Daniel (1973) *Les professionels de la politique.* Paris: PUF.

Gellner, Ernest and J. Waterbury, eds. (1977) *Patrons and Clients.* New York: Duckworth.

Gouldner, Alvin (1979) *The Future of Intellectuals and the Rise of the New Class.* New York: Seabury.

Green, Arnold H. (1979) "Can Iran Happen Here? The 'Ulama and 'Islamic' Political Opposition Movements in Egypt and Tunisia," paper presented to the Round Table on Islam in the Maghreb Today, Aix en Provence.

Hareven, T. ed. (1978) *Family Transitions and the Life Course.* New York: Academic.

Hermassi, Elbaki (1972) *Leadership and National Development in North Africa.* Berkeley: California.

Hughes, Everett C. (1971) *The Sociological Eye.* Chicago: Aldine.

Hussein, Mahmoud (1975) *L'Egypte.* Paris: Maspero.

Ibrahim, Saad (1980) "Anatomy of Egypt's Militant Islamic Groups," paper presented to the Middle East Studies Association, Washington.

Khadduri, Majid (1970.) *Political Trends in the Arab World.* Baltimore: Johns Hopkins.

Klineberg, Stephen L. (1971a.) "Modernization and the Adolescent Experience: A Study in Tunisia," *The Key Reporter*, XXXVII, 1 (Autumn): pp. 2–4.

——, (1971b.) *Adolescents and their Parents under the Impact of Modernization.* Princeton University.

Laroui, Abdallah (1967.) *L'ideologie arabe contemporaine.* Paris: Maspero.

Lenczowski, George, ed. (1975.) *Political Elites in the Middle East.* Washington AEI.

—— (1974.) *La crise des intellectuals arabes.* Paris: Maspero.

Leveau, Remy (1976.) *le Fellah Marocain, defenseur du trone.* Paris: Fondation nationale des sciences politiques.

LeVine, Robert A. (1978.) "Adulthood and Aging in Cross-Cultural Perspective," *Items*, XXXI–XXXII, 4/1 (March): pp. 1–5.

Markham, James M. (1978.) "Spain Seems to Look to Younger Generation for Leaders," *New York Times* June 15.

Moore, Clement Henry (1965). *Tunisia Since Independence.* Berkeley: University of California Press.

Mourad, Kamal-Eddine. (1972). *Le Maroc à la recherche d'une révolution*. Paris: Sindbad.

Paxton, Robert O. (1973.) *Vichy France: Old Guard and New Order*. New York; Knopf.

Roberts, Steven V. (1979.) "Congressional Generation Gap Emerges on Role of Government," *New York Times*, April 1.

Samuels, Richard J. (1977.) *Political Generations and Political Development*. Boston: Lexington.

Schulz, Ann T. (1979.) "A Cross-National Examination of Legislators," *The Journal of Developing Areas*, VII, 4 (July): pp. 571–590.

Shannon, Willian V. (1971.) "Ideals vs Interests," *The NewYork Times*, October 14.

Schlesinger, Arthur Sr. (1939.) "Tides of American Politics."

_____ (1949.) *Paths to the Presidency*. New York: Macmillan.

Tachau, Frank, ed. (1975.) *Political Elites and Political Development in the Middle East*. New York: Schenkman-Wiley.

Tessler, Mark A. (1979.) "Acculturation, Socio-Economic Status, and Attitude Change in Tunisia: Implications for Modernization Theory," *Journal of Modern African Studies*, XVII, 3: 473–95

Toumi, Mohsen. (1978) *Tunisia: Pouvoirs et Luttes*. Paris: Sycomore.

Waterbury, John. (1970) *The Commander of the Faithful*. New York: Columbia University Press.

Welsh, William A. (1979.) *Leaders and Elites*. New York: Holt, Rinehard & Winston.

World Bank. (1980) *World Development Report*. Washington: World Book.

Zartman, I. William, ed., (1980.) *Elites in the Middle East*. New York: Praeger.

_____ .(1964) *Problems of New Power*. New York: Atherton.

2

Morocco: Institutional Pluralism and Monarchical Dominance

MARK A. TESSLER

Morocco is governed by a small group of men who are the offspring of the country's most prominent families and who exercise power through a system of patronage and clientelism that serves first and foremost their own interests and those of the national bourgeoisie. Many members of this elite have held positions of leadership since independence in 1956, and the clientelist system has also been operative since the early days of statehood, suggesting that elite politics is in the first instance marked by continuity. On the other hand, the character of political life has evolved considerably during the last 25 years, there having been important variations in the role and influence of major political institutions and in the pattern of alliances among factions of the elite.

The first decade or so of independence was characterized by a steady decline in the vitality and influence of political parties, resulting in *immobilisme* in policy initiatives, and by growing authoritarianism through an increase of the power of the monarchy. Present-day patterns of clientelist politics solidified during these years, particularly after Morocco's present king, Hassan II, ascended to the throne upon the death of his father in 1961. This period gave way in the late 1960s and early 1970s to an era of political confrontation in general and growing opposition to King Hassan in particular. Key events were attempted military coups in 1971 and 1972, which threatened the life of the monarch and called into question existing elite alliances. Student strikes and demonstrations against the government were also important attributes of this period. The present era began in the mid-1970s, when Hassan initiated policies aimed at liberalizing and democratizing political life and at reinvigorating the country's moribund multiparty parliamentary system. The king's initiatives also included annexation of the former Spanish Sahara. This began with the "Green March" of 1975, in which Hassan amassed hundreds of thousands of civilians on the Morocco-Sahara border, and it has resulted in an ongoing war with the Polisario Front, a Saharan guerilla group opposed to Morocco's takeover of the territory. The initiatives of the mid-1970s have enhanced popular support for the king, undermined the opposition of elite elements traditionally hostile to the government, and quieted lingering uncertainty about the army's loyalty to the existing order.

Observers disagree about the relative importance of continuity and change in contemporary Moroccan politics and about the political future that awaits the country. Positive assessments emphasize change and contend that significant progress has been made in recent years. Those who take this point of view count as extremely important the growing openness of the system, including an increase in freedom of expression and political organization and the renewed vitality of political parties. They also stress heightened elite solidarity, including an expansion of the government's parliamentary coalition and growing areas of cooperation among elites with differing political philosophies. Finally, they note the emergence of political values that stress technical competence rather than political clientelism and/or social connections and they point out that these changes in the criteria of political recruitment are bringing new and younger faces into the elite. All these developments are seen as part of a progressive and an orderly transition away from the dominance of a small and ingrown political elite dedicated principally to the pursuit of its own interests.

Critics of the Moroccan government offer a contrasting view. They see recent changes as largely superficial and wholly obscured by the continuities in Moroccan political life, which leads them to conclude that the current elite will soon come under intense pressure and that the future holds conflict and possibly even violence. These observers point first to the fact that virtually all elite institutions are still in the hands of a privileged few and that the so-called democratization has not brought into the political process leaders and institutions representative of the country's masses. They note also that this democratization appears to have strict limits, with political prisoners continuing to be held and with government interference in critical elections. Finally and most important, they note that the distribution of wealth and privilege has become less rather than more equitable in recent years and that at all levels of society popular discontent and political alienation are growing rapidly. Thus they conclude that the country's liberalization is a sham and that by failing to address fundamental political and economic problems, the Moroccan elite has in fact precluded the long-term survival of the present political system.

The common elements in these competing interpretations provide a point of departure for thinking about Morocco's future. Specifically, the country is on the verge of a major political transition. The elite that has ruled since independence is indeed still in place; but one way or another this leadership cohort will pass from the scene in the not-very-distant future, and the character of the political system it leaves behind will in large measure be shaped by decisions that are only now beginning to be made. It is true that political life has become more active and open in the last few years; but the problems identified by critics of the present system are very real and getting worse, and the policies that current leaders adopt in response to these pressures for change will probably be decisive in determining both the way in which the coming political transition is accomplished and the nature of the government order to which it gives rise.

Much of what follows is an account of elite politics at the present time, of the men and institutions that today dominate Moroccan political life. Descriptive information is presented; and the account is also analytical in that it assesses the causes and consequences of elite behavior and strives to understand the elite within its own sociocultural context. The major changes that lie ahead cannot be ignored, however, and the final sections of this chapter look to the future, returning to the issues summarized above and inquiring about the nature and possible outcomes of the coming transition in Moroccan politics.

DESCRIPTION: BOURGEOIS ORIGINS AND A MONOPOLY OF ACCESS

Morocco's political elite may be viewed as a series of concentric circles, reflecting concomitant variation in the locus and extent of influence and visibility. To begin, there is the monarchy. The person of the king is the institutional and political center of the nation, and King Hassan easily dominates the rest of the elite. Beyond the palace is the inner core of the national elite, which one reliable estimate placed at 200 in the early 1970s (Hermassi 1972a, p. 102) and which appears to have increased to a moderate but not significant degree since that time. Individuals in this category are for the most part political party and union leaders and senior officials in the various ministries. Some also hold or have held positions in the Cabinet or National Assembly, institutions that further structure and delineate elite activity. The members of this inner circle are composed overwhelmingly of highly educated individuals who come from a small corps of urban bourgeois families.

The next circle subsumes the rest of the men who exercise political influence on a national scale. This general elite includes approximately 600–700 individuals, drawn from three discernible categories. First, there are persons of rural origin who have achieved political prominence on the national level, most often through service in the Interior Ministry or one of the rural-based political parties. Adding these individuals to those of the elite's inner circle, a 1965 inquiry concluded that Morocco possessed about 300 "high officials belonging to the ruling class" (Marais 1973, p. 193), and a major study appearing five years later suggested that top political leaders and senior civil servants numbered 430 (Waterbury 1970, p. 86). Second, there are senior army officers, who numbered about 100 in the early 1970s and for whom more recent figures have not been found, although it is certain that their numbers have more than doubled in the last few years. The majority of the army's top officers are men of rural and Berber origin. Finally, there are 100 or 200 influential individuals outside the formal political system, including leaders of business associations, religious institutions, and so forth, who may reasonably be counted as part of the general elite.

The outermost circle is defined by the local and rural subelite. This class of individuals includes about 325 *caids*, or rural administrators; a larger number of influential sheikhs and others over whom the *caids* in theory have jurisdiction; the leaders of approximately 800 local councils; political party officials at the grass-roots level; and those members of parliament with influence only in their home districts. As with urban and national elites, the personnel of these institutions overlap. Individuals sometimes hold multiple offices or, more frequently, move from one position to another during the course of their political careers. Some individuals holding these positions are also middle-level officers in the army. Finally, as previously mentioned, there are again "big men" who exercise influence from outside the formal political system. Attaching numbers to these categories is extremely difficult. Perhaps the rough estimate of 5,000 is as good as any, and obviously there are important variations in power and influence among the individuals in this category.

Although a few individuals of rural origin have served at the highest levels of government, it is the educated sons of the urban bourgeoisie who control the inner circle of national politics and who are the major beneficiaries of high government status. This cadre of elites is socially homogeneous and its bourgeois character reflects a powerful association between political leadership, economic dominance, and privileged origin. The political continuity of the central leadership group is also evident. Its members were prominent in the nationalist movement, assumed important political offices after independence, and have remained the nucleus of the political elite since that time, despite that many changes in Moroccan politics.

Bourgeois families capable of making their impact felt on a national level emerged in only a few cities. Fez is the most notable of these; but Rabat, and to a lesser extent Salé, Marrakesh, and Meknes — more or less in that order — are also important. Tangiers and Tetouan would probably be in this group too, had they not remained outside the national sphere during the Protectorate period. The status and influence of the bourgeoisie in these urban centers derives from three factors: economic prosperity associated with commerce, handicrafts, and later, landholding;

service in the administration of the Alawite dynasty, prior to the establishment of the Protectorate in 1912; and religious importance based on descent from the Prophet and the provision of *ulama*. These factors were not unrelated, but commercial, *makhzan* and *shurafa* families tended to be regarded as separate entities, and it is the commercial families that came through the Protectorate with their influence most intact.

The prosperity of many commercial families increased during the early years of the Protectorate. Opportunities for trade expanded with the pacification of formerly dissident regions and with new import-export activity. In some instances, the availability of lucrative positions in the enlarged indigenous administration also benefited families with educated offspring and/or political connections, contributing further to the wealth and influence of the privileged few. After 1935, the importance of moving heavily into "modern" sectors of the economy became clear and many families, with Fassis in the lead, transferred their businesses to Casablanca. Some subsequently made fortunes during the war. It is the sons of these commercial families, most prominent among which are "thirty or forty sprawling and illustrious" Fassi clans (Waterbury 1972b, p. 76), who were the most important elements of the nationalist movement prior to independence and who are today the foundation of the Moroccan elite.

The educational experiences of these elites are remarkably similar. Until the 1930s, education among the bourgeoisie was principally within the Islamic system, with advanced education at the venerable Qarawiyin Mosque University or, less frequently, the Ben Youssef University in Marrakesh. The nationalist movement, which came to fruition with the creation of the Istiqlal Party (PI) in 1943, was begun by Qarawiyin graduates who were the first generation of bourgeois children educated after the establishment of the Protectorate. But leading urban families increasingly recognized the need to educate their children in European ways, and modern secular instruction soon became preferred in bourgeois circles, not only in Fez but in other cities too. Modern secondary education centered on College Moulay Idris in Fez and College Moulay Youssef in Rabat, schools through which passed virtually all the country's present urban elite, including the few individuals from poor families who used modern education as a passport to elite status. Studies at Moulay Idris and Moulay Youssef included much work in Arabic and preparation for the French *baccalaureat*.

Higher education was probably not viewed as an absolute prerequisite for elite status during this period, but it was highly esteemed and most of those who ultimately achieved high political positions did indeed proceed to university (Duchak, pp. 160 ff., and 233). Seventy-nine percent of the Moroccan cabinet ministers in 1964, for example, had received a higher education, all but one of these at French universities (Quandt, p. 185). Compared to other North Africans in France, Moroccans were distinguished by their relatively small number, their privileged origins, and a playboy image. But most were in fact quite politically conscious. They joined the North African Muslim Students Association (AEMNA), established ties with the future leaders of other North African countries, and discussed colonialism and independence with students and intellectuals from many countries. Most also flirted with Marxism during these years, though the majority was motivated principally by nationalism and, following their studies, joined the older generation of nationalists in the Istiqlal.

Participation in the nationalist movement and the PI is another experience shared by the sons of the urban bourgeoisie on the road to political leadership. By the end of the war, the Istiqlal was led primarily by the younger, Western-educated offspring of Morocco's powerful commercial families. The older generation of traditionally educated men who had founded the party, and who of course were also of Fassi bourgeois origin, remained in the PI in coalition with the young Turks. Also, grass-roots party administration was generally in the hands of individuals with a religious education and a more traditional orientation (Ashford 1964, pp. 31 ff.). Nevertheless, the younger elements assumed leadership roles, worked to transform the party into a modern mass movement and used it as a steppingstone to high political status after independence. The PI's traditional leadership was largely eclipsed during these years and did not regain control of the party until a split occurred in 1959, three years after independence.

The convergence of elite origins, wealth, education, and early political experience has created a leadership group that on the one hand is small, privileged, and divorced from the masses and on the other hand is ingrown and homogeneous by virtue of shared associations. The ingrown quality of the elite is attributable to common as well as similar experiences. Most of its members came to know one another well during their schooling and subsequent nationalist activity. Friendships and rivalries often date from secondary school, for example; and, in at least one instance, men who are today the leaders of rival political factions lived together during their school years in Paris (Waterbury 1970, p. 109). Common clandestine activity or even imprisonment during the nationalist struggle led to yet additional ties among these men. Finally, the families of these individuals are well known to one another and extensive and often deliberate intermarriage among them contributes an institutionalized dimension to these alliances and interconnections. In a few cases, marriages have also helped to integrate into the elite some of its members of more modest origin. Thus most members of the elite are well known to one another and share personal ties as well as comparable life experiences.

The elite is also homogeneous with respect to sex; religion; and among its dominant urban and bourgeois component, linguistic and cultural background. Women are noticeably absent from positions of power and authority. Indeed, among 51 prominent Moroccans listed in the "Who's Who" sections of several recent regional handbooks, the only woman mentioned is Princess Lalla Aicha, who has occasionally served her country as an ambassador. The elite is also composed exclusively of Muslims. A few Jews did hold high positions during the first decade of independence, but they were viewed as representatives of Morocco's then relatively large Jewish community rather than as members of the elite per se. Moreover, they have been absent from national politics for over 15 years, the highest political office held by a Jew since that time being a seat on the Casablanca Municipal Council. The segment of the elite that has been described is also composed almost entirely of Arabs, coming in some cases from families that converted from Judaism to Islam several centuries ago. The absence of Berbers from this component of the elite is attributable in substantial measure to the strong Arab identity of urban bourgeois families, to the establishment of separate educational systems for Arabs and Berbers during the Protectorate, and to the fact that tribal elements and rural areas generally remained outside the nationalist movement.

Age, which in substantial measure is a proxy for generation, does differentiate among the elite's inner circle, introducing potentially important variations in experience and outlook. Men who completed their schooling prior to or during World War II constitute the first generation of the contemporary elite, although there are of course some age differences within this group. These men were born in the 1920s or before and are today in their 50s and 60s. They traveled closely the route to prominence that has been outlined, and their cohort continues to dominate the national elite.

Men who completed their education about the time of independence comprise the second generation of the elite (Ashford 1973, p. 94). These individuals are too young to have participated extensively in the nationalist movement, but they were in their formative years during the period of the most intense nationalist activity, and they were certainly marked by the struggle for independence. Beyond this, their origins and educational experiences resemble closely those of the generation that preceeded them. The number of students completing the *baccalaureat* and proceeding to French universities increased toward the end of the Protectorate but remained extremely small in absolute terms. Only slightly more than 1,000 Moroccans obtained a *baccalaureat* between 1912 and 1955. There were only 134 Moroccans studying at French universities in 1947–1948 and there were still less than 400 in 1955–1956 (Moore 1970, p. 49). Moreover, access to these educational opportunities continued to be dominated by the urban bourgeoisie. Thus the second generation of the elite remains small and privileged and comes from the same mold as the one before it. The members of this cohort are for the most part in their 40s today and many already have considerable tenure in second-level or occasionally even top-level government positions.

The third generation of the elite is the first postnationalist generation. It was educated after independence, when the government expanded dramatically opportunities for schooling and began to shape the academic curriculum. Third generation leaders are today in their 20s or early 30s and, as a group, they have not yet made their mark on the national scene.

The fourth generation is that of the 1980s and 1990s. It is composed of students who have grown up completely since independence and who are today coming out of institutions of higher learning. The impact of the third and fourth generation, both of which are much larger and more heterogeneous than the first and second and no longer tied to the urban bourgeoisie, will be discussed later.

In present-day Morocco there is clearly a strong correlation between status and prestige on the one hand and power and influence on the other. The country's most powerful leaders come from wealthy and prestigious backgrounds; they have the added status that comes with having led the country to independence; and, among comparably aged segments of the population, they have a virtual monopoly on the kind of modern education that is both a source of prestige in and of itself and, more generally, a *sine qua non* for political leadership. Also, as the preceding discussion of education suggests, the elite benefits from the absence of groups that can significantly challenge it for positions of national prominence. Not only was the availability of modern education severely limited during the Protectorate; Morocco experienced a conservative form of colonialism generally, the result being limited social mobilization and few opportunities for the acquisition of political and administrative experience. Thus the Moroccan middle class was very small in 1956, and its members were able to move into the uppermost positions of leadership more or less unchallenged.

Although the king occupies the central position within the Moroccan ruling class, it is important to note that King Hassan's origins and background unite him with the rest of the elite's inner circle. The monarch at independence was Mohammed V, a leader who was revered on religious grounds and also for his contribution to the nationalist movement. But by temperament and education, Mohammed V was a leader of the old school, keeping direct contacts with the people, insulating himself from partisan politics and acting as a generally neutral political arbitrator. Crown Prince Hassan brought to the monarchy a new temperament and political style. Hassan is of the same generation as most of the present urban elite and he has a law degree from France, giving him training comparable to that of most Moroccan politicians and a similar attachment to European culture. Equally important, he has a wide range and long history of personal associations with the elite's most important members, having grown up in the same privileged urban bourgeois milieu and having known many of the country's present leaders during his youth. Finally, he has interacted with the elite regularly and closely since his ascent to the throne, breaking completely with his father's political aloofness and emersing himself in the making of policy and the building of alliances. Thus the king shares the experiences and orientations of the rest of the elite's dominant core, adding further to the homogeneity and ingrown character of this small group of men.

The preceding has focused on the inner core of the political elite, whose origins and experiences tie it to the urban bourgeoisie. Turning to the men who comprise the remainder of the national leadership class, one also finds members of the urban bourgeoisie but, in addition, there are many individuals of rural origin who have used the army, the Interior Ministry, a political party, or some other channel of political mobility to enter the elite at the national level. A summary of the origins of these individuals and of the path most have trod to political prominence will describe the circumstances of a secondary but nonetheless important subset of the national elite. It will also provide descriptive information about the mainstream of the elite's outermost circle, the class of rural notables who exercise power and influence on the regional and local levels.

Prior to the establishment of the French Protectorate in 1912, the Alawite dynasty, from which King Hassan is descended, was the central authority in Morocco. Those parts of the country over which its authority extended were known as *bled el-makhzan*, or land of the government. Territory not controlled by the *makhzan* was known as *bled es-siba*, or the land of dissidence; and while some of these areas consistently remained beyond the influence of the central government, others passed in and out of *siba*, as it were. Under these conditions, the most powerful local personages were *caids* and *pachas*, who were rural administrators in the service of the Alawites; tribal chiefs and other intermediaries who operated on a regional scale, acting as power brokers between the *makhzan* and the regions it did not control; and local religious leaders known as *marabouts*, who were often united in loose confederations and who were particularly influential in the regions of *siba*.

Colonialism radically altered the character of local authority in the rural areas. *Marabouts* lost influence with the pacification of dissident regions and their incorporation into the national sphere, and the class of *caids* and *pachas* that had served the *makhzan* in territories under its control was transformed into a dependent rural bureaucracy. The latter officials were given permanent jurisdiction and permitted to enrich themselves to a moderate degree. On the other hand, their autonomy was greatly undermined because they were strictly supervised by French *officiers*. The French also encouraged an expansion of power by several *grands caids*, individuals who had exercised political authority on a regional level prior to the Protectorate and who thereafter, at great profit to themselves, facilitated French control of large areas in the south of the country. Finally, the French worked to divide Arabs and Berbers, in the hope of isolating the rural world from Arabism and, ultimately, nationalism. College Azrou was founded in 1927 to provide French-oriented postprimary education to the sons of Berber notables. The Berber *dahir*, or decree, which took Berber areas out of the Islamic judicial system, was promulgated in 1930.

The *grands caids* were removed from power at independence. More importantly, most of the 400 *caids* and *pachas* who had been the backbone of rural administration during the colonial period were also removed. Having been compromised by their association with the French, they returned to the land to make way for nationalist cadres, many of whom were not from the regions they were assigned to administer. Nevertheless, substantial continuity of status and influence has been maintained in the countryside. The families of most *caids* were influential prior to the Protectorate, not only because of their administrative role but also by virtue of their wealth in flocks and property, and most used their resources as well as their position under the French to give their sons a modern education. This schooling involved study at a local *école des fils des notables* and, for some, postprimary schooling at Azrou.

Azrou, which prepared students for the *brevet* degree, was the pinnacle of a closed educational network for Berbers. As the French intended, its graduates were poorly prepared to pursue their studies at urban high schools, where facility in Arabic was required. On the other hand, students at Azrou were not completely immune from Moroccan nationalism, although the colonial associations of their families and their physical and cultural separation from the urban mainstream kept most from becoming active in the struggle for independence. In any event, Azrou provided the foundation for much of the present rural elite. A few of its graduates did go on for more advanced training. In addition, some used it as a stepping-stone to the military academy at Meknes and, ultimately, a position in the French and later the Moroccan army. The majority returned to work in the rural areas, however, constituting at independence a nascent rural bourgeoisie that possessed both continuity with prior leadership and the qualifications for effective participation in modern institutions. For these reasons, and also because they sought for their own political purposes a counterweight to the Istiqlal and the rest of the urban elite, Mohammed V and later Hassan II encouraged the political ascendancy of this class of individuals; and as a result of all these developments, present-day rural elites, whether they have moved into the national arena or remained at the local level, tend to (1) be from rural *makhzan* families that have long been prominent by local standards, (2) be products of a closed Berber educational system, (3) have had no more than a high school education, and (4) have associated themselves with the king since independence while remaining apart from the rest of the urban elite.

Since the countryside was not mobilized during the colonial era, established rural notables had little competition for elite status. After independence, the PI did attempt to exercise political leadership in some rural areas; but, in general, the rural bourgeoisie has maintained and even enhanced its advantaged position, replicating on a smaller scale the association between wealth and political influence that exists at the national level and among urban elites. Old guard families retain influence through their children and other family connections, and many have been able to consolidate their wealth, particularly in terms of landholding. Further reinforcing social and economic disparities is the slow rate of rural development since independence, including the fact that the proportion of children attending school is far lower in the countryside than in the cities. So far as politics per se is concerned, members of established rural families are disproportionately likely to be elected to and to preside over local communes (Leveau, pp. 24–25); political parties and the national administration are most likely to seek their rural candidates and civil servants from among the same advantaged population categories; and political power at the local level is often exercised by men of wealth and high status who do not hold office but who manipulate their resources to influence political decisions.

The preceding description of elites of rural origin must be supplemented with three additional observations. First, intergeneration differences among rural elites are not yet significant but may have dramatic long-term consequences. Younger rural notables are somewhat more ideological in orientation than older elites. They are also more urbane. Continuity and agreement on prevailing patterns of leadership seem more important than these differences so far as first and second generation elites are concerned, but changes will become more substantial with the emergence of succeeding political generations. The closed Berber educational system disappeared at independence, with the result that rural children in general, and the sons of established rural families in particular, today attend the Arabic-oriented schools of the Ministry of Education. Moreover, the children of rural notables often pursue their secondary studies at a *lycée* in Casablanca or some other major city, intensifying the difference between their training and experience and that of their parents. Beyond introducing intergenerational differences among rural elites, this means that urban-rural differences and Arab-Berber differences generally, to the extent these are not proxies for social class, will also be less important in the future.

Second, the presence of rural elites with a traditional religious education — graduates of Qarawiyin and Ben Youssef universities — should be noted. Urban graduates of these institutions tended to join the nationalist movement, and after independence many continued to serve as middle-level cadres in the PI. Political activity was less pronounced among rural graduates, many of whom have preferred to return to their land. On the other hand, these men are often highly respected and sometimes participate in what might be called a "secondary elite," those who influence the people who rule (Eickelman 1978, p. 489). In addition, they have not been totally absent from more active political roles, occasionally serving as parliamentary representatives from rural-based parties, for example.

Third, the presence of wealthy and influential men of rural origin in several cities, especially Casablanca, should be noted. Traders from the Suss area in southern Morocco have dominated commerce in foodstuffs since late in the Protectorate period, becoming an important category of retail merchants in the city and also assuring the distribution of many products from the city to the hinterland (Waterbury 1970, pp. 133 ff., and 1972b). Some Sussi traders have amassed large fortunes and built important ties to urban elites, though they remain too closely tied to their rural origins to enter into the urban elite per se (Adam, p. 339). Their potential political significance resides in the fact that they have helped political parties reach rural immigrants in urban slum neighborhoods, that they can serve as a link between urban politicians and the rural areas, and that much of their wealth returns to their home areas to reinforce the position of the local bourgeoisie.

STRUCTURE: THE MONARCHY, POLITICAL PARTIES, AND OTHER INSTITUTIONS

The Moroccan constitution formally establishes the king as the leader and symbol of the nation. It also grants him wide powers of appointment, providing a legal foundation for his active involvement in political life. Beyond the legal basis of his authority, however, the preeminent position of the monarch reflects a moral foundation for the king's leadership, his control and manipulation of a national patronage system, and his willingness and ability to suppress political opponents when he deems it necessary. Each of these considerations need be summarized only briefly at present; the sources of monarchical power will be more fully elaborated later.

The moral foundation of the king's leadership is composed of several elements, all of which provide a reservoir of loyalty and support among the rural masses. One such source of legitimacy is religion. The king is recognized in both orthodox and popular Islam as the spiritual leader of the nation; he is thought by some to have almost magical powers (as evidenced by his escapes from death in 1971 and 1972); and he has encouraged popular beliefs about his religious importance by sponsoring religious activities and festivals in the countryside, by presiding over national Islamic celebrations, and by avoiding any policy that would put him in opposition to the religious establishment. Another important source of legitimacy is the historic role of the monarchy, including the present king's position in a dynasty that has ruled Morocco since 1664; the success of Mohammed V in tying the monarchy's traditional role with a popular, nationalistic one during the Protectorate; and historic divisions between Arab and Berber and between city and country that make the king the only available focal point for national unity. Finally, there is the king's ability to associate himself prominently with nationalist causes. For example, fearing his position after attempted military coups in 1971 and 1972, Hassan sought to identify himself with popular aspirations by nationalizing foreign-owned business and property and by sending soldiers to fight the Israelis in 1973. His principal success came in 1975, however, when he launched the "Green March" into the Spanish Sahara and gained enormous popularity by recovering lands that nationalists had been claiming as Moroccan since before independence. Hassan had been calling upon Spain to relinquish its colonial dominion in the western Sahara, and thereby enable Morocco to reintegrate this part of its historic territory; and the "Green March" involved assembling 350,000 Moroccan civilians on the frontier between Morocco and the Spanish Sahara in support of this demand and then making a short symbolic march across the border. In the face of these developments, Spanish authorities agreed to turn over to Morocco the northern two-thirds of the territory and, with Moroccan approval, to cede the remainder of the colony to Mauritania.

The king's popular legitimacy not only strengthens his own position but also gives him a commodity to share with his followers in return for their loyalty. The support of the monarchy can increase the legitimacy of a candidate for local office, for example. Nevertheless, the king's alliances are based primarily on instrumental rather than affective exchanges, and the dispersion of his charisma is of interest to other elites and to most of their followers as but one element of a more comprehensive system of patronage. In other words, while the king uses traditional and affective sources of legitimacy to maintain his popularity among the masses and to strengthen his hand against other elites, he exercises influence among the elite itself by orchestrating and dominating a clientelist system that permits him to keep others dependent upon him. Major political and administrative positions are appointed by the king and accepted by the rest of the elite as legitimate foci of royal patronage. This enables the monarch to reward supporters; to punish or coopt opponents; and since "there are always plenty of Moroccans willing to assume public responsibility regardless of the strictures placed on their freedom of action" (Waterbury 1970, p. 270), to play off against one another the various members of the ruling class. In addition to the monarch's unrivaled access to political and economic resources, the king's control of a national political machine is further enhanced by the institutional fragmentation of the elite and its isolation from the masses, both of which the palace does nothing to discourage.

A final point is that Hassan has not hesitated to suppress serious opposition. Members of opposition political parties have frequently been arrested and their newspapers have been censored or seized. Following the 1963 elections, for example, some PI members and many leaders of the rival Union Nationale des Forces Populaires (UNFP) were arrested. Some were reportedly held in solitary confinement and even tortured. UNFP followers were also arrested and tried for treason in 1970 and 1971, and press seizures were specifically defended by Hassan in a 1972 speech because "attacks on institutions rather than policies" cannot be tolerated. Yet another round of political trials took place early in 1974. While numerous other examples of the suppression of opposition could be given, it is also important not to overemphasize the authoritarian character of the Moroccan regime. Opposition parties and newspapers have been permitted to operate and considerable criticism of the regime has in fact been tolerated, making the Moroccan political system at least somewhat more open than that of many other developing countries (Hudson, p. 228). In addition, political prisoners have frequently been pardoned and, if willing to work within the system, permitted to return to positions of influence. Nevertheless, for most of the period since independence, the king has had the power and the will to suppress serious challenges from rival politicians; and this coercive ability, as well as the monarch's traditional legitimacy and his control of the national spoils system, is responsible for his political dominance.

In addition to being a constitutional monarchy, Morocco is also a multiparty parliamentary political system. The vitality of these institutions waned greatly in the years following independence, however, with, once again, a steady transfer of political control to the king. The fate of the once powerful PI, which shared center stage with the monarchy during the nationalist era, illustrates the beginnings of this process.

As the party of Moroccan nationalism, the PI was allied with the king prior to and immediately following independence. But the Istiqlal was plagued by internal dissention after 1956 and lost many of its most dynamic and militant leaders when it split in 1959. The defection of these younger and relatively radical elements, who left to form the UNFP, a new party on the political left which in 1974 evolved into the Union Socialiste des Forces Populaires, or USFP, cost the PI much of its support among the urban masses. The PI also encountered trouble in rural areas during this period. A number of new parties were founded in the late 1950s, and some made rapid gains in the countryside, due in part to support from the monarchy but also because the PI showed little sensitivity to established patterns of rural politics and attempted to replace local leaders with its own cadres. As a result of these developments, even though the Istiqlal remained the best organized of Morocco's political parties, its base of popular support diminished greatly and its appeal was soon limited almost exclusively to religious, bourgeois and petty-bourgeois urban elements. Finally, in 1963, the PI passed into the political opposition when the king turned away from his previous alliance with the party and expanded his association with rural notables and the army.

The decline of the PI was not associated with the acquisition of power by newer political parties; and, more generally, parliamentary activity was carried out only intermittently during the decade and a half following independence, and when parliament did convene it was characterized by *immobilisme* and the absence of effective political power. The parliament elected in 1963 was disbanded in 1965, and elections for a new parliament did not take place until 1970. Further, the new elections were boycotted by opposition parties, who consequently held only 22 seats in the 240-member chamber, and as a result the parliament was no more than a rubber stamp for policies put forward by the king and his ministers. Even more important, the new parliament was itself disbanded after the 1971 coup attempt. A new constitution, which remains in effect at the present time, was promulgated and approved in 1972; but the PI and the UNFP, already longstanding members of the opposition, declined the king's invitation to join a government dedicated to this constitution. Thus, in sum, parties and the parliament were important in defining the institutional structure of national politics and the formal roles played by some of the elite's leading members, but they were not associated with the exercise of autonomous political influence and contributed little to the shaping of public policy.

A new phase in Moroccan politics began in 1974, the most important trends being increased political liberalization and a reinvigoration of political parties. These developments have not altered the central position of the monarchy. Nor have they substantially modified the composition and character of the national elite. But it is possible that the seeds of a more long-range political transition have been sewn, and in the short run there have been measureable changes in the relative importance of elite institutions.

The roots of the present political configuration are in the attempted coups of 1971 and 1972, which will be discussed further in connection with the military. Prior to this period, the king had to a degree emulated the former French colonial strategy of building an alliance with the rural and Berber world, thereby contributing to the fragmentation of the elite, to the isolation of the urban bourgeoisie and, ultimately, to his own political supremacy (Hermassi 1972a, pp. 104 ff.). He had also come to rely heavily on the largely Berber army for institutional support, permitting it to expand its influence with the decline of political parties in the 1960s

(Zartman 1973, p. 253). But the coup attempts showed that the military's traditions of loyalty and neutrality could not be counted on to override personal and political discontent. Indeed, some observers wondered in the wake of the coup attempts not only whether the king could still count on the army but whether Berbers in general would continue to support the monarchy. Student strikes in 1972 and 1973 and armed attacks by leftists in the latter year added further to the mood of uncertainty.

Hassan responded with political and policy initiatives, including a new constitution and nationalizations at home and increased militancy in foreign policy. The situation did not change significantly until 1974, however, when an atmosphere of national unity emerged in response to developments in the Sahara and when the king made new overtures to the long inactive political parties. Elections were announced and, though later postponed, considerable political activity was set in motion. The major opposition parties, the PI and the USFP (formerly the UNFP), held party congresses early in 1975, for example.

The king's popularity soared with the "Green March" in November 1975 and, in 1976, he made a major speech announcing municipal, provincial, and national elections and calling for cooperation from all political parties. Observers noted that Hassan had apparently decided on parliamentary democracy. He stated in his address that he had been preoccupied with the Sahara in 1975 but now his attention would be turned to politics. Local elections were held at the end of 1976 and provincial elections early in 1977. The abolition of press censorship was another manifestation of the growing openness and vitality of political life.

In March 1977, after considerable debate, the PI and the USFP agreed to join the government, principally in the hope of assuring that the parliamentary elections scheduled for June of that year would be conducted fairly. Conservative and progovernment candidates had won over 60 percent of the seats in the local and provincial elections, and the opposition claimed that there had been irregularities in the balloting. Independents were again the big winners in the parliamentary elections, but this time the PI was successful too, with the USFP being the major loser. The June election was not completely free of government interference, but most observers were more impressed by what they saw as a successful return to parliamentary democracy. The present configuration took final form when the Istiqlal entered the new government in October 1977 and the USFP became the nucleus of a small parliamentary opposition. It may also be noted that the reintegrated Saharan territory participated in the election and sent three representatives to parliament.

In addition to reinvigorating the party system and changing at least the outward character of political life, the king also managed to improve remarkably his own political fortunes. His personal popularity was never higher, his rule was supported by democratic or quasi-democratic political institutions, and his political opposition was reduced and divided. Since

1977, however, the evolution of the situation in the Sahara has made it likely that important new changes will occur in the future.

Morocco's Saharan problems began in 1976, when a group of Saharan intellectuals known as the Polisario (Popular Front for the Liberation of Saguia el Hamra and Rio de Oro) asserted that the indigeneous population of the former Spanish colony wanted independence of rather than unification with Morocco. The Polisario declared their country's independence in February of that year and raised a guerilla army that undertook its first raid on occupying Moroccan forces several months later. The Polisario is based in Algeria, from which it receives substantial assistance, and the Saharan Arab Democratic Republic it claims to represent was by mid-1980 recognized by a majority of the African states, plus several other countries. Fighting with increasing effectiveness in 1977 and 1978, Polisario raids helped to bring about a coup d'etat in Mauritania in July 1978, leading to the formation of a new government that renounced that country's claims to Saharan territory. Morocco quickly annexed the land ceded by Mauritania; but the Mauritanian coup was nonetheless a setback for Morocco, reducing the latter country's international support. Even more important, the military threat from Polisario forces continued to mount, even as Morocco itself devoted ever more troops and resources to the war effort. Throughout 1979 and 1980, the Polisario roamed over large amounts of Saharan territory, regularly inflicting heavy casualties on the Moroccan army and frequently staging raids within Morocco itself.

Inability to win the Saharan war and severe economic dislocations associated with its conduct have led many to predict that popular support for the prevailing political order in Morocco will soon decline dramatically. Between 1977 and 1980, however, the overwhelming majority of both the masses and the elite enthusiastically endorsed the country's territorial claims in the Sahara and strongly supported the king and the government in their determination to secure this claim, whatever the cost. Indeed, in the short run, the war in the Sahara and attempts by the Polisario to win international support have actually strengthened the domestic position of the king and the government that came to power following the 1977 parliamentary elections. Thus, whatever the problems that lie ahead, the reinvigorated parliamentary system that emerged in the wake of the "Green March" continues to function actively and to structure much of the activity of the present-day elite.

There are seven political parties with representatives in the 264-member parliament elected in 1977. These are the Rassemblement National des Independants (RNI-141 seats); the Istiqlal Party (PI-49 seats); the Mouvement Populaire (MP-44 seats); the Union Socialiste des Forces Populaires (USFP-16 seats); the Mouvement Populaire Democratique Constitutionnel (MPCD-3 seats); the Parti de l'Action (PA-2 seats); and the Parti du Progres et du Socialisme (PPS-1 seat). There are also eight nonparty members of parliament, of whom six represent the Moroccan Union of Labor (UMT). A brief overview of these parties will further clarify the nature of the present political situation, as well as give additional descriptive information about the institutional foundations of contemporary elites. The PI can be mentioned first, since many of its major characteristics should already be clear.

Despite its early prominence and organizational strength, the PI lost much of its influence after independence and joined the parliamentary opposition in 1963. It remained conservative in orientation and outlook, however. Indeed its leftist partners in opposition, with whom it made an informal "common front" in the early 1970s, considered it reactionary. The PI was associated in particular with the orthodox religious establishment and with the most conservative elements of the old urban bourgeoisie; and thus by the time the party reentered the government in 1977, it was widely regarded as a party of "the past, the right and the privileged."

At present the Istiqlal is attempting to move in new directions, claiming to stand for egalitarianism and national development. Some recent party publications even assert that the PI embraces socialism. Partly for this reason, negotiations for cabinet positions in the government formed in 1977 were laborious, with the PI insisting that it wanted important ministries in order to be able to launch development initiatives. Also, although the PI continues to profess that its philosophy is inspired by Islam, it has moderated some of its traditional conservative policies, such as opposition to the use of French in schools. Finally, it has been active in calling for the recovery of Spanish territory in northern Morocco. This rhetoric notwithstanding, however, the Istiqlal has not yet taken the lead in establishing any dramatic new programs, and it remains to be seen whether the party will be able to balance its participation in a government dominated by the king, the long-established interests of its traditional supporters, and a proclaimed desire for new policy initiatives.

The USFP began in 1959 as an offshoot of the PI. Its leader was Mehdi Ben Barka and it was known at the time as the National Union of Popular Forces (UNFP). The UNFP participated in the government briefly after its creation. As a party oriented towards the urban masses, however, with radical positions on economic and cultural issues and with strong ties to the trade union movement, it represented the most important challenge to the king, and accordingly it was the object of repressive measures by the army and the palace after 1960. The party also suffered from a weak organizational base, being more of a "movement of opinion" than a formal political party, and in addition it was severely hurt by internal divisions. Many of its leaders were criticized by younger and more radical elements for their ties to the rest of the elite and for their willingness to work within the prevailing political system. The USFP was formed by dissident elements in the Rabat section of the party, who broke with the UNFP in 1972 and then formally established their new party in 1974; and thereafter the UNFP declined in significance, failing to participate in the 1977 elections and permitting the USFP to emerge as the foundation of the political left. The experience of the UNFP illustrates the left's historic weakness, despite the importance of the population categories to which its appeal is directed, and most of its old problems now confront the USFP.

Although the USFP rejoined the government for several months prior to the 1977 legislative elections, the party was the big loser at the polls. Even its leader, Abderahim Bouabid, was defeated in his district. Since the USFP is the only viable representative of the Moroccan left, with an audience that is certainly larger than the small percent of the vote it received, the honesty of the elections has inevitably been questioned. On the other hand, supporters of the USFP themselves acknowledge that they were to a considerable extent swept away by the euphoria of the "Green March." In any event, the party is in a delicate position, not unlike its situation in the past, and its principal leaders are struggling to define their role in the new parliamentary system. These men have considered joining the government but realizing that younger elements within the party would oppose such a move, they have abandoned the idea in order to keep control of the movement. At the same time, they are attempting to avoid a total break with the king and the rest of the elite.

The position of the USFP leadership has been made even more delicate by the evolution of the Saharan war. Like almost all other segments of Moroccan opinion, the political left supports the government position on the Sahara and in the wake of recent war-related difficulties has found it difficult to resist pressures to close ranks behind the king. Thus, USFP leaders agreed in 1979 to participate in a newly formed National Security Council (NSC), created to oversee the conduct of the war. Interviewed about this development, the leader of the USFP acknowledged that it reflected greater elite solidarity and support for the king on the issue of the Sahara. He denied, however, that the NSC was a disguised national unity government and stressed that his party still opposed the king on domestic issues. Nevertheless, the decision to join the NSC was strongly criticized by younger and more radical elements within the USFP and by external observers normally sympathetic to the party. These critics charged that the party had allowed the king to use the Saharan situation to undermine the position of the political left and, more generally, that the credibility and effectiveness of the USFP's claim to offer an alternative to the government had been severely weakened.

A final point about elites of the left is that they also include a small nucleus of individuals who have broken completely with the prevailing political system, going far beyond the self-styled "constructive opposition" of the USFP. These individuals are Marxist-Leninists, rather than socialists, and some of them currently reside in France. Among their positions are support for the Polisario and criticism of their own country's

Saharan policy and, more broadly, condemnation of the existing social and political order in Morocco, which they see as exploiting the masses and serving only a priviledged bourgeoisie. For the present, their efforts are limited to polemics and have little influence within Morocco, although Hassan has nonetheless felt it prudent to suppress their activities vigorously. Perhaps their greatest potential for exerting influence over the long haul is in undermining the USFP and thereby winning converts among party members who believe their leaders are unwilling to function as a serious opposition.

The RNI is the majority party in parliament, although it was more of an electoral alliance than a formal political party at the time of the 1977 balloting. It was fashioned in the mold of the former Front for the Defense of Constitutional Institutions (FDIC), which was a coalition of independent candidates pledged to the king in the 1963 parliamentary elections. The independents are unconditional monarchists, who sometimes even describe their program as "Hassanism," and their success shows the extent to which the king dominates the political system.

The RNI became a formal political party in October 1978. Four thousand delegates to a party congress elected a national council of 355 individuals, who in turn elected a central committee of 60, from which an executive committee of 15 was then chosen. The composition of the RNI's leadership is diverse, creating some ambiguity about the party's politics. Over half of its parliamentary delegation is composed of men from the liberal professions, and many have had previous experience in the upper echelons of government. The party has also attracted a number of defectors from other parties, including the USFP and the communist PPS. These characteristics make the party representative of much of the elite establishment and *"les grands interests."* On the other hand, the party's parliamentary delegation contains many young men in their 30s and 40s with less political baggage, and there have in fact been some spirited exchanges in substantive discussions. The party has also dedicated itself to programs of social justice, though its emphasis is on technical competence rather than the ideology of the socialist left.

The MP is the party of rural conservatism, its largest base of support being Berber notable families in the north and central mountain regions. The party was established in 1957, by men who had led the resistance when Mohammed V was deposed by the French, and its principal commitments involved loyalty to the king and opposition to the PI and the urban bourgeoisie. In the legislative elections of 1963, the party joined the FDIC in support of the king, although it was careful to maintain its organizational autonomy.

Though generally regarded as the party of Berberism, the MP does not stand for ethnic nationalism and has sought the support of younger and less self-consciously Berber rural cadres. What the MP has historically represented is the alliance between the palace and the rural notables against the Istiqlal, even though it is not of course the totality of that alliance. In 1972, following the second coup attempt and with the PI and the UNFP in opposition, the MP was the only party in parliament, and it responded positively to Hassan's call to form a new government. This was particularly important since the coups had raised questions about Berber loyalty to the king. At present, the party continues to play an important role in the government. It did well in the 1977 legislative elections and received four ministries in the cabinet formed later that year. Some also regard the MP as a stabilizing force within the reinvigorated parliamentary system. On the other hand, the party's importance could well diminish in the future, with the emergence of the RNI, the decline of Berber consciousness among the young, and increased social mobilization in the countryside.

The remaining groups in parliament are far less important. The UMT, which is not a party but has historically been allied with the UNFP, holds six seats. It obtained these seats in the second stage of the 1977 elections, wherein one-third of the chamber was chosen by an electoral college composed of councillors in local government and representatives of employers' organizations and labor unions. The UMT is part of the opposition in parliament. The PPS also belongs to the opposition. It is the descendent of the Communist Party, which was suppressed in 1959 but permitted to reform after 1974. The PPS holds only one seat in the present parliament, and this because candidates loyal to the king voluntarily withdrew in the constituency where its leader was a candidate. The party has been strongly supportive of the king's Saharan policy, condemning the Polisario and joining the newly established NSC in the spring of 1979; and thus, though it remains in the opposition, the PPS has been charged with insufficient militancy by many leftists. Some describe its leader as a *pretendu communiste*. The PA is in the opposition too. It was founded in 1974 by a former resistance leader who was briefly associated with the UNFP. The party's strength is in the Rif mountain region, and its platform is social justice and opposition to the elite establishment. The MPCD, on the other hand, supports the government. The party was also formed in 1974, as an offshoot of the MP. Its leader is one of the founders of the latter party but a man of urban origin who has stronger ties to the urban elite than to the rural and Berber world. The party supports the monarchy and does not appear to have an independent platform.

Although policy decisions are turned into legislation by parliament, policy itself is usually formulated by other, smaller political structures. The cabinet, with its leaders often operating in consultation with the king, is the obvious center of such policy-making activity. There is also a smaller Council of the Throne, composed of the king and top leaders of the parties in the government's parliamentary coalition. Little is known about its workings, but it appears to be the institutional setting within which are held discussions between the king and the elite's most influential members on matters of major significance, such as Morocco's position on the Sahara or the Middle East dispute. Finally, there is the newly created NSC, which is the center of at least some deliberation concerning the war in the Sahara. The NSC is notable in that it includes representatives of opposition parties, as well as those belonging to the government. In the reinvigorated parliamentary system that has structured political life since 1977, these institutions are the vehicles by which leaders of the elite articulate their views and translate them into policy initiatives.

In addition to these structures that are formally responsible for the making of public policy, there are also organizations that act as interest groups in the articulation of political preferences. One category of interest groups is composed of national associations of manufacturers and businessmen, an example of which is the Moroccan Association of Textile Industries. These associations have historically been stronger in Morocco than in other countries of the Maghreb, due in part to the fact that wealthy commercial families supplied much of the elite. Nevertheless, economic organizations have never been more than informal channels for facilitating communication with political authorities and, moreover, most have steadily declined in importance, as a result of both a general political climate that discourages autonomous centers of influence and expanding government control over the economy and foreign trade. Thus, economic associations have political relevance principally in that they are led by individuals who are strategically placed within the economy and who have personal ties to the leaders of more overtly political organizations or to senior government bureaucrats. Many of these men have also been able to articulate their views through intermittent membership on the king's private economic council, which advises the monarch on matters of economic policy.

Labor and student unions are a second category of interest groups. The largest and strongest labor union is the UMT, which is associated with the remnant of the UNFP but is not really independent of the elite establishment. Like other elements of the political left, it opposes the government on the substance of policy but accepts the rules of the political game. UMT leaders are regularly consulted by the king on important policy issues and many also hold government positions, leading younger union militants to question the validity of their so-called constructive opposition. Not surprisingly, the UMT has historically maintained its position among its own rank and file by emphasizing jobs and economic benefits rather than ideology and political symbolism.

Another labor organization is the General Union of Moroccan Workers (UGTM), associated with the PI. The UGTM is almost as large as the UMT but even less independent of the rest of the elite. There are also three smaller unions, the Moroccan Union of Autonomous Labor, the Free National Syndicate, and the National Union of Moroccan Workers, which is associated with the MPCD; but no evidence exists that any of these exercises significant or independent political influence. Finally, a new socialist-oriented union, the Democratic Workers Confederation, has recently emerged and is expanding its membership in such important fields as education, transportation, and the phosphate industry.

The National Union of Moroccan Students (UNEM) is the structural foundation of the student movement. The UNEM, which has long been one of the government's most militant critics, has historically been well-organized and used its institutional strength to politicize students and recruit members for the left opposition. Moreover, it was able to organize extensive protest strikes by high school and university students in 1972 and 1973. On the other hand, UNEM effectiveness in influencing government policy has been limited. Its strikes and demonstrations in the early 1970s failed to shake the regime or elicit major gains. Instead they resulted in the union being banned. The UNEM was legalized again in 1978, and it is presently returning to an activist posture. Its organizational capacity is now limited, however, and most of its leaders do not simultaneously hold other positions that enable them to participate in the political process. Thus it remains to be seen whether the UNEM will be able to exert any more political influence in the future than it has in the past.

Three additional sets of institutions structuring elite activity should be discussed. The first concerns local government. The second concerns religious leaders and institutions. The third concerns the military. With respect to the first, *caids*, sheikhs and other local officials, and local communes may be considered. The approximately 325 *caids* provide the linkage between the national administration and the rural population. Above them are the provincial and regional officials, including *chefs de cercle*, popularly known as *supercaids*, and provincial governors in that order. Below them are sheikhs and other representatives of local society at the subdistrict level. There are also 24 *pachas*, who are the administrative equivalents of *caids* in the urban areas. Following independence, these positions were at first given to former nationalists; but, as local administration was standardized, the *caids* gradually emerged as an identifiable class of career officials. Most today are educated, competent, and apolitical, except in the sense that they are of course servants of the established order. *Caids* are rarely from the districts they administer. Many are graduates of Azrou, and some are army officers working within the Interior Ministry. Still others are younger men, some of whom have been trained in a special school established in 1964, and many of these are of urban origin. As previously stressed, *caids* also tend to be drawn from bourgeois families that were influential prior to independence and used their position to secure a modern education for their offspring.

Below the *caids* are the *khalifas* of urban quarters, the *muqaddems* of rural villages, and the sheikhs of tribal or clan fractions. In contrast to *caids*, who are often regarded as agents of an alien political system, these individuals are regarded as representatives of local society rather than as officials of the national administration. They are of course from the areas in which they exercise authority; and, partly for that reason, they often have more local influence and prestige than do the *caids*, to whom they are presumably responsible. In a sense, sheikhs and others have the position held by the *caids* themselves during the colonial era, being the real points of contact between the people and the government. They are the only officials who live among the people and know them intimately, and their position is enhanced by the fact that the administration relies on them heavily to collect information and allocate resources. Officials at this level are usually persons with high status in traditional society. In addition, however, an important qualification for leadership is the ability to form associations with and extract resources from higher political officials.

Local councils, or communes, were established in 1959, and the first communal elections took place in 1960. Councils have as few as 9 members in sparsely populated districts. The largest council is in Casablanca, with 51 members. The total number of communes is about 800; and each has an elected president and, if it is large enough, an executive committee. Communes and communal elections are technically arenas for party competition, but individuals loyal to the administration have tended to dominate and charges of election interference on behalf of the government have been common. In addition, candidates for council positions are usually chosen from among the members of the local establishment; and council presidents are particularly likely to be comparatively well-educated sons of rural bourgeois families, in other words the same kind of men who tend to be chosen as *caids* outside their home districts.

The influence of local councils is generally restricted to minor economic matters. The legislation creating them provided for significant budgetary powers; but while Mohammed V apparently regarded them as schools for rural democracy, Hassan has had no interest in using them to increase individual political participation. Thus, *de facto*, councils remain subservient to the *caids* who control their agenda, and the governor has the power to veto any council action of which he disapproves. This is not to say that the councils are of no significance, however. Rural commune members are often viewed by the population as legitimate representatives of local society. Further, there are at least some instances where a council has raised meaningful objections to the actions of a *caid* (Leveau, p. 59). Finally, a position on a local council, especially the presidency, can be an important steppingstone to higher office.

The political role of Islamic leaders and institutions must also be considered, especially since Morocco, like other Muslim countries, is experiencing a religious revival. At present, religious figures are at best secondary members of the national and local elite and, in general, they have been on the defensive against a secular and Western-oriented leadership class. At the same time, the present and latent political significance of Islam should not be underestimated.

In the countryside and in the villages, the direct political significance of *marabouts* and *fuqaha,* or local religious teachers, is minor. Most have no following outside their immediate localities and restricted influence even within their home districts. One study of village-level *fuqaha,* for example, assessed the ability of these men to influence local attitudes toward family planning and found it to be limited. The *fuqaha* addressed the matter exclusively in terms of Islamic theology while most people, and especially women, were influenced by social and economic considerations (Bowen). On the other hand, other investigations report that many rural individuals have strong personal ties to Sufi orders and other religious institutions, that socializing in the context of worship at brotherhood lodges often fosters important political and economic relationships, that popular religious figures are still highly esteemed by some segments of the rural population, and that religious ties and piety are often factors in local prestige, enhancing an individual's status and perceived fitness for leadership (Dwyer 1978a, pp. 36 ff., and 1978b, p. 586; Eickelman 1976, pp. 218 and 236, and 1977, p. 10; Leveau, pp. 206 ff.; and Maher, 1974, p. 90). Thus, while traditional men of learning are rarely members of the local bourgeois and bureaucratic elite, upon which the king has based his rural strategy, their presence and continuing prestige represents a possible alternative to the leadership of the present class of rural notables. Further, their influence could increase significantly should growing material disparities or other problems intensify political discontent in the villages and rural areas.

In the cities and at the national level, Morocco's *'ulama* retain popular appeal and are of political significance. As with other religious figures, these teachers and scholars hold no formal office and do not possess direct political authority. But, viewing themselves as protectors of Islam and the welfare of Muslims, they will speak out if they believe government policy is injurious to Muslim well-being; and thus they are widely consulted by political authorities, who are eager to avoid the appearance of being in opposition to Islam. In particular, the king is loathe to appear as anything other than a total supporter of the religion, given that Islamic attachments have traditionally contributed to his legitimacy and popularity among the masses, and this gives the *'ulama* something approaching a veto on religious issues and assures that they will be visibly present at many political functions. There is no evidence that the *'ulama* are discontent in this important but informal political capacity, and to date most remain faithful supporters of the monarchy and the prevailing political order. Also, in contrast to local-level religious leaders, most have a view of Islam that permits them to support government efforts at limited social and cultural change, as in the areas of education and family planning, for example. Thus, in sum, the *'ulama* are secondary members of the elite who operate comfortably within the present-day context.

Like other Muslim countries, Morocco is experiencing a religious revival, and this raises the possibility that the political significance of Islam could change in the future. At the nonelite level, this revival involves increased individual piety generally and growing interest in popular culture among the better-educated strata of society; the formation of Islamic study groups and increased membership in other religion-oriented organizations; greater popular followings for religious figures having strong personalities; and a rise in the sale of books, records, and cassettes devoted to Islamic themes. The extent and political significance of these activities are not well known, but one observer suggests that some young workers and students seek to put more Islamic content into their lives as a reaction against Western cultural and economic dominance (Lambert). The religious revival is particularly pronounced among young urban men with some but not extensive modern education, and the political importance of this fact lies in the possibility that their heightened religious consciousness derives in substantial measure from economic and political discontent, as in some other Muslim countries (Tessler 1980, p. 13). The circumstances of these individuals permit them to be politically mobilized with comparative ease; and if their intensified interest in religion reflects a belief that modern and Western political formulae are inextricably linked to bourgeois privilege and exploitation of the masses in contemporary Morocco, then an Islamic revival clearly signifies latent opposition to the present political system.

At the level of the elite itself, the Islamic revival has the potential to strengthen critics of the present regime who have religious connections. One of these is Abdesslam Yasine, an admirer of Iran's Ayatollah Khomeini and a leader of religious opponents of King Hassan in Morocco. Yasine was arrested in 1974 for his denunciations of the king and was held in detention for three and one half years. He publishes a small Arabic-language magazine devoted to criticizing the current political system and advocating a return to Muslim principles; and with growing popular interest in Islam, his activities are closely watched by political authorities. One observer quotes Yasine as saying, "At the beginning we did not think of changing politics or the world. But now the mosques are full of young people" (Markham, p. 125). Another notable critic of the government is Fqih Mohammed el Basri, leader of the external opposition. Basri is a former PI resistance leader and newspaper editor who helped to found the UNFP. He was arrested in 1959 on charges of plotting to assassinate the Crown Prince but was released four months later without coming to trial. Basri now resides in Switzerland, and in 1979 he visited Tehran and was warmly received by Iran's revolutionary leaders. During his visit, he compared the Shah and King Hassan and called for the overthrow of the latter. Whether the Islamic revival will continue and expand and, if so, whether it will increase opposition to the present Moroccan elite, are of course possibilities whose prospects for realization are sharply debated and extremely difficult to predict.

The army, which plays a particularly important political role, is the last institutional structure of elites to be considered. During the first 15 years of independence, military elites were a source of support for the palace, quashing rural uprisings in the Rif Mountains and quelling urban riots in Casablanca in 1965. The Royal Armed Forces (FAR) have historically been staffed by Berbers, being fashioned at independence from the Army of Liberation and Moroccans in the French and Spanish armies. The former was dominated by Berber soldiers, who subsequently entered the rank and file of the FAR. The officer corps of the new army was composed principally of men educated at Azrou and Meknes who had served with the French forces. As with other educated rural elements, these men also tended to be sons of wealthy and prominent families.

Given their rural and Berber character, army elites served not only to maintain order for the king but also as a political counterweight to the Istiqlal and the urban establishment. Army officers, for their part, were generally eager to participate in this alliance. They believed in an apolitical military loyal to the state. They also believed that strong ties to the palace were the best way to preserve the rural and Berber world from being dominated by the urban elite, although this is not to suggest that they were advocates of Berber nationalism. Finally, they recognized that the army provided an important avenue for personal mobility and for access to resources, enabling them to participate in the same national spoils system as other elite elements. With the coup attempts of 1971 and 1972, however, the alliance between the military and the king was badly shaken.

The motivations of the rebellious officers in 1971 and 1972 are not fully known. Sincere frustration over widespread political corruption appears to have been one factor. But these officers' concern with their own status and future may also be relevant, and this includes a fear that younger officers would take the initiative and sweep them away along with the rest of the elite. Both civilian politicians and loyalists within the army insisted that the rank and file remained faithful to the king during this period, and it is clear that during the first coup troops were very specifically told they were being brought in to protect the monarch. Nevertheless, doubts about whether the king could continue to rely on the army were inevitably raised; and the harsh punishment of coup leaders, including the execution of many senior Berber officers, increased these doubts because many loyal officers were embittered by the loss of friends or relatives (Waterbury 1972a, p. 417). Indeed the king's harassment and degradation of the army after the events of 1971 contributed to the disaffection of his chief of staff and fostered a new bitterness toward the palace, which led to the second coup attempt 13 months later.

The monarch's response to this crisis of confidence has been twofold. First, he has sought to associate the military prominently with popular and prestigious national causes, most notably the Saharan venture but also participation in the 1973 Middle East war and more recently the fighting in Zaire. This has rebuilt the prestige of senior army elites, tied them more firmly to the king, and given the latter an opportunity to provide them with substantially increased material resources, including personal comforts. The army's budget doubled between 1974 and 1978, for example. Hassan also finds occasions to praise the army publicaly for its loyalty and bravery. Second, as previously discussed, Hassan has permitted the reemergence of political parties, giving him a larger number of actors to utilize in maintaining a balance of political support. Prior to this period, the influence of the army had increased as a direct result of the decline of the party system.

In part as a result of these strategies, army elites appear to be staunchly loyal to the king at the present time. This could well change in the future, however. The character of the officer corps is changing and this could have political consequences over the long haul. In the short run, frustration within the military is growing as a result of recent difficulties in the Saharan war, and this too could threaten the relationship between the king and the armed forces.

So far as the character of the officer corps is concerned, younger military men are more ideological and less unconditionally tied to the existing political order than older officers. They are also more likely to be of urban and Arab origin than the generation that preceeded them into the military. Urban families have actively worked to launch their offspring in military careers, and the more stringent educational requirements for admission to the military academy, necessitated by the sophisticated nature of modern weapons, have also tended to favor middle-class young men from the Arab coastal cities. These changes mean that a new type of politicized army officer is beginning to appear, and these men could be particularly hard to please should they conclude that their personal advancement is being retarded by conservative older officers. In this situation, personal and political grievances could converge, undermining loyalty to the king and possibly even providing a stimulus to political action.

A source of more immediate concern about the army's political role has emerged in relation to Morocco's Saharan campaign. Although the country has about 80,000 of its 115,000 troops tied down in the Sahara and is spending approximately 40 percent of its national budget on the war, the fruits of this effort have been limited. Moroccan troops control the major Saharan towns and the phosphate rich Bu Craa area, but Polisario forces roam freely throughout most of the rest of the territory, including parts of southern Morocco. Moreover, Morocco has been struck by bold and successful Polisario raids within its own territory and is reported to be suffering 100–150 military casualties a month. Finally, the Saharan issue has brought Morocco to the brink of war with Algeria and cost it considerable international support. Twenty-six African states had sided with the Polisario by mid-1980, for example. Yet Morocco refuses to admit the possibility of compromise and has resisted attempts at external mediation, insisting that the Saharan affair is an internal matter. The attitudes of the military toward this situation are not well known; but the best guess is that troop morale is low and senior officers are being kept happy by the privileges and opportunities for enrichment that civilian politicians are careful to provide. In any event, should a negotiated solution remain elusive and the military situation continue to be unfavourable, possible scenarios include the army forcing the king to call for an all-out attack on Polisario sanctuaries, which could bring full-scale war with Algeria, and lower army ranks turning against civilian politicians and senior officers for sending them to fight a war they cannot win.

POWER SOURCES: CLIENTELISM AND THE THREAT OF COERSION

The exercise of power takes place only secondarily through the utilization of formal organizations. Parties and other political institutions are not irrelevant. They structure a substantial amount of elite interaction in the political arena, and they articulate in institutional terms the philosophical differences that divide a socially homogeneous elite. Also, in the last few years they have assumed increased importance as foci of parliamentary activity and as agents of contact between elites and their constituents. Nevertheless, organizational roles and affiliations remain secondary factors in determining a politician's ability to advance specific political interests.

Alternatively, political power is accumulated and exercised principally though participation in a system of political and economic clientelism, by being able to situate oneself in the upper levels of a series of intersecting networks of patron-client relationships (Waterbury 1970). To accomplish this, members of the elite use their connections with one another and with the palace to obtain access to resources, which are employed not only for self-enrichment and the benefit of one's immediate clientele group but also for the construction of broader alliances and interdependencies. The objective of these alliances is to preserve or improve one's position within the overall system, and such connections are pursued by (1) establishing onself as an important link in the chain by which higher authorities and other elites distribute resources in order to increase loyalty to themselves; (2) acquiring political debts that offset one's obligations and that can be called in when one's position is challenged; (3) expanding the scope of one's affective ties or of alliances that give others a stake in the maintenance or enhancement of one's position; and (4) avoiding immutable positions or a permanent rupture with competitors and their client groups. Success in accomplishing these objectives permits one to increase the number of his clients and to acquire patrons of greater prominence, and this is tantamount to the enhancement of political power.

This system of clientelism, which has operated more or less continuously since the early days of independence, may not endure for many more years. It is fundamentally conservative and has severely limited absorptive capacity. For the time being, however, these patterns prevail. One factor that makes clientelism possible is the elite's strategic placement in the nation's economy, including numerous directorships of banks, credit agencies, business associations, and the like. This gives the elite special influence in such areas as customs, currency, import-export, and public and semipublic finance, all of which provide numerous opportunities for economic favoritism. It also assures ties to the palace, which is the ultimate repository of patronage and where decisions about the distribution of resources among the elite itself are most often made.

Further encouraging and shaping the character of clientelist politics are the ingrown nature and small size of the elite. Interconnections among the elite are based on common bourgeois origins, shared educational experiences, joint involvement in the nationalist movement, and intermarriage among prominent families. Most elites are also known to one another and interaction among them is frequent and extensive, being based on far more than shared participation in formal political institutions. Indeed, the elite has been described as a sort of "kingdom of cousins" (Moore 1970, p. 284). There are also divisions among political leaders, based on personal jealousy or, less frequently, ideology; but in the aggregate differences are cross-cutting rather than coinciding. Client groups of competing individuals often find themselves allied on other issues, as indeed may the individuals themselves, and this creates patterns of "bet-hedging," which preserve freedom of action and permit adversaries to join together when a new challenge arises. The stability of this "segmented" system is also abetted by the availability of family ties that may be called upon to limit centrifugal tendencies and by the elite's ability to predict one another's values and behavior after years of regular contact. Finally, the small size of the elite is important. Without it, the degree of intimacy and homogeneity necessary to keep the clientelist system operating smoothly would be extremely difficult to achieve. Even more critical, if the elite were substantially larger, available resources would not be sufficient to satisfy all political actors and the system's absorptive capacity would rapidly be overwhelmed.

Traditional Moroccan values concerning political relations and the exercise of power are consistent with the political style of the national elite, and it is possible that the former also help to determine the character of the latter. Relevant norms include segmentary patterns of social relationships, whereby individuals view themselves as members of intersecting corporate entities (linked in traditional society by alleged patrilineal descent) that divide or coalesce depending on the degree of external challenge; a related view that the manipulation of kinshiplike sentiments for sociopolitical objectives is appropriate and legitimate; and a belief that the purpose of alliance-building and manipulation is to minimize dependence on others while maximizing personal autonomy and authority. One scholar asserts that these values are "applicable to situations of political conflict far from the tribal context" and that elite behavior is "founded upon a shared cultural tradition" that "comes naturally and spontaneously to members of the elite" (Waterbury 1970, pp. 8 and 63). Thus the centrality of patron-client relationships and segmented alliances in the national political arena may in part reflect the influence of Morocco's social and cultural heritage.

At the same time, it would probably be inaccurate to endow the association between traditional political values and the elite's contemporary style with too much explanatory power. The national elite is far removed from the segmented patterns of traditional rural society by virtue of both its origins and education. In addition, an explanation of its clientelist political system that emphasizes agreement on the rules of the political game in order to maximize collective self-interest and assure that the greatest rewards go to those at the top of the political hierarchy is highly compelling. In any event, whatever the relative contribution of the various factors that have given rise to and perpetuated these patterns for exercising political authority, patron-client relationships and participation in the spoils system of a top-heavy political machine have "displaced and dwarfed all other forms of politics" (Waterbury 1973, p. 534; Moore 1977, p. 258). They are the mechanisms that organize elite interaction, and they define the behavioral norms according to which the elite seeks to gain and exercise power.

Clientelism also defines the most important mechanism by which power is acquired in the countryside. Describing the way that political influence is exercised generally, one observer writes that "an ambitious man no longer acquires or maintains a following unless he himself has patrons in the administration; he has become a broker rather than a leader, and a patron only by virtue of his support and recognition from above" (Seddon 1972, p. 138). This conclusion also emerges from two studies of the 1963 legislative election campaign. On the other hand, candidates tended to come to a disproportionate degree from wealthy and established families (Leveau, pp. 213 ff.). On the other hand, most candidates employed campaign slogans emphasizing a superior ability to aid constituents by virtue of good relationships with higher political elites (Marais and Waterbury; Zartman 1975, p. 501). Thus rural politics is dominated by a class of wealthy landowners and bureaucrats who are enriched through their ties to the national spoils system and who use their connections to that system to reward their followers and, at the same time, maintain or enhance their own position. These rural elites have no illusions about the social order they are helping to perpetuate; but for themselves at least, and possibly for the rural world in general, they consider this system to be preferable to any plausible alternative (Marais 1972b, p. 282).

Participation in this system by rural elites is not motivated solely by the desire for personal gain, and popular support for local notables does not depend entirely on the ability of the latter to extract resources from the national system. Less instrumental considerations are also present. One such factor, though of only limited significance, is Berberism. Berbers frequently prefer to vote for other Berbers in local elections (Leveau, p. 99), and they are often conscious of their ethnic identity in other political situations. On the other hand, a Berber will usually vote for an Arab when to do so is in his material interest (Rosen, pp. 162–163), and in any event there is broad agreement that Berber nationalism is not a significant political force.

An expressive factor of greater significance may be rural concern about dominance by alien and disdainful urban politicians. Many conservative rural leaders tend to distrust the Western-oriented national elite. More broadly, rural cadres, and presumably rural inhabitants in general, resent being made to feel backward and inferior by urban politicians (Leveau, p. 23). Further, piety, knowledge of tradition, and personality all influence popular attitudes toward elites in the rural areas, affecting an individual's ability to attract support and accumulate political influence. These considerations do not override clientelist connections, but they are significant nonetheless. Moreover, they could become substantially more important should rural stagnation and growing economic disparities lead the peasantry to question whether support for a rural bourgeoisie with ties to the national elite really does serve its material interests.

Returning to the national level, clientelism provides for elite cooperation by requiring agreement on the rules of the game. A few politicians of the political left have abandoned the system, and there are also complaints from students and some professionals without the connections necessary to enter to game at a meaningful level. Further, as will be discussed shortly, there is growing pressure from younger, emerging elites. But most of the present elite shares an interest in preserving the clientelist system and is willing to see resources distributed so as to minimize challenges from within. Clientelism also structures elite competition, but in the context of a relatively closed and stable system of influence-seeking. Attempts to improve one's position in the political hierarchy by gaining access to increased resources and by attracting a larger clientele group are regarded as normal and legitimate political actions. Attempts to mobilize support on the basis of ideological appeals that involve challenges to the regime or to the rules of the game are not legitimate and have been regularly suppressed. Politicians who have flirted with the latter strategy may be reintegrated into the elite, however, after they have been shown the folly of their action and demonstrated a willingness to participate in the prevailing system.

Though based on a quest for personal influence rather than the achievement of normative goals, competition within the elite can be intense. Individuals jockey for position within their immediate political spheres (for example, a party, a ministry, the cabinet) and also with respect to the elite as a whole. The instruments of this competition are service to more established political actors or if possible directly to the palace; the judicious use of resources acquired from one's benefactors, in order to enlarge one's own clientele; and appeals to the clients of rival patrons, using personal and family ties as well as material inducements.

On the other hand, competition among individuals and combinations of interest organizations makes the clientelist system seem much more dynamic than it actually is and has in fact tended to work against social change and political development. There are several reasons for this. First, political position is defined principally on the basis of personal loyalties and only secondarily on the basis of technical competence. Second, frequent changes in political appointments, reflecting shifting or expanding alliances or attempts by senior officials to reduce the autonomy of those below them, create discontinuities that hamper effective planning and policy-making. Finally and most important, the maintenance of the clientelist system and the ability of the present elite to dominate requires that social transformation be limited. This is necessary to retain the support of clients, almost all of whom have an interest in the status quo and would deny their support to patrons who seemed to be forging new alliances, and because the mobilization of new groups would add unpredictable actors to the system and threaten to overwhelm its resources. The competition within the elite, intense though it may be on occasion, is thus one of style rather than substance, pertaining to the pursuit of personal gain and not to the accomplishment of a political program.

The king presides over the political system and, as previously mentioned, his preeminent position is based on (1) popular support derived from affective bases of legitimacy, (2) access to resources and control of appointments that enable him to dominate in clientelist politics, and (3) coercive ability that permits him to eliminate or suppress elites unwilling to accept the rules of the game. The palace is thus the ultimate repository of power, with king accepting the role of guarantor of the prevailing political order.

Despite a widespread belief that his religiosity is to a considerable extent motivated by political considerations, Hassan is an impeccable Muslim in public and finds many occasions to demonstrate his devotion to Islam. In a 1979 speech, for example, he warned against those who would divide Islam from present-day reality and called upon the *'ulama* to increase their participation in the country's daily life. Whatever the degree of his sincerity, such expressions are calculated to bolster the king's image among both religious leaders and the Muslim masses. Hassan's approach to other historically derived sources of royal legitimacy has been similar, the most notable of these being his personal association with traditional Moroccan nationalism in the context of the Sahara. On the other hand, Hassan has never possessed the religious or historically derived charisma of his father, Mohammed V; and more generally, such affective bases of popular support appear to be declining in political significance in contemporary Morocco. They are still important. But they are relatively minor determinants of political loyalty among younger and better-educated Moroccans, and among others, they are increasingly unlikely to be strong enough to transcend attitudes based on economic and social considerations.

As a result of the preceeding, clientelism has become increasingly important to King Hassan. Although at a higher and more inclusive level, he employs the clientelist political system as do other elites, fashioning alliances and coopting or isolating political rivals. His most important alliance in this connection is with the rural-based parties and the rural bourgeoisie. The army is generally regarded as part of this coalition as well, although, as noted, its future position is less certain. This alliance, though called into question briefly in the early 1970s, has been dominant since independence and has been generally impervious to challenges from would-be rivals. Indeed it is the core combination of political factions that has been most successful in penetrating and undermining the solidarity of others. Connections with the palace give rural elites access to resources on the national level and provide them with the power and authority necessary to retain a preeminent position in their respective local communities. They, in return, give Hassan a broad base of grass-roots support and provide him with a counterweight to the more powerful and politicized elites of urban origin, whom he accordingly is able to isolate and prevent from developing an independent national clientele. Over the long haul, local-level opposition to the rural political elite seems destined to increase because of growing disparities of wealth and opportunity in the countryside. So long as these elites remain in power and persist in their alliance with the monarchy, however, the king will be the orchestrator of the national elite, rather than its puppet.

Control of the patronage system also gives the king other resources with which to dominate the national elite. Having effectively isolated them from the rural masses, he imposes his will on the restricted sphere of their interaction by simultaneously coopting them and keeping them in a state of dependency. On the one hand, he sees to it that their stock in the existing order remains high and holds out the promise of even greater wealth and influence. On the other, he keeps them in competition with one another and makes sure they understand that their own well-being and that of their followers is the result of his continuing pleasure. Both of these mechanisms of control are made possible by the monarch's ability to influence government decisions about resource allocation and by his direct and widespread power to appoint, transfer, and dismiss public officials. In the latter context, for example, cabinet positions and high civilian and military offices are all by constitution royal appointment. Senior judges are also appointed by the king, following nominations by a superior judicial council, as are ambassadors and other high-ranking officials. Thus it is not surprising that loyalty to the king is a major factor in the upward or downward mobility of individual members of the elite.

Most members of the elite have willingly accepted this arrangement. First, they welcome the benefits they derive from the existing order. Even the leaders of the USFP, the PPS, and the UMT — the core combination of institutions that is the nucleus of the political left and the parliamentary opposition — have shown themselves to be as interested in clientelist politics as in ideological purity. Second, they know that challenges to the position of the king have the potential to undermine the whole clientelist system. Rather than enhancing the influence of individual elites at the expense of the monarch, these challenges threaten the privileged status of almost all elites. For both these reasons, there is little enthusiasm for radical alterations of the prevailing political style.

Having opted for the maintenance of the present system, most elites appear to recognize that dependence on the king is an unavoidable fact of political life. Few if any are indispensible to the monarch; each knows that he could easily be replaced with a rival politician eager to do the king's bidding and that Hassan would not hesitate to carry out such an exchange if given cause. Also, few members of the national elite, even when aggregated into political organizations, have the kind of independent and reliable popular following that might limit their dependence on the king. The PI, despite its early importance, has been cut off from the rural masses by its own early insensitivity to local norms and, more significantly, by the king's alliance with the rural bourgeoisie. The PI has little following among the urban masses either, however, having by its own policies abandoned this clientele group to the parties of the left. But the left, which in principle should be able to challenge the alliance of the king and the rural world, has found its potential following divided, uncertain, and difficult to mobilize. Its ideological appeals stressing economic justice have, temporarily at least, been eclipsed by those based on nationalism coming from the palace, and which the left itself now echoes. Alternative appeals, based on access to resources rather than ideology and principle, may be more effective; but these depend on an ability to extract benefits from the political center, which of course means playing by the rules of clientelism and maintaining good relations with the king. All this, then, leaves King Hassan comfortably atop the political system, using his superior access to resources and his unmatched alliance-building capacity to dominate easily the rest of the elite.

While most elites have been willing to accept the rules of the game, Hassan has had the ability and will to use coercion against political rivals when other mechanisms of control have proved unsuccessful. Troublesome figures, most notably on the political left but occasionally in religious or other circles, have been exiled or arrested, with there sometimes being documented charges of torture in the latter connection. Force has also been used against antigovernment demonstrations and opposition publications have frequently been censored or seized outright. Critics charge that the government's unchecked ability to engage in political repression supports the entire edifice of Moroccan politics, eliminating those who would seriously threaten the status quo and intimidating most others into accepting the existing system, even though they recognize that it produces stagnation and injustice. Other observers suggest that while specific acts of repression have indeed occurred, the regime is at least comparatively tolerant of dissent and grants citizens relative though admittedly not complete political freedom. Moreover, the latter tend to add, the return to parliamentry rule in the late 1970s has been associated with increased liberalization and democracy, making criticism of the authoritarian side of Moroccan political life increasingly outmoded. Strongly held convictions of both varieties can readily be found among observers of the Moroccan scene.

Compared to both its own recent past and to many other Middle Eastern countries, Morocco today does enjoy considerable political freedom. The 1976 abolition of press censorship appears to have been respected. The press of the USFP, for example, was able without interference to report on political prisoners in December 1977, and accounts of a hunger strike among prisoners was reported in the Istiqlal press in May 1978. There are also spirited debates taking place within the major political parties, and opposition leaders have been free to raise sensitive issues in parliamentary discussions, which has led the latter to acknowledge, while continuing to criticize the government on specific policy issues, that an evident democratization is indeed taking place. In addition, the king continues to make statements pledging himself to the maintenance of democratic forms and has released many political prisoners. Thus Morocco has been praised for its liberalization and some believe its movement toward democracy is irreversible.

On the other hand, repression still exists in present-day Morocco, current liberalization may reflect a reduction in the need to suppress dissent rather than an irreversible commitment to democracy, and there are still no effective political mechanisms that would prevent the king from using force against rivals should he wish to do so. With respect to the first consideration, leftist dissidents were arrested in 1975 and again in 1977. Further, Amnesty International reported in 1977 that torture had been used on persons sympathetic to the Polisario, although the government denied the charges. There have also been more recent reports of the arrest and mistreatment of opponents of the king's Saharan policy. In addition, as noted earlier, there were many instances of interferences in the elections of 1976 and 1977. Thus the advances that Morocco has made must be measured against the abuses that remain. Beyond these and other continuing limits on political freedom, it must also be noted that the real test of Morocco's proclaimed commitment to democracy lies ahead. With the king's popularity higher than it has been in years and the formal opposition weak and divided, there have not been effective challenges to the political status quo in the last few years. Indeed the return to parliamentary rule, coupled as it is with the Saharan campaign, has been an effective strategy for enhancing the king's political position. Yet the faltering performance of Morocco's forces in the Sahara and the increasingly disastrous economic situation of the masses will almost certainly place new pressures on the present elite in the not-very-distant future, and only then will it be clear whether Morocco is prepared to tolerate and respond in a democratic fashion to serious political opposition. Finally, before Morocca can be said to have made significant strides away from authoritarianism, there must be structural reform that makes political freedom more than another commodity to be granted or withheld at the pleasure of the king. To date, however, there has been little progress toward such a restructuring of power relationships; and thus the king's coercive powers, as well as his affect-based legitimacy and his ability to manipulate a national machine, is a critical source of power that enables him to dominate an institutionally diverse political scene.

SOCIALIZATION: POLITICAL CYNICISM AND ATTACHMENTS TO EUROPEAN CULTURE

It is difficult to establish precise linkages between the early life experiences and present-day attitudes of Morocco's elite. Nevertheless, the social origins of the elite should already be clear, and it is reasonable to conclude that the values and behavioral norms of these men reflect their privileged background and near monopoly on preparation for national leadership. Those fortunate enough to have had the family connections and/or educational qualifications necessary to enter the leadership class at the outset have thereafter had a privileged position; and the result has been a small, ingrown and essentially closed elite that sees itself as the natural rulers of the nation and that makes at best a hazy distinction between its own interests and those of the country as a whole.

Elite attitudes in this context have tended to be characterized by the absence of sharply held ideological positions and by shared values of economic self-interest. It is true that many members of the present elite turned to Marxism during their studies, but only a very few retained this interest after returning to Morocco. It is also true that the PI's 1959 split was based mainly on differences of ideology, with younger and more militant elements leaving to establish the institutions of the political left. But the radical character of these institutions should not be overstated. Their leaders belong to and share many of the sentiments of the rest of the urban bourgeoisie; indeed younger and more radical leftist today regard these men as hopelessly compromised and lethargic. On the other hand, militant Islamic conservatism and other ideologies of the right have also been relatively unimportant. The lifestyle of the elite is heavily influenced by European cultural patterns; the primary elite in even second-tier cities, such as Marrakesh, comes out of secular educational institutions; and since rejoining the government in 1977, even the Istiqlal has moderated some of its fundamentalist positions on issues like Arabization and educational policy.

The relative unimportance of ideologically inspired political values, coupled as it is with an emphasis on shared economic interests, creates a low sense of civic purpose. The elite is in some ways disenchanted with the corruption and influence-peddling that permeates the clientelist political system, yet this system supports their privileged position and they have little inclination to sacrifice themselves. Moreover, their dependence on the king adds to their frustration, as did the factionalism that made it impossible to come to grips with significant national problems during the early years of independence, before the autonomy of their parties was destroyed. The result of all this has tended to be attitudes of cynicism and apathy regarding political life and the exercise of power, frequently accompanied by retreat from the political mainstream and withdrawal into one's business ventures or other economic institutions accessible to the elite (Zartman 1973, pp. 253 ff.; Hermassi 1972a, p. 212). Rather than constituting a coherent set of values, these orientations suggest the absence of any belief system per se. But the coming together of political cynicism and economic self-interest defines the political culture underlying much of the elite's behavior.

These political attitudes are changing, albeit slowly, both as a function of generational shifts starting to occur within the elite and in the wake of recent developments in Moroccan politics. Second-generation elites are not quite as firmly tied to the historical associations and mental habits of the urban bourgeoisie as are those who preceded them; but on the whole, similarities between the two cohorts are much more striking than differences, with respect to both political style and attitudes toward politics. The situation will change with the maturation of third- and fourth-generation elites, however. While educational minima associated with elite status have risen from high school to university, difficulty in absorbing new elites, though slow in coming, is inevitable and will strain severely the clientelist system of the present elite. New values about politics and society will also be introduced, including an increase in the importance of ideology and greater emphasis on technical competence. The potential for change associated with the emergence of these new elites will be discussed more fully in the next section.

A more immediate, if limited, stimulus to political cultural change is the opening up of political life after 1975. The reemergence of political parties and the greater tolerance of political dissent have led to a tapering off of political apathy, despite continuing elite skepticism. The government has called for major new development programs and has strongly proclaimed its determination to effect a social revolution. Further, such proclamations emphasize economic justice as well as aggregate growth, and it is interesting to note in this connection that in a 1979 speech the king called for popular appreciation of the socialist character of Islam. Another aspect of these normative changes is the beginning of a gradual shift in patterns of political recruitment and the standards by which elite performance is evaluated. Specifically, there have been numerous calls for an emphasis on technical competence, rather than on political savvy in the traditional sense. For example, the RNI, as previously mentioned, is presenting itself as a party devoted to technocratic efficiency. "Classical politics," its leaders have asserted, "is a waste of time." A statement by the Minister of the Interior following the 1977 elections is particularly clear on this point: "There is a new generation of 'independent' technocrats ready to take over from the men over fifty who have been playing musical chairs for over a decade." Even the king has declared to the nation that "We cannot keep turning around with the same personnel and the same functionaries."

Despite these proclamations, one must wonder about the depth of the elite's commitment to new values and about the impact that any incipient normative trends will have on government activity in the foreseeable future. With respect to the called-for social and economic revolution, it seems unlikely that the elite will break with its long past and translate its statements into meaningful action. Historically, almost no elements of the elite have acted as innovators or catalysts for change. The monarchy has been unwilling to sponsor development programs for fear that they would result in social upheaval; and the elite more generally, despite its resemblance to a capitalist bourgeoisie, has been unwilling to invest in programs that would contribute to national development. Not only have its members had little sense of civic purpose, they also do not possess the economic attitudes that have stimulated growth in capitalists societies.

The paradox, as one observer notes, is that there is capital in the industrial and financial sectors but there is no capitalist class (El Malki, pp. 552–553). Other reasons for scepticism or pessimism about the prospects for dramatic change are that the gap between rich and poor has grown rather than diminished in recent years and that the country's general economic situation has deteriorated to the point that there may not be sufficient resources for any significant development efforts.

With respect to changing values about elite recruitment and performance, the salience of ideological commitment and technical competence seem destined to rise in the long run, at the expense of family and political connections and of skill in building patron-client relationships. Rapid movement in this direction is unlikely, however. Moreover, for quite some time it will probably be more significant among middle-level bureaucrats than among senior political officials. Thus, despite at least some verbal repudiation of the political values that have underpinned elite behavior since the early years of independence, a meaningful transformation of elite political culture is unlikely to occur until the generation of future leaders that grew up and was socialized after independence reaches the center of the political stage. Until that time, the orientation of the dominant elite will be marked by a disinterest in ideology and by political cynicism and an emphasis on clientelism, values that reflect the context of social and political privilege within which this elite acquired its conceptions of political leadership.

Although only indirectly related to the nature and origins of elite political attitudes, a few observations about the acquisition and transmission of political information among contemporary elites may be offered. First, newspapers are more important sources of political information than other formal media channels, with foreign papers and to a lesser extent French-language Moroccan papers being the favored source of information about international events. Second, in matters involving domestic and especially behind-the-scenes political activity, word-of-mouth communication may be the elite's most important source of information. This is because the government gives the press little news about private political discussions and provides it with few opportunities to investigate internal decision-making procedures. Thus many newspaper reports, even if not deliberately biased, are superficial, forcing elites to rely on conversations with colleagues and friends for much of their political information.

By way of conclusion, a brief summary of the elite's cultural orientations may be added to this account of the nature and origins of political values. On the one hand, European and especially French cultural forms are often preferred. French has maintained its status among a leadership class educated in that language and fluency in it continues to be both a prerequisite for success generally and a condition of membership in the elite's inner circle. In addition, European educational institutions are more highly esteemed than domestic ones. Most elites send their children to secondary schools run by the French Cultural Mission, for example, and overseas university training, especially in France, is considered the most prestigious training ground for future leaders and the best guarantee of status mobility. Similarly, so far as Moroccan educational establishments are concerned, modern and secular institutions of higher learning are accorded much more respect than traditional mosque universities. Graduates of the latter have even less chance of entering the political elite than was the case in the past; and, despite the beginnings of an Islamic revival, the kind of ideological transformation that would be necessary to change this situation is highly unlikely. Turning to religion per se, most of Morocco's present and future leaders possess a secular orientation. Few present elites appear seriously interested in religion, and studies have shown that religiosity is negatively correlated with political interest among students (Moore 1970, p. 283). Finally, Western forms tend to predominate in the area of entertainment. French is the principal language of cinema and the theatre so far as the elite is concerned. Also, most of the best known Moroccan writers and intellectuals work in French.

Despite the preceding, Moroccan leaders, like other North African elites, remain deeply attached to their national traditions. Their perspective is bicultural rather than purely European, and the weight of Arabism and Islam in the cultural equation of the elite is destined to grow. The government has worked since independence to Arabize education. Even the parties of the left support this objective. As a result, the first grades of primary school are now conducted completely in Arabic, and latter grades involve heavy usage of both Arabic and French. Also, most classes at the country's secular universities are now in Arabic. There has been progress in Arabizing government administration as well. The Judiciary Ministry was the first to be Arabized, followed by the bureaucracies of the police and the Ministry of Religion. In still another area, it is notable that while Morocco has few Arabic-language writers of international repute, the Moroccan Writers' League has selected as its president a man who works in Arabic. Finally, there is the possibility of increased elite interest in Islamic values. Some politicians of the left have moved to increase their familiarity with religious principles and popular culture, for example, apparently as part of an attempt to make their revolutionary programs more meaningful to the masses, and there have also been instances where French educated professionals have made common cause with the '*ulama* and with PI conservatives in defense of traditional cultural patterns.

The importance of the latter set of observations can easily be overemphasized, at least in terms of any immediate impact. While elites are sincerely attached to their country's traditions of Arabism and Islam, seeking by their reassertion to secure the linguistic and cultural independence of Morocco, the personal behavior and orientation of these men perpetuate a system that limits the social and political mobility of individuals without a thorough knowledge of European culture and the French language. Moreover, this situation reflects a cultural gap between elites and masses that will take on added political significance if expanding interest in Arabism and Islam among the educated middle sectors of society results in the cultural isolation of the present elite.

CIRCULATION: GENERATIONAL CHANGE AND PRESSURE FROM NONELITES

Although the king and the government have been pledging since 1976 to broaden the base of the political elite, parliament and the parties are today dominated by the same elements that have governed Morocco since independence. The leaders of all major parties are members of the privileged bourgeoisie described earlier. The same is true for the trade unions. The economically disadvantaged, on the other hand, have little or no representation at this level. The parliament, though the scene of many pronouncements about the need for social equality, is not representative of the Moroccan nation and includes few persons from those population categories that traditionally have had little political influence. Thus, five years after the proclamation of a return to democratic rule, the demographic character and social composition of the elite inner circle has not changed appreciably.

Looking ahead, the character of the elite can be expected to change more significantly in the future, as individuals educated after independence enter the elite and assume positions of prominence. But since the absorptive capacity of the present political system is severely limited, the emergence of a third and then a fourth generation of educated Moroccans will probably affect the political system most dramatically through external pressures brought by would-be elites who are frustrated at the inability to realize their ambitions. Though not an elite phenomenon, the present regime will also come under intense pressure from sectors of society whose economic position is deteriorating, sectors that could be sources of spontaneous opposition to the political establishment and that certainly will provide a fertile field for those emerging elites outside the leadership group who are seeking to challenge older and entrenched politicians. These pressures from emerging elites and the economically disadvantaged will be the most significant forces for political change in the years ahead.

As previously discussed, the current elite is composed principally of men educated prior to independence, men who make up the first two generations of the Moroccan elite. But a third generation of educated Moroccans is presently coming onto the scene, and a fourth will reach adulthood in the late 1980s and the 1990s. The third generation is very much larger and much more diverse than those that preceded it, even if only university-trained individuals are regarded as potential elites. The establishment of a national educational system following independence greatly expanded opportunities to acquire a modern and secular education; and the creation of a modern university system, based on Mohammed V University with faculties in Rabat, Casablanca, and Fez, provides for domestic as well as foreign university study. Thus in 1968, for example, a year during which much of the presently emerging third generation was still in school, there were over 11,000 Moroccan university students studying at local institutions of higher learning and approximately 3,000 more studying abroad. Only 7 percent of the individuals in the former category were attending traditional religious universities, however, and almost all in the latter category were studying in France. Most of these individuals, as well as the thousands of others who graduated from university during a period spanning roughly the years between 1960 and 1975, are now in their 30s, and it is reasonable to assume that the great majority of them aspire to enter the national elite. The number of potential elites constituting the fourth generation will be even larger. In 1979 alone there were about 70,000 Moroccans attending institutions of higher learning at home and abroad, of whom only 5 percent were in mosque universities.

In the aggregate there are important differences between the characteristics of older and more recent university graduates. Access to a modern education is still not distributed evenly. In rural areas, for example, the opportunity to acquire a solid educational foundation still remains far more limited than in the cities. Also, religious schools are often the most important educational institutions among the urban and the rural poor, and whatever their merits these schools rarely provide for continued educational mobility and subsequent entry into the elite. Another continuing inequity concerns women. Women are still substantially less likely than men to be in school. This is true at all levels, including university where in 1975 women comprised only 18 percent of the Moroccans at domestic and foreign universities. Nevertheless, despite all these limitations, the break with the past is dramatic. University graduates of modest origins number in the thousands, probably even the tens of thousands, and the number of young women with a higher education can reasonably be estimated at over 10,000. Thus the third generation of educated Moroccans will be far more diverse than the first and second generation and at least somewhat more representative of Moroccan society.

Beyond its greater size and demographic diversity, the third generation is also distinguished from its predecessors by less-rigorous academic training, by greater exposure to the study of Arabic, and by more radical political views. It was probably inevitable that the democratization of education would result in lower standards. The academic qualifications of students themselves have declined as the children of the poor enter the system. Many have illiterate parents and few have a home environment conducive to study. The quality of the system has also declined under the weight of these students, as inexperienced and ill-prepared teachers have been pressed into service and as limited financial resources have been stretched even thinner. The significance of these educational limitations is greatest at the primary and secondary school level, but they also mean that today's university students, in the aggregate, are less likely than those of a generation ago to have had a rigorous and high-quality education.

Studies are also more uniquely Moroccan, with much more work being done in Arabic. The generation of Moroccans educated after independence studied according to a curriculum developed and approved by the Ministry of Education. Most also completed much of their primary and some of their secondary schooling in Arabic, and many younger individuals who have attended university in Morocco have also been able to do some of their advanced study in Arabic. Differences between present and future elites with respect to the cultural and national orientation of their studies will be particularly pronounced when the fourth generation of educated Moroccans comes on the scene. Most of the latter will have completed all of their preuniversity schooling in the educational institutions of independent Morocco, subsequent to educational reforms and advances in Arabization. Studies from other Arab countries suggest that younger university graduates are less nationalistic and more oriented toward cultural reform than comparably educated older individuals, despite the fact that their education has been more national in character (Tessler 1976b). Yet there is also evidence that they remain attached to Arabism, Islam, and other cultural traditions that help to define their national identity. Taking changes in the quality and content of education together, some observers have predicted that future elites in Morocco will be less open to the external world than their predecessors and will not have the high cultural levels of their elders. They will, on the other hand, be more representative of the nation and less distant and alienated from nonelites (Marais 1973, p. 199).

Students educated after independence tend to be more politically radical than those who preceded them. Studies in the early 1960s concluded that as many as half the university students were openly critical of the government and supported the parties of the left opposition (Ashford 1973, p. 105); and subsequent surveys reported that the average Moroccan student felt intense hostility toward the regime (Moore 1970, p. 291). The period of greatest student protest was between 1965 and 1972. In the former year, students and teachers were joined by the poor in the streets of Casablanca and hundreds were killed in the riots that followed. Order was restored by the army, and numerous student leaders were arrested.

In late 1971 and early 1972, university and *lycée* students went on strike, prompting another round of arrests and the closing of most branches of Mohammed V University. Additional disturbances and more student arrests followed as 1972 drew to a close. The intensity of student protest has diminished since 1972, but this is irrelevant for third-generation elites, who passed through their student years in the 1960s and early 1970s. Moreover, reduced agitation does not mean that today's university students are any more supportive of the government than those of a decade ago. One observer reports that present-day students are not only sensitive to "traditional" Marxism but are often Maoist in orientation (Knapp, p. 295). A more recent study, based on survey research conducted in 1978–1979, reports that most university students are high in political alienation and judge the government to be unresponsive to the nation's needs. They hold the country's political institutions in low regard, condemning public officials for playing clientelist politics and stating that attempts to achieve political goals by democratic means are almost totally hopeless (Nedelcovych and Palmer). Finally, still another investigation reports that most educated young women are committed to feminism (Maher 1978, p. 88), yet another sign of militant and ideological orientations.

Third-generation elites tend to be trained in the humanities and liberal professions, rather than in the technical fields where cadres are still sorely needed; and thus, despite their high educational levels, they are likely to have difficulty finding jobs consistent with their aspirations. One consequence of this is a continuing shortage of trained personnel in many specialized fields. But the inevitable frustration and increased alienation of third-generation elites is of equal or even greater significance. A survey in the 1960s found students highly optimistic about their career possibilities (Moore 1970, p. 294), and this can only increase the radicalism of graduates who do not obtain a satisfactory position within the elite. It is worth noting that early estimates project a diminution of this problem among fourth-generation elites (Waterbury 1970, p. 304), although too much optimism may not be warranted. Figures from 1975 indicate that 74 percent of all Moroccan students were still majoring in either letters, law, education, or social science.

Though different in the aggregate from earlier generations, the emerging elite is not a homogeneous group. For one thing, many children of the bourgeoisie and the present elite attend schools of the French Cultural Mission. Thus the quality and orientation of their education is different from that of most other Moroccans educated after independence. In contrast to the majority of third-generation elites, for example, these individuals may actually have had less rather than more exposure than their elders to Arabic and Moroccan studies. Third-generation elites also differ with respect to their university training. Most children of the present elite and some others have studied in France. A larger number, for the most part of more modest origin, have studied at home. Political orientation is yet another dimension with respect to which there is considerable variation among emerging elites. While criticism of the government is high, accompanied in most instances by radical political attitudes in general, observers in the 1960s noted differences between students who are "extreme and heavily politicized" and those who decline to express political views (Ashford 1967, p. 265). Politically active students were less likely than others to be religious and, significantly, radicalism was associated with small-town origin, low parental socioeconomic status, and an inferior knowledge of French (Moore 1970, pp. 283 and 296).

Given this diversity, the impact of emerging elites on the Moroccan political system will depend in part on which of its various segments succeeds in penetrating the inner circle of leadership. Although the evidence is somewhat fragmented, the offspring of bourgeois families and the present elite are to a degree set apart from other highly educated young Moroccans. They are more likely to have received a high quality education that is highly French in orientation, and they are less likely to possess radical political attitudes and to be critical of the government. Thus, to the extent that future leaders come from this segment of the third- and fourth-generation elite, the break with the past will not be as dramatic as might be expected given generational differences in the aggregate. Moreover, it is reasonable to assume that if the current political system continues to prevail, future leaders will indeed come from this group to a disproportionate degree, given their superior training, their more acceptable political attitudes, and their ties to the present clientelist system.

Even if this does turn out to be the case, future leaders will not be anywhere near as homogeneous a group as present elites. Also, at least some of the values and experiences that are typical of younger university trained Moroccans will be carried into the ruling class. Indeed, now that third-generation elites are beginning to enter national politics in a visible way, there are signs that this is in fact occurring. For example, press reports about the establishment in 1978 of the RNI, the party of the king, note that "young wolves" are challenging the old guard for leadership, expressing themselves freely and vigorously and arguing for greater attention to economic and social reform. Thus, the intimacy and ingrown character of the elite can be expected to diminish, accompanied by a waning of the isolation from the rest of the country and the general disinterest in social transformation that has characterized the current leadership group.

Because the absorptive capacity of the political system is limited, most emerging elites will be forced to remain outside the ruling class. Yet their exclusion threatens the entire system, raising the possibility of political challenges much more dramatic than any resulting from the inclusion of some younger elements among the country's leadership. The nature of the challenge was well-described a decade ago (Waterbury 1970, pp. 299 ff.), it being argued at the time that the incumbent elite would remain for a while but that over the long haul it would either break apart under outside pressure or submerge its traits in an onslaught of new recruits. Subsequent observers have also been struck by the seriousness of the challenge (Zartman 1974, p. 485), and political developments during the last few years seem at best to have bought the present elite a little more time.

A number of factors contribute to the absorption crisis that looms on the horizon. First is the sheer size of the emerging elite. A leadership group that numbers in the hundreds cannot possibly accept thousands of new members into its ranks. Second is the professional obsolescence of the third generation. There is a need for competent middle-level managers in government bureaucracies, but few would-be elites are trained for these jobs. Thus, even those who do gain entry-level positions are unlikely to rise rapidly or acquire the status and authority they desire. Opportunities for satisfying employment outside the civil service are even more limited, given the lack of technical training among young university graduates. Third, there is a scarcity of jobs apart from the question of professional competence. The size of the government civil service is expanding but relatively few new positions are being created at the level to which future elites aspire. Moreover, the upper echelons of most bureaucratic units are occupied by relatively young second-generation elites, men who are far from retirement and who constitute a bottleneck blocking the advancement of those coming after them. The slow rate of economic growth also contributes to the problem, there being relatively few new career openings generated by economic expansion; and the scarcity of suitable employment may be even more severe by the time fourth-generation elites reach adulthood. Bottlenecks at the top of the civil service will be greater, and most middle-level positions requiring technical competence will by then be filled. All this means than many and probably most would-be elites will not obtain the kind of prestigious and influential position upon which they have set their sights.

The response of would-be elites with little hope of realizing their ambitions is not difficult to imagine. They have little esteem for present leaders and view the prevailing political system with hostility and contempt. They also have but limited confidence in politicians of the left, whom they consider to be partners in the corrupt clientelist system orchestrated by the palace. While the alienation of well-educated young Moroccans has been evident for some time, however, the present elite has been slow to recognize the seriousness of the problem or the threat that it implies. The grasp of the situation among established political leaders was described in 1970 as "bemused and abstract," and the containment strategy that the king and his supporters were inclined to follow was also described at that time (Waterbury 1970, pp. 311–314). It included (1) the encouragement of emigration; (2) preemptive appointments of the most promising would-be elites; and (3) the harassment or suppression of critics too hostile or numerous to coopt. The inadequacy of this strategy over the long haul is obvious. Cooptation and emigration will not alter fundamentally the character of the challenge from third- and fourth-generation elites, and the suppression of growing numbers cannot continue indefinitely. On the contrary, suppression will increase the bitterness of would-be elites and create pressures that could blow away the entire system when they finally erupt. In the meantime, the cooptation of some young leaders may weaken the solidarity of those committed to the old order, given that the homogeneity of the elite will diminish, and emigration will produce an external source of opposition, possibly organized around a few more senior elites who have gone into exile.

It is too early to say whether political liberalization and the reinvigoration of political parties will change the character of the absorption problem. The best guess, however, is that they will not. The size of the emerging elite still precludes its incorporation into the upper echelons of government and the problem of professional obsolescence is only beginning to be felt. Thus, if the movement toward democracy continues, disgruntled would-be elites will swell the ranks of the opposition, enabling the left to challenge the regime from within the system; and the legality of the challenge will not make it any less of a threat to the existing political order. On the other hand, if the movement toward democratization is not extended to embrace emerging elites, the system will gravitate back toward the confrontation between supporters of the monarchy and opposition elements that existed through the early 1970s.

Pressures on the regime would be less severe if the challenge were limited to disgruntled university students. But the problem of emerging elites is in reality only part of a much broader maldistribution of economic and political opportunity. Hundreds of thousands of high school students seem destined to share the frustration and bitterness of the third- and fourth-generation elite. They may aspire to no more than middle-level positions in either the public or the private sector, but their limited qualifications and the scarcity of jobs relative to demand portend an absorption crisis in the middle as well as the elite sectors of society. The plight of the peasantry and the urban masses is even worse. The unemployment rate among persons aged 20–40 is estimated at 40 percent, and the situation of the poorest population categories is far worse than per capita income figures indicate.

Making all this even more discouraging is the fact that the present elite is prospering, widening the gap between rich and poor, and that while political leaders are beginning to recognize the need for greater equality, a gloomy economic picture is unlikely to allow much opportunity for action. The bourgeoisie has never been richer. Wealth is concentrated in the hands of landowners and a small corps of urban industrialists and merchants, the same groups that have been in a privileged position since independence. But many private fortunes are much larger today than they were before the Saharan crisis. Even the king acknowledged in a 1978 speech that the war has enriched some people and that Morocco is "heading for a society where the poor will be very poor and the rich will be very rich." At the other extreme, as suggested, the plight of the poor is getting worse. Not only are unemployment and underemployment high but many of the poor are also victimized by corruption and administrative abuse, and indications of the breakdown of social order, like prostitution, juvenile delinquency, and alcoholism, are increasingly in evidence.

The government has called for greater attention to economic development and social equality but has not the resources to launch many initiatives. Morocco has one of the lowest growth rates in the Arab world and its economic situation has been particularly difficult in recent years. Among the reasons for this are (1) declining world prices for Moroccan exports, most notably phosphate, whose price had increased dramatically between 1973 and 1975; (2) massive defense expenditures in the Sahara; (3) a few large development projects that have tied up an unusual amount of capital; (4) poor harvests on top of already declining food production; and (5) rapidly rising fuel costs. As a result of these considerations, Morocco is able to finance virtually no investment out of its regular budget and has run up a hugh international debt; and this in turn has led to austerity measures in recent years, including the postponement of many development initiatives. Further compounding these problems are rapid population growth and an inflation rate that exceeds 25 percent.

Morocco's long-term economic potential is much greater than the present situation indicates. But the current economic crisis coincides with the problem of political absorption and intensifies significantly the pressure on the elite. Since 1978 there have been sporadic strikes and increased agitation among students, leading some critics to draw comparisons with the turbulent years of 1970–1972. Indeed, a United States' CIA report appearing in 1979 suggested that these domestic pressures, coupled with Morocco's declining fortunes in the Sahara, might conspire to bring down King Hassan's regime in the months ahead.

A potentially important related phenomenon is the Islamic revival occurring in Morocco, the political significance of which is as yet unknown. As mentioned, studies of other Muslim countries suggest that growing interest in Islam may be fueled by economic and political discontent and may be an important vehicle for organizing and directing opposition to the government. Further, comparisons with the recent Islamic revolution in Iran are inevitable in this context, given the structural similarity of domination by a monarch in league with a national bourgeoisie in both prerevolutionary Iran and contemporary Morocco and given also that the shah was welcomed in Morocco after his departure from Iran. Contacts between Moroccan opponents of the king and Iran's revolutionary leaders are significant in this context as well. For the present at least, these considerations appear to be outweighed by King Hassan's personal association with the religion and his good relationships with Morocco's Islamic leaders, and also by important differences in the origins of the monarchy in Morocco and Iran. It is regarded as indigenous in the former instance and was a focal point of nationalism during the colonial era, while in the latter case it was imposed and, in more recent times, it has been associated with foreign influence. Despite these differences, there is at the very least a simultaneous intensification at popular levels of Islamic sentiments and economic discontent, and this coming together could lead many nonelites to conclude that a radically different form of government would be appropriate, both for themselves as individuals and for the nation as a whole. In any event, rising pressures from below must be added to the list of challenges confronting the present political elite, and this collection of challenges leads many to believe that the Moroccan political elite is approaching a critical point in its evolution.

CONCLUSIONS: A CHOICE BETWEEN AUTHORITARIANISM AND RADICAL CHANGE

The Moroccan political system is characterized by both continuity and change. Continuity is evident in that the majority of the country's present leaders have been in positions of authority since the early days of statehood. Further, the major institutions and structures of government have also been in existence since the period following independence. On the other hand, patterns of interaction and alliance among Moroccan elites and the character and role of key political institutions have evolved considerably since 1956. In particular, the last few years have witnessed a reinvigoration of Morocco's parliamentary system, with the increasing vitality of long dormant political parties and with greater freedom of expression and political organization. The present period has also been marked by increasing national solidarity, based on both popular and elite support for the king's policy of incorporating into Morocco the former Spanish Sahara.

To the superficial observer, political life in Morocco appears to be going through a happy period of development and maturation. However, while political life is indeed more open and vigorous than it has been for some time, and this is not an insignificant development, serious problems threaten to undermine the political system that has, in one form or another, been in place since 1956. The first problem concerns the coming to adulthood of university educated Moroccans who have grown up since independence. These individuals are far too numerous to be absorbed by the present political system, if indeed they would even be willing to play by the rules of the prevailing political game, and thus they seem destined to become frustrated would-be elites, swelling the ranks of the regime's opponents.

A second and even more severe challenge concerns absorption problems at nonelite levels, a challenge defined by the concatenation of expanding social mobilization, growing disparities of wealth and opportunity, and general economic stagnation. Such agents of social change as education, urbanization, the mass media, and domestic and international labor migration have oriented hundreds of thousands, or more likely even millions, of Moroccans toward the modern sectors of society, raising expectations about new opportunities and an improved standard of living. The country is poorly prepared to satisfy these expectations, however. On the one hand, the individuals involved are very numerous and even an expanding economy would be able to absorb them only in the long run. On the other, the country is in the midst of a severe economic crisis, with growing inflation and debt and little money for development projects. This alone would be enough to produce substantial political alienation, but the situation is made worse by the fact that the present political and economic system has permitted the wealthy to thrive in the midst of this crisis, distributing unevenly the nation's economic burden and widening the gap between rich and poor.

A final problem concerns the Sahara. The king gained enormous popularity after 1975 by launching the "Green March" and annexing large amounts of Saharan territory. Moreover, the campaign came at a time when Hassan's popularity and political support were extremely low, enabling him to rebuild his power and prestige. On the one hand, it has undercut the opposition of rival politicians, most of whom are in fact in personal agreement with the government on this issue. On the other, it has enabled the monarch to rebuild and reward the military, renewing with it the alliance that was called into question in the early 1970s. But while this strategy has been effective until the present, the war effort has gone badly of late. The army has been unable to suppress attacks by the Polisario Front and it continues to sustain heavy losses, leading some observers to argue that rising discontent among the military could, conceivably, be directed as much against civilian politicians as foreign adversaries. Moreover, the war effort has contributed significantly to the country's disasterous economic situation and to the maldistribution of wealth, raising still additional questions about whether the Saharan campaign will continue much longer to enjoy popular support. The Saharan issue does not pose the same long-term threat as do the absorption problems discussed above. Also, there is at least some chance that a negotiated settlement will resolve the matter quickly, before it can produce much domestic tension. Nevertheless, at least in the short run, the foreign adventure that undermined political opposition and set in motion trends of democratization and solidarity now threatens to turn sour and intensify pressure on the regime.

In the face of this pressure, it will be difficult for the Moroccan regime to maintain its movement toward liberalization. With popular discontent mounting and a growing number of would-be elites destined to be frustrated in their political ambitions, freedom of expression and organization can be expected to lead to increasingly severe challenges to the regime by groups working within the political system. Thus, it appears that the present elite will be faced with a choice between retreat from parliamentary democracy on the one hand and accepting the emergence of radically new political values and institutional arrangements on the other. There is little in the history of independent Morocco to suggest that the king and the present elite will willingly accept the latter alternative. If there is a return to authoritarianism, however, the conflict, latent instability, and general uncertainty of the late 1960s and early 1970s will reemerge, as will questions about the price the present elite will have to pay to maintain its dominance, if indeed it can do so at all in the face of an increasing mobilized populace. In any event, it is unlikely that the established clientelist political system and the present trend toward democratization will be able to survive in tandem for very long; and thus, although it is always dangerous to assume that the dilemmas of the present will be be decisive, it is difficult to avoid the conclusion that the current political system cannot survive in its present form very much longer.

Given a choice between authoritarianism and radical change, it is to be hoped that the country's leaders will have the courage to see through to their logical conclusion the trends that they have initiated — to tolerate, in other words, the emergence of a political system in which the interests of the bourgeoisie will no longer predominate and in which active steps will in fact be taken to affect a more equitable distribution of Morocco's resources. The emergence of such a system would maximize development and orderly change over the long haul, and even in the short run it would produce less disruption and tension than any plausible alternative. Moreover, it would permit the present elite to play a part in affecting the political transition that cannot be put off much longer, enabling it to remain active in political life even if it no longer monopolizes power.

REFERENCES

Periodicals and References Books

Africa Confidential.
Africa Yearbook and Who's Who 1977. London: Africa Journal Limited, 1976.
Afrique-Asie.
Annuaire de l'Afrique du Nord. Paris: C.N.R.S.
Jeune Afrique.
Le Monde.
Machreb Machrek.
Marchés Tropicaux et Mediterranéens.

Middle East and North Africa. London: Europa Publications, 1980.
New York Times.
L'Opinion.
Quarterly Economic Review of Morocco.
Record of the Arab World 1972. Beirut: The Research and Publishing House.
Who's Who in Africa. London: Africa Buyer and Trader, 1973.

Bibliography

Accad, Evelyne (1978) "The Theme of Sexual Oppression in the North African Novel," in L. Beck and N. Keddie (eds.) *Women in the Muslim World.* Cambridge: Harvard University Press.

Adam, André (1972) "Berber Migrants in Casablanca," in Ernest Gellner and Charles Micaud (eds.) *Arabs and Berbers: From Tribe to Nation in North Africa.* Lexington: D.C. Heath.

Amin, Samir (1970) *The Maghreb in the Modern World: Algeria, Tunisia, Morocco.* Baltimore: Penguin Books.

Ashford, Douglas E. (1961) *Political Change in Morocco.* Princeton: Princeton University Press.

—— (1964) *Perspectives of a Moroccan Nationalist.* Totowa, New Jersey: The Bedminster Press.

—— (1965) *Morocco-Tunisia: Politics and Planning.* Syracuse: Syracuse University Press.

—— (1966) "Political Aspects of Rural Development," in L.C. Brown (ed.) *State and Society in Independent North Africa.* Washington: The Middle East Institute.

—— (1967) *National Development and Local Reform: Political Participation in Morocco, Tunisia, and Pakistan.* Princeton: Princeton University Press.

—— (1973) "Second- and Third-Generation Elites in the Maghreb," in I. William Zartman (ed.) *Man, State, and Society in the Contemporary Maghreb.* New York: Praeger.

Ben Kaddour, Abdaslam (1972) "The Neo-Makhzan and the Berbers," in Ernest Gellner and Charles Micaud (eds.) *Arabs and Berbers: From Tribe to Nation in North Africa.* Lexington: D.C. Heath.

Berque, Jacques (1972) "Tradition and Innovation in the Maghreb," in S.N. Eisenstadt (ed.) *Post-Traditional Societies.* New York: W.W. Norton.

—— (1974) "Dans le Maroc Nouveau: Le Role d'une Université Islamique," *Annales d'Histoire Economique et Sociale*, 10: 193–207.

Bowen, D.L. (1980) "Islam and Family Planning in Morocco," *The Maghreb Review*, 5 (Jan.–Feb.): 20–29.

Braun, Frank H. (1978) "Morocco: Anatomy of a Palace Revolution that Failed," *International Journal of Middle East Studies*, 9: 63–72.

Brett, Michael (1978) "Islam in the Maghreb: The Problem of Modernization," *The Maghreb Review*, 3 (Jan.–April): 6–9.

Brown, Kenneth (1972) "The Impact of the Dahir Berbere in Salé," in Ernest Gellner and Charles Micaud (eds.) *Arabs and Berbers: From Tribe to Nation in North Africa.* Lexington: D.C. Heath.

—— (1976) *People of Salé.* Cambridge: Harvard University Press.

_____ (1977) "Changing Forms of Patronage in a Moroccan City," in Ernest Gellner and John Waterbury (eds.) *Patrons and Clients in Mediterranean Societies*. London: Duckworth.

Brown, Leon Carl (1966) "The Role of Islam in Modern North Africa," in L.C. Brown (ed.) *State and Society in Independent North Africa*. Washington: The Middle East Institute.

Chambergeat, Paul (1973) "The Moroccan Communal Elections," in I. William Zartman (ed.) *Man, State, and Society in the Contemporary Maghreb*. New York: Praeger.

Clement, Claude (1974) *Oufkir*. Paris: Editions Jean Dullis.

Cohen, Mark I. and Lorna Hahn (1966) *Morocco: Old Land, New Nation*. New York: Praeger.

Coram, A. (1972a) "The Berbers and the Coup," in Ernest Gellner and Charles Micaud (eds.) *Arabs and Berbers: From Tribe to Nation in North Africa*. Lexington: D.C. Heath.

_____ (1972b) "Note on the Role of the Berbers in the Early Days of Moroccan Independence," in Ernest Gellner and Charles Micaud (eds.) *Arabs and Berbers: From Tribe to Nation in North Africa*. Lexington: D.C. Heath.

Duchak, René et al. (1973) *La Formation des élites politiques maghrébines*. Paris: Librarie Générale de Droit et de Jurisprudence.

Duclos, Louis-Jean (1972) "The Berbers and the Rise of Moroccan Nationalism," in Ernest Gellner and Charles Micaud (eds.) *Arabs and Berbers: From Tribe to Nation in North Africa*. Lexington: D.C. Heath.

Dwyer, Daisy Hilse (1978a) *Image and Self-Image: Male and Female in Morocco*. New York: Columbia University Press.

_____ (1978b) "Women, Sufism and Decision-Making in Moroccan Islam," in L. Beck and N. Keddie (eds.) *Women in the Muslim World*. Cambridge: Harvard University Press.

Eickelman, Dale F. (1976) *Moroccan Islam: Tradition and Society in a Pilgrimage Center*. Austin: University of Texas Press.

_____ (1977) "Ideological Change and Regional Cults: Maraboutism and Ties of 'Closeness' in Western Morocco," in R.P. Werbner (ed.) *Regional Cults*. London: Academic Press.

_____ (1978) "The Art of Memory: Islamic Education and Its Social Reproduction," *Comparative Studies in Society and History*, 20: 485–516.

El Malki, Habib (1976) "Maroc," *Annuaire de l'Afrique du Nord*. Paris: C.N.R.S.

Gallagher, Charles (1963) *The United States and North Africa* Cambridge: Harvard University Press.

_____ (1966) "Language and Identity," in L.C. Brown (ed.) *State and Society in Independent North Africa*. Washington: The Middle East Institute.

Gaudio, Attilio (1972) *Allal el Fassi: ou l'Histoire de l'Istiqlal*. Paris: Alain Moreau.

Gertz, Clifford (1968) *Islam Observed: Religious Development in Morocco and Indonesia*. New Haven: Yale University Press.

Gellner, Ernest (1969) *Saints of the Atlas*. Chicago: The University of Chicago Press.

_____ (1972a) "Introduction," in Ernest Gellner and Charles Micaud (eds.)

Arabs and Berbers: From Tribe to Nation in North Africa. Lexington: D.C. Heath.

——— (1972b) "Patterns of Rural Rebellion in Morocco During the Early Years of Independence," in Ernest Gellner and Charles Micaud (eds.) *Arabs and Berbers: From Tribe to Nation in North Africa.* Lexington: D.C. Heath.

Halpern, Manfred (1963) *The Politics of Social Change in the Middle East and North Africa.* Princeton: Princeton University Press.

Hart, David M. (1972) "The Tribe in Modern Morocco: Two Case Studies," in Ernest Gellner and Charles Micaud (eds.) *Arabs and Berbers: From Tribe to Nation in North Africa.* Lexington: D.C. Heath.

Hermassi, Elbaki (1972a) *Leadership and National Development in North Africa: A Comparative Study.* Berkeley: University of California Press.

——— (1972b) "Political Traditions of the Maghreb," in S.N. Eisenstadt (ed.) *Post-Traditional Societies.* New York: W.W. Norton.

——— (1976) "Towards a Comparative Theory of Revolution," *Comparative Studies in Society and History,* 18: 211–235.

Hudson, Michael C. (1977) *Arab Politics: The Search for Legitimacy.* New Haven: Yale University Press.

Knapp, Wilfrid (1977) *North West Africa.* New York: Oxford University Press.

Lambert, Pierre (1978) "Point de vue sur les jeunes marocains," *L'Afrique et l'Asie Moderne,* 1177: 57–62.

Leveau, Remy (1976) *Le fellah marocain: defenseur du trône.* Paris: Presses de la Foundation Nationale des Sciences Politiques.

Maher, Vanessa (1974) *Women and Property in Morocco: Their Changing Relation to the Process of Social Stratification in the Middle Atlas.* London: Cambridge University Press.

——— (1978) "Women and Social Change in Morocco," in Lois Beck and Nikki Keddie (eds.) *Women in the Muslim World.* Cambridge: Harvard University Press.

Marais, Octave (1972a) "Berbers and the Moroccan Political System After the Coup," in Ernest Gellner and Charles Micaud (eds.) *Arabs and Berbers: From Tribe to Nation in North Africa.* Lexington: D.C. Heath.

——— (1972b) "The Political Evolution of the Berbers in Independent Morocco," in Ernest Gellner and Charles Micaud (eds.) *Arabs and Berbers: From Tribe to Nation in North Africa.* Lexington: D.C. Heath.

——— (1973) "The Ruling Class in Morocco," in I. William Zartman (ed.) *Man, State, and Society in the Contemporary Maghreb.* New York: Praeger.

Marais, Octave and John Waterbury (1970) "Thèmes et vocabulaire de la propagande des élites politiques au Maroc," in Charles Debbasch et al., *Pouvoir et Administration au Maghreb.* Paris: C.N.R.S.

Markham, James M. (1980) "King Hassan's Quagmire," *The New York Times Magazine,* April 27, 1980.

Maxwell, Gavin (1966) *Lord of the Atlas: The Rise and Fall of the House of Glaoua, 1893–1956.* New York: E.P. Dutton.

Micaud, Charles (1972) "Conclusions," in Ernest Gellner and Charles Micaud (eds.) *Arabs and Berbers: From Tribe to Nation in North Africa.* Lexington: D.C. Heath.

Moore, Clement H. (1966) "Political Parties in Independent North Africa," in

L.C. Brown (ed.) *State and Society in Independent North Africa*: Washington: The Middle East Institute.

———— (1970) *Politics in North Africa: Algeria, Morocco, and Tunisia*. Boston: Little, Brown.

———— (1977) "Clientelist Ideology and Political Change: Fictitious Networks in Egypt and Tunisia," in Ernest Gellner and John Waterbury (eds.) *Patrons and Clients in Mediterranean Societies*. London: Duckworth.

———— (1978) "A Review of *North-West Africa* by Wilfrid Knapp," *International Journal of Middle East Studies*, 9: 419–420.

Murphy, Dermot (1977) "Colonial and Post Colonial Policy in the Maghreb," *The Maghreb Review*, 2: 1–9.

Nedelcovych, Mima and Monte Palmer (1980) "The Political Behavior of Moroccan Students: Democratic Indicators in a Quasi-Democratic Environment," paper presented at the Annual Meeting of the Midwest Political Science Association.

Ortzen, Len (1970) *North African Writing*. London: Heinemann.

Pascon, Paul and Mekki Bentahan (1971) "Ce qui disent 296 jeunes ruraux," in Abdelkedir Khatibi (ed.) *Etudes Sociologiques Sur Le Maroc*. Rabat: Bulletin Economique et Social du Maroc.

Paul, James A. (1975) *Professionals and Politics in Morocco: A Historical Study of the Mediation of Power and the Creation of Ideology in the Context of European Imperialism*. New York: New York University, unpublished Ph.D. dissertation.

Quandt, William B. (1970) *The Comparative Study of Political Elites*. Beverly Hills: Sage Publications.

Rabinow, Paul (1975) *Symbolic Domination: Cultural Form and Historical Change in Morocco*. Chicago: The University of Chicago Press.

Rosen, Lawrence (1972) "The Social and Conceptual Framework of Arab-Berber Relations in Central Morocco," in Ernest Gellner and Charles Micaud (eds.) *Arabs and Berbers: From Tribe to Nation in North Africa*. Lexington: D.C. Heath.

Rousset, Michel (1971) *L'administration marocaine*. Paris: Editions Berger-Levrault.

Schaar, Stuart (1968) "The News Media in Morocco," *American Universities Field Staff Reports*. Hanover, N.H.: AUFS.

———— (1973) "King Hassan's Alternatives," in I. William Zartman (ed.) *Man, State, and Society in the Contemporary Maghreb*. New York: Praeger.

Seddon, J. David (1972) "Local Politics and State Intervention: Northeast Morocco from 1870 to 1970," in Ernest Gellner and Charles Micaud (eds.) *Arabs and Berbers: From Tribe to Nation in North Africa*. Lexington: D.C. Heath.

———— (1978) "Review of *Fellah Marocain* by Remy Leveau," *The Maghreb Review*, 3 (Jan.–April): 33–34.

Shuster, James R. (1973) "Bureaucratic Transition in Morocco," in I. William Zartman (ed.) *Man, State, and Society in the Contemporary Maghreb*. New York: Praeger.

Tessler, Mark A. (1976a) "Development, Oil and Cultural Change in the Maghreb," in Naiem A. Sherbiny and Mark A. Tessler (eds.) *Arab Oil: Impact on the Arab Countries and Global Implications*. New York: Praeger.

_____ (1976b) "Political Generations," in Russell Stone and John Simmons (eds.) *Change in Tunisia.* Albany: SUNY Press.

_____ (1979a) "Minorities in Retreat: The Jews of the Maghreb," in R.D. McLaurin (ed.) *The Political Role of Minorities in the Middle East.* New York: Praeger.

_____ (1979b) "The Political Culture of Jews in Tunisia and Morocco," *International Journal of Middle East Studies*, 11: 59–86.

_____ (1980) "Political Change and the Islamic Revival in Tunisia," *The Maghreb Review*, 5 (Jan.–Feb.): 8–19.

Vinogradov, Amal R. (1972) "The Socio-political Organization of a Berber Taraf Tribe: Pre-protectorate Morocco," in Ernest Gellner and Charles Micaud (eds.) *Arabs and Berbers: From Tribe to Nation in North Africa.* Lexington: D.C. Heath.

Wansbrough, J. (1977) "A Review of *Moroccan Islam* by Dale Eickelman," *The Maghreb Review*, 2 (March–April): 29.

Waterbury, John (1970) *The Commander of the Faithful: The Moroccan Political Elite — A Study in Segmented Politics.* New York: Columbia University Press.

_____ (1972a) "The Coup-Manqué," in Ernest Gellner and Charles Micaud (eds.) *Arabs and Berbers: From Tribe to Nation in North Africa.* Lexington: D.C. Heath.

_____ (1972b) *North for Trade: The Life and Times of a Berber Merchant.* Berkeley: The University of California Press.

_____ (1973) "Endemic and Planned Corruption in a Monarchial Regime," *World Politics*, 25: 533–555.

Zartman, I. William (1964a) *Destiny of a Dynasty: The Search for Institutions in Morocco's Developing Society.* Columbia: University of South Carolina Press.

_____ (1964b) *Morocco: Problems of New Power*: New York: Prentice-Hall.

_____ (1973) "Political Pluralism in Morocco," in I. William Zartman (ed.) *Man, State, and Society in the Contemporary Maghreb.* New York: Praeger.

_____ (1974) "The Study of Elite Circulation," *Comparative Politics*, 6: 465–488.

_____ (1975) "A Review Article: The Elites of the Maghreb," *International Journal of Middle East Studies*, 6: 495–504.

3

Algeria: Technocratic Rule, Military Power

JOHN P. ENTELIS

INTRODUCTION: CHANGES AT THE TOP

Politics in postindependence Algeria is characterized by a stable system of rule with power concentrated among relatively few individuals within select institutions. While incumbent elites remained relatively unchanged during the Boumediene years (1965–1978), significant changes in the state's institutional life took place since the early and middle 1970s culminating in back-to-back referendums on a National Charter (1976) and a new Constitution (1976) paving the way for national presidential (1976) and legislative (1977) elections. These nation-wide participatory efforts were preceded by a number of carefully prepared local and regional assembly elections and followed by a systematic series of conventions of the various national organizations. A party congress of the National Liberation Front (FLN) was convened in January 1979 following Boumediene's death, and a single presidential candidate was selected (Chadli Benjedid) and confirmed a month later by the electorate in a national election (February 1979).

This accelerated pace of political activity following nearly a decade of authoritarian single-man rule at the national level reflects the growing importance of institutional life and the concurrent deemphasis of informal, patron-client, and personalized politics at the highest levels of power. The National Charter, which elaborates in detail the role of party and ideology in "Arabic, Islamic, socialist" Algeria, provides the ideological rationalization for this increased reliance on institutional patterns of elite and nonelite behaviour. This is not to say, however, that the historically pervasive influence of informal politics or the importance of clientelist, personal, and other face-to-face ties have been completely eradicated from Algerian political life; rather, such behavior has now been incorporated into more formal and regularized settings under closer public scrutiny.

The peaceful transfer of power from Boumediene to Chadli attests in part to the credibility and effectiveness of these various institutional arrangements put into place by Boumediene and his colleagues during the last decade of his life. Particularly significant has been the emergence of a powerful and interlocking technocratic system with its tripartite mobilizational, managerial, and military components working collectively to ensure a relatively effective and unchallenged operation of the state.

This study of postindependence elites in Algeria emphasizes the most recent period, including some preliminary assessments of Chadli's first two years (1979–1981); there is little discussion of the ben Bella years (1962–1965). The overall analysis seeks to provide a general profile of the significant party, military, and administrative elite as situated in their various institutional settings.

Algerian politics in the Boumediene period (1965–1978) were dominated by a relatively small yet stable civil-military oligarchy with remarkably little participation on the part of the masses, notwithstanding the numerous noncompetitive and plebiscitary elections that have taken place nation-wide and within functional organizations since mid-1976.[1] Under the country's first elected president, Ahmed ben Bella (1962–1965), Algerian political elites were composed of "numerous clans, factions, and cliques, none of which [had] power enough to dominate the entire political system" (Quandt 1969, p. 11). From 1965 to 1978, however, Algeria was ruled by a "collegial group of slowly varying size, cohesion, and importance around a single central figure, [Houari Boumediene]" (Zartman 1978, p. 13).

In the 1968–1978 decade especially, the Algerian leadership moved unhesitatingly toward a more homogeneous coalition of professional military men and technically competent administrators. When Boumediene fell seriously ill in 1978, effective and legal rule was transferred, on November 22, 1978, to the defense ministry under the dual authority of Col. Chadli Benjedid, commander of the second military region (Oran), and Col. Abdallah Belhouchet, commander of the first military region headquartered in Blida. As members of the remaining nine-man Council of the Revolution, Chadli and Belhouchet were supported in their interim leadership positions by a coalition of three influential moderates on the Council, with their former and current positions: Abdelaziz Bouteflika, uninterrupted foreign minister under ben Bella and Boumediene from 1963 to 1979 and thereafter presidential advisor and one of seven members of the FLN's Political Bureau, functioning as the president's key advisory council; Col. Ahmed Draïa, a former transportation minister and, until the April 1977 cabinet reshuffle, head of the *Sûreté*; and Col. Mohamed ben Ahmed Abdelghani, former commander of the fifth military region in Constantine, ex-minister of the interior, and incumbent prime minister.

With the death of Boumediene on December 27, 1978, of a rare blood disease, executive power was constitutionally transfered to Rabah Bitat, president of the National Assembly (Assemblée Populaire Nationale, or APN) and the only remaining politically active member of the revolution's original nine "historic chiefs." Article 117 of the 1976 Constitution stipulates that in case of the death or resignation of the president, the incumbent head of the APN is automatically designated interim chief of state for 45 days until new presidential elections take place. Such elections are to be held under the organizational and political auspices of the FLN in an extraordinary session convened especially for purposes of selecting a presidential candidate. The head of the National Assembly is constitutionally prohibited from running as a candidate for the presidency.

Presidential aspirations were contested in the numerous committee meetings and closed sessions of the FLN congress on 27–31 January, 1979 with several political factions emerging and revolving around individuals within the Council of the Revolution: Mohamed Salah Yahiaoui, former commander of the prestigious Cherchell Military Academy and for nearly three years (October 1977–July 1980), "responsable exécutif, chargé de l'appareil du parti," represented "left-wing" interests with an emphasis on accelerated Arabization, "hard line" socialism, Islamic fundamentalism, and continued Soviet frienship. Bouteflika's relatively moderate posture, pro-Western sympathies, and call for greater liberalization of Algerian society had the support of Draïa and Abdelghani. Col. Ahmed Bencherif, the hydraulics minister in the April 1977 cabinet and former gendarmerie commandant, represented himself but with the outside support of such key military figures in the Ministry of Defense as Abdelhamid Latrach, secretary general in the ministry, and four loyal followers: Lt. Col. Cheloufi of the gendarmerie; Lt. Col. Lakhal Ayyat, commander of the army's armored attack division; Lt. Col. Salim Saadi, in charge of the frontier troops along the Moroccan border; and Kamal Abderrahim who heads the army's operational division. Finally, Col. Chadli Benjedid, representing army-national interests, which are normally viewed as standing above any parochial or special political considerations, constituted the "independent" candidate who had the full support of the 640-ANP (Algerian People's Army) delegation.

On the last day of the congress, the so-called moderate majority defeated a movement by leftists to gain greater influence in the FLN's leadership by selecting Chadli as the new secretary-general of the party and the only candidate for the February 7, 1979, presidential election. With the confirmation of election results on February 9 (94.23 percent approval of the electorate) Chadli Benjedid assumed the presidency as the country's third elected head of state.

Unlike Boumediene's concentrated personal powers and wide-ranging authority—at the time of his incapacitation he was president of the republic, of the Council of the Revolution, and of the Council of Ministers; head of the army (since 1967); minister of defense (since

1963); and head of the FLN—the new president's formal powers were ostensibly reduced with the creation of a 17-member Political Bureau and a 160-member Central Committee (30 alternates) of the FLN and the selection of three vice-presidents and a prime minister by the Central Committee rather than by the president.

Since independence, therefore, top political leadership in Algeria has evolved from a heroic yet flamboyant and unpredictable authoritarian style, to one dominated by a single, powerful individual whose "no-nonsense" leadership was balanced by a reliance on collegiality and consultation for effective rule, to one apparently reflecting greater institutionalization, broader consultation, expanded participation and politicization, and a regularized and legitimized political style. Yet it is too early in the new regime to make conclusive judgments regarding the balance of political forces at the top, for within a year and a half after the January party congress, Chadli reduced the Politburo's membership to seven; failed to select any vice-president; weakened the office of the prime minister by stripping its incumbent of the powerful Interior Ministry, which he also held; dismissed Yahiaoui from his leadership position as party coordinator although retaining him in the Politburo; and reestablished the army General Staff, which had been dissolved 13 years earlier by Boumediene in the wake of the aborted coup against his regime. These acts of power consolidation, however, do not undermine Chadli's basic policy of pragmatic accommodation on social and economic issues and commitment to a more regularized system of rule, thus distinguishing himself from his more authoritarian and narrow-minded predecessor.

DESCRIPTION

Notwithstanding the future performance of such popular institutions as the national, regional, and local assemblies (APN, APW, and APC respectively) and the revitalized mass party (FLN) in the latter half of the 1970s power remains concentrated in the hands of a technocratic elite whose claim to authority is based on the modern skills that they possess and for which there is a high value in the society. This technocratic system is made up of three major units that although they have very different internal characteristics, are united in an overriding new allegiance to the state and its developmental objectives. The military, party, and administrative technocrats, who all share a common socializing background in the Armée de Liberation Nationale (ALN, the Algerian People's Army—ANP—predecessor) and its experience in the revolutionary war, monopolize the state's critical military, mobilization, and managerial affairs. In the decade following his consolidation of power in 1968, Boumediene depended on this triumvirate to maintain and aggrandize power as well as to erect his socialist state using the crucial technical skills that this group possesses. For the better part of this 1968–1978 period, however, these elements were unevenly aligned, with the FLN reduced to a minor, functionary role while the military and the administrative elite were elevated to predominate positions.

Initially, with the elimination of the past political elite and the establishment of an internal cohesion within the army's structure of authority, the new Boumediene regime sought to strengthen its hold on the economy and administration by "recruiting civil servants and technicians in such a way that the congruence between military and managerial elites was maximized" (Hermassi 1972, p. 167). Yet to a certain extent this was achieved at the expense of the single party, which was left in the hands of faithful party hacks like Ahmed Kaid, who, while they did not lack enthusiasm, loyalty, and "personality," were clearly second-rate by the educational and technical standards used to recruit and maintain the military and administrative elites.

The balancing of forces began to take place in the mid-1970s when Boumediene, at the time of the tenth anniversary of his June 19, 1965 coup d'etat or *"redressement révolutionnaire,"* launched a campaign to revitalize political life at the national level through the formulation and implementation of a National Charter and a new Constitution in 1976 and 1977 followed by presidential and legislative elections all organized under the political guidance of the FLN. The "acid" test came rather suddenly with Boumediene's passing, as the single party, in its formal structures and statutory language at least, was significantly enhanced in power and prestige and its Political Bureau and Central Committee replaced the dissolved Council of the Revolution as the Country's "supreme political body."

Until such time as the party tests and sustains its newly acquired political clout, however, the military remains the most decisive elite group in Algerian politics today. This has been the case since the old dissensions between the conventional nationalist army (ALN) and the *moujahidin* or *wilayists* (who fought in the interior of the country during the war of independence) were resolved in favor of the former renamed the Algerian People's Army (ANP) in 1963.

Military elites' claim to privileged status is not limited to the obvious fact that they monopolize the nation's coercive instruments of force or that the late president himself was the former chief of staff of the wartime ALN who later, as defense minister and head of the army, provided the critical support that brought ben Bella to power until overthrown by Boumediene himself. Equally important has been the fact that the military continues to possess a revolutionary mystique, that it was determinative in imposing law and order in the chaos that followed independence, that it possesses the special skills of organization and management that has enabled society to stabilize and develop, that it has become directly involved in local rural affairs thus gaining popular support at the mass level, and that, finally, it has continued to hold firmly on to the notion that it alone is the guardian of the revolution. This latter consideration was clearly in evidence when the army once again demonstrated its instrumental, indeed decisive, role in the final selection of Chadli Benjedid — one of its own — as Boumediene's successor.

Yet, despite the numerous advantages they possess vis-à-vis other elite groups in the society, military elites have so far played a guardian role. They become involved directly in politics only when the situation so requires, as they did in 1962, when the external ALN coalesced behind ben Bella in his struggle for power with the GPRA (Algeria's pre-independence provisional government) and dissident *wilaya* leaders and in 1965 following ben Bella's attempt at the 1964 FLN party congress to remove military representation from the Council of Ministers, which led the military to remove him instead (Zartman 1970c, 1975b). After each of these two examples of direct military army intervention, the military followed a policy of "returning to the barracks" to observe the political process carefully, with a discreet but always present eye. Representation in all elite political institutions, including the Council of Ministers, the National Assembly, the Political Bureau, the Central Committee, and the FLN party congress permits military elites to oversee directly all political activities. The military's influence and prestige have been recently reinforced, possibly at the expense of the party once again, with the recreation of the Army General Staff in July 1980. It is headed by three close military associates of Chadli: Col. Abdallah Belhouchet, a former member of the Council of the Revolution, head of the first military district centered in Blida from 1967 to 1979, inspector-general of the army, a vice minister of defense, and one of seven members of the newly reconstituted Political Bureau; Col. Kasdi Merbah, a presidential advisor, vice-minister of defense, former secretary-general of the defense ministry, ex-head of the powerful and much-feared Securité Militaire (SM), and then responsible for military support and industry; and Lt. Col. Mustapha Belloucif, the newly designated secretary-general of the Ministry of Defense.

In addition to their role in national bodies, military elites are also active participants at the local and regional levels. On the local level, for example, "its members work closely with the local administration and the favors that the party is not able to distribute are often obtainable from military influence." At the intermediate level, the heads of the country's five military districts function in capacities as regional governors often with more influence than the heads of the 31 APWs (Zartman 1975b, p. 276). Finally, the qualitative and quantitative improvement in manpower (70,000) and equipment that has been in evidence since the 1967 Arab-Israeli war, when Soviet military assistance and training accelerated noticeably, has made the Algerian military a credible threat and a force to contend with in regional Arab and African affairs. Its aspiration to regional military predominance has had the added effect of further increasing its domestic standing among elites and masses alike.

The administrative elite constitutes a second important component of the Algerian technocratic system. In fact, it is no exaggeration to say that with the increasing industrialization and complexity of Algerian society, the administrative stratum may soon replace the military as the paramount elite force, especially if the post-Boumediene system of rule with its emphasis on dispersed and countervailing powers is sustained and institutionalized.

Under this category is included both the civil service, whose activities extend beyond the actual administration of the country into the substantive functions of various other ministries and their local networks, as well as a more narrowly defined new class of technocrats who have the authority and responsibility for the planning, development, operation, and expansion of the nation's industrial complex, particularly the petrochemical central base. In the process of nationalizing and socializing the many aspects of the petroleum and natural gas industries, numerous national companies (state monopolies) have been established with the most important being the oil empire, SONATRACH, and the technical administrators of these companies have become the most important technocrats.

There are, in addition, economic technocrats included in the administrative elite — namely, the economic and financial planners and managers for the government-owned and government-operated banks, insurance companies, import and export controls, and related commercial activities.

This administrative elite has expanded enormously ever since the Boumediene takeover, so it has tended to break down into component groups. In fact, ever since the technocratic predominance began in the late 1960s, bureaucratic politics within the ministerial and presidential councils have been largely conducted among the leaders of technician subgroups. This multiplistic administrative group constitutes an important subelite and has been the most noticeable recipient of new class status including conspicuous wealth and other tangible signs of social advantage (Etienne 1977; Zartman 1975b; Lazreg 1976; Farsoun 1975).

Unlike the other two technocratic elite groups of the military and the party, "the bureaucrats are a highly productive elite with a real impact on the country's development and hence, on the production of new elites. Whether it is the school, the factory, or the local assembly, the policy output of the administration creates new skills, new opportunities, new demands, and new sources of power" (Zartman 1975b, p. 277).

While the role of the FLN in the achievement of national independence was a decisive one, it did not manage to maintain its power and prestige after independence. The factionalism that had been suppressed in the name of national unity during the revolution quickly reappeared as the party leaders vied with one another for positions of power. The quality of

FLN leadership at the local level declined, and individual party officials in many cases seemed more intent on personal advancement than in building up the party as an effective peacetime organization.

As a consequence, the FLN has not been a very credible force in stimulating political activity or in mobilizing the masses. The heavy hands of the state and the army have not allowed it any independent political activity. It is unattractive to young people with an educated and intelligent interest in politics because they are required, as members, to be more conformist than nonmembers. Most debilitating has been the virtual powerlessness of the party as a dispenser of even the most minor favors and services. For the better part of Boumediene's 13-year rule, the FLN was anything but a vanguard party; indeed its role was simply to propagate others' policy or defend others' candidates (Zartman 1975b).

Yet with all these shortcomings, the party has managed to retain a dominant position over all other national organizations while party elites remain nevertheless, distinctly inferior to the military and administrative elites. But even this subordinate status may have undergone a transformation of sorts in the aftermath of the fourth party congress held to select a new presidential candidate in January 1979. Should this new power advantage be maintained, it would reflect the logical growth of authority and prestige that the FLN has achieved as part of Boumediene's prodigious effort to revitalize the party via an array of mobilizational campaigns intended to gain support and legitimacy for the 1976 National Charter and new national Constitution, both of which institutionalized the FLN as an integral force in national politics. The legitimizing process is reflected in Part Two of the Charter which, for example, devotes a lengthy section to the "avant-garde" nature of the party that is to become the ideological vanguard of the socialist revolution. Moreover, the Charter now stipulates that political participation at any level of political organization requires FLN membership. All this reflected Boumediene's desire to create a viable national political organization that would permit citizen participation in the political life of the state, thereby decentralizing authority and enhancing the populist quality of the regime. Thus, despite earlier predictions of the FLN's demise or, at best, its sustained insignificance (Lewis 1966), the party elites of 1979 have now been given new responsibilities, power, and resources that may yet transform Algeria into an effective single-party system. As Boumediene told an assembly of mayors back in early 1973 when he initiated his campaign to reactivate party life: "A revolution needs revolutionaries and the socialist revolution socialist militants. Whoever has faith in the revolution and its objectives must join the party. Otherwise he can have no place at any level of responsibility." Boumediene's immediate successors seemed to have taken his words to heart.

The various national organizations, including the workers' union (UGTA), farmers' organization (UNPA), the youth association (UNJA), the veterans organization of former *moujahidin* (ONM), and the women's association (UNFÁ) are all subordinated to the party with little or no independent power or authority. The only group that sought to challenge centralized authority and assert its own view, the student union (UNEA), was finally suppressed in 1971 following a series of student boycotts, strikes, and demonstrations. It has not been revived since and is conspicuously absent from the list of national organizations included in the party section of the National Charter. Its activities have been incorporated into the more docile and politically inefficacious UNJA. At its most recent yough congress held in January 1979, however, more radicalized and politicized elements known as "Pagsistes" managed to achieve several positions of leadership in the UNJA with the potential for transforming it into a meaningful representative of independent student interests. It has also been reported that Pagsistes were elected in March 1979 to the executive commission and national secretariat of the UGTA. The Pagsistes, referring to membership in the Parti de l'Avant-Garde Socialiste (PAGS), is a party of opposition devoid of legal standing and heir to the principles of the defunct (1962) Parti Communiste Algérien (PCA). It is constant and continuous in its criticism of the regime, especially since the onset of the Agrarian Revolution in 1971. It has also been active in the various committees of the Volontariat, a national service organization for youth and students.

The increased complexity of Algeria's technocratic system has made it difficult to determine with any reasonable accuracy the size of its incumbent elites. Part of the difficulty at elite identification has to do with the precariousness of institutional life and the predominance of conspiratorial politics during periods of transition and consolidation. (For earlier studies on Algerian elites see Quandt 1969; Michel 1973; Ottaway and Ottaway 1970; Humbaraci 1966; and Zartman 1975a.) Increasingly, however, as political processes have become more regularized, the identification of the country's top national elite in the state, government, military, and party utilizing institutional criteria has become more valid. Until recently, for example, the core of power was concentrated in the Council of the Revolution, the Council of Ministers, the General Staff, the FLN executive, and the National Assembly president (Zartman 1975d, 1978).

Some major institutional modifications have taken place as a consequence of the decisions taken at the recent FLN congress. Specifically, the Council of the Revolution has been officially dissolved and its remaining nine members incorporated into a 17-member Political Bureau of the FLN. This number was changed to seven and then ten as a result of decisions of the Central Committee in late June 1980 and in early July 1981. The 160-member Central Committee of the party has been officially designated as the country's "supreme political body," and the president's powers have been noticeably reduced and dispersed within the Political Bureau, Council of Ministers, and National Assembly.

A preliminary estimate of the core elite would identify 50 or so separate individuals as constituting the top political decision makers in post-Boumediene Algeria. They would be located in the Political Bureau of the FLN (n = 10); Council of Ministers (n = 30, with 5 duplicative representative in the Political Bureau); the General Staff of the ANP (n = 3); the president and executive council of the APN (n = 5); and the commanders of the five military regions (n = 5). All key military, governmental-administrative, and party elites are represented in one or more of the above bodies.

The size and composition of this core elite varies according to a cyclical pattern. During periods of executive transition (every decade or so) the core elite is expanded to the maximum. Once the power relations have been worked out, however, the core elite narrows to a smaller, stable group that maintains itself until the next change in the chief of state. This is exactly what has been happening in the latter half of 1980, beginning with the Central Committee's decision in May to give Chadli "full powers" and followed by the extraordinary session of the FLN party congress held on June 15-19, 1980 to discuss the new Five Year Plan (1980–1984), a document that reflects Chadli's desire to moderate some of Boumediene's excesses, especially in the field of heavy industrialization. The extraordinary session of the Central Committee on June 28-29 confirmed the reduction of the Politburo membership by more than half, replaced Yahiaoui as party coordinator, and recreated the army General Staff, and the cabinet was reshuffled on July 15. All attest to Chadli's determination to consolidate and refine political powers in a manner consistent with Algeria's parainstitutional character.

In general, this core elite is regionally balanced but above all originates from small towns with strong underrepresentation of the large cities. More than 75 percent possess a modern higher education gained either in Algeria or France, rarely in other Arab countries. The dominant professional backgrounds of this core elite are in education, administration, and the military, with very few coming from labor, business, or the legal profession. This group is somewhat older in average age (49) than its predecessor, which during the Boumediene period averaged 43 years. As a group, this core elite is reasonably close knit having been formed during the period of the revolutionary war. Their technical competence was also obtained during this period or immediately thereafter. As a rule, the core elite consciously seeks to bring new members into the broader, general elite from somewhat diverse backgrounds and form them in its own image.

A broadened interpretation of national decision makers incorporating elements of the general elite would result in a tenfold increase of elite incumbents involving the Central Committee of the FLN (160 full and 30 alternate members); the 31 *wilayal* governors (*walis*) and an equal number of presidents of the Assemblées Populaires de Wilaya; the total

National Assembly membership (n = 261); general secretaries of ministries and presidents and directors of the 15 or so major state-owned industries; the top ambassadorial and diplomatic corps; the presidents and executive councils of the five national organizations (UGTA, UNFA, UNPA, UNJA, and ONM); and heads of the 12 or so professional associations (lawyers, doctors, teachers, and so on) (see Leca and Vatin 1975, pp. 132–133; Zartman 1975b).

Biographic data on Algeria's core and general elite[2], such as ethnicity, geographic origin, religious sect, age, sex, family background, and occupation, are all of uncertain importance in understanding the rise and fall of particular leaders and leadership groups, the instruments of power used to maintain political dominance, or the ideological rationalizations put forth to legitimize authority. For example, studies have shown that, while conflicts within the Algerian political elite have at times been intense, only with rare exception have they revolved around issues of regionalism, separatism, or ethnicity. Therefore, while Berbers—Kabyles, Shawiyas, Mozabites, and Tuareg—and Arabs in Algeria are aware of their distinctive identities and often express hostility to one another, at the level of elite politics, ethnic background has been a minor source of friction (Quandt 1972, pp. 285–303). This does not prevent mass-based expressions of cultural discontent, however, as was experienced in the main Kabylia center of Tizi-Ouzou in April 1980 through violent strikes and riots by students against perceived suppression of Berber culture, language, and traditions by the Arab-dominated Algerian elite.

Looking simply at the Council of Ministers, FLN executive, ANP General Staff, and, later, the Council of the Revolution, two relatively distinct phases in the backgrounds of Algerian elites are identifiable. On accession to power, for example, the revolutionary elite was broadly composed: "there was a rough balance among regions, a wide age spread, a broad spectrum of social origins with a large representation of villagers, a nearly even split between those who had modern higher education and those who did not, and a wide distribution of professional origins with some concentration in liberal professions and in labor" (Zartman 1975c).

In the period preceding the Boumediene coup in 1965, there were signs that the top political elite was both broadening for support and changing in direction: "it increased in size and regional balance, but it was younger and somewhat less spread out in age, and nearly a third of its members came from rural agglomerations smaller than a commune." The leadership shift that occurred in 1966 was different from those it replaced or coopted "only in that its numbers increased and its members were a bit younger with a smaller age spread; two-thirds of its members came from communes or douars" (Zartman 1975c).

Boumediene's consolidation of power following the attempted Zbiri coup in December 1967 constitutes a turning point in the make-up of the top elite and initiates the second phase. "Now a narrow, transforming, technocratic elite came fully into its own, by elimination rather than by replacement. Numbers were cut in half, the age span was sharply reduced, the rural base maintained, and three-quarters of the members were modern college graduates" (Zartman 1975c). The only constant characteristic cutting across both phases was the village but nonpeasant base of the elite.

Zartman best summarizes the two stages in the postrevolutionary politics of the Algeria "type": "from 'those who made the revolution' to those who are making a revolution, from consumers to producers, from representation to restructuring, from a broad—even a great—coalition to a narrow transforming coalition" (Zartman 1975c).

Based on preliminary evidence of the newly reconstituted elite structures, it appears that the post-Boumediene "phase" will continue to expand the "rule of the technicians" but within a broadened coalition involving the recruitment and cooptation of less-educated and less-urbane, loyal party militants to reflect the FLN's diverse membership and the increased powers assigned to it. This should mean that among the top and secondary Algerian elites of the 1980s there will be a wider age spread, a modest increase in size, a wider distribution of professional types, and a probable increase of those without modern college educations with geographic and rural origins likely remaining constant. The regional identity factor, however, especially among the ethnically-conscious Kabyle, may begin to make itself felt politically and socioeconomically especially if large numbers of the mostly Kabyle 750,000 Algerians working in France are forced to return home.

Based on the most recent data available (1980) and looking strictly at the membership of the Council of Ministers, the Council of the Revolution, and the FLN executive, the following statistical summary of one segment of the top elite can be made: of the 28 total members, 14 were carry-overs from the previous realignment in 1975 with over 75 percent originating from the Algiers (25 percent), Constantine (30 percent), and Oran (22 percent) regions; they averaged 49 years of age, with social roots predominantly in the village (32 percent) and the town (22 percent) over the city (Algiers, Constantine, and Oran; 7 percent); 82 percent possessed modern higher educations while teachers (22 percent), the military (18 percent), and administrators (18 percent) constituted the largest professional categories (Zartman 1978 p. 31). An incomplete biographical survey of 1980 incumbents in the Political Bureau (n = 7) and Council of Ministers (n = 30) finds a carry over of 10 from the 1977 government with an average age of 48. (A 15-year profile of these elites is provided in Table 1.2 in the Introduction.)

The socioeconomic characteristics of the general elite as reflected in the three popular assemblies—communal (APC), *wilayal* (APW), and national (APN)—duplicate the two-phase process evident among the top elite. "Collaborators are out. The old politicians are gone. Prominent *moujahidin* are absent. In their place on all three levels are new representatives from a modern middle class of technicians and professionals, mixed with people from all other walks of life" (Zartman 1978, p. 24).

In the APC elections held in 1967, 1971, and 1975, the largest categories of members were farmers (29 percent), lower bureaucrats (15 percent), workers (14 percent), and school teachers (13 percent) (Grimaud 1973; Zartman 1978). In the departmental or *wilaya* assemblies elected in 1969 and 1974, the largest categories of members were lower bureaucrats (22 percent) and higher bureaucrats (14 percent) (Zartman 1970a; *Maghreb-Machrek*, #64 (July–August, 1974), 3). Finally, in the National Assembly elections of February 25, 1977 — the first held since Boumediene dissolved parliament in 1965 — high officials and civil servants on the one hand and school teachers on the other obtained about 25 percent of the vote, each constituting the two largest categories of representatives in the 261-member legislative body (Grimaud 1977; Zartman 1978).

In terms of the kinds and sources of higher education previously received by Algerian elites and currently being obtained by elite aspirants, the role of foreign universities or "foreign" pedagogical and administrative models applied to indigenous institutions still tend to be influential. Among the administrative component of the technocratic elite, for example, French remains the principal language of professional training and communications whether obtained in France or, as increasingly the case, in Algeria at such institutions as the Ecole Nationale d'Administration (ENA) modeled after its more prestigious counterpart in Paris.

Relatively large numbers (1977–1978: 2,500) of Algerian students are also currently being educated at American colleges and universities mostly in technical, business management, and scientific fields. Should this trend continue, elites-to-be in the technocratic system may begin to incorporate some of the features and values of American technological-scientific knowhow with particularly significant impact on the key oil, gas, and petrochemical industries upon which Algeria is depending for its developmental "takeoff." In due time, English may come to replace French as the *lingua franca* in the system's technological education.

While the military's "legitimacy" is rooted in some form of participation in the revolutionary war, its growth has been primarily influenced by events since independence (Zartman 1975b, c). In both instances, however, French education and training remain a constant feature although not uniformly applied. For example, while the professionalization of the military has been universal, there still remains a slight but not insignificant distinction between "gallicized" and "Arabized" elites, with both types still in evidence at the highest level of military-administrative power. Yahiaoui and Benjedid, for example, represent differing "socializing" experiences in regard to linguistic-cultural identity with Yahiaoui more

Arabized and Islamicized than Benjedid, who is a product of a formal French military education. Both are undisputed nationalists, however, with the badge of revolutionary authenticity firmly imprinted. In the future, this distinction will probably wane altogether as all components of the technocratic elite, save the party, will be exposed to similar professionalization experiences, including bilingualism, technical know-how, loyalty to the "organization," and certain foreign experience.

Most elite incumbents and aspirants to elite positions in the army, administration, and, less so, the party, continue to receive their professional training and formal higher education in a foreign language (French but increasingly English), in foreign countries (Europe and the U.S.), taught by foreign instructors (*coopérants* from many nations but teaching in French), and learning "foreign" ideas — in other words, institutionalizing the socioeconomic distance between themselves and the mass of illiterate and semi-literate, devoutly Muslim, Arabic and Berber-speaking, tradition-bound, underemployed and unemployed rural and urban people, with all its implications for social harmony, economic development, and political stability in the post-Boumediene era.

STRUCTURES

The June 1965 coup suspended the national Assembly and constitution which had been put in place under ben Bella in 1962 and 1963, respectively. At the national level, for over a decade thereafter, Algerian political life was strongly centralized under the Council of the Revolution and the Council of Ministers, both headed by Houari Boumediene. In the absence of a constitution, the Council of Ministers became responsible for the day-to-day administration of the government and thus became the effective executive and legislative body. The FLN and other national-level institutions were allowed to atrophy in order that Boumediene's vision of a strong, secure, centralized government could evolve free of the challenge that such organizations could present. Instead, he believed that institutional development could only emerge from the base upward via a systematic process of political education supervised from the top.

In accordance with this strategy, communal (Assemblée Populaire Communale) elections first took place in February 1967 and were renewed in February of 1971 and 1975 and in December 1979. Likewise, APW (Assemblée Populaire de Wilaya) elections were held in May 1969, five years later in May 1974, and most recently in December 1979, where 71.35 percent of the registered voters participated in the elections. However, these local and regional assemblies are largely administrative in function without significant political authority. A congress of the presidents of these assemblies is held annually and, although there is no juridical basis for these meetings, they have attained quasi-institutional status.

Until recently the Council of the Revolution, whose original 26-member body was eventually reduced — through deaths (natural or otherwise) and resignations — to nine loyal followers of Boumediene, constituted for over a decade the *noyau dur* ("hard core") of political power in the state notwithstanding its assumed "withering away" (Zartman, 1978: 22) by "natural" and constitutional "causes." Observations that by 1968 the Council had lost its "independent existence" later to be formalized by the 1976 Constitution were somewhat premature as the ANP-dominated body resurfaced at the time of Boumediene's incapacitating illness to take undisputed control of political authority in the state. The effective and stable transition of power via institutional means was guaranteed by the Council's surface cohesion and subsequent decision to liquidate the Council as a formal body while incorporating its remaining members into an enlarged Political Bureau of the FLN.

Within the elite of these national-level institutions, three types of figures can be identified: national decision makers associated with and beholden to the incumbent president, national decision makers with independent sources of power, and top-level technicians. "Each of these figures has his own following down into the next levels of government and politics, among the technicians within the ministries, party and military. Some of the 'top national elite', notably the top level technicians, are leading clients of one of the national decision-makers while at the same time being a patron in his own right for lower client levels" (Zartman, 1978: 13).

The Boumediene years were characterized by a relatively high degree of elite and institutional stability, making promotion slow and difficult. As a consequence, new graduates tended to aspire towards positions which provided security over mobility. The years 1967–68 and 1977–78 "were times of placement and maneuvering, preludes to longer periods of bureaucratic stability." A new "scramble" for political advantage began almost immediately after the onset of Boumediene's illness in Fall 1978. Notwithstanding the apparently smooth selection of his successor in late January 1979, the placing of clients undoubtedly will be an intensive if not prolonged affair with "winners" and "losers" undetermined for some months to come. Hence, 1979–80 can also be considered a time of "placement and maneuvering" — without, however, the same guarantee that a long period of bureaucratic stability will ensue.

A secondary stratum of technical elite is found within each structure of the party, government, and military. Directly below the Political Bureau of the FLN, for example, is the party's Central Committee, a broadly inclusive body representing diverse functional, professional, and regional interests. It is organized into numerous functional commissions, some paralleling governmental ministries, responsible for formulating party policy on such matters as foreign, financial, economic, and social affairs, military and judicial matters, education, Arabization, and political orientation. The Committee is also responsible for establishing the various party organs, managing party finances, executing congressional decisions, and, most importantly, electing the members of the Political Bureau.

Technically the FLN Congress is the highest organ of the party, given responsibility for establishing general party policy, adopting and modifying FLN statutes, and electing both the party secretary-general and the Central Committee. Betweeen party congresses the Central Committee functions as the county's "supreme political body." In its meeting of January 1979, for example, the Congress was constituted into three commissions. The first was charged with working up amendments to the constitution. A second was responsible for formulating permanent statutes for the party which, since June 19, 1965, had been operating under provisional statutes. Finally, the third commission screened and approved all candidates to the Central Committee and the president of the republic (Kaidi, 1979: 16).

Among the 3,290 delegates attending the fourth FLN party congress in January 1979, for example, virtually all of the core and general elites were present. The party organization had 1,759 delegates, including: 1,216 "militants de base" (cellule and Kasma representatives), 491 members from mass organizations (such as UGTA, UNPA, and UNFA), and 52 representatives of the various professional unions (lawyers, doctors, etc.). Other congress delegates included: the Armée Nationale Populaire (640), local elected officials and National Assembly deputies (323), governmental and administrative officials (537), and the presidents of the 31 APWs. The next congress, originally scheduled for 1984, was convened in extraordinary session in June 1980 to debate and adopt the Five Year Development Plan (1980–1984).

Other national organizations within the party hierachy where general elites can be found are the labor (UGTA), farmers' (UNPA), women's (UNFA), and youth (UNJA) unions as well as the veterans' association (ONM). The presidents and, to a lesser extent, the executive councils of these bodies constitute separate but not autonomous elite groups. Not all these groupings are of equal influence, however, with the UGTA probably the most important given its history of independent action (Grimaud, 1978: 57–63). Sporadic wildcat strikes and general labor protests in recent years have led authorities to come down hard on rebellious strike leaders while simultaneously granting large pay increases to workers in the hope of preempting future difficulties. Yet, while the UGTA is firmly in hand under the authoritative control of the party, Algerian workers do not satisfy easily, and valuable union experience gained in

France is readily transferable to the Algerian situation where the potential for labor unrest and violence remains high. This was most strongly evident in the massive unrest and violent disturbances by students and workers in the Kabyle in mid-April 1980.

General elites tied to the party structure can also be found among the dozen or so professional associations which group under direct government supervision such professions as the plastic artists (UNAP), accountants (UNPC), journalists (UJA), architects (UAA), translators and interpretors (UNIT), writers (UEA), engineers (UIA), physicians, dentists, and pharmacists (UMA), those working in the audio-visual field (UAAV), musicians (FNAL), moviemakers (FNCC), and others (Leca and Vatin, 1975: 132).

Immediately below the Council of Ministers, where the top governmental-administrative decision makers are located, are the general secretaries of ministries. Below the APN's five-member presidential council with Rabah Bitat at its head stand the Assembly's eight permanent commissions each with their three-member executive staffs (president, vice-president, and secretary). These parliamentary committees qualify as general elite structures situated above the APN's 261 general membership. Similarly, the *wilayal* assemblies and their elected presidents, representing the country's 31 administrative districts, constitute another important category of secondary elites. Finally, governmental leadership at the local level is provided by the executive councils of the Assemblées Populaires Communales (APC) (composed of a president and several vice-presidents, ranging from two to eighteen, depending on the size of the commune) (Leca and Vatin, 1975: 197).

The strictly administrative structures include both the civil service and those bodies responsible for running the state's major nationalized industries. Hence, while those in charge of the major components and subcomponents of the expansive administrative structure may not be core decision makers, within their own areas of bureaucratic and technological competence they hold significant power. This is especially true of the presidents and directors-general of the principal state-run industries such as SONATRACH (oil and gas), SNS (iron and steel), SONAREM (mining), SONACOME (heavy industry), SN METAL (metallurgy), SONEL-GAZ (gas and electricity), SNIC (chemicals), SONITEX (textiles), SNMC (building industries), SNCFA (railroads), CNAN (shipping), and Air Algérie, the largest and most profitable commercial airline in Africa (Gauthier and Kermarec, 1978: 61).

Despite the gradual "civilianization" of the regime since 1968 decisive elite structures in the state include the ANP General Staff, the Ministry of Defense (controlled by Boumediene from 1963 until his death fifteen years later), the head of the Gendarmerie, and the commanders of the five military regions. Their role was clearly demonstrated in the manner and outcome of the selection process for a new president that took place before and during the party congress held for that purpose in January 1979. Not only did the Ministry of Defense assume full powers during Boumediene's illness — notwithstanding Bitat's constitutional designation as interim president for 45 days — but it was a thoroughly professional military man, indeed the highest ranking military officer at age 49 with impeccable revolutionary "credentials" — Colonel Chadli Benjedid — who was eventually chosen to succeed his former commander-in-chief.

The army has always been represented on the key civilian decision-making bodies such as the Council of the Revolution and the Council of Ministers. Although it has never ruled directly, it has continued to expand its presence and influence — as, for example, when Mohamed Salah Yahiaoui, who for eight years was director of the prestigious military academy in Cherchell, was appointed to head the FLN from October 1977 until July 1980, representing a noticeable shift away from old party stalwarts like Cherif Belkacem, Ahmed Kaid, and Mohamed Said Messaadia. This trend has continued with Chadli's election as the FLN's new secretary-general. Likewise, when the new constitution provided for the creation of a National Security Council, it was Colonel Slimane Hoffman who was asked to direct it. When that body was allowed to atrophy, Slimane assumed responsibility for the Central Committee's foreign affairs division. In other words, rather than minimizing their political presence by keeping a low profile, military elites have emphasized their national, professional, and technical attributes, thus making them available for political involvement. This has resulted in a thorough integration of the military into the key decision-making structures in the governmental, administrative, and party spheres, notwithstanding the change in "uniforms." "As much as the military takeover of the party, the [Yahiaoui] appointment represented the integration of top officers into a leadership pool that is available for party, bureaucratic, administrative and diplomatic positions, much as ministers, wilaya governors, and secretaries general are available for each others' jobs. The party is the latest instance in which the regime has taken an important aspect of the revolution and tried to combine it with good management" (Zartman, 1978: 21).

That the army has been able to initiate and maintain such a noticeable presence is due in part to the historical circumstances of the revolutionary struggle and the army's role in it but also stems from its internal composition, guiding principles, and practical policies, which in combination have resulted in a legitimizing and noncoercive framework for participation in the political process. While the early years of Boumediene's regime (1965 –1967) were maintained by the use of coercive force or the threat of it ten years later the military's integral role in the technocratic system was an accomplished fact.

Concerning the army's internal composition, Zartman writes:

> The ANP has a popular base, drawing largely from the lower social strata: sons of fellahin and sons of workers. But social origins are less important for the ANP than social change; the army is composed not of workers and fellahin but of their sons, whose present situation differs from their origins by their training, profession and status ... No single tie, experience, or origin is the key to the army's political action, and no constant hierarchy of ties can be established as a source of motivations. Moreover, no combination of past ties, experiences, and origins is sure to produce the same action, reaction, allegiance, or alliance in any two individuals ... [I]t may also be said that, all things being equal, similarities in ethnic or geographic origins, in war experiences, or in educational promotions, are all causes of friendships, debts, and solidarity feelings, and they can be the basis for lasting ties, lasting enmities, or later appeals for alliances. (Zartman, 1970c: 246–247.)

The army's several guiding principles, which have dictated the military's posture since 1965, work to maintain cohesion and continuity, both within the military and the society at large: (1) The army identifies with the people; (2) the revolution to them that made it; (3) political unity is natural but division is an artificial counterrevolutionary trick; (4) a strong state structure must be built; (5) the army as guardian of the revolution has the primary task of safeguarding its own group interests; (6) the army's primary military task is to build itself into a modern professional armed force; (7) as a military organization the army must have control over its own force; and (8) the most important precondition of an effective army is its military unity (Zartman, 1973a: 217–221; Zartman, 1978: 11).

Military elites' direct involvement in rural and developmental projects, as discussed earlier, has gained them wide, popular appeal further enhancing their legitimacy as the "authentic" instrument for organizing, directing, and implementing the socioeconomic goals of the revolution (Leca and Vatin, 1975: 398).

POWER SOURCES AND USES

The principal sources of power in Algeria's technocratic system are *organizational* in nature. Colonialism and the revolution severely disrupted and undermined the impact of *traditional* and *religious* bases of power on national decision-making processes. Power predicated on *class* consciousness and other forms of socially determined group association may emerge in the future but do not yet exist, notwithstanding arguments to the contrary put forth by class-oriented and Marxist scholars (see Lazreg, 1976; Raffinot and Jacquemot, 1977; Etienne, 1977; Farsoun, 1975). *Personal* power tied to some exceptional or charismatic qualities of a leader with only incidental or marginal institutional ties has most likely diminished with the death of Boumediene, whose regime was characterized at its apex by strong, single-man rule. *Clientelist* relations constitute important sources of power, but in their "modernist" (that is, bureaucratic) rather than traditional form. The technocratic character of the system put into place by Boumediene and his army colleagues in 1965 has elevated organizational sources of power above traditional-religious, class, personal, and clientelist sources. Since the late 1960s, technical competence rather than political orientation or prior wartime record have become the distinguishing criteria for elite incumbency and the powers associated with it. Boumediene was unambiguous in this regard when he told a French interviewer in 1975: "La génération de dirigeants algériens, qui a participé à la guerre de libération, a joué un certain rôle pendant une période donnée. Cette époque est pour moi définitivement révolue" (*Jeune Afrique*, #912 (June 28, 1978), p. 33).

The term "technician" has often meant not being identified with any specific clan, nor commanding a fief anywhere in the country, nor possessing an independent political power base of one's own. It is in this regard that the new managerial, military, and party elites can be defined as technicians. While the wartime ALN experience has remained an important heritage for them, "it has become subordinate to their membership in one of the new groups [administration, army, party], with its own natures and demands" (Zartman, 1975b: 272). Furthermore, the overwhelming majority of these elites have been without strong antecedent ties and obligations and are therefore ready to identify with their particular groups. One consequence of all this has been the technical elites' strong identification with the new organizations. "Unlike scions of old families who take their place in institutions...as 'delegates' from their social groups, the new elites of Algeria became organization men with the particular imprint of their organization. Because both were new, the elites and the organizations grew together, the elites using the organizational power to defend and promote the organization's interests" (Zartman, 1975b: 273).

Organizational power is manifest in all three principal ruling hierarchies. The power imbalance so evident in the 1960s has given way to a veritable *redressement institutionnel*, especially as regards the once impotent party. Now all three institutions — party, administration, army — possess legitimacy and influence at each of the national, regional, and local decision-making levels, can and do dispense political favors and patronage, recruit and retain ambitious and qualified cadres, have adequate managerial, mobilizational, and military resources to assure the noncoercive application of popular and not-so-popular socioeconomic programs and policies, and, in general, command response and respect from a populace that increasingly is being socialized to accept rational-legalistic rather than traditional or charismatic forms of authority and power.

While this institutionalization process is still in its "infancy" a decade of stable rule (1968–78) and gradual institution building from the bottom up (beginning with communal elections in 1967 and evolving to national legislative elections ten years later) has resulted in one of the few instances where a nonviolent, constitutional transfer of power has taken place in the Third World.

Obviously the power resources available to the military, however discreetly used, are superior to those held by the party and administration but only if a narrow definition — military hardware — is employed. Since technical skill increasingly is a "resource" onto itself once attached to legitimate organization, it becomes a power "equalizer." Hence, in the current scheme of things, a regional military commander is no more or less "powerful" than a director-general of a major nationalized industry, a *wali* of an administrative district, a Central Committee member of the FLN, or a president of one of the National Assembly's eight permanent commissions. Indeed, that same military figure is eligible to fill any one of these managerial, administrative, party, and governmental posts reflecting the interchangeability of incumbents in a technocratic system. Revealingly, however, civilian technicians are *not* available for military appointments demonstrating that in the final analysis, authoritative decision making in transitional societies remains in the hands of the armed forces whose strong sense of group identification and cohesion leads them to jealously guard their rights and protect their interests against the incursions of "outsiders." The implicit or explicit threat of "intervention" constitutes the military elite's "bottom line" of available power, one permanently denied to other elite groups in the society. Yet, if the Iranian case is at all instructive, the threat of military intervention can be neutralized under conditions of imperfect or incomplete institutionalization. Such a realization is important in understanding the integrative nature of the Algerian elite system with its interchangeability of technocratic parts designed to insure that no decision-making component of the political system becomes disengaged from its popular base. In a sense, the Algerian experiment is an empirical working-out of the "crises of development" fundamental to the building of state and nation; indeed, the nature and sources of power available to the national-level elite and their ruling structures are aimed at resolving the crises of identity, legitimacy, participation, penetration, and distribution in a harmonious, nonconflictual manner. The military's commitment of its diverse power resources to this functional enterprise coupled with its participatory but noninterventionary posture in civilian politics has been central to the system's stability and relatively effective political performance in the last ten years.

The power resources available to the administrative elite are the most expansive and politically significant inasmuch as the ministerial, bureaucratic, and technological-economic activities of the state are under its control and jurisdiction. The party's once modest human, material, organizational, and symbolic resources have dramatically altered in recent years, especially at the national level. Yet only time will tell whether the party elites, as FLN leaders in their own right rather than as the president's men or transplanted military officers, can command the kind of authority and power now possessed by the army and administration. Yahiaoui's recent removal (July 1980) as party coordinator to be replaced by the aging functionary, Cherif Messaadia, in his new capacity as permanent secretary of the Central Committee, may compromise the party's incipient power and prestige returning it to its more modest role as the country's principal "Ministry of mobilization" to be used at ad hoc moments such as elections and discussions of major government initiatives.

Nonorganizational sources of power become relevant only within existing institutional arrangements. For example, despite the importance accorded religion, traditional values, and other components of the Islamic belief system, Algerian elites have not permitted religious authorities or leaders to establish an independent power base, at least not as it impacts on national politics. Boumediene, himself a devout Muslim and a strong advocate of a religiously based traditional culture, made certain to directly attach the minister in charge of religious affairs — Mouloud Kassim Nait Belkacem — to the presidency, thus insuring "official" Islam's cooperation in the cultural revolution, the third component along with industry and agriculture of Boumediene's tripartite revolution. Similarly, single individuals, whether as power brokers in their own right or as clients to more influential patrons, assert their authority and flex their political muscle as men of the organization, rarely as independent spokesmen or popular heroes. Outstanding examples of organization men who have no clan identification or control of a regional fief include: Belaid Abdesselam, ex-minister of light industry, former minister of heavy industry and energy, and an *eminence grise* of Algeria's aggressive oil policies within OPEC who, although in current disfavor with the regime, remains available for future elite-level assignment; Kamel Abdallah Khodja, former secretary of state for planning; Ahmed Ghozali, former hydraulics minister, ex-minister of energy and petrochemical industries, and former head of SONATRACH; Mohamed Liassine, minister of heavy industry and former director of SNS (iron and steel); and Ahmed Taleb Ibrahimi, former minister of culture and continuing ministerial counselor to Chadli. All of these men have their origins either in the wartime GPRA or student movement of the prerevolutionary and revolutionary periods. Their distinguishing characteristic is the specialized skills they possess and their ability to effectively manage the ministries or industries under their jurisdiction (Raffinot and Jacquemot, 1977: 124).

Heads of "secondary" ministries and former military officer-technicians such as Abdelmajid Aouchiche (housing and construction), Mohamed Zerguini (PTT), Said Ait Messaoudene (light industries), and Mohamed Amir (ex-labor) were direct clients of the late president; as such they have had no power base of their own.

Likewise, Bouteflika, who was Boumediene's protégé and foreign affairs minister for over fifteen years, certainly lost more than a friend in the new government formed on March 8, 1979, after a three-day meeting of the FLN's Central Committee which designated Mohamed Seddick Benyahia, the former finance minister, as Bouteflika's replacement; this designation is interpreted as a mild dilution of Bouteflika's previous influence — an influence and prestige which would be more difficult to maintain in his new capacity as presidential adviser to Chadli Benjedid and a member of the Political Bureau. Then, direct clients of the former foreign minister such as Abdellatif Rahal (ex-higher education), Djamal Houhou (sports), Abdelmalek Benhabyles (ex-justice), M'Hamed Yala (finance), and Mohamed Said Mazouzi (ex-*Moudjahidin*) could also be reduced to secondary elite status. Redha Malek (ex-information and culture) and Mostefa Lacheraf (ex-education), respected intellectuals who were, among other things, responsible for drawing up the National Charter, are clients of and patrons to no one with all the advantages and liabilities that this entails.

While much of this remains highly speculative, it is clear that the resources and tactics that enable the elites to remain in power are and will continue to be organizational in nature. To the extent that patron-client relations and horizontal coteries maintain themselves, and that other forms of traditional and personal power develop, they will interact within a highly regularized technocratic system leaving little room for the kinds of personal intrigues, elite conflicts, clashes, and dissentions that so paralyzed the ben Bella regime and the early governments of Boumediene.

SOCIALIZATION

The content and method of elite socialization in Algeria is conditioned by the attitudes toward the "proper" role of government held by the current generation of incumbent elites. Historically and contemporaneously, such attitudes have been marked by coexisting contradictory impulses and fundamentally inconsistent views.

The colonial and war experiences have had particularly profound impact on the elites' perception of the proper role of government. Specifically, Boumediene's successors believe, as he did, in the need for strong centralized state, often referred to as state capitalism or *étatisme* when applied to economic development and organization. Simultaneously, and in apparent contradiction, Algerian political elite place a great stress on the role of the impoverished masses, reflecting a populist orientation.

In its essentials, populism consists of two fundamental principles: first, the supremacy of the will of the people which is identified with justice and morality above all other norms; and secondly, the importance of a direct relationship between the people and their leaders in which non-governmental intermediary institutions and mediating structures can only play a secondary role (Leca, 1975).

These unreconciled perceptions of the role of government originate from a strongly felt sense of nationalism and a less clearly defined attachment to the rhetoric and symbolism (and, much less frequently, the content) of socialism. Among the political elite, these dual notions of nationalism and socialism have assumed sacrosanct status. The *étatiste* policies of Algerian developmental elites are in fact justified in nationalist terms wherein the state is viewed as having the "right" to intervene in many areas of national life. In particular, it is felt that the state must control its own resources and territory. Yet there remains a genuine commitment to the masses which transcends the excessive revolutionary and socialist rhetoric. This is reflected in the areas of welfare, education, and social services where government policy has been progressive and enlightened. In recent years there has also been a commitment to the idea of mass political participation and administrative decentralization as has been demonstrated by the National Charter debates, the new constitution, and the legislative and two presidential elections in the 1976–79 period.

Other elements of elite political culture and ideology in Algeria include belief in a continuing revolution, Arab unity, and the resurrection of an Algerian Arab-Islamic culture through the means of Arabization and Algerianization under the guidance of a mass mobilizational political party. The Islamic component of socialism remains a salient feature of contemporary ideology. For Algerian ideologues, socialism can have no meaning outside the realm of Islamic belief. In the Algerian context, socialism refers to a belief system whereby a centralized structure is concerned with the allocation of resources whose objective is the control and utilization of national economic wealth so as to prevent one class from monopolizing the products. Yet this takes place within the world of Islam, which constitutes the "heart, mind, and soul" of Algerian consciousness. Thus, not only is there no apparent contradiction between scientific socialism and religious belief, but in fact such socialism has no meaning outside the Islamic essence of Algerian national and cultural identity. This perspective is reaffirmed in both the National Charter and new constitution, which explicitly extol Islamic socialism as the road to political, economic, social, and cultural salvation. The new Algerian leadership under Chadli Benjedid seems committed to the continuation and concretization of these principles notwithstanding other elements of the "de-Boumedienization" process already under way in certain areas of political, economic, and social policy.

In practical terms, this perspective has permitted incumbent leaders to sustain a conservative, indeed puritanical, policy in the area of personal, religious, and moral affairs while simultaneously pursuing a radical modernization policy involving rapid and sweeping economic growth, the use of advanced technology and scientific know-how, and dependence on Western secularists for organizational, technological, and financial expertise. Inevitably, the coexistence of socialist-revolutionary, French republican, and Arab-Berber-Islamic-traditional influences generate unexpected tensions and contradictions which the previous and current rulers have not yet adequately reconciled. These conflicts and contradictions are reflected in the socialization process itself, espeically in its important educational component through which aspirant elites are created.

A technocratic system dependent on tripartite mobilizational, managerial, and military sources for system maintenance and development requires appropriate educational instruments to provide (1) the technical skills required for such maintenance and (2) concurrent attitudinal orientations supportive of the elite political culture and ideology thereby providing legitimacy to the policy process. The educational system has thus been created with the dual goals of transforming Algerians into participants in a modern, technological society and at the same time rejuvenating the country's Arab-Islamic heritage.

The government's educational efforts since independence have indeed been impressive if not spectacular at least in statistical and quantitative terms. In 1962, for example, there were only about 750,000 Algerian children enrolled in primary school; sixteen years later, in the 1977–78 academic year, nearly three million (2,900,000) students were registered, or about 81 percent of the total primary school age group in the country (Dufour, 1978: 34–35). At the secondary school level progress has been even more impressive: the figure of 32,000 at independence was multiplied ten-fold by 1974–75, with over 400,000 enrolled constituting nearly 20 percent of all children of secondary school age. Finally, while there were only 3,000 Algerian university students enrolled in 1962, by 1978–79 the figure had topped 70,000, distributed unevenly throughout the country's four major universities and six university centers with over 70 percent on full government scholarship (Remili, 1978: Junqua, January 4, 1979; Dufour, 1978; Minces, 1978: 69).

For the last decade, more than 30 percent of the Algerian national budget and 11 percent of its GNP has been spent on education (in the Middle East-North Africa region only Tunisia compares favorably in this regard); despite marked regional, social, and economic imbalances (for example, while only 63.8 percent of Tiaret's primary school age group was enrolled in school Tizi-Ouzou had a 95 percent enrollment figure [Dufour, 1978: 34]), a comprehensive network of full-scale universities (Algiers, Oran, Constantine, and Annaba), regional university centers (Tizi-Ouzou, Setif, and Batna in the east, Blida and Tiaret in the center, Mostaganem, Bel-Abbes, and Tlemcen in the west, and new ones planned), and technical, agricultural, vocational, and teacher training institutes as well as army, navy, and air force military academies have all been put into place to service the nation's educational needs—including those of its adult, female, religious, and peasant populations. At the university level, scientific, technical, biological, and medical studies were and continue to be the most encouraged; nearly 50 percent of all university enrollment in the 1974–75 academic year specialized in these fields (Dufour, 1978). While interest and concentration in the humanities, social sciences, and juridical studies continues to be high, authorities are placing greater emphasis on "scientific" studies aimed at creating the necessary technical cadres needed to staff, manage, and run the administrative but not necessarily political machinery of the state. In fact, Algeria's educational policies are aimed at four different sectors of society reflecting different pedagogical philosophies, levels of human and material investment, and expected outputs. Among the mass of illiterate peasants, Bedouins, and semi-nomadic groups, for example, the government has been working conscientiously—with mixed results—to establish a minimal functional literacy regarded as necessary for effective participation in the country's modernization and development process. At a slightly higher level there is another mass-oriented effort to create necessary, utilizable skills involving vocational training, special institutions, and other non-academic programs that could integrate teenage and adult "dropouts" into jobs that would provide acceptable benefits to the individuals involved as well as blue-collar-level labor for the state's numerous industrial and manufacturing enterprises. A third category of "mass" education involves those pursuing formal academic programs paralleling or slightly exceeding secondary school standards designed ultimately to train the bulk of bureaucratic, technical, administrative, and clerical personnel that the public and, increasingly, the private sector will need in the next decade. In a sense, this politically obedient, clerical-administrative stratum constitutes the mainspring of the regime's expanding technocratic base. At the apex of this educational pyramid stands the 1 to 3 percent who are destined, because of the kind and level of education, family and personal connections, acquired wealth and influence, multilingual fluency, and technical-scientific accreditation, to assume the top and secondary-level decision-making positions in each of the principal institutional components of the technocratic system. These four sectoral targets reflect the mass-elite dichotomy characterizing educational policy in Algeria today. Thus the overwhelming thrust of educational efforts is to create a minimally educated, participant but obedient mass public trained to assume the technical requirements of a scientifically developing society while maintaining—indeed, reinforcing—the Arab-Islamic cultural identity for purposes of ideological congruity and political legitimacy. For a very small segment of the society, however, an elite-oriented educational structure exists for purposes of forming the managers of this technological system. Yet this latter process is directed more at producing administrators than politicians, doers than thinkers, imitators than inventors, technicians than scientists, and organizational men rather than independently minded and creative decision makers.

How successful has this socialization process been among the elites-to-be as they are trained in the country's universities and other educational institutions?

Pedagogically, Algeria's university system is in a stage of painful transition from its colonial heritage to an independent, academically credible, and culturally authentic national system of higher education. This transitional stage is undergoing serious discontinuities and conflicts regarding its impact on student socialization. For example, while foreign instructors (mainly French) have virtually been eliminated from the primary and, to a lesser extent, secondary school systems, they still predominate (over 50 percent) at the university level at ranks (*Maîtres de conférence* and *professeurs*) and in fields that have policy and prestige significance (science, technology, law, and economic sciences). That is to say, French-language competence — notwithstanding the government's official Arabization policy — continues to insure access to disciplines and academic specializations which are most rewarded in the economic market place. Indeed, increased Arabization of primary and secondary school curricula without concurrent language uniformity at the higher levels has created enormous tensions and frustrations for those *Arabisants* unprepared to deal effectively in French-language instruction and therefore destined to "dead-end" jobs, since nearly all openings in the public and private sectors require some level of bilingualism and, in certain fields, trilingualism. Here immediately one sees the practical and potentially dysfunctional consequence of seeking to promulgate a dual system simultaneously aimed at providing technical training and establishing the foundation for a culturally meaningful sense of national identity. The creation of parallel *sections arabophones* and *francophones* in many faculties and disciplines at the four major universities has led to severe competition and conflict between both groups as regards academic status, job potential, cultural authenticity, nationalist credibility, and so forth. Sometimes these conflicts turn violent, as occurred in 1974, 1975, and, most recently, in fall 1976, at the University of Constantine where representatives of both groups clashed technically over the question of which legal system the country should adopt and maintain — traditional Islamic or modern secular. In reality the conflict reflected increased student dissatisfaction with the quality, purpose, and usability of an all-Arab education in a society that still puts a substantive although not symbolic premium on bilingual training and other features of modern, secular education regarded by incumbent decision makers as integral to the development process. Even in a minor ministry such as the postal and telephone service, for example, Arabization has barely taken hold.

In political terms these pedagogical incongruities have future import, not so much for aspirant elites as for counterelites-in-the-making. Notwithstanding the inflated rhetoric of ideologues quoting the National Charter and other official statements regarding the importance of "nationalist-revolutionary elements" as prerequisites for elevation to leadership roles in the economic, social, and administrative sectors student Arabophones perceive their educations and teachers as second-rate and inappropriate (for example, it is common knowledge that students regard French faculty as superior in every regard to the many Egyptian instructors who staff the Arabic sections of university faculties). From the perspective of these students, such redundant training virtually excludes them from all positions of political significance save the minor functionary roles available at the lower echelons of the party or at local levels of government and administration.

In addition to pedagogical discontinuities, there are severe socio-economic disparities at both the "input" and "output" end of the educational-socialization process which have significance for elite attitudinal formation.

In absolute terms it is quite evident that nonelite children dominate elementary and secondary school enrollments. In this sense Algeria has created a truly "mass" educational system without, however, eliminating inequalities in relative and absolute terms at the lowest and highest levels of education. For example, if one measures relative chances that elite children will enter secondary school one finds fairly marked inequalities, while absolute figures indicate that schooling remains very much open to nonelite children. At the postsecondary school level, however, the mass feature of the educational system disappears altogether in both relative and absolute terms. Recent studies have shown a consistent relationship between socioeconomic level and chances for entrance into unversity. One such study, for example, has shown that a son of a blue-collar worker has a 15 times better chance than the son of a farm laborer to enter university, while a son of an agricultural manager has a 30 times better chance than the farm laborer's son to go on to university. The son of a technocrat or a businessmen has a 285 times better chance of going on to university than does the son of an agricultural worker (Dufour, 1978: 45). By whatever indicator one uses, it is evident that there is an imbalance favoring those whose families already hold power, wealth, or status in the society.

This situation is exacerbated by the fact that children of the well-to-do also tend to be the ones who enroll in the universities' *sections fran-cophones*, thereby gaining immediate advantage over their lower-class counterparts in the *sections arabophones*. Not infrequently, many of these same elite children receive their primary and secondary school training in the 50 or so French-run educational institutions (in 1978–79: 5 *lycées*, 4 *collèges d'enseignement général*, and 40 primary schools) that have been permitted to be established in Algeria under the jurisdiction of the Office

Universitaire et Culturel Français (OUCF) ostensibly to meet the educational needs of the children of diplomats, *coopérants*, businessmen, and other segments of the large foreign community living and working in Algeria. In fact what has happened is that the Algerian well-to-do, some married to foreigners but many not, have been sending their children to these OUCF schools to avoid the hopeless overcrowding and mediocrity of the all-Algerian schools as well as to gain the necessary linguistic and educational advantage that the OUCF schools are perceived as possessing. In the 1977–78 school year alone, for example, over 50 per cent of OUCF enrollment was composed of Algerian students in direct opposition to a 1976 government law giving the state exclusive responsibility for educating Algerians (Dufour, 1978: 38–39).

Beyond the major universities themselves are several newly developed specialized institutes under the direct jurisdiction of appropriate ministries that are gaining in technical importance and, with it, increased influence. The Ecole Polytechnique d'El Harrach, Ecole d'Ingénieurs des Travaux Publics, Ecole Nationale d'Administration, and the Centre Africain des Hydrocarbures et des Textiles are major examples of functionally oriented training institutes from which state employment is immediately guaranteed. In a real sense these are the training centers for the middle-level cadres that the state is developing to ultimately eliminate the system's continuing dependence on foreign technocratic expertise and foreign training institutes. At best, however, only elements of the general, not core elite will emerge from these institutions, with the possible exception of the ENA.

None are so privileged, however, as the military academies — especially the army's prestigious school at Cherchell, a seaside town of 20,000 located about 60 miles west of Algiers. This former French officer school has developed into a "super-elitist" institution providing for its cadets a quality program within an impressive physical environment. Indeed while civilians of all classes experience chronic food and water shortages, confront the daily problems of housing and transportation, and battle the powers of bureaucracy at almost every turn, academies like the one at Cherchell are veritable enclaves of material prosperity and comfort.

Recreational facilities alone, including swimming pools, tennis courts, soccer fields and the like, are unmatched by any other sector of society devoted to education and professional formation. One result is that — while the military has to date not been characterized by elaborate ceremony, uniforms, personal ostentation, or inflated rank (colonel is the highest rank in the ANP, with the number of colonels not exceeding 35 and probably fewer than 250 majors) — their expanding elite status, good pay, extensive fringe benefits, and other tangible and nontangible signs of privilege are creating an officer "caste," with the military in general developing into a preferred and almost separate segment of society notwithstanding the "people's army" label.

Curiously the existence of educational inequalities and socioeconomic discrepancies in professional training have not yet been translated into overt political opposition or general social discontent on the part of incipient elites. It is uncertain whether this relative political docility stems from a successful socialization of the elite political culture including acceptance of the socialist-Arabic-Islamic ideology or simply represents a surface acquiescence to overpowering state authority or, more likely, reflects the existence of sufficient employment opportunities in the public sector access to which is a function both of appropriate technical training and ideological conformity. In any case what is more certain is that, unlike the situations in neighboring Morocco and Tunisia where discontinuous political socialization between incumbent and emerging elites has been observed for the past decade, elite aspirants in Algeria, in general, identify with the ruling class and share in their ideological orientation particularly its technocratic component.

This is not to say that the educated classes are unaware of or insensitive to the system's numerous abuses, inequalities, and injustices. Yet criticism is usually directed less at specific individuals or the elite-generated belief-system than at its arbitrary application. For example, Algerian students resent the dual standards applied by the well-to-do who encourage a producer ethic for the aspirant elite and mass public while espousing and practicing a consumer ethic for themselves.

More serious, perhaps, is the fact that students have not been permitted an independent political status since 1971 when the UNEA (Union Nationale des Etudiants Algériens) was suppressed following a series of disruptive student strikes and demonstrations. Dissolution was facilitated by the relative weakness of the student movement as an instrument of political organization and mobilization. Since that time despite increased student political sophistication the regime has relegated them to a supportive role in the overall revolutionary effort being officially represented in the innocuous Union Nationale de la Jeunesse Algérienne (UNJA) where they have been designated the task of advancing the agrarian revolution through voluntary service (*le volontariat*) undertaken between academic semesters and in the summer. As a result, the UNJA has attracted only a very small portion of available students, although this situation may be changing as radical Pagsistes take over UNJA's leadership. Their natural cynicism and distrust have therefore turned "inward" towards the educational rather than political system, a situation made easier by the relatively high degree of student participation permitted in curriculum and other pedagogical matters (*les comités pédagogiques*) of the various institutes (formerly faculties). Within this narrow sphere of action students have frequently undertaken unilateral strikes, boycotts, and demonstrations to protest everything from excessive course (*module*) requirements to the inadequacy of public transportation in a situation where classes are often assigned on the five or so different campuses of the University of Algiers.

Rarely, however, are these protestations permitted to overflow into the political sphere.

Given the relative rigorous enforcement of the system's "rules of the game," student responses have tended to operate on several different levels. At the *systemic* level there is general support for the regime and its policies, both domestically and internationally, although there is an acute awareness and resentment of the many abuses of privilege and corruption that take place. At the *university* level there is an obsessive preoccupation with success and the need to advance or in any way qualify for that "prestigious" position that awaits the graduate in the expansive public sector, an impression continuously fortified by the government itself. Excessive time and effort are expended at this level as students continuously politic for reductions of course requirements, grade changes, make-up examinations, and whatever else is deemed appropriate to guarantee academic certification. Such politicking may include verbal and physical intimidation of professors, both foreign and native. At the *personal* level as well, student expenditure of time is enormous as they strive to overcome the frustrations and hardships of daily life in a society that offers them virtually no social, cultural, or sexual outlets save the meager diversions of soccer, beaches, and movies — all experienced within a virtually all-male environment.

To date the frustrations and bitterness so evident at the university and personal levels have not spilled over into the political environment, where the regime's appeal for enthusiastic participation in its political institutions and processes has evoked only a mild positive response from university students. Expectations that the material and status rewards now accruing to incumbent elites will one day accrue to them along with their genuine belief in the appropriateness of the socialist, Arab, and Islamic paths to development provide the incipient elite with sufficient psychopolitical sustenance to overcome the travail of "making it" in socialist Algeria.

Yet there is no guarantee that the balance of these forces and experiences will not one day overlap and clash, perhaps violently, as happened in April 1980 among students at Tizi Ouzou. The contradictory messages being received in the students' different socializing milieus — traditional-Islamic at home, participatory-technocratic-scientific at school, political passivity or controlled participation in the political arena, a media mixture of modernist, traditionalist, diversionary, instructional, and superfluous in the press, radio, and television, travel and exposure to Western ideas — all combine to produce a condition of discontinuous political socialization with great potential for social unrest. If the system's reward structures fail to materialize in terms of adequate number of secure jobs and the mediocre and incomplete nature of much of the educational process continues unchecked, a "third" generation of disillusioned and economically "unabsorbable" counterelites, as described by Waterbury and

Zartman for Morocco, may emerge. "The fact that these [third generation counterelites] often tend to be semieducated, traditionalist school-leavers, trained only in Arabic and more hostile than frustrated in their feelings toward modernization, suggests that their reaction will be neo-traditionalist, . . . Islamic, populist, xenophobic, and Qaddafite. This stratum will be one of cynical radicals, suspicious of any leadership . . ., intolerant, impatient, and embittered over being excluded from the public benefits that private [and public] corruption make appear inexhaustible" (Zartman, 1974: 484–485; Waterbury, 1970).

For the immediate future, however, and from the perspective of current power holders, a profile of aspirant elites would look as follows: (1) bilingual, possibly trilingual; (2) trained in scientific, managerial, and/or technical skills; (3) holding advanced degrees and having gained experiences abroad, especially in Europe and the United States; (4) politically participatory but nonoppositional; (5) organizational, conformist, loyal to the "company"; (6) more pragmatic than ideological; (7) holding links, connections, and ties with patrons and within coteries; (8) administrators, not politicians.

CIRCULATION

The recruitment and retirement of incumbent elites has become increasingly regularized, particularly but not exclusively at the secondary level. Even among the national decision makers, neither earlier involvement in the revolutionary struggle nor previous personal association with Boumediene is sufficient criteria for access to or retention in top elite positions. Similarly, the arbitrariness of single-man rule can be expected to diminish with the death of Boumediene and the concurrent dispersal of political authority among various high level institutions. Based on the manner in which the new president and cabinet were recently selected (President: January 1979; cabinet and reshuffle, March 1979 and July 1980 respectively) the consultative process as formalized within the constitutional and party structures seems to have been further institutionalized without, however, eliminating completely the "wheeling-and-dealing" and backdoor personal power struggles virtually inherent in all interelite relations and possibly intrinsic to the whole Algerian political process.

Regular elections to the various local, regional, and national assemblies constitute one important and direct device for elite recruitment at both the top and secondary levels. This applies as well to the Congress, Central Committee, and Political Bureau elections of the FLN. In fact, there has been a veritable electoral "revolution" ever since Boumediene began to create a system of decentralized local government (1967 and 1969 APC and APW elections) to be counterbalanced by a single, centralized party and a well-established administration. Virtually every unit of the party—national organizations (UGTA, UNFA, etc.), professional associations, and governmental and administrative structures—has procedures for regular mandatory elections legitimized under the National Charter's banner of "democratic centralism."

For all top-level technical and civil service positions, expertise and political loyalty continue to be the determinative criteria for elite entrance— with such people as Belaid Abdessalem, Ahmed Taleb, Rehda Malek, Ahmed Ghozali, Mostefa Lacheraf, Abdelatif Rahal, Mohamed Liassine, and Djamal Houhou being outstanding examples, however much policy failures may have "done-in" certain of these individuals (e.g., Belaid, Ghozali, and Rahal). While all of the above participated in the wartime effort in some capacity either at home or in France, they did not play a role in the turbulent politics of the immediate postindependence period; rather, they reemerged to prominence from within the general elite half a decade later with their political reputations unsoiled and their technical skills in demand.

At all levels of bureaucracy and administration the patronage system still prevails which, as one example, entails the obligation to find jobs for war veterans. In fact, most ministries still adhere to an earlier policy that required each government agency to recruit at least 10 percent of its total staff from veterans' groups.

The relatively regularized system of elite circulation currently in effect is in marked contrast to the pattern of constant turnover in top political leadership evident in the decade prior to Boumediene's consolidation of power beginning in 1968. Indeed, the 1968–78 decade was a period of remarkable stability among top elites—in the Council of Ministers alone, for example, there was an uninterrupted seven-year stretch (1970–77) before a personnel reshuffle of any consequence took place—with changes occurring because of resignation, promotion, rebellion, retirement, and death, natural or otherwise.

It has been difficult to determine exactly what causes an incumbent leader to lose favor with the "powers-to-be" and either be 'promoted" out (to embassies like Delici, Bejaoui, and Maaoui or to the National Assembly like Yaker, Zaibek, Fadel, and Guennez) (Zartman, 1978: 15); forced to resign (Mahroug, Kaid, and Cherif Belkacem); or, once in exile, assassinated (Krim in 1970 and Khider in 1967, with the latter murder undoubtedly related to Khider's confiscation of nearly $15 million of FLN funds gathered during the war in his capacity as party treasurer). Even so-called "natural" and "accidental" deaths of those fallen from favor (Kaid of a "heart attack" in Morocco in March 1978, and Medeghri of injuries resulting from a car accident in 1974) are rarely accepted at face value, especially in an environment where even a mild political deviation from the narrowly defined norm is reprimanded.

Such suspicions are reinforced by the fact that, under Boumediene, the game of political "musical chairs," so finely developed by Bourguiba in Tunisia and Hassan II in Morocco, has rarely been played in Algeria. That is, there is none of the "exile-and-reintegration" phenomenon which has always kept incumbent and oppositional elites in Tunisia and Morocco on their feet. For those who so disagreed with Boumediene by reason of temperament, policy, or ideology that they could no longer play by the "rules of the game" the alternatives were few and virtually irreversible. As Zartman indicates: "There [was] elite circulation up and circulation out [under Boumediene], but not circulation back in" (Zartman, 1978: 15).

It is still too early in the new regime to determine whether or not Boumediene's system of collegiality and consultation within a narrrow circle of trusted individuals will be retained or modified and expanded to enable "legitimate" opposition to emerge. A slight but perhaps representative shift along these lines was noted in the reintegration of Major Abderrahman ben Salem into the Council of the Revolution in late December 1978, when Boumediene was dying. Ben Salem had been an original member of the Council until he was unilaterally removed by Boumediene in late 1977. Since there was no opposition to him by the eight remaining members of the Council, he was allowed to be reinstated.

Whether representative or not, the above example does not alter the basic pattern established by Boumediene to handle dissent. To date elite opposition has been successfully suppressed at home and made politically insignificant abroad due in part to the government's close and continuous supervision of people and ideas within and across its borders. Where potentially disruptive oppositional tendencies have manifested themselves, as among incipient counterelites such as university students and urban workers, the government has employed a combined "carrot-and-stick" approach to bring them into line. This has meant that, once public disorders have been terminated, students have been granted increased rights in the determination of university-level policies while being assured of future employment opportunities within the public sector. As for the workers, impressive pay increases have been promised. When dock and railroad workers went on several wildcat strikes in fall 1977, one result was a whopping 30 percent pay raise announced several months later in a presidential address to the fifth annual UGTA congress.

The system's expanding economy, with its productive industrial and manufacturing sectors, provides the regime — in the short-run at least — with sufficient resources to coopt or buy-off potential opposition. Moreover, unlike the situations in Morocco and Tunisia, upward mobility to subordinate elite status within the various components of the technocratic system is still possible for qualified and ambitious university-trained Algerians. Such a situation makes it all the more difficult for oppositional forces at home and abroad to gain credibility and widespread support.

Yet clandestine and occasional public challenges to elite incumbents do take place both at home and in France, where it is more pronounced. A recent case of "above-ground" domestic opposition occurred during the heady days of public debate and discussion preceding the approval of the new National Charter and Constitution in 1976, when a group of former leaders of the revolution issued a series of manifestoes in Algiers and elsewhere beginning with a March 6, 1976 "New Appeal to the Algerian People" condemning the absence of democratic institutions and deploring a foregin policy that had led to a split in North Africa and the danger of war with Morocco. The four men who took the initiative in demanding constitutional democracy were all former leaders in the war of independence, including two ex-presidents of the Algerian government-in-exile (GPRA) — Benyoussef ben Khedda and Ferhat Abbas. (The other two were Hocine Lahouel, former secretary-general of the MTLD — Mouvement pour le Triomphe des Libertés Démocratiques, and Mohamed Kheiriddine, a member of the ex-CNRA, Conseil National de la Révolution Algérienne). All four had criticized Boumediene for totalitarian rule and the cult of personality. For his part, Boumediene rejected these criticisms of his rule as the work of "bourgeois reactionaries" and declared that the revolution had reached the point of no return.

Despite the legitimization of certain democratic liberties implied in the formal approval of the Charter and Constitution, the signatories were placed under house arrest, where they remained until early 1980. Ben Khedda's pharmacy in Algiers was nationalized and Kheiriddine, who owned a plastics factory just outside the capital, was confronted with a strike by his employees, who denounced him as an "exploiter." The factory was also nationalized. As part of Chadli's liberalization decrees, these properties were later returned back to their owners and their pensions (provided to all former GPRA presidents and ministers) were once again activated. The ben Khedda-Abbas experience marked the beginning and end of public declarations of opposition by those who criticized not only policies and their excution — a "lawful" exercise — but policymakers and their legitimacy as well — a subversive act.

It has not been possible to determine.whether any other source of organized opposition exists within the country among current or disaffected elites although it is known that Algeria's economic and military support for the Polisario Front has on occasion divided but not fractured the core elite. In addition, as indicated earlier, there is diffuse dissatisfaction among certain categories of university students and urban laborers, especially in the volatile Kabyle, where recent bloody demonstrations jolted the regime; yet this has not taken concrete political form. One impediment to such a development has been the virtual absence of any respected or popular opposition leader as, for example, exists in Tunisia. Ben Bella, although no longer under house arrest, remains under strict police restraint. While there is some concern for him by French leftist intellectuals and former Algerian political personalities residing abroad, there appears to be no grass roots support evident for the man or his ideology among Algerian incipient or counterelites.

The most visible and vocal, albeit ineffective form of organized political opposition is found abroad, especially in France where several exiled Algerian leaders have formed miniscule opposition "parties" which to date have gained very little support among the thousands of Algerian students and workers residing in France and elsewhere in Europe.

For example, Mohamed Boudiaf, who left the FLN at the time of independence, founded the Parti de la Revolution Socialiste (PRS) which, through its Paris-based newsletter, *PRS Information*, continues its attack on Algeria's "confiscated" revolution, state capitalism, and burgeoning class of *nouveaux riches*. Boudiaf himself lives in exile in Morocco. Hocine Ait Ahmed, who organized the Kabyle revolt against ben Bella in 1963–64, founded the Front des Forces Socialistes (FFS) in 1963. Although centered in Paris, Ait Ahmed himself lives in exile in Switzerland. Ben Khedda's Union Nationale pour la Liberté et al Démocratie (UNLD) is little more than a paper organization reflecting the views of the four signatories of the March 1976 Manifesto. Le Rassemblement National pour la Démocratie (RND) was created in Paris by Ali Mahsas, former minister of agriculture under both ben Bella and Boumediene. It represents another feeble attempt to put forth a "democratic" alternative to Algeria's current socialist path to be legitimized under the personal leadership of such "unanimously respected" individuals as Abbas, ben Khedda, and ben Bella.

Mohamed Lebjaoui, former head of the FLN federation in France, fled to Switzerland in 1966 where he formed the Mouvement Algérien des Forces Populaires et de l'Armée pour la Démocratie et l'Union Maghrebine (MAFPADEUM) as a means of continuing his support for ben Bellist principles.

In August 1975 a group calling itself "Soldiers of the Algerian Opposition" bombed Algerian embassies in three European capitals and issued a communique demanding free democratic elections and an end to dictatorship. Among the leaders of the group was thought to be Colonel Tahar Zbiri who, following his unsuccessful attempt to overthrow Boumediene in December 1967, sought refuge in Tunisia and later moved to Morocco. Other exiled leaders, such as Hocine Zahouane, Mohamed Harbi, Mohamed el Hadi Hadj-Smaine, and Bachir Boumaaza, who were either loyal ben Bellists or early supporters of Boumediene, quickly became disenchanted; they continued to oppose socialist Algeria more as separate individuals, however, than as representatives of a specific political organization or ideological group.

The significant features of all these clandestine and unofficial groups and individuals are that they: (1) represent the past more than the future; (2) have little political support among incipient elites; (3) reflect the political points of view of single individuals with personal "gripes' more than that of ideologically based movements with wide appeal; and (4) possess insufficient resources to adequately confront or seriously challenge the power and authority of the incumbent regime and its leaders who, despite the numerous differences that divide them, are firmly united against the "subversive" claims of discredited former elites. The further institutionalization of the Boumediene-inspired technocratic system with its vanguard single party makes it highly unlikely that the calls for "democratization" and "liberalization" by historical "has-beens" will have any impact on current or emerging elites.

We can conclude our discussion of elite circulation with the following summary generalization. Because of the relative youth of the core elite, there will be little personnel change among the national decision makers for another generation or so. For general elites the picture is more promising as qualified, university-trained, organization men representing each of the three components of the technocratic system begin to capture their share of influential positions in the next decade or until such time as the system's productive capabilities begin to level-off or contract.

The most volatile and potentially disruptive category of incipient subordinates or counterelites are those of the so-called "third generation" as identified above. These partially educated, inadequately trained, monolingual Arabists with strong traditional and religious ties are rapidly swelling the ranks of the urban unemployed. Since it will take at least one or more decades for the country's program of capital-intensive selective industrialization to impact meaningfully on the national employment picture, especially on its minimally skilled and unskilled sectors, the potential for excessive indeed revolutionary demands seems great. The fact that nearly 65 percent of the country's population is under eighteen years of age (based on the latest 1977 census) along with a 3.3 percent annual birth rate combine to aggravate an already precarious situation.

Moreover, these groups seem most vulnerable to psychologically inspired and culturally motivated religious appeals since their bleak economic futures are ensconced within an anomic sociopsychological environment where family ties are disintegrating, sexual frustrations are increasing, crime and other expressive forms of personal disaffection are mounting, and a general social malaise is imposing itself on all of Algeria's burgeoning urban conglomerations. Inasmuch as a socialist revolution is theoretically already in place and a communist one is unacceptable, only a religious Islamic revolution can successfully alleviate the growing sense of social isolation and personal alienation so evident among the third generation of aspiring elites. Much more so than the ineffectual political opposition abroad, these "disruptive dropouts" constitute a direct threat to the system's social stability and an ominous, indirect threat to its political viability not unlike that experienced by Iran in 1978–79.

CONCLUSION

Contemporary Algeria has evolved into a bureaucratic polity — a political system in which power and national decision making are shaped almost exclusively by the employees of the state, and especially by the topmost levels of the officer corps, single party organization, and civilian bureaucracy, including the significant socioeconomic class of managers and technicians. It is this complex political legacy that Boumediene has bequeathed to his successor, Chadli Benjedid.

Since his election to the presidency in February 1979 Chadli has pursued a cautious, middle-of-the-road policy consistent with his strong military identification and institutional loyalty that made him, during the critical five-day FLN congress convened to select a new president, a perfect symbol of the army as guarantor and arbiter of the national interest. "His personal image reinforced his claim — Arabo-Muslim in cultural orientation, a nationalist unsullied by intrigue" (Mortimer, 1979: 11). Chadli's nomination reflected the army's determination to protect its own place at the very center of Algerian politics by preventing a marked shift of power to either the state (Bouteflika) or the party (Yahiaoui).

Chadli's uncertain status and his initial hesitancy to tamper with Boumediene's political legacy have quickly given way to more pronounced political designs that reflect both the continuity and change that have been the hallmarks of postindependence Algeria. Within the narrow ruling elite circle, the anticipated "power struggle" predicted by many in the immediate postsuccession period seems to have gotten under way, if indeed, it has not already terminated in rather swift fashion. The post-Boumediene continuity, apparent, for example, in the make-up of the Politburo, has been "balanced" by changes evident with the appointment of the new government in which Chadli's power and influence above all seem to have consolidated, at the expense of both his immediate rivals — Yahiaoui and Bouteflika — and of some other new individuals and groups seeking entry into the core elite.

One immediate consequence of this seeming realignment is that power is more effectively redistributed among army, party, and government elites, eliminating in the process the single-man concentration of power that for so long characterized Boumediene's system of rule. In theory at least, in the first year of the Chadli era, the premiership and the party leadership constituted alternative bases of power. Yet, all three men had common military origins and associations — indeed, that Chadli, Abdelghani, and Yahiaoui all held the rank of colonel is ample reminder that the ANP has not surrendered its influence — and shared in the belief of the supremacy of a strong and secure state.

This critical realignment had apparently not gone unchallenged, however, if one is to believe the alleged plots to overthrow Chadli and his new government (*An-Nahar* [Beirut June 4–10, 1979, *Al-Mostakbal* [Paris] June 9, 1979). Quoting sources "close to the Algerian presidency" *An-Nahar* indicated that Algerian authorities had uncovered a plot for carrying out a coup d'état aimed at ousting President Benjedid. Supposedly the date fixed for the coup attempt was the 14th anniversary of Boumediene's 1965 overthrow of Ahmed ben Bella. These same sources were quoted as saying that a number of prominent military and civilian figures who had played pivotal roles during Boumediene's regime had formed a bloc against Chadli. Their strategy, according to this report, was to stymie the new President as a first step, then bring him under their tutelage, after which moving him out of office would be relatively easy. Supposedly, these oppositional forces were identified to the President and effectively countered. Along these lines, a military reshuffle of "maximum importance" was carried out on 5 May, 1979 in which Colonel Abdallah Belouchet, an original member of the Council of the Revolution, was removed from his post as commander of the Algiers garrison and appointed instead to an administrative post, thus depriving him of the power to give orders to the troops. While no independent or third party sources have been available to confirm or deny these allegations, their credibility may be somewhat enhanced by the *Al Mostakabal* report which referred to "basic changes" being undertaken at the top of the Algerian leadership involving Chadli's ouster of three prominent members of the FLN's Politburo: Bouteflika, Draïa, and Larbi.

Whether accurate or not, the displacement of Bouteflika's "clique" seems to have suspended, temporarily at least, that current of thought that had pushed for a more visible "opening up" of the political process in the direction of greater Westernization and increasing contacts with Europe, especially France. Symbolic of such "liberalizing" attempts was the apparently innocuous decision to change the day of the sabbath from Friday (Islamic) to Sunday in keeping with standard international business practices. Arabo-Muslims of Yahiaoui's ilk reacted strongly against such measures, resulting in temporarily putting off this decision. Clearly, the strong socialist, puritanical, Arabist, and Islamic current effectively tapped by Boumediene and fully supported by Yahiaoui seems to have been maintained despite recent leadership changes.

Yet such actions do not yet constitute a definitive pattern, and it is to the credit of Chadli that he has been able to pursue other liberalizing policies consistent with the regime's desire to achieve a more "balanced" profile in its domestic and international considerations. Important gestures in this liberalizing direction include the release of ben Bella from house imprisonment in July 1980 as well as the lifting of the surveillance of Abbas and ben Khedda, who had been placed under house arrest following publication of their March 1976 manifesto. In addition numerous political prisoners have been released, including Amar Mellah, a Zbiri colleague who was implicated in both the *coup manqué* of 1967 and the attempted assassination of Boumediene in 1968. Zbiri himself, in exile overseas, has been invited to return to Algeria (Buchet, 1979: 28).

Domestically Chadli is giving greater attention to the pressing social and economic problems besetting his country. The abolishment of the notorious exit permit, that bureaucratic nightmare required of citizens and foreign residents alike for any travels abroad, has been enthusiastically received. This important decision reflects Benjedid's determination to loosen up the overly bureaucratized and enormously inefficient socioeconomic system without, however, undermining the centralized nature of political life at the national level. The purge of the political right is testimony to this effort at maintaining a narrow political concensus. Apparently Chadli's new team wants the institutionalization process to continue while responding more effectively to the myriad demands of an ever increasingly dissastified mass public. It is uncertain, however, to what extent social and economic demands may be adequately satisfied without simultaneously raising political demands that go far beyond the relatively limited political parameters established by the regime. Yet most of this is a problem of the future; for now, attention is directed at untangling the complex maze of redundant bureaucratization that is currently suffocating the country's productive capacities.

One significant consequence of this inward-looking policy currently being pursued is the relative decline of Algeria's Third Worldism and preoccupation with the "big issues" in foreign affairs. The only issue that remains a principal agenda item is the Sahara conflict with Morocco, which seems no closer to resolution under Chadli than it was under Boumediene. Even the so-called "steadfastness and confrontation front" of Arab militants opposed to Anwar Sadat's peace initiative with Israel is not drawing Chadli's attention the way it did for Boumediene, who was a prime factor in originally forging this front.

Benjedis' increasing grasp of the reigns of political power, pragmatically dispersed within key institutional settings, is evidenced by: (1) the reduction and realignment of the Political Bureau from which Yahiaoui and Bouteflika are excluded; (2) Yahiaoui's removal as party coordinator, thereby effectively undercutting his independent power base; (3) recreation of the Army General Staff; (4) reassigning the interior ministry to Boualem Benhamouda, thus reducing Abdelghani's sphere of influence; and (5) adoption of a new five year development plan (1980–1984) by the FLN Congress in June 1980. Chadli has managed to consolidate his authority in a nonauthoritarian manner, gaining the respect of his colleagues without simultaneously arousing the enmity of key individuals or cliques.

At home and abroad, President Chadli Benjedid, supported by an invigorated party-government, is pursuing a cautious and pragmatic policy that is intended to make the Algerian system work more effectively for the people themselves. In this effort he has the apparent support of the system's key men and institutions in their pre- and postrealignment positions. That Chadli is unprepared to transform Algeria into another Egypt is clear enough by the uncertain status of Bouteflika and his brand of liberal political development. Yet Algeria is not Iraq and is far from being another Libya, rhetoric and ideological posturing notwithstanding. What Boumediene started, Chadli is simply pursuing to its logical conclusion — political institutionalization leading to political stability and development; mixed socialist-state capitalism based on oil and gas leading to economic growth and development; and military strength and preparedness insuring regional stability.

NOTES

1. National Charter, June 1976; Constitution, November 1976; President, December 1976; worker's union (UGTA), March 1978; farmer's union (UNPA), April 1978; war veterans (ONM), May 1978; women's union (UNFA), October 1978; youth organization (UNJA), January 1979; party congress (FLN), January 1979; President, February 1979; FLN Central Committee selection of new government, March 1979; party congress, June 1980; Central Committee extraordinary session, June 1980.

2. Background information on elites have tended to be of three types: single individual profiles usually limited to prominent, politically significant personalities such as Boumediene, Bouteflika, and now, Chadli Benjedid (see, for example, Lentin 1972, 1973; Balta 1975; Kaidi 1979; Ottoway 1970; Gordon 1966; Howe 1979; and Buchet 1979); institutionally defined surveys whether at the national level including the top leadership and selected secondary elites located in the National Assembly, Council of Ministers, Council of the Revolution, FLN party executive, and ANP general staff (see, for example, Grimaud 1977; Quandt 1969, 1972; Michel 1973; Barrada 1978; Ottaway and Ottaway 1970; and Zartman 1975b, 1975c, 1978), regional level (APW) (Zartman 1970a), or local level (APC) (Grimaud 1973); and finally, class-oriented descriptions that focus on the so-called ruling elite and its relationships with various social sectors (see, for example, Raffinot and Jacquemot 1977; Lazreg 1976; Farsoun 1975; and Etienne 1977).

REFERENCES

"L'Algérie Indépendante Dix Ans Après," (1972) *Le Monde* (July 5), 3–4.

Ammour, Kader, Christian Leucate, and Jean-Jacques Moulin (1974) *La Voie Algérienne: Les Contradictions d'un Développement National*. Paris: Maspero.

Arab Bessaoud, Mohamed (1966) *Le FFS* [Le Front des Forces Socialistes]: *Espoirs et Trahison*. Colombes: Imprimerie Cary.

Ashford, Douglas E. (1973) "Second- and Third-Generation Elites in the Maghrib," I. William Zartman (ed.) *Man, State, and Society in the Contemporary Maghrib*, New York: Praeger, 93–107.

"Avant-Project de Charte Nationale" (1976), *Révolution Africaine* (April, No. 636—Special Supplement), 80 pp.

Baghli, Sid-Ahmed (1977) *Aspects de la Politique Culturelle de l'Algérie*. Paris: UNESCO.

Balta, Paul (1975) "Les Hommes: Houari Boumediene" *Maghreb Machrek* 69 (July-Aug-Sept): 20–24.

———— (1977) "L'Algérie Aujourd'hui. 1. De la Légitimité Révolutionnaire à la Légitimité Institutionnelle" *Revue de la Défense Nationale* 33 (May): 89–98.

Balta, Paul et al. (1978) "L'Algérie Face à son Développement" *Le Monde Diplomatique* (June, supplement): 23–38.

Balta, Paul and Claudine Rulleau (1978) *La Stratégie de Boumediene*. Paris: Sindbad.

Barrada, Hamid (1978a) "Ben Bella: Où est-il?" *Jeune Afrique*, 912 (June 28): 29–60.

———— (1978b) "Algérie, Révélations Exclusives: La Lutte Secréte pour la Succession" *Jeune Afrique* 936 (Dec. 13): 15–18.

———— (1979) "Quand le tombeur de Ben Bella trébuche . . ." *Jeune Afrique* 967 (July 18): 30–37.

Belloula, Tayeb (1977) *De L'Organisation Socialiste des Entreprises*. Algiers: Librairie-Edition du Parti.

Belguedj, Mourad (1977) "Algerian Natural Gas—The Political Economy of Diversification." PhD Dissertation, Fletcher School of Law and Diplomacy, Tufts University.

Ben Yahmed, Bechir (1976) "Le Maghreb Bouge" *Jeune Afrique*, 794 (March 26): 14–23.

Bennoune, Mahfoud (1976) "Algerian Peasants and National Politics" *MERIP Reports*, 48 (June: 3–24.

Bernelas, Jean-Louis and Patrick Lecomte (1977) "Le Parti Selon la Charte Nationale Algérienne" *Maghreb-Machrek*, 75 (Jan-Feb-March): 60–67.

Berque, Jacques (1973) "Tradition and Innovation in the Maghrib" *Daedalus*, 102 (Winter): 239–250.

Berri, Younès (1975) "Algérie: La Jeunesse s'organise, la Révolution se porte Bien" *Jeune Afrique*, 753 (June 13): 20–21.

Blair, Thomas L. (1970) *The Land to Those Who Work It: Algeria's Experiment in Workers' Management*. Garden City, N.Y.: Anchor Books-Doubleday.

Boudiaf, Mohammed (1964) *Ou Va l'Algérie?* Paris: Etoile.

Bouhali, Larbi (1963) "The Algerian Revolution Goes On" *World Marxist Review*, 6 (No. 1): 43–46.

Boularès, Habib (1976) "Algérie: l'Offensive de l'Opposition" *Jeune Afrique*, 797 (April 16): 16–19.

Boumediene, Houari (1968) 'The Future of the Algerian Revolution" *Journal of Modern African Studies* 6 (No. 3): 425–439.

———— (1973) "The Third Anniversary of Algerian Independence" I. William Zartman (ed.) *Man, State, and Society in the Contemporary Maghrib*. New York: Praeger, 127–130.

Bourdieu, Pierre (1962) *The Algerians*. Boston: Beacon Press.

———— (1973) "The Algerian Subproletariat" I. William Zartman (ed.) *Man, State, and Society in the Contemporary Maghrib*. New York: Praeger, 83–92.

———— (1979) *Algeria 1960*. New York: Cambridge University Press.

Bourges, Hervé (1967) *L'Algérie à l'Epreuve du Pouvoir (1962–1967)*. Paris: Grasset.

Buchet, Jean Louis (1978a) "Pourquoi Boumediene a 'disparu'," *Jeune Afrique*, 929 (Oct. 25): 34–35.

———— (1978b) "Ce qui Pourrait Changer en Algérie et au Sahara" *Jeune Afrique*, 934 (Nov. 29): 17–21.

———— (1979a) "L'Algérie à l'Heure du Congrès," *Jeune Afrique*, 941 (January 17): 25.

———— (1979b) "Qui est réellement le Nouveau Président [Chadli Benjedid]?" *Jeune Afrique*, 945 (February 14): 28–30.

———— (1979c) "Les limites de l'ouverture" *Jeune Afrique*, 963 (June 20): 28–29.

Burke, Edmund (1971) "Parties and Elites in North African Politics: Algeria and Morocco" *Africa Today*, 18 (No. 4, October): 50–59.

Buy, François (1965) *La République Algérienne Démocratique et Populaire*. Paris: La Librairie Française.

Camau, Michel (1971) *La Notion de Démocratie dans la Pensée des Dirigeants Maghrébins*. Paris: Editions du Centre National de la Recherche Scientifique.

Centre de Recherches et d'Etudes sur les Sociétés Méditerranéennes (1968) *La Succession d'Etat en Afrique du Nord*. Paris: CNRS.

———— (1969) *Mutations Culturelles et Coopération au Maghreb*. Paris: Editions du Centre National de la Recherche Scientifique.

———— (1970) *Pouvoir et Administration au Maghreb: Etudes sur les Elites Maghrébines*. Paris: Editions du Centre National de la Recherche Scientifique.

———— (1973a) *Elites, Pouvoir et Légitimité au Maghreb*. Paris: CNRS.

———— (1973b) *La Formation des Elites Politiques Maghrebines*. Paris: Librairie Générale de Droit et de Jurisprudence.

———— (1974a) *Indépendance et Interdépendance au Maghreb*. Paris: CNRS.

———— (1974b) *Les Influences Occidentales dans les Villes Maghrebines à l'Epoque Contemporaine*. Aix: Editions de l'Université de Provence.

———— (1975) *Introduction à l'Afrique du Nord Contemporaine*. Paris: Editions du Centre National de la Recherche Scientifique.

————(1979) *Développements Politiques au Maghreb: Aménagements Institutionnels et Processus Electoraux*. Paris: CNRS.

Chauleur, P. (1975) "Problèmes Algériens" *Etudes* (July): 27–43.

Chaliand, Gérard (1965) *L'Algérie est-elle Socialiste?* Paris: Maspero.

Chaliand, Gerard and Juliette Minces (1972a) "L'Algérie Algérienne: Bilan d'une Révolution Nationale" *Le Monde Diplomatique* (July): 11–16.

———— (1972b) *L'Algérie Indépendante: Bilan d'une Révolution Nationale*. Paris: Maspero.

Colonna, Fanny (1975) *Les Instituteurs Algériens*. Paris: Colin.

Criscuolo, Josiane (1975) *Armée et Nation dans les Discours du Colonel Boumediene: Etude Comparative des Editions Française et Arabe*. Montpellier: Université Paul Valery.

Cubertafond, Bernard (1974) *L'Algérie Indépendante: Idéologie et Institutions*. Unpublished PhD dissertation, University of Paris II.

―――― (1975) "Réflexions sur la Pratique Politique Algérienne" *Maghreb-Machrek*, 69 (July-August-September): 25–32.

―――― (1977) "La Constitution Algérienne du 22 Novembre 1976" *Maghreb-Machrek*, 75 (Jan-Feb-March): 68–74.

Dahmani, Mohamed (1979) *L'Algérie: Légitimité Historique et Continuité Politique*. Paris: Le Sycomore.

Damis, John (1974 "The Free-School Phenomenon: The Cases of Tunisia and Algeria" *International Journal of Middle East Studies*, 5 (No. 4, September): 434–449.

Descloitres, R., C. Descloitres, and J.C. Reverdy (1973) "Urban Organization and Social Structure in Algeria" I. William Zartman (ed.) *Man, State, and Society in the Contemporary Maghrib*. New York: Praeger, 424–438.

Douence, Jean-Claude (1964) *La Mise en Place des Institutions Algériennes*. Paris: Fondation Nationale des Sciences Politiques.

Duclos, Jean-Louis, Duvignaud, Jean and Jean Leca (1966) *Les Nationalismes Maghrebins*. Paris: Fondation Nationale des Sciences Politiques.

Dufour, Dany (1978) "L'Enseignement en Algérie" *Maghreb-Machrek*, 80 (April-May-June): 33–53.

Duprat, Gérard (1973) *Révolution et Autogestion Rurale en Algérie*. Paris: Armand Colin.

Durand, Jean-Pierre (1979) "Exacerbation des Contradictions Sociales et Resserrement des Alliances Politiques en Algérie," CRESM, *Développements Politiques au Maghreb*. Paris: Editions du Centre National de la Recherche Scientifique: 123–140.

Entelis, John P. (1979) "Algeria, Myth and Reality" *The New York Times* (December 1): 21.

―――― (1980a) "Democratic and Popular Republic of Algeria" David E. Long and Bernard Reich (eds.) *The Government and Politics of the Middle East and North Africa*. Boulder, Colorado: Westview Press, 415–436.

―――― (1980b) *Comparative Politics of North Africa: Algeria, Morocco, and Tunisia*. Syracuse, N.Y.: Syracuse University Press.

―――― (1981) "Elite Political Culture and Socialization in Algeria: Tensions and Discontinuities," *Middle East Journal*, 35 (2, Spring).

Estier, Claude (1964) *Pour l'Algérie*, Paris: Maspero.

Etienne, Bruno (1973) "Le Vocabulaire Politique de Légitimité en Algérie" Marcel Teitler and Others (eds.) *Elites, Pouvoir et Légitimité au Maghreb*. Paris: CNRS, 73–105.

―――― (1975) "Le Socialisme Algérien", Centre de Recherches et d'Etudes sur les Sociétés Méditerranéennes, *Introduction à l'Afrique du Nord Contemporaine*. Paris: CNRS, 359–374.

―――― (1977) *L'Algérie, Cultures et Révolution*. Paris: Editions du Seuil.

Etienne, Bruno and Jean Leca (1974) "La Politique Culturelle de l'Algérie" *Annuaire de l'Afrique du Nord*, XII. Paris: CNRS, 45–75.

Etienne, Mallarde (1975) *L'Algérie Depuis*. Paris: La Table Ronde.

Farsoun, Karen (1975) "State Capitalism in Algeria" *MERIP Reports*, 35 (Feb): 3–30.

"La Formation des Cadres Administratifs en Afrique du Nord" (1968) *Maghreb*, 30 (November-December): 31–35.

Francos, Ania (1975) "Algérie, Les Etats Généraux de la Jeunesse" *Jeune Afrique*, 748 (May 9): 34–35.

Francos, Ania and Jean-Pierra Sereni (1976a) "Algérie: La Soif de Démocratie" *Jeune Afrique*, 806 (June 18): 32–35.

——— (1976b) *Un Algérien Nommé Boumediene.* Paris: Stock.

Gallagher, Charles F. (1963) *The United States and North Africa: Morocco, Algeria, and Tunisia.* Cambridge, Mass.: Harvard University Press.

Gallissot, René (1969) "Les Classes Sociales en Algérie" *L'Homme et la Société* (October-November): 207–225.

——— (1977) *Marxisme et Algérie.* Paris.

Gauthier, Yves and Joël Kernarec (1978) *Naissance et Croissance de la République Algérienne Democratique et Populaire.* Paris: Edition Marketing.

Gellner, Ernest (1974) "The Unknown Apollo of Biskra: The Social Base of Algerian Puritanism", *Government and Opposition*, vol. 9, no. 3 (summer).

Gendzier, Irene L. (1978) "Algeria and Modernization" *Government and Opposition* 13 (No. 2, Spring): 247–258.

Gharbi, Samir (1977) "Algérie-Etats-Unis: Un Marriage de Raison" *Jeune Afrique*, 869 (Sept. 2): 14–17.

Gordon, David (1966) *The Passing of French Algeria.*. London: Oxford University Press.

Gourdon, Hubert (1976) "L'Ordonnance en Algérie (1965–1975): Essai d'Analyse du Système Politique" *Annuaire de l'Afrique du Nord*, XIV. Paris: CNRS: 323–361.

——— (1979) "Citoyen, Travailleur, Frère: la Deuxième Constitutionnalisation du Système Politique Algérien", CRESM, *Développements Politiques au Maghreb.* Paris: CNRS: 99–122.

Grimaud, Nicole (1972) "Réformes de Structure en Algérie" *Maghreb*, 49 (Jan–Feb): 36–39.

——— (1973a) "The Elections of February 5, 1967" I. William Zartman (ed.) *Man, State, and Society in the Contemporary Maghrib.* New York: Praeger: 3400–343.

——— (1973b) "Approfondissement de la 'Révolution Socialiste' en Algérie" *Maghreb-Machrek*, 56 (March-April): 12–17.

——— (1973c) "Evolution du Syndicalisme en Algérie" *Maghreb-Machrek*, 57 (May-June): 26–30.

———(1976a) "Une Algérie en Mutation à l'Heure de la Charte Nationale" *Maghreb-Machrek*, 73 (July-August-Sept.): 70–77.

——— (1976b) *La Charte Nationale Algérienne (27 Juin 1976).* Paris: La Documentation Française.

——— (1977) "Algérie: Election d'une Assemblée Nationale et Formation d'un Nouveau Gouvernement" *Maghreb-Machrek*, 76 (April-May-June): 29–33.

——— (1978) "Les Relations de Travail en Algérie: Le Cinquiéme Congrès de l'UGTA" *Maghreb-Machrek*, 80 (April–May–June): 57–62.

Guerin, Daniel (1964) *L'Algérie Qui Se Cherche.* Paris: Presence Africaine.

——— (1965) *L'Algérie Caporalisée.* Paris: Centre d'Etudes Socialistes.

Hadj Ali, Bachir (1966) *L'Arbitraire.* Paris.

Hahn; Lorna (1965) "Politics and Leadership in North Africa" *Orbis*, 9 (No. 3): 729–759.

Halpern, Manfred (1963) *The Politics of Social Change in the Middle East and North Africa*. Princeton, N.J.: Princeton University Press.

Harbi, Mohamed (1973) "The Party and the State" I. William Zartman (ed.) *Man, State, and Society in the Contemporary Maghrib*. New York: Praeger, 159–167.

———— (1975) *Aux Origines du FLN: Le Populisme Révolutionnaire en Algérie*. Paris: Christian Bougois.

Heggoy, Alf Andrew (1969) "The FFS: An Algerian Opposition to a One-Party System" *African Historical Studies* II (No. 1): 121–140.

Helie, Damien (1973) "Industrial Self-Management in Algeria" I. William Zartman (ed.) *Man, State, and Society in the Contemporary Maghrib*. New York: Praeger, 465–474.

Hermassi, Elbaki (1972) *Leadership and National Development in North Africa: A Comparative Study*. Berkeley, Cal.: University of California Press.

———— (1973) "Political Traditions of the Maghrib" *Daedalus*, 102 (No. 1 Winter): 207–224.

Horne, Alistair (1978) *A Savage War of Peace: Algeria, 1954–1962*. New York: The Viking Press.

Howe, Marvina (1979) "Algeria's Next President: Benjedid Chadli" *The New York Times* (February 2).

Humbaraci, Arslan (1966) *Algeria: A Revolution That Failed — A Political History Since 1954*. New York: Praeger.

Ibrahimi, Ahmed Taleb (1976) *De La Décolonisation à La Révolution Culturelle (1962–1972)* Second Edition. Algiers: SNED.

Icheboudene, Larbi (1974) "Armée et développement — les cooperatives industrielles de l'armée en Algérie." Ph.D. Dissertation, Paris V.

Jackson, Henry F. (1977) *The FLN in Algeria: Party Development in a Revolutionary Society*. Westport, Conn.: Greenwood Press.

Jacob, Alain (1963) *D'Une Algérie à L'Autre*. Paris: Grasset.

Joesten, Joachim (1964) *The New Algeria*. Chicago: Follett.

Judet, Pierre (1979) "L'Economie Algérienne et la Logique de l'Indépendance" *Le Monde Diplomatique*, (February): 12–13.

Junqua, Daniel "L'Algérie au Milieu de Gué: I: Le Défi Industriel, II: La Jeunesse, Atout et Menace, III: Du Pain et du Beton," *Le Monde*, December 28, 1978, January 4 and 5, 1979.

———— (1978) "Une Succession Difficile" *Le Monde* (December 28).

Kaidi, Hamza (1979a) "Et si Bitat Succédait à Bitat . . ." *Jeune Afrique*, 940 (Jan. 10): 24–28.

————(1979b) "Algérie: Le Congrès de la Succession" *Jeune Afrique*, 944 (Feb. 7): 16–17.

Kerr, Malcolm H. (1976) "Political and Economic Trends in North Africa" A.L. Udovitch (ed.) *The Middle East: Oil, Conflict and Hope*. Lexington, Mass.: Lexington Books, 383–426.

al-Kholi, Lutfi (1975) *In the Revolution, About the Revolution, By the Revolution: Conversations With Boumedienne*. Beirut: Dar al-Qadaya.

Knapp, Wilfrid (1977) "Algeria" *North West Africa: A Political and Economic Survey*. (Third Edition). Oxford: Oxford University Press, 51–173.

Knauss, Peter R. (1977) "Algeria's 'Agrarian Revolution': Peasant Control or Control of Peasants?" *African Studies Review*, vol. XX, No. 3 (December): 65–78.

_____ (1980) "Algeria Under Boumedienne: The Mythical Revolution 1965 to 1978" *The Performance of Soldiers as Governors: African Politics and the African Military*. Isaac J. Mowoe (ed.). Washington, D.C.: University Press of America, 27–100.

Lacheraf, Mostefa (1965) *L'Algérie*: Nation et Société. Paris: Maspero.

_____ (1968) *La Culture Algérienne Contemporaine: Essai de Définitions et Perspectives*. Algiers: Services Culturels du Parti.

Lacouture, Jean (1965) "Anatomie d'une Armée" *Le Monde*, July 14.

Laks, Monique (1970) *Autogestion Ouvrière et Pouvoir Politique en Algérie (1962 –1965)*. Paris: Etudes et Documentation Internationales.

Lamrani, Fadela (1977) "Charte Nationale et Mobilisation des Masses en Algérie" *Les Temps Modernes* (Oct.): 185–202.

Lapassat, E.J. (1968) *La Justice en Algérie*. Paris: Fondation Nationale des Sciences Politiques.

Lawless, Richard I. (1972) *A Bibliography of Works on Algeria Published in English Since 1954*. University of Durham, Centre for Middle Eastern and Islamic Studies.

_____ (1976) *Algerian Bibliography: English Language Publications 1830–1973*. London and New York: Bowker, In association with the Centre for Middle Eastern and Islamic Studies of the University of Durham.

Lawless, Richard I. and Gerald H. Blake 1976) *Tlemcen*: Continuity and Change In An Algerian and Islamic Town. Boulder, Col.: Westview Press.

Lazreg, Marnia (1976) *The Emergence of Classes in Algeria: Colonialism and Socio-Political Change*. Boulder, Colorado: Westview Press.

Lebjaoui, Mohammed (1970) *Vérités sur la Révolution Algérienne*. Paris: Gallimard.

Leca, Jean (1966) "Le Nationalisme Algérien Depuis l'Indépendance" Louis-Jean Duclos (ed.) *Les Nationalismes Maghrebins*. Paris: Fondation Nationale des Sciences Politiques, 61–82.

_____ (1968) "Parti et Etat en Algérie" *Annuaire de l'Afrique du Nord*, VII, 13–42. Paris: CNRS, 1969.

_____ (1973) "Administration Locale et Pouvoir Politique en Algérie" Marcel Teitler and others (eds.) *Elites, Pouvoir et Légitimité au Maghreb*. Paris: CNRS: 207–236.

_____ (1975) "Algerian Socialism: Nationalism, Industrialization and State-Building" Helen Desfosses and Jacques Levesque (eds.) *Socialism in the Third World*. New York: Praeger, 121–160.

Leca, Jean and Jean-Claude Vatin (1975) *L'Algérie Politique: Institutions et Régime*. Paris: Presses de la Fondation Nationale des Sciences Politiques.

_____ (1977) "Le Système Politique Algérien (1976–1978): Idéologie, Institutions et Changement Social", Annuaire de l'Afrique du Nord, vol. XVI Paris: CNRS, 1979, 15–80.

Lentin, Albert-Paul (1972) "Les Hommes: Abdelaziz Bouteflika" *Maghreb*, 52 (July-August): 7–10.

_____ (1973) "Les Hommes: Mohamed Ben Yahia" *Maghreb-Machrek*, 56 (March-April): 9–11.

Lepoul, Georges (1977) "'100 Villages Socialistes' en Algérie," *Maghreb-Machrek*, 77 (July, August, September): 40–48.

Lewis, William H. (1966) "The Decline of Algeria's FLN" *The Middle East Journal*, 20 (2, Spring): 161–172.

—— (1969) "Algeria: The Cycle of Reciprocal Fear" *African Studies Bulletin*, 12 (No. 3, December): 323–337.

Lucas, Philippe and Jean-Claude Vatin (1975) *L'Algérie des Anthropologues*. Paris: Maspero.

Maalouf, Amin. (1978) "Algérie: les moments difficiles", *Jeune Afrique*, No. 935 (December 6): 15–16.

Mahl, J. (1977) "L'Evolution de la Politique de Formation en Algérie comme Indicateur d'une Situation de Classe" *Les Temps Modernes* (October): 234–248.

Mameri, Khalfa (1977) *Citations du Président Boumediene*. (3rd edition). Algiers: SNED.

Markham, James M. (1978) 'Algiers is Calm Awaiting Word of Boumediene," *The New York Times* (November).

—— (1979) "Algerian Minority May Pose Problems" *The New York Times* (January [Kabyles].

Masmoudi, Mohamed (1977) *Les Arabes dans la Tempête*. Paris: Jean-Claude Simoen.

—— (1978) "L'Autre Boumedienne" *Jeune Afrique*, 937 (Dec. 20): 37–38.

Mazouni, Abdallah (1969) *Culture et Enseignement en Algérie et au Maghreb*. Paris: Maspero.

Micaud, Charles (1974a) "Bilingualism in North Africa: Cultural and Socio-Political Implications" *Western Political Quarterly*, 27 (No. 1, March): 92–103.

—— (1974b) "Maghribi Politics: Old and New Commentaries" *Africa Today*, 21 (No. 1): 82–92.

Michel, Hubert (1973) "L'Algérie: Elites et Conquête de l'Indépendance: Données Générales", Centre de Recherche et d'Etudes sur les Sociétes Méditerranéennes, *La Formation des Elites Maghrebines*, Paris: Librairie Générale de Droit et de Jurisprudence, 87–122.

—— (1975a) "Le FLN en Mutation" *Rev. Franc. et Etude Politique Medit*, I (Jan.): 72–85.

—— (1975b) "Les Elites Politiques du Maghreb: L'Algérie", Centre de Recherches et d'Etudes sur les Sociétés Méditerranéennes. *Introduction à l'Afrique du Nord Contemporaine*, Paris: CNRS, 98–106.

—— (1975c) "Administration et Développement au Maghreb", Centre de Recherches et d'Etudes sur les Socités Méditerranéennes. *Introduction à L'Afrique du Nord Contemporaine*, Paris: CNRS, 283–299.

Miette, R. (1977a) "Réalité Algérienne" *L'Afrique et l'Asie Modernes*, 113: 52–56.

—— (1977b) "Le Système Politique Algérien" *L'Afrique et l'Asie Modernes*, 114: 25–41.

Minces, Juliette (1978) *L'Algérie de Boumediene*. Paris: Presses de la Cité.

Miner, Horace and George De Vos (1960) *Oasis and Casbah: Algerian Culture and Personality in Change*. Ann Arbor, Mich.: University of Michegan Press.

Moore, Clement Henry (1966) "Political Parties in Independent North Africa"

Leon Carl Brown (ed.) *State and Society in Independent North Africa.* Washington, D.C.: The Middle East Institute, 22–40.

―――― (1970) *Politics in North Africa: Algeria, Morocco, and Tunisia.* Boston: Little, Brown & Co.

―――― (1974) "Old and New Elites in North Africa: The French Colonial Impact in Comparative Perspective" Centre de Recherches et d'Etudes sur les Sociétés Méditerranéennes (ed.) *Les Influences Occidentales dans les Villes Maghrebines à l'Epoque Contemporaine.* Aix: Editions de l'Université de Provence, 17–37.

Moore, Clement H. and Arlie Hochschild (1968) "Student Unions in North African Politics" *Daedalus*, 97 (No. 1, Winter): 21–50.

Mortimer, Robert (1977a) "Boumedienne Redesigns His Regime" *Africa Report*, 22 (No. 4, July-August): 14–18.

―――― (1977b) "Algeria and the Politics of International Economic Reform" *Orbis*, 21 (No. 3, Fall): 671–700.

――――(1979) "Algeria: Which Way Ahead?" *Africa Report* (May-June): 9–14.

Mourtdah, Abdelmalek (1971) *Renaissance de la Littérature Arabe en Algérie.* Algiers: SNED.

Mrabet, Fadela (1969 *La Femme Algérienne.* Paris: Maspero.

Mussard, A. (1976) "Impressions d'Algérie" *L'Afrique et l'Asie Modernes*, 110: 50–60.

Nellis, John R. (1977) "Socialist Management in Algeria" *Journal of Modern African Studies*, vo. 15, no. 4 (December): 529–554.

―――― (1980a) "Maladministration: Causes or Result of Underdevelopment? The Algerian Example," *Canadian Journal of African Studies*, 13 (3): 407–422.

―――― (1980b) *The Algerian National Charter of 1976: Content, Public Reaction, and Significance.* Washington, D.C.: Georgetown University Center for Contemporary Arab Studies.

Nelson, Harold D., ed. (1979) *Algeria: A Country Study*, third edition. Washington, D.C.: USGPO.

Nesson, Claude; Sari, Djilali; Peillon, Pierre (1978) *Recherches Sur L'Algérie.* Paris: Editions du Centre National de la Recherche Scientifique.

Nouschi, André (1962) *La Naissance du Nationalisme Algérien.* Paris: Ed. de Minuit.

Nyrop, Richard F. and others (1972) *Area Handbook for Algeria.* Washington, D.C.: U.S. Government Printing Office.

Ottaway, David and Marina (1970) *Algeria: The Politics of a Socialist Revolution.* Berkeley, Cal.: University of California Press.

Ottaway, David B. (1968) "Algeria" Donald K. Emmerson (ed.) *Students and Politics in Development Nations.* New York: Praeger, 3–36.

Parpais, Galisette (1974) "Formation Professionnelle et Formation Sociale: Le Cas de l'Algérie Indépendante" Ph.D. dissertation, Paris VIII.

Paul, James A. (1977) "Algeria's Oil Economy: Liberation or Neo-Colonialism?" Russell A. Stone (ed.) *OPEC and the Middle East.* New York: Praeger, 240–250.

Perera, J. (1977) "Algeria: Building Socialism on a Bitter Heritage" *Middle East*, no. 38 (December): 51–55.

Peroncel-Hugos, J.P. "Les Métamorphoses de l'Algérie" *Le Monde*, Part I (July 1, 1972) Part II (July 2–3, 1972) Part III (July 4, 1972).

Perroux, Francois (1963) *Problèmes de l'Algérie Indépendante*. Paris: Presses Universitaires de France.

Quandt, William B. (1969) *Revolution and Political Leadership: Algeria, 1954–1968*. Cambridge, Mass.: M.I.T. Press.

—— (1970) *Algeria: The Revolution Turns Inward* Rand Corp. (May).

—— (1972a) *Algerian Military Development: The Professionalization of a Guerrilla Army*. Santa Monica, Cal.: The Rand Corporation (March): 30pp.

—— (1972b) "The Berbers in the Algerian Political Elite" Ernest Gellner and Charles Michaud (eds.) *Arabs and Berbers: From Tribe to Nation in North Africa*. Lexington, Mass.: Lexington Books, 285–303.

—— (1972c) "Can We Do Business with Radical Nationalists? Algeria: Yes." *Foreign Policy* (No. 7, Summer): 108–131..

Raffinot, Marc and Pierre Jacquemat (1977) *Le Capitalisme d'Etat Algerien*. Paris: Maspero.

Remili, Abderrahmane (1968) "Parti et Administration en Algérie" *Annuaire de l'Afrique du Nord*. 7. Paris: CNRS.

——, (1975) *Les Institutions Administratives Algériennes, 1971–1975*. Algiers: SNED.

—— (1978) "Vers une Refonte Totale du Système de Formation" *Le Monde Diplomatique* (June): 37.

Revere, Rober B. (1970) "Consensus in Independent Algeria, 1962–1965," Ph.D. dissertation, New York University.

Robert, Jacques (1966) "Opposition and Control in Tunisia, Morocco, and Algeria" *Government and Opposition*, 1 (No. 3, April).

Rondot, Pierre (1978) "Quelques réflexions sur l'Effort Algérien" *Defense Nationale*, 34 (January): 85–97.

Saivetz, Carol R. (1976) "The Soviet Assessment of Third World Socialisms: The Cases of Egypt and Algeria, 1960–1973," Ph.D. Dissertation, Columbia University.

Salem, Mohamed "Algérie: Faut-il Compter avec les Opposants?" *Jeune Afrique* 938–939 (Dec. 27, 1978–Jan. 3, 1979): 56–58.

Sanson, Henri (1979) "Le Peuple de la Révolution Socialiste Algérienne," CRESM, *Développements Politiques au Maghreb*. Paris: CNRS: 81–98.

Sbih, Missoum (1977) *Les Institutions Administratives du Maghreb: Les Gouvernements de l'Algérie, du Maroc et de la Tunisie*. Algiers: ENA.

Schaar, Stuart (1968) "Reflections on Algeria's Crisis of Participation" *AUFS Reports, North Africa Series*, 14 (No. 1): 1–19.

Schemeil, Yves (1978) "Les Elites Politiques au Proche-Orient: Quelques Examples d'Analyse Comparative" *Revue Française de Science Politique*, 28 (No. 3, June): 537–573.

Sheehan, Edward R.F. (1972) "The Algerians Intend to Go It Alone, Raise Hell, Hold Out and Grow" *The New York Times Magazine* (April): 18–43.

Sivan, Emmanuel (1976) *Communisme et Nationalisme en Algérie, 1920–1962*. Paris: Presses de la Fondation Nationale des Sciences Politiques.

Smith, Tony (1975) "The Political and Economic Ambitions of Algerian Land Reform, 1962–1974" *The Middle East Journal*, 29 (No. 3, Summer): 259–278.

—— (1978) *The French Stake in Algeria, 1945–1962*. Ithaca, N.Y.: Cornell University Press.

Souriau, Christiane (1975) "L'Arabisation en Algérie" W.K. Ruf and others (eds.) *Introduction à l'Afrique du Nord Contemporaine.* Paris: CNRS: 375–397.

Spillman, G. (1974) "Algérie 1974" *Afrique et Asie Modernes*, No. 4:3–18.

Sutton, Keith (1976) "Industrialization and Regional Development in a Centrally-Planned Economy: The case of Algeria" *Journal of Economic and Social Geography* (2): 83–94.

_____ (1977) "Population Resettlement—Traumatic Upheavals and the Algerian Experience," *Journal of Modern African Studies*, vol. 15, No. 2 (June): 279–300.

"The Two Aspects of Algerian Socialism (1st Part)" (1978) *Civilisations*, vol. 28, nos. 1–2: 2–30.

Vallin, Raymond (1973) "Muslim Socialism in Algeria" I. William Zartman (ed.) *Man, State, and Society in the Contemporary Maghrib.* New York: Praeger, 50–64.

Vatikiotis, P.J. (1973) "Tradition and Political Leadership: The Example of Algeria" I. William Zartman (ed.) *Man, State, and Society in the Contemporary Maghrib.* New York: Praeger, 309–329.

Vatin, Jean-Claude (1974) *L'Algérie Politique*: Histoire et Société. Paris: Presses de la Fondation Nationale des Sciences Politiques.

_____ (1979) "Religious Resistance and State Power in Algeria" Middle East Studies Association Annual Meeting, Salt Lake City, Utah, 24pp.

Viratelle, Gerard (1968) "Le Régime Militaire Algérien" *Revue Française d'Etudes Politiques Africaines*, 38 (February): 63–78.

_____ (1970) *L'Algérie Algérienne.* Paris: Editions Economie et Humanisme.

Waterbury, John (1973) "Land, Man, and Development in Algeria: Part III, The Four Year Plan" *AUFS Report*, North Africa Series, 17 (No. 3, March).

_____ (1974) "The Soviet Union and North Africa" Ivo J. Lederer and Wayne S. Vicinich (eds.) *The Soviet Union and the Middle East: The Post World War II Era.* Stanford, Cal.: Hoover Institution Press, 78–120.

_____ (1978) "The Maghreb" John Waterbury and Ragaei El Mallakh (eds.) *The Middle East in the Coming Decade: From Wellhead to Well-Being?* New York: McGraw-Hill: 55–64.

Weexten, Raoul (1976) "Algérie: Le Pays se donne les Moyens d'être Mâitre de Lui-Meme" *Le Monde Diplomatique* (November): 11.

Younger, S. (1978) "Ideology and Pragmatism in Algerian Foreign Policy" *World Today*, 34 (No. 3, March): 107–114.

Zartman, I. William (1963) *Government and Politics in Northern Africa.* New York: Praeger.

_____ (1970a) "Les Elections Départementales Algériennes du 25 mai 1969" *Annuaire de l'Afrique du Nord*, VIII: 1969. Paris: CNRS: 311–327.

_____ (1970b) "Research Facilities in Algeria" *Middle East Studies Association Bulletin*, 4 (No. 1, February 15): 42–50.

_____(1970c) "The Algerian Army in Politics" Claude E. Welch (ed.) *Soldier and State in Africa: A Comparative Analysis of Military Intervention and Political Change.* Evanston, Ill.: Northwestern University Press, 224–249.

_____ (1970d) "Party and Elections in Algeria" Working Paper for Fellows Colloquia, Center for International Studies, New York University (April 29).

────── (1973a) "The Algerian Army in Politics" I. William Zartman (ed.) *Man, State, and Society in the Contemporary Maghrib.* New York: Praeger Publishers, 211–224.

────── (1973b) (ed.) *Man, State, and Society in the Contemporary Maghrib* New York: Praeger Publishers.

────── (1974) "The Study of Elite Circulation: Who's on First and What's He Doing There?" *Comparative Politics*, 6 (No. 3, April): 465–488.

────── (1975a) "The Elites of the Maghreb: A Review Article" *International Journal of Middle East Studies*, 6 (No. 4, October): 495–504.

────── (1975b) "Algeria: A Post-Revolutionary Elite" Frank Tachau (ed.) *Political Elites and Political Development in the Middle East.* New York: Schenkman Publ., Co., 255–292.

────── (1975c) "Toward a Theory of Elite Circulation." paper presented to the Workshop on Elites in the Middle East, Social Science Research Council, at New York University, March 14–15.

────── (1975d) "Elites, Revolution, and Mideast Politics: Algeria" Paper presented to the Annual Meeting of the American Political Science Association San Francisco, Cal., Sept. 2–5.

────── (1978) "The Rise and Passing of the Algerian Radical Military Regime," unpublished paper.

Zenati, Hassen (1975a) "Ahmed Medeghri: Le Bâtisseur de l'Etat" *Afrique Asie*, 73 (December 30, 1974-January 12, 1975): 34–

────── (1975b) "Algérie: Le Second Souffle" *Afrique Asie*, 87 (June 30-July 13): 29–58.

Newspapers, Periodicals, and Reference Books

Afrique
Afrique-Asie
Algérie-Actualité
L'algérien en Europe
Annuaire de l'Afrique du Nord
Christian Science Monitor
El Djazaira
El Djeich
L'économiste du Tiers Monde
Jeune Afrique
Maghreb Machrek
Middle East and North Africa, 1978–79; 1979–80
Le Monde
Le Monde Diplomatique
El Moudjahid
New York Times
Révolution Africaine
L'université

4

Tunisia: A Single Party System Holds Change in Abeyance

RUSSELL A. STONE

The Tunisian political elite is a small, although not truly homogeneous group of leaders, almost all of whom can be considered a part of the institutional elite. That is, research evidence to date suggests that almost all active members of the elite exercise their influence through political structures, rather than in alternate frameworks such as the military, economic organizations, or cultural organs. Leadership in the country is concentrated in relatively few national-level organizations, which emerged before or right after independence (1956) and became the sole foci of leadership when the "colonial" elite departed. The necessities of immediate nation building, undertaken by a unified nascent political organization under the charismatic leadership of President Habib Bourguiba, pressured Tunisian society into accepting and actively supporting a single-party (Neo-Destour) political system. The party minimized political debate, eliminated potential opposition (cf. assassination of Salah ben-Youssef in 1961), and devoted itself to the tasks of mass education and economic development. Thus, the leadership of the country exerted economic and sociocultural as well as political dominance throughout the first 10 to 15 years of independence, and the incumbent political leadership appeared to be the only elite worthy of recognition until very recently.

The few systematic studies we have of the elite in independent Tunisia fall into two categories: They either focus on the emergence of this elite in the pre-Independence period and show its continuity through the early years of independence (Micaud, Moore, and Brown, 1964; Moore, 1965, 1970; Rudebeck, 1969; Amin, 1970; Hermassi, 1972), only raising questions about its continuing viability and stability as concluding speculations; or they attempt to identify, enumerate, and describe the characteristics of the elite based on the assumption that the only relevant elite is "up front" and visible. Camau, Dubray, and Sraieb (1973) and Emmecey (1975) define the elite as members of the ruling political organizations (government ministers, political bureau, and central committee members of the Neo-Destour party, whose name was (changed to Parti Socialist Desturien — PSD — in 1964). Clausen (1976) used a slightly broader definition which includes members of the National Assembly, all of whom were also Neo-Destour party members, plus leaders of national organizations and economic administrations, the national union movement, etc. Most broadly of all, ben Salem (1969b, 1976) included all high-level manpower carrying out administrative or technical jobs of leadership and responsibility. While this latter definition encompasses an extremely wide range of people and occupations, it was still apparently a clearly definable group ten years after independence, when the study was undertaken. Depending on the definition chosen, the Tunisian elite can be taken to number about 100 people in 1969 (Camau, *et al.*, 1970) 130 people in 1973 (Emmecey, 1974); about 480 people in 1975 (Clausen, 1976); to a maximum of about 6,550 people in 1965 (ben Salem, 1969, p. 109), of which 4,446 are Tunisians (the rest being "foreign" experts, advisors, teachers, etc.); over 4,100 of these work in the government or public sector, the others in the private sector. Thus, the group is small and identifiable, as evidenced by these empirical definitions as well as by more general characterizations of the elite in post-independence Tunisia.

Published information based on studies of the elite, or biographical data sources, is not more recent than 1975, despite the fact that the situation can change quickly. For instance, an updating of a 1973 study (data to 1969 — Camau *et al.*) in 1975 (data to 1973 — Emmecey) shows changes even in a four-year period. More recent years undoubtedly show continuing change, but information must be gleaned from daily newspapers (*Le Monde, London Times,* or Tunisian newspapers), news journals or summaries (*Jeune Afrique, Maghreb-Machreq, Le Monde Diplomatique, Afrique-Asie*), or from area yearbooks (*Annuaire de l'Afrique du Nord, The Middle East and North Africa*). The discussion below concentrates on the contents of knowledge of elites, rather than the form, although references are supplied throughout. It is based on a mixture of studies and analyses, journalism and interpretation of news events, and personal observations. It must be remembered, however, that the systematic data are most out of date, focusing on the first 10 to 15 years of independence, when the elite appeared rather unified and well organized in a voluntaristic pattern. Evidence of disunity and dissension, plus greater compulsion in the political system, has emerged more recently and is not as clearly documented.

DESCRIPTION

Observers have described the elite in general terms as a "humane, intellectual, petit bourgeois, mildly socialistic" group whose orientations have remained relatively stable over time, although individual careers have had their ups and downs" (Poncet, 1974, p. 62), or,

Tunisia has been the sole society in North Africa in which the generation that achieved independence continued to assume the tasks of nation building. A long tradition of leadership, combined with a liberal bent, has generated an approach that is fundamentally gradual and pragmatic .... (T)he flexibility of party recruitment has enabled men of varied political perspectives to come to power at the same time, giving Tunisia both a liberal elite of aristocratic and middle class origins and a group of civil servants, intellectuals, and labor leaders entirely committed to state intervention in the economy, ... provision of free education, and the initiation of symbolic reforms, such as the nationalization of Habous, the introduction of mass media, and the expulsion of religion from the temple of politics (Hermassi, 1972, p. 162–3).

Similar characteristics of early homogeneity, consensus, and smooth working of the elite within the framework of a single-party system can be found in the works of Micaud, Moore, Ashford, and Carter. All agree that Tunisia's elite was more successful in the early years of nation building and managing independence than most Third World nations, and attribute it to the single-party system for producing consensus under Bourguiba's charismatic leadership.

More recently, however, cracks have appeared in the edifice. In a review of Moore's *Politics in North Africa*, Micaud indicated that by 1971 it was clear that the "first generation of observers" had ignored weaknesses in the system. "The much publicized concensus among the political elite did not exist."

Political development required

... the subordination of individual and collective claims to a grand strategy of structural reforms of the economy. Two conditions were essential to the success of the strategy: a strong, alert and cautious leadership and a homogeneous political elite united behind the official ideology and strategy of change. In 1969 these two conditions no longer availed. ... (Micaud, 1971, p. 61–62)

He further cited

... the lack of political homogeneity among the political elite, made up in part of bourgeois elements with vested economic interests. Revolutionary rhetoric hid the fact of profound differences concerning the scope and tempo of social change. The bourgeoisie was well represented in the high councils of state and party and ready to defend its interests if they were directly threatened. A class analysis of the composition of political elites ... would probably show greater heterogeneity in Tunisia (than in Algeria). (Micaud, 1971, p. 62)

While it is not entirely true, as he claimed, that "This class analysis has not been made," it appears correct that "we neglected to study the antagonisms created by social origins and vested interests, as well as by personal rivalries in the scramble for influence. ...." (Micaud, 1971, p. 62–

63) Evidence of these antagonisms among the elite has emerged in more recent years, but is yet to be documented in systematic studies.

As for the class background of the political elite, studies from the Mediterranean Societies Research Center in Aix-en-Provence, France, provide information on the age, education, occupation, father's occupation, and geographic origin of the members of the government, Destour party political bureau and central committee from 1955 (just before independence) through 1969 (Camau et al.), and all the variables except age are updated through 1973 in a subsequent study (Emmecey). This upper elite, once considered young and vibrant, is indeed aging over time, not being replaced at a fast enough rate to keep the average age stable. Despite this, some turnover was identified beginning around 1964, when many of the old "militants" whose claim to elite status was based on resistance to the French and the fight for independence began to be replaced by younger, more highly trained if not better educated people. (The level of education was always generally high, as will be seen below, but the shift was from people with liberal-humanistic, or at best legal training to those with more specialized studies in economics, engineering, and so forth.) Many of the "old guard" were born in the period of 1910–14 (29 percent), but the largest concentration of elite members was born in 1920–34 (62 percent).

Close ties among elite members of similar age is reinforced by a feature of their secondary education. More than half of the elites attended one rather small institution, Sadiki College. This school provided a bilingual education, Arabic as well as French, and was the school which over half of the studied sample attended (57 percent of the 1955–1973 elite). The school graduated only 215 students between 1911–1940 (Chenoufi, 1975, pp. 388–393), and half of these were in the last decade of the period; it is therefore highly likely that strong informal social ties among members of the elite were established as early as their high school days. Another 23 percent graduated from two other secondary institutions in Tunis (Lycée Carnot, a French school, and Zitouna, a traditional Islamic institution) meaning that over three fourths of the elite were educated in Tunis and had already become oriented to life in the capital city during their school days, although only 24 percent came from families who lived in the capital.

The great majority of this elite group went on to higher education, with 77 percent having a postsecondary degree. This is a remarkably high rate of higher education for a Third World elite. It also means that most of the elite was educated abroad (75 percent), mostly in France (70 percent), as the only institutions for higher education in Tunisia were the Zitouna University for Islamic studies, and after 1945, the Institut des Hautes Etudes, which became the University of Tunis after independence, but before then only offered the first years of study (Emmecey, p. 92). Emmecey stresses the large number who undertook Arabic studies (21 percent), either alone or in conjunction with another discipline, like law or humanities. He also noted, however, that in the later portion of the sample this number was reduced, and more people with technical degrees entered the elite, continuing a trend which Hermassi (p. 164–5) and Camau (p. 208–211) identified as beginning in 1964. The predominant academic specialty is law, studied by over one third of the elite, followed by Arabic/humanities and engineering in about equal proportions. Very few specialized in Islamic studies, reflecting the secular orientation of the Neo-Destour movement. However, some of those who joined the elite after 1969 did have a Zitouna education. It is interesting that at about the same time, a Tunisian sociologist published a paper suggesting that a reemergence of a religious traditionalism was taking place in the country (Zghal, 1973).

The elite is disproportionately drawn from Sousse and the surrounding Sahel (coastal plain) area, from where the President originates and from where the Neo-Destour party drew its original strength. That area, representing only 11.5 percent of the population, supplied 24.4 percent of the elite, followed by Tunis, which supplied 23.8 percent of the elite from 17.4 percent of the population. The other area overrepresented in the elite is the tiny island of Djerba in the south, with 1.5 percent of the population but 8.2 percent of the elite. Djerbans have a long tradition of commercial activity (Stone, 1974). Sfax, the second largest city after Tunis, and the Kairouan region are represented proportionately to their population (9 and 7 percent), and all other areas in the country are underrepresented. These regional disparities were well recognized in the elite study literature even before these systematic data were published. There exists some corresponding regional favoritism in economic investments and development programs.

Ben Salem's data (1969b, 1976) on a more broadly defined concept of the elite show similar trends in overrepresentation, although the disparities are not so great. Another study she conducted of Tunisian university students likewise shows that rates are highest in Tunis, Sousse, and the Sahel, although Sfax is also overrepresented among university students (Ben Salem, 1969a). Regionalism is an integral part of Tunisian political life. Journalistic accounts of a recent Destour Socialist party congress made reference to "clans" from various parts of the country, referring not to family ties but to local interests, and care was taken to assure that replacements for an elite member dismissed from the party central committee and the government were from the same city (Sfax) (Stemer, 1974, p. 21).

Similar findings emerge from previously unpublished work by Zartman which focuses on the core elite in Tunisia, members of the government and party Politburo, numbering 30 or less. His findings are summarized in table 1.3 in the introductory chapter, which reflects changes over the years 1956–1980. They show that the core elite aged 12 years in two and a half decades, half the rate of passing time, but with a fairly constant (and narrow) age spread, reflecting generational homogeneity of leadership in the Bourguiba period. The predominance of elites with higher education, primarily from French universities, is also clear, as is the primacy of Sahelians after 1970.

A salient indicator of class interests is occupational background. Here, an important difference which has been overlooked in the literature appears between the elites and their fathers or family interests. The elites themselves are predominantly "professors" (including high school instructors) and teachers, followed by high-level administrators (mostly in government or public service) and other professionals, mostly lawyers (Camau et al., Emmecey). These occupations are often considered "petit bourgeois," and this has become part of the image of the elite, a "new class" without substantial wealth from private economic interests. This reinforces the image of a humane, intellectual group, who could conceivably be mildly socialistic, as suggested above (Poncet, p. 62). However, they would have to come from families sufficiently well off to send their sons to university in the years before independence, or to encourage the brightest to study with the help of scholarships. (After independence, all education was made free and access was based primarily on merit, although some financial burden for purchasing supplies, and loss of earnings or contribution to family support, were still incurred.)

Looking at the occupations of fathers, however, reveals a very different structure (Camau et al.; Emmecey). The two largest categories were landowners and large merchants, comprising almost one half of all responses (although data were not available for fully one third of the sample, so this proportion might be as low as one third). Next came officials and administrators, and smaller merchants who can be considered the petite bourgeoisie, but they were out-numbered by the more substantial bourgeois class with private economic and commercial interests which were threatened by the socialistic tendencies of official government policy through the 1960s. The richer "went along" with these policies, partly out of fear and, possibly, partly because their interest could be protected by sons who were active in government. This also suggests the existence of a "shadow" elite — relatives, parents, or siblings of elite members who were not directly involved in the public sector, and thus never became identified as leaders. However, they might be able to influence their kin in elite positions along lines consistent with their social or economic interests. The study of ties between the recognized elite and indigenous wealth or traditional high status has yet to be done, and would be most difficult to carry out without intimate knowledge of the society and the courage to uncover privileged information. (It must be noted that researchers find this sort of research difficult, even in open and overstudied societies such as the United States, Canada, or England.)

More recent cabinet shuffles (late 1979, early 1980) have brought even more "technocrats" into the government, particularly engineers. They are often men with experience both as government officials and administrators, brought into public service due to former Prime Minister (1970–80) Hedi Nouira's preference for technocrats rather than lawyer-politician types. (See, for example, *Jeune Afrique*, November 21, 1979, p. 43.) The family ties of these newer members of the upper elite likewise have not been systematically studied, but their access to higher education again suggests they come from relatively rich families. Behind-the-scenes influence from a "shadow elite" of influential families is still not ruled out by these trends.

A listing of almost 500 members of the elite from whom biographies are available, or who are members of important government and party committees or leaders of national organizations (Clausen, 1976), reveals that most family names appear once, or at most twice. Many Tunisian families tend to be large, and when two or more generations of people are active, it could well be that many families have one representative in the political elite, while others work at family private interests. Such "hedging of bets," like the classical French habit of devoting sons to both "the red and the black," if it exists, would both indicate a continuing influence of family and clan (in the true sense) interests in modern Tunisian society, and provide further explanation for the widening gap in elite concensus and conflict which appears to be emerging in recent years (to be discussed below).

Conspicuously absent from the elite (at least so far) are military leaders. Little is known about the Tunisian army (Belhassen, 1980), and no "generals" are active in public life. The military has remained completely subordinate to civilian control (Belhassen, 1980, p. 182). The national guard has been called out in recent years to deal with strikes and riots by students and unionists. It has, however, always returned to the barracks under orders. Disturbances in early 1978 saw the public emergence of a militia-type group under the control of the Destour Socialist party leadership, and possibly another organized group from the temporarily dissident trade union movement (UGTT). This might signal the potential for an active power struggle among elements of the elite in the future. Also, when the Minister of Interior was dismissed in December, 1977, partly because of labor unrest, the Director of Tunisian National Security, a civilian, was also replaced —— by a colonel. Another colonel was named Director of Telecommunications within the ministry. Internal security is formally under the control of the Interior Minister, but this change in command structure was immediately noticed by critics of the regime and by the foreign press (*Maghreb-Machreq*, 79, p. 18; *Le Monde*, Jan. 8, 1978, p. 6; Toumi, 1978, p. 138). It has turned out, however, that the move was an interim administrative expedient by Defense Minister Abdullah Farhat, temporarily named acting Interior Minister, to avoid personal in involvement in domestic security while a new interior minister was being chosen, and not a "trial balloon" to test acceptability of military people in political positions.

Toumi (1978, p. 83) warns that the military budget increased six-fold in the two years 1976–78. He interprets this as indicating a growing tendency for the regime to use repressive force. It can also signal a future potential for a military role in politics, and for army officers to become members of the active elite. This has not been the case up to the present in Tunisia, which makes the country exceptional in the context of African politics. Recent trends suggest that military officers might be considered a potential "shadow" elite, which could even emerge to active leadership. This possibility was curtailed in late 1979, however, when Abdullah Farhat was removed as defense minister, then expelled from the P.S.D. Political Bureau by President Bourguiba. Farhat had organized the party congress in September 1979, with considerable military pomp. He also influenced the popularity of various candidates in the elections to the party central committee, such that supporters of his and Prime Minister Nouira's "hard line" in dealing with the social unrest of the previous two years emerged with more popular votes than the "moderates" whom President Bourguiba favored. The firing of Farhat from his ministerial post after the congress (*New York Times*, October 6, 1979), and from the Political Bureau of the party a week after the November 1979 elections to the National Assembly was interpreted in many press reports as a sign of Bourguiba's continuing control. (See, for example, *Maghreb-Machreq*, #87, 1980, p. 64.) However, it also signaled the president's disapproval of the use of the military in politics and for control of civil strife. This lessened the possibility that military leaders might attempt to enter the political arena, so long as Bourguiba retains his supreme control over Tunisian politics.

Official representatives of large-scale private economic interests are also absent from the elite; such groups are considered to be rather weak and unimportant politically (Poncet, p. 202–203), which may be a mistake. It is true that there are no private banks, large insurance companies, or private import-export firms any more. Most were foreign owned and departed, or were nationalized shortly after independence. However, Tunisian large landowners do remain, industrial investment is encouraged (fitfully), and much invisible capital might well exist in various commercial branches. If so, interests from these groups are pursued behind the scenes, and the people involved are not visible members of the active elite.

Few women are in the elite, despite the President's strong advocacy of women's rights. The head of the Tunisian National Women's Union is active in politics and public life, and subject on the same liabilities of disfavor that face all members of the elite. (These liabilities are outlined later under *Circulation*. The dismissal of Radhia Haddad after her public support of the "liberal" group is reported by Martel, 1975, p. 48 and 51.)

Beyond this, few women play an active part in public life or very high-level administrative leadership. For instance, of the 2,236 members of municipal councils in 1975, less than 5 percent (117) were women, although this was a gain from the 23 elected in 1972. (*Annuaire de l'Afrique du Nord*, 1977, p. 374.)

As for political affiliation, in the early years of independence, virtually the entire political elite were active members of the Neo-Destour party for years before acquiring formal elite status by membership in top bodies or government. Although the appearance of solidarity is almost completely maintained to the present, it frequently happens now that new government members, or appointees to high office, while they may be "officially" members of the party, are not party "militants" of long standing or high activity level. Other political groups (described in the next section) are beginning to emerge, although they are not officially sanctioned.

No religious leaders are visible, active members of the elite. The secular orientation of the Neo-Destour pushed religious leaders into the background, and official government policy of supporting religious institutions and encouraging Islamic practice in a manner consistent with modernization (Tessler, p. 10–11) has received wide enough public support that the 'ulama have no independent political influence. However, beginning in late 1977, journalistic sources have indicated the existence of a nascent religious revivalist movement, similar to the Egyptian Muslim Brotherhood, although spokesmen deny the similarity. The leaders are sheikhs and imams acting as individuals. (Belhassen, 1979; Schaar, 1977, p. 71; *Le Monde*, Oct. 15, 1978, p. 3; *Jeune Afrique*, Nov. 15, 1978, p. 67; Tessler, p. 12–13.) The movement is not unified, but its leaders actively preach and practice religious involvement in politics — a trend which has grown recently in the Moslem world, with Iran as an extreme example. This trend is of concern to the Tunisian political elite: "Muslim fundamentalist movements" were denounced in two public speeches, by the director of the P.S.D. and by the Prime Minister in December 1979, (*Maghreb-Machreq* #87, 1980, p. 64), and the two publications of the religious movement were suspended. The leaders of these Muslim groups can be considered another "shadow" elite, generating the potential to exercise political influence in the "parallel society" (*Jeune Afrique*, No. 15, 1978, p. 67) they are forming.

STRUCTURES

The dominant elite structure within Tunisia is the Destour Socialist party, which until 1964 was known as the Neo-Destour (Constitutional) party. It was formed in 1934 from an earlier nationalist party, the Destour, and has been headed since its beginning by Habib Bourguiba. Bourguiba has also been President of the country since independence, and was named chairman-for-life of the party and president-for-life of the country in 1974. This one-man dominance of the elite structure, and one-party dominance in politics (no other parties are legal, although several groups operate informally or clandestinely of late) accurately characterizes the nature of the Tunisian political system. The elite either actively cooperate (although some mild criticism is tolerated within the structure from time to time), or risk expulsion, removal from public life, and even imprisonment, if deviation from party discipline is interpreted as "treason" or an attempt to overthrow the regime ("harm internal security").

The Neo-Destour led the fight for independence, and early governments as well as leadership groups throughout the elite structures were composed of party "militants," people active in the fight for independence. More recently, occupational specialization has begun to replace militance as qualification for access to high position in the party, although as mentioned above the elite has always been relatively well educated. After independence, a rather large underground movement was converted into a mass political party—the sole political organization permitted in the country after the elimination of early opposition groups, including the assassination abroad of one leader, Salah ben Youssef, who had strong regional support from the south. (Note that Bourguiba's regional support centers in the Sahel.) The structure has a grass-roots basis in local-level party cells in villages, city neighborhoods, large economic organizations, and administrations. Regional coordination committees centralize the structure. At the top of these is a central committee with elected national representation, and above it is a political bureau, the top leadership of the structure, appointed by the president. This ability to appoint (and dismiss) at the highest level of the party enables the president to "legitimize" political appointees to elite positions (and banishments), although, in practice, most of the visible elite are at least official members of the party and usually have been active enough to rise to positions of elected status in the local, regional or national frameworks, which number about 300. The party name was changed to Destour Socialist party in 1964, but now the name is more symbolic than substantive after a brief attempt at socialistic reorganization of the economy that lasted only until 1969.

Parallel to the party structure is the government administration—which also begins at the local level with elected municipal councils in larger towns and cities and appointed officials in rural areas. At the regional level governors are appointed by the president of the republic, and other government officials by the interior minister. At the national level, the President appoints ministers, who in turn run their respective ministries, staffed by a permanent civil service, with some political appointees at high levels. There is an elected National Assembly of 121 representatives, who run on a party list basis, so all are Destour members. (In the

December, 1979 elections, each seat was contested by two candidates, for the first time in Tunisian history. However, in each case both candidates were party nominees, so Destour hegemony was assured. In only one instance was a central committee member defeated by an alternate candidate, (*Maghreb-Machreq*, #87, 1980, p. 64). The Assembly debates and ratifies legislation. It can originate laws, but presidential proposals take precedence — which, in fact, means the Assembly can initiate little legislation on its own. Furthermore, when the Assembly is in session, legislative procedures assure support for government proposals before they are introduced for plenary debate. (Details of the legislative procedure are succinctly described in the *Area Handbook*, 1971, 1979, Chapter 13. The 1976 modifications to the constitutional and organic laws are reported in *Annuaire de l'Afrique du Nord*, 1976, p. 881–887.) Clausen (1976) uses National Assembly membership as an indication of elite status.

The important feature of government structure and party leadership is the almost complete overlap in membership, so that exercise of government elite function is carried on entirely by the party elite. At least lip service to party loyalty is required of all active elites, and the accusation that this system is undemocratic is consistently countered with the ideological stand that full debate, criticism, and opposition are permitted *within* the party structure and councils, so that the one-party system can both provide democracy and aggregate national unity. The issue of whether or not formally to join the party has long been a serious question in the minds of young potential elites, intellectuals, and university students. On the one hand, many are opposed to the principle of the single-party system or to its policies. On the other hand, mobility to elite status, and access to positions from which it is possible to influence the direction of change in the country, are very likely to require at least symbolic adherence to the party, throughout the forseeable future. The party has succeeded in raising the political consciousness of the country's elite, even if not always with the desired outcome.

Most other national organizations are formally affiliated with the Destour Socialist party (PSD), and were formed or supported by the party. Most of the time they indeed tow the partly line and cooperate actively in political and government activities. Thus, organizations such as the National Women's Union (UNFT), the Farmers Union, the Union of Industry, Commerce, and Crafts (UTICA), and various "National Offices," government monopolies in various branches of the economy are solidly in support of the party. There are two important exceptions, however: the Tunisian Trade Union movement (Union Générale des Travailleurs Tunisiens — UGTT) and the University Students Union (Union Générale des Etudiants Tunisiens — UGET), which have actively opposed the government and party from time to time.

The most recent example occurred in January, 1978, when a general strike was organized by the UGTT, the first in the history of independent Tunisia. Union supporters and government forces clashed violently on January 26, following several months of labor unrest, which the government had tried to resolve by dismissing the Interior Minister, who was replaced along with four other cabinet ministers who either resigned or were dismissed. The general strike and conflict left numerous dead and wounded. The entire union leadership was arrested and tried several months later, resulting in convictions for 24 union leaders, ranging up to 10 years at hard labor for harming the internal security of the country. The large number of convictions (300 rioters had been quickly tried and convicted), as well as the number of deaths (estimated at from 50 to over 200) and injuries indicated the existence of a fairly powerful opposition group (Bishtawi, p. 25; Disney, p. 12; Toumi, 1978, p. 112).

The opposition may have been crushed, but the UGTT has a long history of independent militant action. For most of its history it worked in cooperation with the Destour party, but this was a cooperation of two independent organizations and not a "puppet" relationship which characterizes most other groups' relations with the party. The UGTT emerged as an effective union as early as the 1930s (calling itself a "confederation" — CGTT — until 1945) and was permitted to operate under the French protectorate. In the struggle for independence, the outlawed Destour used the UGTT as a front for nationalist activities. After 1956, the union was generally in accord with the party but maintained an independent stance. The union has always published its own newspaper. Ideologically, it is socialist but clearly anticommunist, having overcome a challenge from a competing communist union shortly after independence.

Many national leaders have been associated with the union, including Ahmed ben Saleh, who was ousted from UGTT leadership in 1956 for being too radical. He returned to attempt to institute his ideas in the 1960s within the government. The union head at the time of the general strike in 1978, Habib Achour, a close associate of the President, was a long-time Destour party militant. He resigned from the Political Bureau shortly before the strike and his arrest. He was replaced as union head within a few weeks by a regional union official who was not involved in the strike and was considered politically safe, a loyal member of the party who was also a member of the National Assembly. The "election" of new union leadership took place in a closed UGTT convention which was clearly dominated by the party. The Union has thus returned to the "fold" of national unity, but the experience raises the question of whether organized labor might become a competing political force in the future. Achour himself had previously been deposed from UGTT leadership in 1966 on a charge of mismanagement, behind which lay political motives. He returned to the leadership in 1970 after the deposition of Ahmed ben Saleh. One cannot rule out the possibility of another return, either by Achour or by other like-minded leaders. In fact, first moves in this direction were made in 1979–80. Achour's sentence was modified to house arrest in August 1979 and a series of presidential pardons in 1980 freed all of the more than 100 UGTT leaders and activists imprisoned following the January 1978 riots. (*Le Monde*, July 10, 1980; *New York Times*, August 4, 1980). This "softening" of the hard line is part of the policy change being introduced by a new prime minister, Mohammed M'zali, appointed in spring 1980 (see *circulation*, below). M'zali admitted that union activism and labor unrest were continuing problems his government must face (*Le Monde*, ibid., p. 3). In the future, it would not be surprising if President Bourguiba coopted one or more of the formerly imprisoned union leaders into the party and/or government elite echelons in return for labor peace.

University students are another structural source of occasional elite dissidence. Entelis (1974) has characterized Tunisian students at home and abroad as an "emerging counterculture." Sometimes the Destour student organization itself (UGET) opposes government or party actions, and sometimes student demonstrations, riots, or strikes emerge in opposition to UGET, or outside its jurisdiction. In 1971–72, student unrest and demonstrations at the University of Tunis resulted in its closing for several months, and in a heavy-handed attempt by the government to reconstitute the student leadership at a UGET convention held in the small town of Korba in a rural area of the Cap Bon peninsula. This signaled both the fact that the student leadership was out of accord with the party, and the party and government's intention to control student politics. Three years later, a widespread one-day strike of secondary school teachers was led by young teachers, recent university graduates, reflecting an activist orientation to politics among this group. Previously, after riots at the time of the 1967 Middle East war, many student leaders and young intellectuals were arrested and tried for political dissidence. Again, following the events of January 1978, unrest was at a high level at the university, with many classes boycotted or poorly attended; and in 1980, antigovernment demonstrations by engineering and law students followed an abortive attack on Gafsa by disgruntled migrant workers, backed by Libya. In response, classes were suspended in those two faculties (*Le Monde*, Feb. 26, 1980). While no formally organized opposition by students or young intellectuals has crystallized, this group is inherently likely to be a potential power center when the occasion arises. Unlike other organizations, however, the composition of student groups is unstable, turning over every few years as students graduate and move on to other pursuits, often occupying elite-level positions in society.

A related, and potentially important elite structure is comprised of students and young Tunisian intellectuals studying and working abroad, particularly in France. UGET has groups in many French and other European universities, and other temporary Tunisian émigrés are organized into informal associations as well as opposition groups. For instance, following the general strike of January 1978, *Le Monde* reported several times the existence and activities of the Tunisian 26th of January Collective, a group apparently involved in publicizing the government repression and violence surrounding the strike, riots, and trials of UGTT leaders. Little documentation on such groups has been located, although the headquarters address of the Collective in Paris is published in *Le Monde* each time that organization is mentioned in a news item (cf. various issues since January, 1979).

Alternate political organizations are beginning to appear in Tunisia. Although none have been legally recognized as political parties, they are becoming a political force in Tunisia (for the first time in 1978, the Europa Yearbook on ,he *Middle East and North Africa* listed "clandestine" political organizations in addition to the dominant Destour Socialist Party). The most important are:

1. The Tunisian National Progressive Front, consisting of three nationalist and socialist groups — one Nasserist, one Baathist, and one Youssefist. (The Youssefists are followers of the assassinated opposition leader, Saleh ben Youssef, who had regional support from the south of Tunisia and socialist support.)

2. The Popular Unity Movement (MUP) headed by Ahmed Ben Saleh, deposed former head of the Tunisian economy and planning ministries, who spearheaded an eight-year drive to convert the country to a guided socialism based on cooperatives in all branches of the economy. He was arrested in 1969, tried for treason, and convicted in 1970. He escaped from prison in 1972, first to Algeria and then to Europe, where he maintained a low profile for a few years. More recently, he permitted a memoir to be published (Nerfin, 1974) and has begun to make public comments on Tunisian affairs, as well as organizing supporters in Tunisia and abroad into a movement advocating radical reform.

Toumi suggests that the MUP and the Tunisian Communist party are closely allied ideologically, if not organizationally, and together could rally 9 to 10 percent of voter support in a free election (1978, p. 380). The Communist party continues to exist both in Tunisia and abroad; the last politbureau was elected in 1962 (p. 328) before the party was outlawed, but three members of the committee were actively identified with the unrest in January 1978 (p. 330), which indicates that long-time Communist activists are still involved in politics. Further evidence of Tunisian Communist party operation was its request in 1980 for permission to publish a newspaper to be called *al Jadid* (*Le Monde*, May 21, 1980). Permission was not granted by the government.

3. The Socialist Democratic party, headed by Ahmed Mestiri and Hassib ben Ammar. Mestiri particularly has long advocated a liberalization of the regime, both by permitting a liberal political party to

function, and by allowing a freer political system with multiple parties if the people are so inclined. Mestiri has had a checkered political career, falling in and out of favor with the Destour party and national leadership several times. (Political careers in Tunisia will be discussed in the section on *Circulation*, below.) At the Destour Socialist party congress in 1971, the "liberal faction" within the party, led by Mestiri, almost staged a takeover of policy, based on support by about half the delegates. Mestiri lost out in a showdown with President Bourguiba, but his demonstrated popularity made it impossible to do more than banish him from the party. Pressure for recognition of the liberal movement has continued since that time. At the 1974 Party congress, Bourguiba noted that many others with liberal tendencies have remained within the party, and while he decried their ideas he stressed that political disagreements should be worked out within the framework of the single-party system. Then, shortly after the congress, eight prominent liberals were expelled from the party.

The liberals have continued their pressure for recognition, however. In June 1977 they organized an international conference on human rights to be held in Tunis. The conference was forbidden by the government at the last minute, but not before it had generated attention and participation from human rights activists in other countries (Schaar, 1977). In early 1978 the liberal group began publishing two newspapers, a weekly in Arabic and a monthly in French, which required government permission. The Arabic language *Er-Rai* (Opinion) has grown to a circulation of 25,000, half as much as the leading party newspaper, when it was suspended for three months in early 1979, after one year of operation, for excessive criticism of the government. A formal request by the liberal group to be recognized as the Socialist Democratic Party, presented to the government in June 1978, was denied. However, the movement continues to function and receive recognition by the foreign press. It apparently has the support of considerable middle-class interests who no longer identify with Destourian socialism.

The pendulum swung in a more favourable direction for the liberals in 1980. Bourguiba held two informal meetings early in the year with Ahmed Mestiri. Then, with Prime Minister Nouira disabled by illness, the path was cleared to readmit Mestiri and seven of his supporters to the party (PSD). The reconciliation was strengthened when Nouira was formally replaced by Mohammed M'zali in a major cabinet shuffle on April 23, 1980. One member of the liberal faction, Sadok ben Djamaa, was given a minor cabinet post, and three more important positions were awarded to elite members who advocated concilliation with the liberal and unionist factions. (*Le Monde*, April 26, 1980.) In July permission for publication of two more weekly newspapers (one Arabic and one French) was granted to the liberals.

Other nascent political groups which could conceivably take part in a multiparty or multifaction political system include the communists, long suppressed and illegal in the political system and the labor movement but continuing in existence (*Jeune Afrique* Nov. 15, 1978, p. 66, and Toumi, 1978), and the religious revivalist group mentioned above (Belhassen; Schaar; Tessler). The role of Islam in politics has long been rejected by the modernist Destour ideology; however, recent years have seen a resurgence of Islamic movements in politics in other Arab and Muslim nations, and religious traditionalism has been recognized within Tunisia itself (Zghal, 1973; Tessler). Since 1979, the popularity of the Islamic revival movement in Tunis has been growing (Belhassen, 1979). Six religious leaders were specifically identified in that article, including Mourou, two other sheikhs and three leaders from the university. It is not yet clear whether the religious leaders have political aspirations as individuals, but this has generally been the case elsewhere in the Muslim world. Traditional Islam does not draw a distinction between religion and politics, and this principle has been confirmed by at least one Tunisian religious leader (Tessler, p. 13). The example of Iran will raise the possibility of Islamic neotraditionalism as a viable political force. Also, in Libya and Algeria, Tunisia's immediate neighbors, leaders stress the role of Islam in government and politics. While a religious political movement is not likely to gain widespread support in Tunisia, it could possibly form part of a multifaction mosaic in the future. One religious leader, Hassen Ghodbani, only 26 years old, speaking before a university student audience, was reported to have attacked communists and atheists, the former presumably referring to supporters of Ben Salah (Belhassan, 21 March 1979, p. 68). The popularity of these leaders and the Islamic "revivalist" idea could contribute a new, conservative, "traditionalist," nonsocialist elite to the Tunisian political picture.

Elite activity is concentrated in the capital city, Tunis. Although more elite members originate outside the city, and regional background shows regularities (discussed above), the capital is very much a "primate city." Tunis is the center of power for political and economic decision making and for cultural and social life. Although heavy industry is somewhat decentralized geographically, the country is small, and high-level administrators can commute to work, so their families can enjoy the advantages of life in the capital. Of the other main cities, Sousse and Bizerte are so close to Tunis that daily commuting is possible. Only Sfax, the second largest city, is both far enough from Tunis and large enough to be an alternate elite power center. While much independent economic power is concentrated in Sfax, which has a long tradition of commerce and its own port facilities, no strong regional elitism is apparent, although in the past there was support for ben Youssef there. Care is taken in the government, at party congresses, and in the central committee and political bureau to ensure adequate participation by Sfaxiens (for example, see Stemer, p. 21).

Concentration of elite activity in Tunis, the relatively small size of the elite, and indeed the small scale of the country mean that social and cultural life takes place in a relatively small circle, and informal social contacts among elite members must be quite regular. No systematic information has been recorded concerning informal social contacts or interlocking of elite groups through intermarriage or business associations. Although the elite is by no means a single social circle, or closed to newcomers, many formal and informal crosscutting ties do exist. Of the known high-level examples are the fact that President Bourguiba was divorced from his first wife, a French woman, in 1961, and in 1962 married Wassila ben Ammar, of a rich and powerful bourgeois family of Tunis, with large land holdings in the north of the country. Five members of this ben Ammar family are listed in the index of Clausen (1974), more than any other Tunisian elite family. Another example, from the area of business, concerns Habib Achour, the leader of the UGTT-sponsored general strike, jailed in 1978: When Achour was deposed from office a previous time, 1965–69, he ran a travel agency in Tunis which received considerable business from the Central Bank, headed by Hedi Nouira, who subsequently became Prime Minister of Tunisia, 1970–1980, (*Jeune Afrique*, Nov. 1, 1978, p. 63) They continued to work together closely in reorienting the ideology of the PSD in 1970, but apparently grew apart politically and ideologically through the 1970s. In the long run politics overcame personal ties, and Achour was convicted in 1978. Sources such as Clausen's (1976) compilation of published biographies can be used to trace links of intermarriage and association among the elite, but such analysis has not been done. It would likely be hampered by incomplete information. However, it appears that the small, Tunis-centered elite forms a fairly dense social network.

In the first two decades after independence, the Tunisian elite did depend upon foreign experts for technical guidance in various aspects of national planning and development. The extent and composition of such advice has not been well documented. A study focusing on one year only (1971–72) indicated 428 French technical advisors in Tunisia on long-term assignments (one year or more), and 89 short-term visiting experts (Flory, 1975, p. 253). These advisors work closely with individual top leaders in clearly defined areas such as economic development planning, international relations, publicity, and many technical fields such as industrialization, irrigation, etc. Some work on personal service contracts directly with government or administration leaders, and some are provided within the context of international or bilateral governmental aid agreements in fields like agriculture, public health, etc. Foreigners have direct contact with top or second-level decision makers in these frameworks, but their positions are strictly advisory, and the responsible Tunisian officials make all decisions. Tunisian development has relied upon large amounts of foreign aid, so that pressures from fund-granting agencies such as the World Bank, USAID, the French government, etc. have affected Tunisian decision making, sometimes very directly. For instance, the refusal to extend aid to agriculture in 1969 unless agricultural cooperatives were limited and improved contributed to the demise of Ahmed ben Saleh and the complete reorientation of the Tunisian economy and the ideology of the PSD.

Formally, all national ideological orientations and development policies are formulated and debated within the PSD, at local, regional, and national meetings, and particularly at the party congresses held approximately every four years. Three- or four-year national plans, begun in 1961, are created via a planning·process which is supposed to originate at local levels·and work its way up to the national government, which balances all demands and establishes priorities in line with available means and development goals. In practice, however, both the planning process and political "interest aggregation" have been criticized for being entirely one-way in nature, originating from the top leadership for transmission downward, with little upward flow of information or input.

POWER SOURCES AND USES

Almost all exercise of legitimate power in Tunisia derives directly or indirectly from the unanimous legitimacy accorded President Bourguiba, and is institutionalized in the single-party form of government, which he heads in the dual capacity of President of the Republic and head of the Party, both posts accorded him for life, as of 1974. This centralization of power had been consolidated by 1959, when no member of the upper elite studied by Camau et al. (1973) was not a member of the Neo-Destour, and the Youssefist opposition had been suppressed. All high-level appointees serve at the pleasure of the President, and he actively cultivates a paternalistic, benevolent image as the "supreme combatant" in the struggle for independence and national unity, and the legitimate father-figure destined to guide the people to national development until his death.

Bourguiba's death and a resulting power struggle have been predicted for at least the last 15 years but have not yet happened, despite failing health and frequent long absences from the country for medical treatment. He has consistently demonstrated the remarkable capacity to remain in at least symbolic control of all affairs of state, returning to take over active leadership whenever dissension or power struggle threatens to break the national concensus into opposing factions vying for power. For reasons difficult to comprehend, the elite have always agreed to abide by Bourguiba's decisions and recognize his legitimacy. Individual opponents or small groups of potential dissidents have been unable to break away from party discipline because of peer pressure or lack of support. Active dissidents have been removed or isolated from power by means of control and concensus of the majority. Even unreasonable policies are seldom opposed openly. Perhaps the elite deeply fear the inevitable power struggle which will follow Bourguiba's death, and prefer to defer the inevitable as long as possible.

Part of Bourguiba's strategy has been a pragmatic flexibility which originated in the strategy used to gain independence from France, gradualism in overcoming resistance, and willingness to compromise, to forgive, and to alter policies in line with changing realities. In terms of postindependence leadership, this has been manifest in: (1) an ability to alter or even reverse national policies if opposition becomes too strong, as happened to the policy of socialism and cooperativization in 1969; (2) strong loyalty and confidence placed in close political collaborators and supporters (there were only two prime ministers in the first 23 years of independence, with a third appointed in 1980); and (3) a willingness to forgive individual opponents and dissidents in return for renewed loyalty, as witnessed by numerous examples of elite members expelled from government and party only to return in later years. Recently, it appeared that this flexibility and toleration was receding with age, being replaced by a much firmer, more authoritarian, even "fascistic" form of government (Toumi, 1978, p. 374–5). As Prime Minister Nouira and his appointees assumed more control, they found themselves unable to generate the charisma Bourguiba used to mediate disputes and unite disparate factions. Instead, they relied upon force or threat of force to maintain order and put down opposition. However, with Nouira's removal from power in 1980 due to illness, the typical Bourguiban leadership traits just enumerated reappeared. Amnesty has been granted to all "political prisoners," (*New York Times*, Aug. 4, 1980) many opponents and dissidents have been reinstated into party and government, and policies are "liberalizing" within the existing single party structure. Many political dissidents are reported to be returning from abroad, or have been issued passports permitting them freedom of movement.

The military has been completely isolated from power, and entirely subject to civilian control to date. The one, apparently minor exception was the naming of colonels to command national security forces and direct communications during the labor unrest at the end of 1977, but these are second-level administrative posts, responsible to the Interior Minister. Security forces have been called out on occasion to control civil unrest, from the time of the Middle East war in June 1967, through the 1970s at times of student and worker unrest, to the most recent example of the general strike in January 1978, when a curfew was imposed on the large cities for several days. However, in none of these instances was there any question of the military exercising power on its own. In fact, the defense minister responsible for the 1978 moves, Abdullah Farhat, was dismissed from public office and the party in October, 1979. Since then, the army was used to quell the attack on Gafsa in January, 1980, but this was an example of legitimate use of force, under government control.

A private militia of the PSD made an appearance in the 1978 riots. While its size was officially reported at about 500, observers claim its true size was closer to 2,500 (Disney, p. 12, who quotes *Jeune Afrique*, March 1, 1978). This might signal a growing authoritarian tendency among high party officials or fear of a future power struggle, but up to now none has been apparent. Mob power with some small arms was also used by the UGTT during the strike, in reaction to police tactics employed by the regime. An airline hijacking by a group demanding the release of Achour in December 1978 represented the first attempt by an opposition group to use international terror in the history of Tunisia. The airplane, on a domestic flight, was diverted to Libya, where the hijackers eventually released it and took refuge with the Qaddafi regime, which has supported Tunisian dissidence over the last several years. In 1973, Foreign Minister Mohammed Masmoudi had engineered a 'union between Tunisia and Libya which was quickly reneged upon by Tunisia, resulting in Masmoudi's dismissal and temporary exile followed by house arrest for two and a half years. Achour also had support from Libya and had visited the country, together with Mestiri, not long before the general strike. These and the 1980 attack on Gafsa are the only bits of recent evidence that might signal a potential violent power struggle within Tunisia. All include the active involvement of Libya, whose leader Qaddafi appears committed to destabilizing the Bourguiba regime. Competition for political power and legitimacy by other dissident groups has been mentioned in the previous section.

The power of popular support rallying behind religious leaders with political aspirations in another potential force for legitimizing a new elite in a Muslim country experiencing religious revival. The case of Iran could be replicated in Tunisia and elsewhere, as popular support is apparently growing (Belhassan, 1979).

SOCIALIZATION

For older members of the high-level elite, the process of socialization has been documented in research. A majority have the common education experience of Sadiki College, which provided informal social contacts among them as well as a bilingual education, Arabic and French. This bilingual capability is strong among the old elite, but may be somewhat weakened (less adequate French) among the young (Entelis, 1974, p. 559). Of the old guard, all were active in the nationalist struggle, and specifically in the Neo-Destour Party. Education levels are high, and most have university degrees relevant to a political career (law, education, etc.) which involved study abroad, mainly in France. "Generations' of high-level leadership have been recognized in the literature (Camau et al.; Hermassi, *Maghreb-Machreq*, 79, p. 16). Militant activism during the fight for independence was the primary socialization experience common to the elite first in power after independence. Cabinet and high-level party changes in 1964 reflected a stress on technical competence and specialized training among new elites brought into power. In 1969 and again in 1977, major cabinet changes and recruitment to high-level positions brought in people with top administrative experience in the civil service, government ministries, or national organizations. As indicated above, more recent cabinet shuffles (1979 and 1980) have brought even more "technocrats," particularly engineers, into elite positions. Recruitment was from among safe, active, and loyal party members, so that a background in Destour youth or student organizations, then in party cells or committees on the local or regional level, is a required part of the socialization process. Usually, elite recruits will also have reached positions of importance in national-level party organizations, as delegates to party congresses and members of the central committee. The only exemption from this part of socialization is for people who have spent most of their early careers abroad.

As the elite is small and closely knit, with high-level appointments made directly by the President and leaders serving at his pleasure, it is undoubtedly true that family and social contacts, private influence, and ties through marriage, business association, and regional origins play an important part in actual incumbency to high-level positions. For instance, the new Prime Minister, Mohammed M'zali, is from Bourguiba's home town of Monastir, as was his predecessor Hedi Nouira. The regime maintains an ideology of openness and mobility based on universalistic criteria of competence. However, as the supply of elite incumbents has grown to exceed the demand, while competence has become increasingly *necessary*, it is unlikely to be a *sufficient* condition for access to elite status.

Lower-level elites and skilled manpower were in short supply in the early years of nationhood, so advancement was rapid for those with the requisite skills, and stress was place on solid education and adequate technical training. The government made massive investments in education, for which it allotted about one-fourth of government budgets (Toumi, 1975, p. 38), access was open to all Tunisian youth who qualified free of charge,[1] and incumbency to elite positions was based primarily on achievement. Nevertheless, university students and skilled cadres come predominantly from middle- and upper-middle-class social strata, and from the urban areas or other traditional sources of elite incumbents, the Sahel and Djerba. (Ben Salem 1969a, 1969b, 1976).

Of course, adherence to Destourian organizations was a necessary part of the socialization process, but it was fairly universal, too. True believers and followers had easy access to party membership, and dissidents or doubters found it more expedient to be hypocritical and join rather than to draw attention by making a point of avoiding adherence. Also, the government could and did use the expedient of revoking the scholarships of dissident students.

In recent years supply has caught up with and overtaken demand for elite incumbents and cadre. Mobility channels to elite positions have become blocked. (This situation was anticipated by Allman, 1976). A university degree or a certified technical skill no longer warrants anticipation of mobility to elite status, as previous studies assumed (Stone, 1973). Under these conditions, the quality or degree of party activism should figure more prominently in the socialization process, as should excellence in training as reflected by grades, etc. Advanced degrees or training in foreign institutions provide a competitive advantage, as do informal ties to, or influence with the elite, described in French as *"piston."*

While these problems in mobility are known to exist, there have been no studies of recent problems of social mobility or elite composition to document the exact nature of the problem or measures to cope with it. It is well known that unemployment is high, and labor unrest is growing. University students are restive and apprehensive about their future (Entelis, 1974), although to date the sentiments have not been justified. Most of the recently trained and educated cadres have found employment (Toumi, 1978, p. 403) although not necessarily access to elite status. Most do not approve of Destourian leadership or the single-party system, yet are forced to cope with the reality of its existence as well as the uncertainty of its endurance. Future Tunisian elites are squarely faced with the problem of "socialization for an unknown future."

No studies deal with attitudes or knowledge on alternative political or ideological orientations among students or among any segment of Tunisian society. However, the society is fairly open to ideas, and to publications from around the world, plus broadcast media from Europe and the Arab world. Therefore, it can be assumed that the range of choices and thought that students elsewhere are exposed to also make the rounds among Tunisian students. If Europe is an example, many leftist ideologies of varying intensity and extremity are more popular among students than among older elites. From the Arab world, notions of Pan-Arabism, socialism, support for the Palestinian movement, and Islamic nationalism are likely components in political awareness.

Among older elites, the strongest alternative ideology appears to be the liberal tendency of the Socialist Democratic movement, which stresses individual freedom, human rights, and a certain amount of economic liberalization in the direction of free enterprise. Among the newly emerging elites, increased freedom is more likely to be associated with the growth of leftist or socialist tendencies. These may be directly tied to the trade unionist opposition that was headed by Achour, to ben Salah's clandestine and foreign-based Popular Unity Movement, or the long-outlawed Tunisian Communist party, but many other tendencies are likely to emerge. On the other hand, rightist political tendencies associated with religious traditionalism and Islamic revival also appeal to some of the younger emerging elites, especially some students (Belhassen; Tessler). These movements advocate equal access and status for all adherents. Entelis' (1974) data show general agreement among students that the present single-party system cannot survive the passing of Bourguiba, nor can the Destour leadership and administrative style as now constituted. The same study also indicates that students perceive inequality of opportunity for social mobility and access to jobs, with the system favoring people of higher social status.

As this chapter was being written, an event took place which could affect the Tunisian elite for years to come. The Arab League decided to move its headquarters from Cairo to Tunis, in reaction to the Egyptian-Israeli peace agreement. This will create an important new outlet for employment of Tunisian elites and highly educated manpower. It will also draw Tunisia more closely into the Arab world sphere of influence, increasing the importance of the Arabic language (classical or modern standard) as a medium for elite communication with foreign Arab leaders and Arab League officials. It may also cause a shift in cultural ties and geopolitical orientations of the Tunisian elite, away from Europe (particularly France) in the direction of the Arab East. The change could affect Tunisia much more than it did Egypt, because Tunisian society is on a much smaller scale, and the capital city is much more compact, thus liable to be influenced by a new "foreign" presence. The extent to which these changes will take place will not be evident for several years and will depend upon the permanence of the Arab League move and the extent to which the organization grows in importance and activity, if at all. However, the potential impacts on the Tunisian elite should be closely watched in the future.

CIRCULATION

Within the existing regime, circulation of high-level elites requires the direct involvement of President Bourguiba, who controls the composition of the cabinet and the political bureau of the party at will. One victim and interested observer of this process, Ahmed ben Salah, has pointed out that by the 1974 PSD congress the Political Bureau had no members from the first postindependence central committee, signaling a complete "rejuvenation" of party leadership (quoted in *Maghreb-Machreq*, 66,

1974, p. 21). Appointments and dismissals are made, of course, in consultation with other officials, but the "court"-like setting for intrigue, plots, and backbiting which this situation can evince makes political life precarious and arbitrary. Many high-level political careers are characterized by cycles of rise to favor, then dismissal and banishment, followed by renewed gaining of favor and reintegration into the upper elite. In some cases this cycle has been repeated more than once. Sometime high-level officials who have been subject to this process at least twice include: Habib Achour; Mohammed Masmoudi (former minister of foreign affairs, removed after the near union with Libya in 1974, who went into exile, then returned, but was under house arrest until 1980); Tahar Belkhodja (interior minister until the labor unrest in late 1977); Habib Chatti (foreign minister removed at the same time as Belkhodja, but who returned to favor in December 1977); and Ahmed Mestiri, who consistently has pressured the government for liberalizaton. Expelled from all official status in 1971, Mestiri was joined by eight other former high elites expelled after the party congress in 1974 in forming the Socialist Democratic movement. He was readmitted to the party in 1980, and one of his supporters received a minor cabinet post in the new M'zali government.

All political appointees are fully aware of these and numerous other examples of cycles of favor and disfavor, which is one of the more arbitrary aspects of Bourguiba's long single-party rule. The seesawing of support for socialist-leftist and bourgeois interest groups over the years, as well as alternation between humane, personal freedoms and the "hardening" of rigid civil control, has created insecurity — if not confusion — among the elite who try to influence the President and predict his reactions. The adoption of socialism by the party in 1964, the dropping of ben Salah and reversal of socialism in 1969, and massive cabinet turnover at the end of 1977, when 9 new ministers (out of a total of 25) were appointed following dismissals over the labor unrest are some of the more extreme examples of enforced elite "circulation."

Through 1979, a presidential change of heart was considered less likely with Bourguiba's increasing age and the expansion of powers of Prime Minister Nouira, who appeared willing to use force to maintain order. However, action was forced by the sudden disablement of Nouira due to a brain hemmorhage in February 1980. A few weeks before this, Bourguiba had met with "liberal" leader Mestiri, shortly after his reinstatement into the PSD. This hint of "liberalization" was facilitated by Nouira's illness. Mohammed M'zali, then minister of education, and previously minister of youth and sport, was appointed acting "coordinator of government activity." He was known for his sympathy for younger Tunisians' interests. After two and a half months, he was formally named prime minister, in a cabinet shuffle which brought in four sympathizers of previously isolated political interest groups, the liberals and prounionists

(*Le Monde*, April 26, 1980). Thus, another "round" was evident in Tunisian elite circulation, a move of compromise and concilliation, confirmed by a series of presidential pardons for political opponents imprisoned in the violence of past years.

Journalists continue to watch closely for changes in the status of other political outcasts, who may succeed in rapidly returning to favor and power. Two potential alternate political elite groups are currently visible, involving past incumbents to power together with new, unknown elements. On the left is Ahmed ben Salah, who heads the Popular Unity movement (MUP) from exile in Europe, apparently supported by other Tunisian leftist dissidents in Tunisia and abroad (Toumi, 1978, p. 266). The 26th of January Collective, formed in Paris to protest government force, repression, and mass arrests and trials following the 1978 general strike, is ideologically similar, but efforts to bring the two groups together have not been successful (*Le Monde*, Jan. 26, 1979, p. 4). A nonunified opposition increases the temptation to "divide and rule" by bringing one of the factions into favor, although any presidential move of reconciliation with ben Salah would have to involve overlooking the fact that he was convicted of treason and serving a ten-year jail sentence at hard labor when he escaped. He was tried in absentia and sentenced to an additional five and a half years for escaping. He has already refused one offer of amnesty on condition that he return to Tunisia. Instead, it may be possible to "split" the leftist opposition by according some recognition to the TCP, which has recently requested permission to publish a newspaper.

On the right is the rather large group of "liberals" associated with the Socialist Democratic Movement, headed by Mestiri and including many former cabinet ministers and elites who have fallen out of favor and been dismissed from high posts. This group is large and talented enough so that if the President chose to support it, a viable new administration could be formed very quickly. Another important out-of-favor leader who sympathizes with one or more of the SDM policies is Mohammed Masmoudi, whose "error" was support of a union with Libya. Contacts with that country have also been established by Mestiri, and by Habib Achour, the jailed UGTT leader. Achour's group of unionists is more leftist than Mestiri's on economic policies; however, both identify with the struggle for individual freedom and human rights, as does Tahar Belkhodja and the group of cabinet ministers deposed along with him at the end of 1977, among whom Habib Chatti has already made his return, regaining presidential favor at the end of 1978. Although the SDM was refused recognition as a legitimate political party in 1978, it was permitted to publish its weekly newspaper for a whole year, before *Er-Rai* was suspended in December 1978, for three months, after which it was permitted to resume publication. The editor, Hassib ben Ammar, is another former minister who has fallen from presidential and party favor.

It appears that this "liberal" tendency is being kept in the wings, not accorded official legitimacy, yet not completely suppressed. As it functions over time, it can only gain more strength and leadership experience. What is not clear is whether it is favorably viewed as a "safety escape route" for a shift in power (its ideology is closer to the Destour than is the MUP platform), or whether it is considered too strong to suppress in view of widespread public support, despite a desire to eliminate the opposition. At present, Bourguiba appears to have adopted a tactic of "cooptation," resuming contacts with Mestiri and his followers within the context of the PSD.

Thus, in terms of future elite circulation, at least four possible contending groups are identifiable outside of the incumbent party and administrative elites, each with its identifiable leadership. The most clearly defined clusters of political alternatives are: (1) the leftist groups — including ben Salah and other leaders of the MUP, the Communist Party leadership identified by Toumi (1978), and the organizers of the 26th of January Collective, operating from Paris; (2) the (relatively) rightist (liberal) faction of Mestiri and the Socialist Democratic movement; (3) the growing Islamic revivalist movement, with its elite of religious leaders, teachers and scholars, including some traditionalist university instructors; and (4) the enigma of the military, which is growing in strength but appears submissive to government (civilian) control. Its leadership is least known of the four groups, but there has been some evidence of army officers beginning to assume political roles. Also, Toumi (1978, p. 374–75) cites two 1978 changes in the National Service (military) laws. The first provides for military service to be served "on the job" for workers with militarily relevant occupations (factory workers, etc.). During the time of military service, workers cannot strike or leave work without permission of the military. In addition to bringing some individuals under military control in important industries, this law has the further effect of justifying a military police presence on a permanent basis (there will always be some people doing national service) in a wide range of enterprises. The second legal change created a compulsory one-year "civilian service" for all unemployed men between the ages of 18 and 30. The term of service is renewable at the discretion of the authorities, and is served in special work centers. In 1979, newspaper reports indicated that unemployed youth were being rounded up in public places (cafés, etc.) for this service (*Le Monde*, June 22, 1979, p. 4). These developments could have signaled a growing influence of the military, as well as suggesting that the government feels confident that it is in control. Such potential for increased military involvement in social control has, in other Middle Eastern and African countries, led to take-overs by military elite groups, so the possibility cannot be ruled out in Tunisia. However, by mid-1980 it was reported that these programs were no longer operative, and most "civilian service" camps had been emptied (*The Economist*, January, 5, 1980). The potential of the military for involvement in a power play for leadership has correspondingly diminished.

There is also recent evidence of a fifth source of alternate elites, which may or may not be related to the groups identified above. Small, dissident political groups are emerging; their existence is evidenced by trials of 38 people in June 1979 for membership or activity in illegal political organizations such as the Revolutionary Party of the Tunisian People and the National Front for the Liberation of Tunisia (*Le Monde*, June 9, 1978, p. 6). Another group, Ech-Chaàb Clandestin, was apparently responsible for organizing strikes in at least three provincial centers, which resulted in more trials (*Le Monde*, June 22, 1979, p. 4). *Ech-Cha'ab* was the name of the trade union (UGTT) newspaper, suspended when union leader Habib Achour was arrested in 1978. Thus, this group evidently has trade union ties and continued illegally publishing an underground newspaper through 1978, for which some members were tried (*Le Monde*, March 5, 1980) after reports of its editor having been tortured during imprisonment (*London Times*, December 31, 1979). All three groups' names suggest leftist revolutionary identity and may signal the emergence of a fifth potential source of elite incumbency. Such a wide range of identifiable alternate elite groups is a new development in the previously unified and (outwardly) peaceful Tunisian politican scene.

At lower levels, current (young) elite aspirants face a nearly insurmountable problem of blocked mobility. Positions were occupied in the early years of independence by available incumbents who may have been marginally qualified for the jobs. Over the years, all necessary positions were filled, at the same time that new aspirants to elite status were entering the job market better trained and more highly qualified than their elders (Allman, 1976). People who found positions often grew to realize they were more competent than their superiors but could not aspire to replace them; this created a "generational tension" which is mounting over time. Thus, at lower levels, the problem is lack of elite circulation.

The most pressing question on Tunisian elite circulation is: What happens after Bourguiba? He has been in poor health for so long that speculation on this issue has appeared in the literature for at least 15 years. This long-standing uncertainty over the timing of his demise is a major contributing factor to tension among the Tunisian elite. It is clear that opposition forces advocating system transformation will remain in abeyance until he dies or retires from public life, although how he has managed to avert overthrow is puzzling. A plausible explanation, suggested above, is that the elite, among themselves, have dreaded the succession question enough to agree to defer it as long as possible. While Bourguiba lives, Tunisian political change is characterized as being in "suspended animation" (*New York Times*, June 10, 1979). The succession question is complex, involving at least three issues—personality, party, and political structure.

The issue of personality is at present determined, if the structure holds. A 1975 constitutional amendment clarified that the Prime Minister would take over on the death of the President. However, M'zali's ability to do so, and to maintain the Bourguiba style of leadership, on which the system hinges, is questionable. Will another single "leader" emerge? Will he be from within the existing single-party structure? from one of the alternate elites identified above? from another source of support? Answers to these and other questions can drastically alter the nature of Tunisian elite structure.

What will become of the Destour party after Bourguiba is equally uncertain. Can it remain unified, or will it break down from within? Active participation has waned at the grass roots level, but the formal mass party structure has remained in place and membership has grown in recent years.[2] Can its popular activity be rejuvenated? Will it be broken apart by regionalism? by ideological disputes? by personal power struggles? Informal evidence in support of all these possibilities can be gleaned from observation of elite composition and activities, but no systematic studies are available. Furthermore, the ability of elite analysis to predict future events or assess alternate scenarios must be questioned.

A third possibility is a complete change in the political structure, either through replacement of the Destour party by another political organization (several alternatives have been identified in this chapter), or by transformation of the system into a two-party or multi-party competitive system, or a no-party dictatorship, military or otherwise. Support for all system transformations except the last have been reported among the elite, and no aspiring dictator can be expected to signal his intentions ahead of time. Of all the unknowns indicated here, the likelihood of system transformation involving the legitimation of competing groups seems greatest, but this evaluation is hardly subject to prior testing through research.

CONCLUSION

This chapter has been based on an uneven and eclectic amalgam of published sources and personal observations and interpretations. Among the published sources, systematic research is in the minority, and many published "findings" are nothing more than the observations and interpretations of others, journalists and social scientists who have lived and worked in Tunisia. This approach can be justified because many of the inherently most interesting questions about elites cannot be translated into systematic field research—either because of the nonresearchable nature of the question (future events, alternate scenarios, orientations to action), or because the sensitivity of the issue prevents the research from being carried out (official suppression of research activity, non-cooperation, nonresponse, or dissimulation by subjects or respondents). Sources consulted or relevant to this chapter are listed in the bibliography.

To some extent, existing research approaches do not address (or cannot address) the most relevant questions, given the "state of the art" and because research has been made less possible by increased hardening of government policies, suppression of civil freedoms, and resulting caution by elites. In fact, many important insights cannot be anticipated ahead of time for inclusion in a research plan, and conclusions are often based on informal observation rather than directly interpretable results of objective field research. Much more direct field experience by researchers is required, in a role which will legitimize access to elites and exposure to ongoing events and elite interpretations of them (Stone, 1980).

As for topics requiring further research, in addition to following developments already mentioned in this paper, the experiences of young, highly educated and trained cadres are worthy of observation as they graduate from educational institutions and either integrate into the occupational structure or fail to be absorbed, as the case may be. The combination of high education and expectations, and blocked mobility can be politically explosive, or it can lead to various other forms of coping behaviour such as withdrawal, search for new philosophies or lifestyles, or turning to alternate forms of political organization. However, Toumi claims that to 1978, at least, problems had not appeared (Toumi, 1978, p. 403). Subsequent events, described above, suggest the situation may have changed. Another, low-level elite group worthy of study are young teachers, educated in Tunisia, who are now filling out the needs of the mass education system, replacing French "cooperants." Their own orientations and their approaches to teaching will be crucial to the attitude formation of future generations. (Secondary school teachers staged an independent one-day strike in 1975) (*Maghreb-Machreq*, 68, p. 26–27). Also important are the large numbers of Tunisians studying and working abroad, particularly in France. From the point of view of elite studies, émigré students and those in highly skilled jobs are more important than the many "guest workers" performing manual labor and low-skilled jobs in Europe and richer Arab countries. However, in terms of disruptive political action, "guest workers" have proven to be potentially powerful. In January 1980, the town of Gafsa in southern Tunisia was "attacked" by a group of Tunisian dissidents who had been working in Libya and presumably had been trained there, although they crossed into Tunisia from Algeria. About 40 Tunisians were killed in the raid. After trials two months later, 15 of the accused were condemned to death, of whom 13 were executed (*Le Monde*, March 29, April 17, 1980).

Another 18 remain in jail, despite amnesties for all other "political prisoners" in 1980 (*New York Times*, Aug. 4, 1980).

If experience in other Arab and Moslem countries is any example (including both of Tunisia's neighbors, Algeria and Libya), then the role of religious leaders and institutions, plus religious ideas and practice among elite members, is a topic worthy of observation. In fact, the tie between religiosity and regionalism might be particularly important in Tunisia. For instance, Djerba has a separate religious tradition within Islam (Stone, 1974), and Sfax is reputed to be a more religiously traditional city than Tunis. Saint cults and brotherhoods remain in some other centers, such as Kef. Finally, a system for systematically covering foreign and Tunisian journalism, or periodic intensive content analyses, can yield a view of the overall pattern of evolving events, although the *Annuaire d'Afrique du Nord* now produces excellent annual interpretive chronologies of events.

NOTES

1. Even university tuition is free to all students who qualify. In addition, needy students receive grants for living expenses. In 1976–77, for instance, almost two-thirds (62.4%) of the 23,137 university students received government aid. (*Annuaire d'Afrique du Nord*, 16, 1977, pp. 676–678).

2. Figures for 1971 showed 345,000 P.S.D. members, which grew to 552,000 in 1976. (*Annuaire d'Afrique du Nord*, 16, 1977, pp. 533–534)

REFERENCES

Allman, James (1976) "Social Mobility After Independence," in Russell A. Stone and John Simmons, Eds., *Change In Tunisia*. Albany, New York: State University of New York Press.

Amin, Samir (1970) *The Maghreb in the Modern World*. London: Penguin (English translation of:) *Le Maghreb moderne*. Paris: Editions de Minuit.

Area Handbook (1978–1979) *Area Handbook for the Republic of Tunisia*. Washington, D.C.: U.S. Government Printing Office.

Ashford, Douglas Elliott (1965) *Morocco-Tunisia; Politics and Planning*. Syracuse, N.Y.: Syracuse University Press.

Ashford, Douglas Elliott (1967) *National Development and Local Reform, Political Participation in Morocco, Tunisia and Pakistan*. Princeton, N.J.: Princeton University Press.

Belhassen, Souhayr (1979) "L'Islam Contestaire en Tunisie," *Jeune Afrique*, 949, 950, 951 (March): 81–84, 65–69, 89–92.

Belhassen, Souhayr (1980) "L'Armee Tunisienne, Une Grande Inconnue," *Jeune Afrique*, 1043 (December): 178–184.

Ben Salem, Lilia (1969a) "Démocratisation de l'enseignement en Tunisie." *Revue Tunisienne de Sciences Sociales* 16 (March): 81–135.

Ben Salem, Lilia (1969b) "Origines Geographiques et Sociales des Cadres de l'Administration Economique des Offices et Sociétés Nationales en Tunisie," in *Annuaire de l'Afrique du Nord*—1968. Paris: Centre National de la Recherche Scientifique, 107–127.

Ben Salem, Lilia (1976) "Development et problème de cadres. Le cas de la Tunisie—Les cadres superieurs de l'économie tunisienne." *Cahiers du C.E.R.E.S.* (Série Sociologique) 3 (juin): 1–234.

Bishtawi, Kathleen (1978) "Tunisia at the Crossroad." *The Middle East* 42 (April): 25–29.

Boukraa, Ridha (1974) "Industrialisation et Industrialité: Les Attitudes des cadres superieurs de la nouvelle industrie Tunisienne." *Revue Tunisienne de Sciences Sociales* 36–39, 155–173.

Camau, Michel (1973) "Le Discours Politique de Légitimité des Elites Tunsiennes," in M. Teitler *et al.*, *Elites, Pouvoir et Legitimité au Maghreb*. Paris: Centre National de la Recherche Scientifique, 29–72.

Camau, Michel, Gérald Dubray and Noureddine Sraieb (1973) "La Tunisie," Chapter VII in Lhachmi Berrady *et al.*, *La Formation des Elites Politiques Maghrébines*. Paris: Librarie Générale de Droit et de Jurisprudence.

Carter, Gwendolen, (Ed) (1962) *African One-Party States*. Ithaca, New York: Cornell University Press.

Chenoufi, Ali (1975) "Note sur le Collège Sadiki 1875–1975." *Cahiers de Tunisie* 26 (No. 91–92): 371–394.

Clausen, Ursel (1976) *Tunisie Notes biographiques*. Hamburg, Germany: Deutsches Orient-Institut.

Disney, Nigel (1978) "The Working Class Revolt in Tunisia." *MERIP Reports* 67, 12–14.

Emmecey, Jean (1975) "La Tunisie," p. 83–97 in Chapter V "Les Elites Politiques du Maghreb," in W.K. Ruf *et al.*, *Introduction a L'Afrique du Nord Contemporaine*. Paris: Centre de la Recherche Scientifique.

Entelis, John P. (1974) "Ideological Change and An Emerging Counter-culture in Tunisian Politics." *Journal of Modern African Studies* 12, 4, 543–568. The introductory footnote to this article contains a full bibliography of the Tunisian political development literature.

Flory, Maurice (1975) "Etats Maghrébins et Cooperation pour le Développement," in W.F. Ruf *et al.*, *Introduction a L'Afrique du Nord Contemporaine*. Paris: Centre Nationale de la Recherche Scientifique, Chapter 9 241–253.

Hahn, Lorna (1972) "Tunisian Political Reform: Procrastination and Progress." *Middle East Journal* 26: 4 (Autumn): 405–414.

Hermassi, Elbaki (1972) *Leadership and National Development in North Africa*. Berkeley, California: University of California Press.

Holley, Charles (1977) "Tunisia After Bourguiba: On Verge of Succession Crisis." *The Middle East* 37 (Nov.): 51–53.

Kacem, Abdelaziz (1974) "La Politique Culturelle Tunisienne." *Annuaire de L'Afrique du Nord*, 1973: 29–44.

Kerr, Malcolm H. (1976) "Political and Economic Trends in North Africa," Chapter 14 in A.L. Udovitch (ed), *The Middle East: Oil Conflict and Hope*. Lexington, Mass.: Lexington Books/D.C. Heath.

Martel, Pierre-Albin (1975) "Tunisie, Le Temps des Gestionnaires." *Maghreb-Machreq* 67, 46–51.

Micaud, Charles A. (1971) "Politics in North Africa—Tunisia." *Africa Today* 18: 4 (Oct.): 60–64.

Micaud, Charles A. (1974) "Bilingualism in North Africa: Cultural and Sociopolitical Implications." *Western Political Quarterly* 27, 1 (March): 92–103.

Micaud, Charles A., Clement Henry Moore, and Leon Carl Brown (1964) *Tunisia: The Politics of Modernization.* New York: Praeger.

Moore, Clement Henry (1970) *Politics in North Africa: Algeria, Morocco and Tunisia.* Boston: Little Brown.

Moore, Clement Henry (1965) *Tunisia Since Independence: The Dynamics of One-Party Government.* Berkeley, California: University of California Press.

Nerfin, Marc (1974) *Entretiens avec Ahmed ben Salah.* Paris: Francois Maspero.

Poncet, Jean (1974) *La Tunisie à la Recherche de Son Avenir: Independance ou Neocolonialisme?* Paris: Edition Sociales.

Rudebeck, Lars (1969) *Party and People: A Study of Political Change in Tunisia.* New York: Praeger.

Said, Rafik (1970) *Cultural Policy in Tunisia.* Paris: UNESCO.

Schaar, Stuart (1977) "Le Jeu des Forces Politiques en Tunisie." *Maghreb-Machreq* 78, 70–73.

Sraieb, Noureddine (1973) "Enseignement, Elites et Systèmes de Valeurs: Le Collège Sadiki de Tunis," in M. Teitler *et al., Elites, Pouvoir et Légitimité au Maghreb.* Paris: Centre Nationale de la Recherche Scientifique, 107–140.

Stemer, Elisabeth (1974) "Le IXe Congress du Parti Socialiste Destourien." *Maghreb-Machreq*, 66, 20–23.

Stevens, Paul B. (1973) *Language Use Patterns of Tunisian Elites.* Washington, D.C.: USIA, Office of Research and Assessment, August, Doc. R-18-73, Mimeo. The bibliography in this paper is a complete source of studies relating to Tunisian elite communications and language use to 1971. The paper contains a detailed analysis of existing studies, with policy-relevant conclusions.

Stone, Russell A. (1973) "Anticipated Mobility to Elite Status Among Middle Eastern University Students." *International Review of History and Political Science*, X, 3 (Nov.): 1–17.

Stone, Russell A. (1974) "Religious Ethic and Capitalism in Tunisia." *International Journal of Middle East Studies*, V, 3 (June): 260–273.

Stone, Russell A. (1980) "The Impact of Elites and their Future Study," Chapter 7 in I. William Zartman (ed.) *Elites in the Middle East.* New York: Praeger.

Tessler, Mark A. (1980) "Political Change and the Islamic Revival in Tunisia." *The Maghreb Review*, 5, 1 (Jan.–Feb.): 8–19.

Tiers, Joëlle and Werner K. Ruf (1975) "La Press en Tunisie," in W.K. Ruf *et al., Introduction a L'Afrique du Nord Contemporaine.* Paris: Centre National de la Recherche Scientifique, Chapter 13, 319–337.

Toumi, Mohsen (1975) "La Scolarisation et le Tissu Social en Tunisie." *Revue Francaise d'Etudes Politiques Africaines*, 10, 109 (Jan.): 32–61.

Toumi, Mohsen (1978) *Tunisie, Pouvoirs et Luttes.* Paris: Le Sycomore.

Zartman, I. William (1975) "The Elites of the Maghreb: A Review Article." *International Journal of Middle East Studies*, 6, 495–504.

Zghal, Abdelkader (1973) "The Reactivation of Tradition in a Post-Traditional Society." *Daedalus*, 102, 1 (Winter): 225–238.

Newspapers, Periodicals, and Yearbooks

Le Monde
The Times of London
The New York Times
The Economist — London
Jeune Afrique
Maghreb-Machreq
Revue Tunisienne de Sciences Sociales — CERES — Tunis
Annuaire de L'Afrique du Nord — CRESM-Aix
The Middle East and North Africa — Europa Publications

5

Libya: Personalistic Leadership of a Populist Revolution

RAYMOND A. HINNEBUSCH

THE LIBYAN REVOLUTION: CRUCIBLE OF A NEW ELITE

The Libyan Arab Popular Republic of Mu'ammar Qaddafi is the youngest of the "family" of authoritarian nationalist-populist states which emerged throughout the Middle East in the last three decades as direct imperialism receded from the area and traditional oligarchies gave way before new social forces. The new Libya, radical nationalist in orientation, based on an alliance of middle- and lower-class political forces, and authoritarian in political structure — is the handiwork of a wholly new political elite. This elite and the state it has forged are best understood as the products and expression of a national and social revolution in Libya.

The new elite must first of all be seen as part of an Arab nationalist revolt against imperialism and its local residues and consequences — local client elites, the fragmented regional state system, and an outward-looking, dependent economy. Under the monarchy, Libya did enjoy nominal political independence but was in fact a creature of the West. The foreign military bases and great oil companies on her soil overshadowed a deferential traditional elite, dependent wholly on Western subsidies or oil royalties. The rise of oil production only made Libya more of an appendage of the Western capitalist market as agricultural self-sufficiency gave way to the exchange of oil for imported consumer goods and as a proliferating comprader bourgeoisie forged hundreds of new bridges Westward. The oil sector remained an enclave in the Libyan economy, fueling a disproportionate growth of the tertiary sector but contributing little to the development of a national productive base. Moreover, as Libya's integration with the West grew tighter, so was she alienated from the Arab-Islamic world to which a majority of the newly politicizing classes felt a strong attachment. By the late sixties, the traditional Libyan elite was increasingly perceived by the growing segment of politically conscious Libyans as a client of the West and underserving of political legitimacy on that account. The officers who carried out the *coup* in September 1969 were perhaps chiefly motivated by a desire to break Libya's dependency on the West and reintegrate her into the Arab-Islamic world.

Once in power, the new elite reacted swiftly against the Westernization and appendization of the country, making palpable efforts, if incomplete in their effect, to reverse these processes. The foreign bases have been removed; the oil has been nationalized, its proceeds now funneled into the creation of a productive base; the comprador bourgeoisie has been weakened; and the economy has been made less outward oriented and potentially less dependent. A stronger, more modern state seems to be in formation. Libya has, in spirit at least, rejoined herself to the Arab-Islamic world. Yet, as in many of the Arab mini-states left behind by imperialism, the project of building a new nation-state remains profoundly ambiguous. Loyalties and identities are caught between the big nation — the Arab *umma*, that seemingly unattainable but most desired political community — and the little potential nation — Libya — attained, but, for Libyans like Mu'ammar Qaddafi, an entity hardly able to evoke strong identifications. Thus, a constant crisis of nation building pervades Libyan politics, fueling conflict over Libya's place in the Arab world and the world arena. It is Libya's relatively late confrontation with these problems of emerging statehood as compared with her neighbors (especially Egypt and Tunisia, well advanced beyond the early nationalist stage), which accounts for her role in inter-Arab politics — the radical anti-imperialist, anti-Zionist, and Arab unionist stance which the more "mature" modernizing states have largely discarded.

The new regime in Libya must also be seen as part of a social revolution. Briefly, it represents the breakthrough of the emergent middle class, and subsequently of elements of the politicized lower classes into a political system heretofore dominated exclusively by the traditional upper classes. This breakthrough resulted from the special conditions of a distinctive state of development.

By the late 1960s, the Libyan monarchy and the traditional establishment appear to have been moribund. This was in good part the result of social changes let loose in the country by the impact of oil wealth: massive migration to the cities produced by new opportunities in the oil sector or the expanding state bureaucracy snapped many of the ties of dependency and clientage constituting the substructure on which the monarchy rested, while the growth of new appetites stimulated by petrodollars and imports eroded the puritanical Islam which was the ideological cement of the regime. The growth of non-agricultural employment, and the oil-financed expansion of the instruments of social mobilization — infrastructure, education, mass media — began to generate new social forces only tenuously integrated into the traditional structure and increasingly susceptible to political alienation from it. A middle class emerged which, though still small, was strategically situated at a time of traditional breakdown. A significant entrepreneurial bourgeoisie hardly existed, but there were clusters of old families in importing and contracting, and their sons, often educated in the West and exposed to nationalism, liberalism, and the idea of modernization, were rapidly losing sympathy with the monarchy. Of greater social weight was a salaried new middle class or petit bourgeoisie emerging from the masses, nourished by the bloating of the bureaucracy and the creation of a new army. In addition to national grievances, demands issued from this new political force for a redistribution of wealth and power and a more serious modernization effort. The new officer corps in particular was rapidly crystallizing into a radical reformist center of political ferment. The lower classes, albeit at a slower rate, were also politically awakening. Partly proletarianized, partly lumpenproletarianized and atomized, and sharing many of the grievances of the middle class, they were increasingly "available" for political mobilization.

Yet the development of these new forces had not, by the end of the sixties, translated into a qualitative change in the practice of Libyan politics; for, although the traditional tribal elite and the bourgeoisie which dominated politics were now occasionally joined in such activity by small groups of middle class students and intellectuals and conspiritorial circles in the officer corps and although the semi-proletarianized masses occasionally took to the streets in anti-regime disturbances, the political game largely remained the province of small personalized groupings lacking organized mass bases. The old regime possessed neither the desire, the legitimacy nor the political infrastructure to absorb the political discontents of the new groups into organized participation, and they, in turn, lacked the political resources and habits to organize on a significant scale from below. Thus, by the eve of the revolution, no one political force or alliance of forces any longer controlled the political arena, while rising new social forces on its rim were on the verge of being mobilized into it. Into this political vacuum moved the Free Officers. They intended to carry out a social revolution — of some kind — in Libya.

The conditions from which the new elite emerged have greatly shaped the subsequent development of the regime. Dependent on and accountable to no other political force, the new leaders had no need — or intention — of sharing power and diluting their conception of revolution. Indeed they set out to centralize power in a stronger, bigger state and to drive competing forces from the political arena. This does not mean that they were unconcerned to build a popular support base or encourage participation on certain terms. But their relative monopoly of power, the weakness of rivals, and the fluidity of the socio-political structure at the time gave them a unique chance to shape the political arena — and indeed the whole social system — in their own way and on their own terms. Seeking to curb the social power of higher status opponents and to build support among the classes from which they came and identified, they have used populist policies to redistribute resources to the lower-middle and lower classes. Taking advantage of the favorable conditions of post-coup Libya — nationalist self-assertion and the emergence of newly politicized groups — the leader of the revolution, Colonel Qaddafi, has made a credible bid for charismatic leadership. Not satisfied with passive support, he has encouraged the rising of the masses and their active participation in politics — albeit on his own terms. In this way the regime has mobilized a mass constituency into the political arena on its side. Its experimentation with new political forms meant to institutionalize this participation — forms which bear equal resemblance to the mass organization of "popular democracies" and to traditional "desert democracy" — have given Libya a political structure unique in the contemporary world. As a result, the originally exclusively military character of the regime has been substantially altered. The new Libyan state which has emerged over the last decade is, thus, more than most others, a conscious creation of a political elite. The following pages will explore how and why Qaddafi and his comrades in arms have so shaped Libya according to a personal vision of revolution.

ELITE DESCRIPTION

The description of Libyan political elites can conveniently start with a brief sketch of the pyramid of power, distinguishing the various levels of the elite. The leader, Colonel Qaddafi, and his close associates in the Free Officers movement — as initially institutionalized in the Revolutionary Command Council (RCC) — can be taken as the *core elite*. High state officials and managers, especially ministers, and lesser members of the Free Officers movement, can be seen as the *general elite*. Local officials and the activists of mass organizations and popular councils can be seen as the *sub-elite*.

The Core Elite

The core elite in Libya has been a quite small group, consisting originally of twelve officers, only five of whom are today still politically active (marked below by an asterisk). The majority of those politically inactive have lost out in intra-elite conflict since 1969.

*Mu'ammar Qaddafi
*Abdel Salam Jalloud
*Mustafa Kharubi
*Abu Bakr Yunis
*Khweldi al-Hameidi

Muhammed Najm
Mukhtar Qarawi
Bashir Hawadi
Abdel Munim al-Huni
Awad Ali Hamza
Omar Muhayshi
Muhammed Magaryef

Mu'ammar Qaddafi is, by far, the most powerful of this core elite, and indeed it would not be an exaggeration to see the dynamics of Libyan politics since the revolution as chiefly growing out of the attempt of Qaddafi to impose his gradually unfolding messianic vision on a sometimes recalcitrent society. As such, a description of the Libyan political elite cannot dispense with a brief analysis of Qaddafi's belief system, its strengths, and its vulnerabilities.

Elite Ideology: Qaddafi's Belief System

Mirella Bianco's depiction of Qaddafi as a prophetic "voice from the desert" is not entirely fanciful. Qaddafi clearly does see himself as a man with a messianic vision and does seem to have that supreme inner conviction that he alone in a corrupt world is righteous and right, which is typical of the prophet; and, like other prophets, he too must contend with the cynicism of the worldly and the competition of "false gods" (Bianco 168–70). Qaddafi's self-assumed mission is, of course, to regenerate the Arab nation and return it to its once-leading position in the world; this must be done by purging it of the two main causes, in Qaddafi's view, of its decline — its disunity and, owing to foreign cultural invasion, the loss of its authentic Arab-Islamic values. Thus, the first and central component of Qaddafi's belief system is Arab nationalism.

From Arab nationalism springs Qaddafi's abiding preoccupation with inter-Arab politics, his desire to "nationalize" the Arab-Israeli conflict (that is, to bring all Arab resources to bear on the elimination of the most dangerous of all foreign penetrations), and his intense desire to initiate the process of Arab unification — indeed, to make Libya the "Savoy" of the Arab world. For Qaddafi, thus, the focus of national identity is not Libya, but the Arab world; Libya is merely the base — and a poor one at that — from which he has sought to project his vision and leadership to the rest of the Arab world. A Libyan national-state, poorly endowed with human and natural resources — excepting oil — and lacking any distinctive national tradition of its own — in contrast, for example, to Egypt — can hardly be satisfying to Qaddafi. Qaddafi's desire to merge Libya into the Arab world represents, in a sense, a struggle against what might be called the "Kuwaitization" of Libya, the perhaps inevitable tendency of Libyans to look inward and loose their Pan-Arab identity in the enjoyment of the country's oil wealth. From Qaddafi's point of view, this can only be a moral degeneration—a turning of Libya into a nonproducing, Western-dependent, wasteful island of consumerism in a surrounding sea of poverty. From his Pan-Arab point of view, even a concentration on the modernization of Libya, Algerian style, can lead to a dangerous confusion of priorities (Leveau 87–9).

This Pan-Arab vision undoubtedly has enormous emotional and idealistic appeal in a Libya which has only recently recovered its Arab identity; it also, however, has some very clear vulnerabilities. It must pull against the natural course which seeks to preserve Libyan oil wealth for the Libyans. Arab unity requires partners, and Qaddafi has notably failed to find suitable or willing partners; indeed, he has succeeded in antagonizing, at one time or another, all the Arab leaders, at times virtually isolating Libya from the Arab arena. As Ruth First (1974) says, Qaddafi is the only Arab leader with the stomach for struggle with Israel, but Libya is too far from the front line to make much difference in the conflict. Libya, with its tiny population and peripheral location, generally seems ill suited to support Qaddafi's ambitious designs. How long can an ideology be convincing or win converts when its practical realization remains so illusive? It seems very possible that Qaddafi will end up having to content himself with far less than the leadership of a Pan-Arab union—much like the Ba'th party—or burn himself out.

A correlary of Qaddafi's brand of Arab nationalism is his intense rejection of all things foreign—in his view, all the works of imperialism—and his desire to purge Libya of such influences, whether Western capitalist or communist, and to create an authentically nativist "third way" based essentially on Islam. Islam is thus the second major component of his belief system. For Qaddafi there is no conflict between Arabism and Islam; rather, a reinvigorated Islam is the key to Arab rebirth.[1] For Qaddafi, Islam can be the motivating, disciplining source of moral activism needed to mobilize the Arabs for national reconstruction. Moreover, Qaddafi holds that the Quran contains all the answers to the problems of modern men. Despite his puritanism on matters of personal morality—such as consumption of alcohol and relations of the sexes—Qaddafi, is however, no literalist; he is closer to the fundamentalist tradition of Ibn Taymiyya (d. 728/328), which combines stress on inner moral activism with a liberal acceptance of *ijtihàd*, the need to interpret the meaning of the Quran in changing conditions. Far from accepting the accumulated traditions of Islamic law, Qaddafi wants to sweep the *shari'a* away, while arrogating to himself the role of *mujtàhid*, reinterpreter of the Quran for modern Islam. Needless to say, Qaddafi's fundamentalism has not prevented him from adopting and importing on a massive scale all the products of modern technology.

There is no doubt that Qaddafi's Islamism has elicited a considerable response from the deeply religious Libyan masses, especially newly mobilizing elements which have yet to be greatly exposed to foreign influence.

But it too has its vulnerabilities. Qaddafi's radical nativism comes into direct confrontation with a powerful countertrend of cosmopolitanism among the educated classes. His religiosity separates him from secular nationalist intellectuals who otherwise would be natural allies. It is questionable whether the Quran, however interpreted, can serve as the basis for a programmatic ideology of modernization, and Qaddafi's efforts to so reshape Islam open him to attack from the traditional religious establishment. As Herve Bleuchot suggests, Qaddafi may find Islam less effective as an ideology of change than as an obstacle to it, readily invoked by conservative opponents (Bleuchot, 1975a).

The third element in Qaddafi's belief system, "Arab Socialism," was, at least initially, a kind of populistic reformism which preserved, while reshaping, an increasingly capitalist, indeed state capitalist, economy. It has entailed the extension of national control over the economy through state planning, investment and regulation, Libyanization and nationalization of larger enterprises, and a modest redistribution of wealth and opportunity through measures such as minimum wages, progressive taxation, state employment, and the welfare state. It attacks monopolistic capitalism and the big accumulation of wealth but preserves the principle of private property, per se; it seeks to reduce class gaps but accepts class differences as inevitable (Bianco, Breton, 1970, First, Bleuchot, 1975b). Thus, it has all the advantages and disadvantages of populism. It is likely to appeal strongly to the rising petty bourgeoisie as it seeks to turn itself into a state bourgeoisie. It increases the control of the newly emergent state over its own resources, curbing its hitherto extreme extroversion and, in principle, providing a means for state capital accumulation and investment. On the other hand, it may alienate the national capitalist class and undermine capitalist rationality and initiative without creating an alternative principle of motivation and reward, put the economy in the hands of a sluggish and inefficient bureaucracy, and invite the expansion of consumption, especially by the middle sectors of society.

By the late 1970s, however, Qaddafi seemed to be moving toward a more Marxist conceptualization of society. In the *Green Book* he accepted the Marxist argument that hiring the labor of others is exploitation, per se, and, as such, seemed to reject private ownership of the means of production. There subsequently followed major assaults on the private sector and experimentation with worker self-management and cooperative forms of ownership, and, although the final outcome of this experimentation remains uncertain, a more radical variant of the populist model appears to be emerging in Libya today.

The Core Elite: A Social Profile

It is generally accepted that the leaders of the Libyan revolution came from quite modest social backgrounds. Ruth First states that the Free Officers represented the oases and the interior as against the coastal cities, and the minor depressed tribes against the major aristocratic ones. Significantly, many were originally from social strata lower than the petty bourgeoisie (First, 1974).

Qaddafi, at least, can almost certainly be considered as coming from a lower-class Bedouin family. His family lived in a tent, and in order to go to school the young Qaddafi had to walk thirty miles to the nearest town, Sirte, and seek quarters in the local mosque. He and a handful of other students of nomadic background were poorer and of lower social status than other students, and even in a small town like Sirte they were looked down upon by the children of townsmen. But Qaddifi's tent-home was not uncomfortable, and the young Qaddafi's family does not seem to have been destitute. In short, Qaddafi appears to have come from the upper strata of the lower class (Bianco 3–13).

The other members of the original RCC seem to have come, in roughly equal proportions, from middle- and lower-class backgrounds. According to data provided by Fathaly and Palmer (1980: 46), only one of the top Free Officers (Muhayshi) was of "upper-middle class" background, while four (Magaryef, Qarawi, Huni, and Najm) were middle class, and seven (including Qaddafi) were "poor." Thus, the center of gravity of the top elite seems to span the lower-middle lower class divide.[2] As such, it appears that Libya's top political elite resembles less the Tunisian, Egyptian, and Algerian elites, which are more clearly of middle-class origins than the Syrian and South Yemenese elites, which have deeper roots in the lower classes. Thus, it may not be surprising that, politically, many of the Libyan revolutionaries seem to have felt closer to the lower than to the middle classes and that their steadily radicalizing policies continue to draw them toward the leftwing of the populist spectrum. Nevertheless, the Libyan elite-to-be was clearly upwardly mobile through education and recruitment into middle class occupations by the time of the power seizure.[3]

By occupation and educational background, the core elite is exclusively military.[4] Their educational credentials are not impressive: None seems to have gone beyond high school and the two-year period of military training. Since they were mere junior officers at the time of their seizure of power, they lacked even the advanced military-political training that many of the Egyptian Free Officers had acquired, and there is so far no evidence that any of them have subsequently tried to acquire more education — that is, to become "officer-technocrats," as did many of the Egyptian officer elite. Qadafi is said to have sporadically attended history classes at the university and his ideological preoccupations suggest he is trying to educate himself, while Jalloud has evidently acquired a good deal of "on-the-job" administrative training. But generally the Libyan top elite cannot be considered intellectuals except in the loosest sense; indeed, they evince a strong streak of anti-intellectualism. Educational credentials are, of course, no indispensable part of a good politician's background, but the very modest educational exposure of Libya's new elite compares unfavorably with many other Middle Eastern and third world elites. It may certainly be asked whether such educational short-comings do not deprive the elite of technical skills and broadened vision which could contribute to their ability to preside competently over Libya's drive to modernize and to establish her place in the world. Much of the erratic character of Qaddafi's policies, especially his foreign policies, may be attributed to a lack of sufficient educational preparation for dealing with a complex world.[5]

Under the old regime, the basic cleavage among elites was regional; the rivalry between Cyrenacia and Tripolitania and strong localistic loyalties exercised a powerful centrifugal pull on the state. Such tendencies seem to have been considerably reduced under the new elite. The available evidence indicates that the new elite is not drawn disproportionately from certain regions (Fathaly and Palmer 1980: 46). Regional cleavages seem to have largely disappeared as an important factor in politics. If Qaddafi's personal history is typical, localistic identities have been greatly diluted by geographical mobility. Thus, Qaddafi was born on the coast between Tripoli and Cyrenacia, later attended high school in the interior (Fezzan), and then on the coast again, west of Tripoli. The small spaces of Libya, increasingly tied together by modern transport, seem to have eroded localism for Qaddafi's generation; his concerns and those of his followers as they emerged from adolesence were Pan-Arab in focus. The political bases of the new elite, once they came to power, appear to be national institutions — notably the army — and perhaps classes, rather than local constituencies. Nevertheless, in times of severe conflict, political actors often fall back on the smaller communities and persons whom they know best and with whom they feel most secure; thus, it is said that Muhayshi, during his conflict with Qaddafi, relied mostly on officers from Misurta, his home area.[6] Muhayshi himself has accused Qaddafi of favoring his own tribe and region (Bleuchot 1976: 353). Thus, the regional or local factor is not wholly inoperative. One other similar possible cleavage, the Arab-Berber differentiation seems so far of little significance: Khweldi Hameidi and Beshir Hawadi, the two Berbers in the leadership, were on opposite sides in the major intraelite conflict of 1975 (Bleuchot 1974: 323). In general, like Egypt and in contrast to Tunisia, Algeria, Syria, and Iraq, there does not seem to be a noticeably disproportionate representation in the Libyan elite of certain ethnic or regional constituencies, nor do such factors seem to play a prominent role in politics. This may reflect the fact that Libya is a small, rather homogeneous society lacking major vertical cleavages resistant to submergence in a broader identity. The one differentiation which seems to be an exception to this is the urban-rural, center-periphery one. As in Syria, Egypt, and perhaps Algeria and Iraq, the new elite seems to represent the rural periphery against the urban center.

Age is a final characteristic of the Libyan elite worth mentioning; the youth of the new leaders is even more striking than in other populist Arab states. The revolution was the work of junior officers in their twenties rather than, as is more common, middle level officers in their thirties; they deliberately avoided recruitment of older officers into their movement and they subsequently purged such officers from the armed forces. It would be surprising if the generational cleavage were not an important factor in Libyan politics.

The General Elite

The Libyan general elite can be divided into two separate groups. One might be called the second rank of the Free Officer movement, namely those officers, about 60 to 80 in number, who played a role in the coup but remained outside the RCC. Some of these officers have held positions as governors and some have moved into civilian management positions — for example, of state agricultural projects. But in contrast to Egypt, the Libyan army has so far not constituted a dominant political-administrative recruitment pool, and officers have not been seconded on any large scale to the civil bureaucracy or promoted to ministerial rank. Although there is some evidence that the RCC has occasionally consulted with a wider informal body of officers, such a practice appears not to be institutionalized. The officer corps has been confined largely to its professional role — where, indeed, given rapid military expansion, it is most needed — and has played a less overt and continuous political role than in other Middle Eastern "military republics." Nevertheless, it seems safe to say that those who helped make the revolution remain, however informally, major pillars of it and a critical constituency for the core elite.

Civilian ministers and top bureaucrats represent the other component of the general elite. Some of these have been inherited from the old regime, as, given the scarcity of educated talent in Libya, the new elite found it necessary to keep much of the existing bureaucracy intact. Moreover, a few personalities who have served as ministers under the new regime were politically active prior to it — notably Salah Buwaysir, foreign minister for a while, who was a prominent opposition politician under the monarchy. However, subsequent to the revolution, a corps of younger technocratic and administrative elements have been brought into high positions (Leveau 91–6). In addition, there evidently existed a civilian wing of Qaddafi's movement dating back to high school days, and there is evidence that some of its members have received high positions in the state (Bianco 23, 27). Both the older and newer cohorts of the civilian general elite are for the most part said to be well educated, and it seems to be assumed that they are recruited essentially from the urban upper-middle and middle classes. In particular, many carry-overs from the old regime are sons of Tripolitanian bourgeois families educated in the West. This difference in background from the core elite appears to have resulted in serious differences in outlook, straining relations between elements of the core and general elite—a cleavage which, indeed, has been a major source of dynamism in the political system.

The Subelite

The subelite refers to that "second stratum" of local-level leaders charged with mediating between the population and the ruling elite. The regime has fostered two distinguishable groups of subelites. The first, "modernizing officials," were bureaucrats originally appointed in the place of tribal leaders at the levers of local government. They were for the most part urban middle class in origin, often college educated, and on the average somewhat older than the top elite and thus, presumably recruited under the old regime.[7] The "popular revolution" gave rise to a second subelite type. This group, sitting on the popular committees, was younger and of a lower class origin than the modernizing officials and the old tribal chiefs (but above the mass average). Also, they were less educated than the officials, but more so than the traditional leaders (Fathaly, et. al., 1977: 91–102). This group, in short, seems very much like the top elite itself— that is, of lower- or lower-middle-class origin but upwardly mobile through acquisition of some education. The core elite appears to have found the second group more politically congenial, but the first administratively indispensable.

ELITE SOCIALIZATION

The social background variables discussed above have helped determine the basic socialization experiences of the Libyan elite; a closer look at how these experiences have shaped the political attitudes and behavior of the new leaders can help explain the course Libya has taken since the revolution. Some fairly detailed information is available on Qaddafi's socialization experiences, but this is so far largely lacking for the other members of the core elite; as such, one cannot, unfortunately, know just how variations in socialization experience help explain instances of intraelite conflict. But it is Qaddafi's life experience, as it has contributed to his political behavior, which has had the greatest impact on Libya's current development.

Qaddafi's bedouin background, his upbringing in the desert, and his early education in the home by a Quranic tutor contributed the first and doubtlessly the most profound influences to the shaping of his personality and perceptions. To these early life experiences may be attributed Qaddafi's deep sense of attachment to his Arab identity. During this critical period Qaddafi was left almost untouched by foreign influence with the exception that—as his grandfather and father were both involved in the struggle against Italian imperialism—the West was seen as a remote enemy. Thus, as Bleuchot argues, he was left unscarred by that sense of inferiority and profound ambiguity (love-hate relationship) toward his own culture which so characterizes the typical educated Arab. Certainly Qaddafi is the least Westernized of the modernizing Arab elites and stands in considerable contrast to the elites of former French North Africa and Egypt, as well as Libya's own technocratic elite. Also, the deep imprint the Islamic world view has left on him probably owes much to this early upbringing for, as Bleuchot explains, Qaddafi experienced no discontinuity between the world of his childhood and that of the Quran (Bleuchot, 1975a, 70–71). Even today, he continues to look to the desert and the Quran for inspiration; not only does he keep up early habits of Quran reading, but on occasion has returned to his desert tent for meditation.

Qaddafi's early upbringing has also probably helped to shape his social attitudes. The egalitarianism of his style of personal interaction, as well as the simplicity and asceticism of his living habits seem to be characteristic of Bedouin culture. Qaddafi is one of the few heads of state who eschews the pomp and symbolism of office and the inevitable accompanying remoteness from the people, and in this sense, seems to replicate patriarchal desert patterns of leadership.[8] His puritanism and suspicion of the city with its riches, and, in his view, its decadence, corruption, and foreign influence, is not untypical of the desert man. His apparent identification with the less privileged elements of society may also have been shaped by early experiences; for example, he is said to have reacted to the condescension displayed by urban students in his primary school toward those of bedouin background with fierce pride in his bedouin origins.

Finally, his leadership style has certainly been influenced by his desert unbringing. His egalitarian style, and his deep rooted sense of personal honor—and consequent sensitivity to slights—may be part of bedouin culture. So also, may his intensity. Andrew Carvely (1973) argues that Qaddafi exhibits the "clear hardness of belief" which characterizes the desert man; to be sure, the bedouin are also known for unbelief, opportunism, and even treachery, but from Ibn Khaldun's time observers have noticed that, when fired by a religious-ideological vision, the bedouin is transformed into a hardy warrior for his cause. Qaddafi may be such a man.

Central to Qaddafi's socialization as an adolescent was his exposure to modern-style secondary education and simultaneously to Arab nationalism and Nasserism. Going to secondary school meant moving out of the small, localistic milieu; indeed, Qaddafi moved several times from one part of the country to another, helping, perhaps to broaden his "horizons." Significantly, Qaddafi was exposed to modern education mediated by Arabic and Egyptian teachers. In secondary school—glued to Cairo radio—he was agitated by the great struggle being played out between Western imperialism and Arab nationalism. Nasir became the great hero to be emulated; it is well known that Nasir saw his younger self in Qaddafi and that Qaddafi has consciously sought to assume the mantle of Arab nationalist leadership from Nasir. It seems plausible to argue that it was during secondary school, as Qaddafi moved away from the small, tribal milieu into the bigger world, that, searching for a new wider identity, he merged his Bedouinism into an intense, personal identification with the "Arab nation." This identification remains the most distinctive trait of Qaddafi's belief system.

The effect of military education does seem to have left a mark on Qaddafi as well as on the other Free Officers. Qaddafi seems to have learned the value of discipline, hierarchy, and organization as well as a certain contempt for the civilians who lacked all these qualities. He and his colleagues learned certain habits of organization and management of not negligible value in a society where they were very scarce. They also learned habits of command which continue to influence their political style; although their rule has been very unlike that of the conventional military regime, behind much of their political experimentation seems to lurk an ultimate desire to turn all of Libya into a vast citizen army, responsible, motivated, and prepared to take orders from the top. Qaddafi and his military associates do exhibit a clear in-groupness, a suspicion and certain disdain for civilians which has inhibited them from sharing power on a broader basis.

Finally, it seems clear that the 1967 war was, for Qaddafi and his generation, a deeply traumatic experience, comparable to the profound effect of 1948 on the immediately preceding generation. This defeat brought home to Qaddafi how backward and divided the Arab world remained. Whereas for other leaders (like Sadat), its principal effect was a gradual move toward accomodation with the realities of Israel and imperialism, in the youthful Qaddafi, the defeat engendered that spirit of defiance which seems to make him the odd man out among current Arab leaders.

Qaddafi's socialization experiences and the distinctive Arab-Islamic worldview which has emerged from them are both a strength and a vulnerability for his regime. Because they are not dissimilar from those of the semimodernizing masses from which Qaddafi himself has emerged, they represent a sociopsychological elite-mass bond from which has sprung Qaddafi's charismatic leadership and much of the popular support of the regime. But Qaddafi's belief system also sets him apart from many middle- and upper-class Libyans, in particular the general elite elements who, drawn from higher status strata and educated abroad, are much more cosmopolitan in outlook. This represents a basic cleavage in elite political culture and perhaps the major source of instability and conflict in the regime. Moreover, unless Qaddafi can recruit and socialize a new elite which shares his vision, there is little prospect that it can long survive him. In fact, Qaddafi has tried to do this. He has tried to purge the universities — training grounds of future elites — of foreign influence. Compulsory military training is meant to impart to youth a sense of nationalism and civic responsibility. The popular revolution has been used to sponsor the emergence of new elites from the lower strata, whose socialization experiences are similar to the leader's. Nevertheless, there seem to be very serious limits upon how far Qaddafi can hope to go, so long as he is committed to his ambitious modernization program, in effacing the intraelite cultural cleavage. The program has in itself widened, if anything, the exposure of the new generation of Libyans to foreign influence. Foreigners have flooded into the country to do business, while thousands of Libyans sent abroad to acquire modern skills and thereby exposed to cosmopolitan influence are bound to become indispensible elements of the country's leadership. While it is not impossible that in the long run some synthesis of cosmopolitan and nativist values may take place, in the immediate future this intracultural cleavage seems likely to remain basic to Libyan politics.

STRUCTURES

The Libyan Political Model: Ideological and Motivational Roots

The new Libyan elite has invested a great deal of energy since the revolution in forging a new political system designed to embody and facilitate the realization of their values. The outcome of these efforts has been shaped by both the exegencies of power and the elites' conception of certain desirable "models" — notably, Nasserite Egypt and traditional "desert democracy."

The impact of the Naserite experience on Libyan political development since the revolution is, of course, profound; not only were Libyan leaders deeply impressed by Nasir's political style and methods, but, in imitating them, they found themselves facing similar circumstances, problems, and outcomes. Like the Egyptian Free Officers, their movement evolved as a conspiratorial association of army officers bound together more by personal loyalty to the leader and vague nationalistic sentiment than a clear programmatic ideology or formal political organization. This group of friends became, in the aftermath of the coup, the core of the new state, a tight, personalistic network closed to outsiders which, pending the development of more impersonalistic institutions, necessarily constituted the main channels of decision making and the major sinews of collective action at the top. A certain ideological vacuum was also bound to be felt at the top — which Qaddafi has subsequently worked indefatigably to fill. The parallels to Egypt are clear.

As in Egypt, the idea of the military as vanguard of the revolution and of the people became a starting point for the creation of the new state. As in Egypt, so in Libya this translated into a drive to concentrate power in the hands of the military elite and to exclude other political groups from access to decision-making power. The army was held — as the only nationally conscious and popular-based institution — to deserve a special and leading political status. More specifically, the Free Officers who carried out the revolution claim by virtue of this role the continuing right to lead and interpret it; in a sense, it is seen as their "property." While this seems a rather patrimonial concept, it is justified on grounds that the leaders are from and representative of the people. Qaddafi has, with some justification, told intellectuals demanding a broadening of participation in the name of the people that he and his colleagues *are* the people — and by social status far more authentic tribunes of the people than the educated middle class.

Also in imitation of the Naserite model was the repression of (the rudiments of) pluralistic politics in the name of national unity and consensus. Qaddafi shares with Nasir a profound distrust of partisan politics — perhaps partly owing to the military man's contempt for conflict and disorder in the ranks, but more importantly because they are, in his view, a source of division in the Arab nation and conduits for the foreign ideological penetration which he sees as the major causes of the weaknesses of the Arab *umma*. In his *Green Book*, Qaddafi draws on Rousseauist political theory to buttress this position, arguing that a liberal politics of groups results in the exclusive pursuit by different parts of society of their particularistic interests at the expense of other parts and the whole. Likewise, the Marxist-Leninist notion of a single party ruling in the name of proletarian dictatorship is dismissed as the domination of one part of society over another. Thus, as in Nasserite Egypt, all political activity must be on an individual basis and channeled through the all-encompassing mass organization which is supposed to ensure cooperation and peacefully resolve all partisan or social conflicts. No autonomous group political activity is permitted; not only are political parties forbidden, but trade unions, professional associations, and the press are subjected to close government supervision in the name of national unity. It may be argued that Libya has, in any case, little history of organized group politics and that the suppression of its rudiments in the name of consensus is compatible with Libya's traditional political culture; but, by refusing to permit the emergence of group politics based on class or ideology, Qaddafi risks that Libyan political culture will not develop beyond personalistic factionalism based on kinship and locale.

The Nasserite model, in its repression of organized group activity, leaves a political vacuum, a gap between elites and masses which must be bridged if the regime is to develop legitimacy, create stable foundations, and carry out development. In Egypt, this gap was filled by development of a charismatic bond between the leader and the masses, and by the cooptation of the middle class into the bureaucracy and the mass organization. The support thus generated was, however, largely passive, with the result that Nasir was either constrained or content to leave the business of development to the state apparatus. In Libya, the effort to fill the gap has taken a somewhat different form. To be sure, in the person of Qaddafi, the rise of charismatic leadership appealing directly to the masses and unconstrained by institutional checks and accountability procedures can be very clearly seen. Moreover, the regime has been unable to dispense with bureaucratic methods — and not only in technical tasks, for the regime has shown a strong tendency to try to legislate social and even attitudinal change from above by decree law (Bleuchot 1972: 315). Nevertheless, very early Qaddafi showed a tendency to depart from the classic Nasirite model. This can be seen in his efforts to develop a close, direct, face-to-face relation between elite and mass, supposedly a form of "direct democracy." This innovation is meant to by-pass not only bureaucratic structures but also the use of "representatives," parliamentary-style, which Qaddafi insists inevitably usurp the political rights of the people. It can also be seen in his greater concern to stimulate mass activism and his experiments with direct mass action against officials and opponents and in the implementation of social changes. Such a political style is alien to the rulers on the Nile. Qaddafi does seem at times to believe that the voice of the masses, uncontaminated by foreign cultural deformation, should be the authentic guide for the leaders. Yet his attitude toward the masses is profoundly ambiguous, as is evident in his outbursts of impatience with their particularism and their unwillingness to accept responsibility and to work hard for their living and the nation. He desires to transform the people as well as listen to them; thus, he finds himself in the contradictory position of goading the masses to take action, then constantly reproving them for their "mistakes."

Qaddafi's political experiments, legitimized as they have been by appeal to Islamic practices and Arab culture, have inevitably provoked comparison with traditional desert Islamic states or tribal patriarchal forms of government. Bleuchot notes the compatability of Qaddafi's newly created political forms with traditional tribal "democracy" and concludes that they probably do embody authentic if limited forms of participation in the Libyan context (Bleuchot 1975b: 445). There is the stress on *shura*, direct consultation between leader and people, and on reaching decisions by consensus. In some ways, Qaddafi seems to play the role of the tribal chieftian who consults with the people but takes the final decisions and brooks no opposition to them. But if Qaddafi is, in some ways, playing a role legitimized by and expressive of traditional Bedouin or

Islamic practices, it is not that of the patriarch who is merely a broker among the elders nor that of imam bound by the *shari'a*. The role he seems to envision for himself is closer to that of charismatic prophet, ideological innovator, and moral leader in a new *jihad*. There is, of course, a basic tension between the role of charismatic innovator and the effort to create consultative institutions. There may also be a tension between both of these patterns of behavior and efforts to carry out modernization in society through a technocratic elite. Thus does Qaddafi give a new, nativistic twist to the authoritarian populist model. In the following section, these developments will be more closely examined, discussing first interelite and then elite-mass structures.

Central Elite Structures

At the apex of the new Libyan state until 1975 was the Revolutionary Command Council (RCC), the intraelite, policy-making organ headed by Colonel Qaddafi. At the outset, the RCC, as the executive committee of the Free Officers movement, assumed supreme executive, legislative, and judicial powers. Its operations and the relations between the council and its leader, Qaddafi, constituted the main structural underpinning of the core elite.

The functioning of the RCC must be understood by viewing it as an outgrowth of a movement which was, in good part, the creation of Qaddafi. The evidence indicates that Qaddafi was from the beginning clearly dominant figure in the officers movement. He had personally supervised the recruitment and formation of the majority of the movement's cells and many were known only to him. Bianco pictures him as the natural leader of the movement who carefully recruited his followers by winning their personal loyalty and willing compliance with his wishes. Qaddafi is also portrayed as a leader who interacts with his followers in an egalitarian fashion, listens to their opinions, and treats all fairly. But he is definitely rather more than the first among equals. He is clearly the chief activist, ideological innovator, and initiator among the Free Officers. He also appears to be a man so convinced of his mission that he would be unlikely to accept sustained opposition to it from close colleagues.[9] He has undoubtedly dominated top elite councils.

Nevertheless, at least during the initial years of the new regime, the RCC did seem to function as a collective decision-making and conflict-resolution body, and there were incipient tendencies which, though in conflict with a countertrend toward personal charismatic leadership, might have culminated in the institutionalization of some measure of collective leadership. Even before the power seizure, for example, the Free Officer organization had strict rules that decisions of the leadership council could only be taken if all members were present (Bianco 34). In the first years of the revolution the RCC periodically went into extended session behind closed doors; it presented a front of solidarity to outsiders, strictly forbidding members who dissented from its decisions to take conflicts outside the council by seeking public or elite (army or bureaucratic) support (Leveau 92–3). It was possible to disagree with the council or its leader without being purged. Jalloud, observers thought, was even something of an "anti-leader," representative of more pragmatic elements in the regime and as indispensable as Qaddafi by virtue of his growing administrative expertise (although in fact there appears never to have been any irreparable cleavage between the two men). Qaddafi's frequent resignations, in evident reaction to council decisions which went against him, indicated that policy decisions were taken by a majority vote and that Qaddafi could be defied. Even though Qaddafi may in the end have usually gotten his way as the price for withdrawing his resignation, that he was constrained to resort to such tactics seemed to show that his RCC colleagues were not simply his obedient "administrative staff." Still, as Leveau wrote, it was often impossible to know to what extent Qaddafi spoke for a collective consensus and to what extent he acted on his own initiative, with his colleagues hesitant to later disavow his actions (Leveau, 88).

It does appear, however, that, particularly after the failure of some of Qaddafi's Pan-Arab policies and the consequent tarnishing of his image, growing strain was placed on the operations of collective leadership by a conflict between Qaddafi's insistence on having his way, evidently supported by some of his colleagues, and the growing determination of others to curb his independent initiatives. Although his evidence is hardly dispassionate, Muhayshi, Qaddafi's main rival at the time, holds that the "popular revolution" was an effort by Qaddafi to go over the heads of his RCC colleagues and build up personal popular support, that by 1975 RCC meetings had not been held for two years, that Qaddafi used threats and intimidation to get his way, and that, indeed, he had always resented and tried to evade collective leadership constraints (Bleuchot 1975: 451–2). Such claims are probably exaggerated, but in 1975 the RCC did break up when Muhayshi (and at least one other RCC member) tried to topple Qaddafi in a *coup*; when the dust settled, only five of the original RCC members remained (one had been killed previously in an auto accident, so at the time of the break there were eleven left). Clearly, the rules of collective leadership had broken down. While one must be cautious in interpreting the outcome of the conflict, it seems that this event may have spelled the end of collective leadership and the emergence of Qaddafi as undisputed leader, with only those RCC colleagues willing to play the role of loyal lieutenant surviving the showdown. On the other hand, it may be that the surviving rump of the RCC shared with Qaddafi a common policy orientation as against the losers; to the extent this is so, some semblance of team leadership may persist.

Soon after its breakup the RCC was officially disbanded, but, in fact, its rump persisted as supreme policy-making body under the new name of Secretariat of the General People's Congress—the top organ in the new political structure Qaddafi was erecting at the time. Initially the five surviving RCC members alone made up this body, while also dividing up the other strategic regime posts among themselves. Qaddafi remained chief ideologue and policy-innovator, and Jalloud increasingly became the loyal and able chief administrator, a relationship which reminds one of that between Mao and Chou En-Lai. The others—Abu Bakr Yunis, Khweldi al-Hameidi, and Mustafa Kharubi—served as top army and security commanders. In 1979, the new civilian Prime Minister, Ubaydi, joined the Secretariat, but whether his actual political status is equivalent to the officer-politicians seems doubtful. Whether in subservience to Qaddafi or not, the top policy organ has seemed to function harmoniously since the 1975 conflict.

Rather less is known about the structure of relations between the core elite and the general elite. Initially, when relations between the RCC and the cabinet were not clearly defined, there was conflict between the two bodies over how much discretion should be granted to ministers; the first crop of civilian ministers resigned, partly over this issue. Since then a working relationship seems to have been arrived at in which the ministers content themselves with the role of technicians (although on technical matters this could still leave them with considerable discretion, given the modest educational qualifications of the ruling officers.) In the typical cabinet since 1970, RCC members have held only a few of the more critical posts (Prime Minister, Defense, Interior, Foreign Affairs), while civilians have held most of the portfolios. Jalloud, prime minister until 1977, acted as the key link between the RCC as policy-making body and the cabinet as implementor of policy. Leveau has suggested that the minister-technocrats constitute Jalloud's "clientele" and that he has represented their views at the very top (Leveau 95–6). In the absence of formal interest-articulation access points and methods, it seems reasonable to think that civilians would seek a patron in the RCC, if not exclusively Jalloud, perhaps others such as Muhayshi, who served briefly as Planning Minister. It would not be surprising, in fact, if webs of informal personalistic ties between the top and middle elite have developed; in the long run, emergence of the "centers of power" and bureaucratic "fiefdoms" which issued from similar political arrangements in Nasserite Egypt cannot be excluded. Nevertheless, contrary evidence indicative of the relative abstention of the civilian ministers from political and policy conflicts is the fact that not a single minister was purged in the aftermath of the RCC split in 1975. Indeed, the turnover in ministerial portfolios has been remarkably low by Middle Eastern standards, suggesting that politics—whether of the personalistic-patronage or ideological variety—is being kept out of the cabinet by a technocratic ethos. In 1977 Jalloud relinquished his role as prime minister to a civilian, Ubaydi, who, also sitting on the General Secretariat of the General People's Congress, links it and the cabinet in some way. Whether this marks a breakdown in the role segregation between officers and civilians cannot be determined on the basis of available evidence.

As for the second ranks of the Free Officer movement, if any processes of consultation between it and the RCC have been institutionalized, they have not been given public prominence. Leveau refers to a wider consultative body of about fifty persons, including both officers and trusted civilians, but we learn very little definite about it (Leveau 93). Second rank Free Officers do not seem to have been coopted into the inner core or the cabinet to replace officers purged in 1975, as happened under Nasir. Up to now, Qaddafi seems to have excluded both army and bureaucracy from overt political roles, but it seems likely that top unit commanders as part of the general elite carry political weight, if not in the inner councils of the core elite, at least as informal mediators between clients and decision makers.

Elite-Mass Linkage

Qaddafi and his colleagues set out to build structures of elite-mass linkage with dual (to some extent contradictory) aims in mind—namely, to mobilize the active support and participation needed to legitimize the regime and carry out development, but at the same time to channel that participation according to goals determined by the revolutionary leaders (although not necessarily in a vacuum) and to exclude from political action those who would not accept those goals. In doing this their aim was to make the linkage with the masses as direct as possible, minimizing intermediaries. They faced what might be called the "Nasirite dilemma" typical of such systems: Can a regime born of a *coup d'état* by a small group of officers lacking the party "organizational weapon" mobilize the masses from above? The new leaders also wanted to create a new state administrative machine, more modernized and responsive to elite and mass needs. From these felt needs have issued a series of remarkable experiments.

The first structural innovations of the new regime were administrative reforms. At the center there were purges of top elements of the bureaucracy, the introduction of financial controls meant to root out corrupt practices, and an infusion of younger technocrats under the supervision of Jalloud. The central government apparatus was left largely intact, but the following years saw successive efforts to simplify the bureaucratic structure and reduce the duplication of functions and distance between center and periphery.

At the local level, traditional tribal leaders had under the old regime presided over government units corresponding to tribal boundaries. New local government boundaries were now drawn with the aim of breaking up tribal entities, and "modernizing officials" — governors and mayors — were appointed as local chief executives (assisted by elected councils and the local agents of the service ministries). However, the regime was soon dissatisfied with this arrangement: The appointed officials did not perform effectively, did not encourage local participation, and failed, as a result, to become community leaders able to win the masses from the traditional elite on behalf of the modernizing regime (Fathaly, et. al., 1977: 92–99).

The second wave of structural innovation thus followed: an effort to create a Nasirite-style mass organization, the Arab Socialist Union (ASU). It was to answer to multiple purposes: on the one hand it was meant to fill the "vacuum" left by the banning of parties and the effort to dismantle tribal structures, to prevent political activity by both traditional chiefs and party leaders by cutting them off from their bases, and to bring the voluntary organizations, trade and professional unions under government control. On the other hand, it was to mobilize mass support and bring the various social and political forces into a cadre promoting common cooperative activity directed from above. The organization would also function as a check on the bureaucracy and its National Congress as a forum within which policy would be approved.

RCC members themselves launched the experiment, fanning out over the country, presiding over the selection of local leaders, and holding meetings in which they met face-to-face with the masses. By 1972, a pyramid of local, provincial, and national assemblies and committees was elected and set in place. Bianco, who attended some local ASU meetings presided over by the governor in periodic circuits of the province, was impressed by the vigorous level of discussion and the readiness of common folk to criticize officials obliged to defend their performance in these sessions. Problems raised before base level congresses were supposed to be solved by leadership committees in consultation with the administration (Bianco 17–18). Reports stressing the role of the ASU in attending to the problems and grievances of citizens with the bureaucracy and in finding jobs for people have a ring of plausibility. In 1972 Qaddafi presided over the first national congress of 350 delegates (50 appointed) in which vigorous, televised debate took place on the proper form of democracy for Libya. Qaddafi encouraged freedom of expression on the part of the delegates, but stressed that it had to take place within limits: He denounced all foreign political ideologies, liberal or Marxist, as alien to Libya. Conflict over the status of the press went unresolved, but strikes by trade unions were banned. At the next ASU congress in 1973, basic ground rules having been successfully imposed by the regime, debate centered around "who gets what" issues — price rises, taxation, project allocation and delays, regional disparities, and conscription.

The ASU never appears to have generated any great impetus, and it soon appears to have incurred the leader's dissatisfaction. It does not seem necessarily to have neutralized opposition leaders, but instead to have been "infiltrated" by them. In urban areas, nonrevolutionary types or educated middle-class elements lacking in enthusiasm for the regime appear to have reached high places. In rural areas, rather tradition-oriented types had been elected, competition being determined by tribal, personal, and regional solidarities and clientelism. This was hardly surprising in view of the indiscriminate opening of the ASU to all social forces regardless of ideological and political commitments, as well as the prohibition against electoral competition on grounds of alternative policy issues. Moreover, as Qaddafi himself would admit, the organization, created from above, proved little able to mobilize the masses or enlist middle-class commitments. Rather than fighting bureaucracy, the organization itself seemed to be bureaucratized, constituting yet another intermediary structure.

It was evidently in response to these failures of mobilization and control that in 1973 Qaddafi launched his famous "Popular Revolution" (Fathaly, et. al. 1977: 92–99). The Popular Revolution was, in good part, an effort to purge or weaken opposition, but to do so less by police measures than by mass action. One target was the residue of party members in the ASU, the bureaucracy, and the universities. Another was the growing opposition to Qaddafi's projected union with Egypt among middle-class groups and bureaucrats. Qaddafi was also increasingly dissatisfied with the bureaucracy's sluggish performance, lack of service orientation, and tendency to evade political directives by taking refuge in the administrative rules of the old regime. As such, the Popular Revolution signified an effort by the charismatic leader to appeal to the masses over the heads of the intervening bureaucratic and middle strata — in a way not at all unlike the original Chinese model. Muhayshi, indeed, would charge that he also meant to appeal over the heads of the RCC itself (Bluechot 1973: 380–82). Qaddafi, Bleuchot suggests, a genuine populist, expected that the masses, less tainted by foreign influence, were a more congenial base of support for his ideas; unleashing them in the streets would recharge his legitimacy, strengthen his hand in dealing with the middle and subelites, and force the bureaucracy to be more responsive to the citizens. But Ruth First, less convinced, wonders if the Popular Revolution was not more the encouragement of a system of mass informing than a genuine popular rising (First, 1974).

The Popular Revolution appears to have involved two components. First, Qaddafi, in a speech to the crowd, incited the masses to direct "attacks" on various government and social institutions in which, among others, several governors, mayors, managers, and the rector of the university were dismissed. Second, employees were urged to set up "Popular Committees" in their places of work or at the local government level to which those holding authority would be responsible. (At first, at any rate, it seems the committees were given full legislative and executive powers while officials were confined to strictly administrative roles.) The RCC and the Cabinet were exempt from these measures, and Qaddafi undertook to guide the course of mass action, ensuring that it not take on an oppositionist character and reserving for himself the right to tell the new activists when they had not "expressed the general will in a suitable manner."

The incitement of masses to direct action against the structures of the state is certainly unprecedented in the Middle East and could have the effect of altering elements of the political culture which stress subservience to the state and mass political apathy. Fathaly, et al. argue that the Popular Revolution led for the first time to real popular involvement in the selection of local leaders and in the policy-making process. A new type of local leadership did indeed emerge — distinct from both traditional tribal chiefs and educated officials, closer to the masses, and hostile to bureaucratism (Fathaly, et. al., 1977: 97–99). But judging from later complaints about the popular councils, these new political leaders were often poorly prepared to exercise their tasks, were guilty of negligence, incompetence or indiscipline, or took the Popular Revolution as merely an opportunity to leap to positions of power, without showing much concern for popular service. The result seems to have been in some cases an exacerbation of administrative confusion, resulting in increased popular discontent (Bleuchot 1973: 383–84; 1974: 324–25). Accordingly, by late 1973 the committees had been reduced to advisory roles. Throughout 1974 the RCC seemed to be unsure in which direction the popular revolution should be steered. The masses, encouraged to demand better performance from their committees, took to the streets again, often dismissing incumbent committes; frequently, the first group to reach committee headquarters "seized" power, while other groups, later in arriving, set up rival committees. Then, the RCC, dissatisfied with this "anarchy," undertook to organize orderly elections. It is possible that these somewhat divergent signals from the top were an expression of a conflict in the leadership between Qaddafi's more activist policies and more orderly-minded members of the RCC (Bleuchot 1974: 321–144). The old ASU seems also to have thrown its weight against the popular committees in defense of its own role as the central institution for popular participation. In any case, the antipopulist tendency seems to have won out at this time. In the new round of elections, educated middle-class experts tended to replace many of the less cultured mass elements originally incited to action. The role of the committees was officially confined to giving advice, and they were to be subject to supervision by ASU leadership bodies. Thus, popular committees seemed to become a superfluous third structure alongside the ASU and the local government.

In 1975 (subsequent to the breakup of the RCC), however, Qaddafi embarked on another major wave of mobilization and institution building. For the third time, the Popular Revolution was let loose, purging the incumbent popular committees, evidently with the aim of installing pro-Qaddafi militants. Then, in a major organizational rearrangement, the formally disbanded RCC, the Cabinet, the ASU, the unions, professional associations, and the popular committees were all merged into a single institutional structure called "People's Power" (*Sult ash-Sha'b*) in which each of the components assumed a distinct function. People's Power is touted in Qaddafi's famous *Green Book* as a wholly new form of direct democracy—as, indeed, the only real democracy in the world. In actual fact, the new arrangement appears to have been chiefly an effort to systematize and institutionalize the relations and operations of the main political organs which had hitherto emerged from Qaddafi's successive experiments with political structure. The persistence of this structure, largely intact by the turn of the decade, seemed to indicate that this effort had had some success.

The new structure is a pyramid (albeit a flattened one) whose base is constituted of about 186 "Basic Popular Congresses" of around 3,000 persons each, including all the (adult male) population in their territorial boundaries. These basic congresses—the whole people assembled—are, in principle, the locus of all sovereignty, the building blocks of direct democracy. The congresses are too large to sit at once and evidently meet in phases or rotations (but exactly how this works is very unclear). The basic level congresses "choose" leadership committees of ten, including a secretary and two assistants. The leadership committees in a district—the second level of organization—together constitute the district-level congress, which also chooses its (five-man) leadership body. The secretaries and assistants of the basic and district congresses sit in the national level General People's Congress.

Two points as regards the operations of this system peculiar to Qaddafi's conception of direct democracy, must be clarified. First, the leadership organs are not elected by competitive secret balloting. Rather—in traditional tribal fashion—candidates for these positions are chosen by consensus forged through open debate or discussion. Bleuchot points out that this procedure is likely to favor candidates who are known to have the support of the elite and to discourage opponents of the current regime line, who must either withdraw from participation or risk being publically identified as opposition elements. The system may also favor those who enjoy local prestige and who, ensured of support, can afford to offer themselves as candidates (Bleuchot 1975b: 444–45). The second point which must be stressed is that the delegates sent by the basic congresses to the General People's Congress are not permitted to exercise broad discretion in the representation of their constituents—for this, in Qaddafi's view, would allow for the usurpation of the people's political rights by their representatives. Rather, the delegates are bound by the instructions of their congresses and must faithfully reflect their demands. In

Qaddafi's view, the nation-level congress functions only as a mechanism to *register* the views of the sovereign basic congresses (Bleuchot 1975b: 444–45). Presumably, in principle, decisions on all unforeseen questions or resolutions of conflict between delegates can only be concluded through constant consultation of the delegate with his constituent congress (there is at least one case on record where this procedure was resorted to). If this system should actually become practice, it would indeed represent a political anomoly for the modern state (as well as an interesting attempt to deal with the fundamental problems of leadership elucidated by Rousseau and Michels).

"Popular Committees" continue to be "chosen" as well in the various organs of local government, certain government organizations, social institutions, and economic enterprises, evidently from the basic congresses. Their role is evidently administrative for the leadership committees of the basic congresses are given rights of political supervision over them. Although it is not clear in the sources, popular committees seem to be formed of a mix of career administrators and political activists, providing for a balance between needed expertise and popular participation in local government. In another reform designed ostensibly to bring administration and people together, the regime abolished the governorate level of administration (between the district and central government) and, in its place, each ministry created an inspectorate which deals directly with local popular committees. Many governorate level powers were transferred to the center and local popular committees began to deal directly with it (thus, it is unclear whether the actual effect of this change is the centralization or decentralization of power). Popular Committee chairmen represent their committees in the General People's Congress.

The General People's Congress is composed of around 1,000 delegates from the basic congresses, popular committees, and syndical associations together with the government (renamed General People's Committee) and the remaining members of the RCC, which now functions as the General Secretariat of the Congress. Qaddafi is the congress chairman. The General Congress has the right, in principle, to replace the government; and in its sessions, the ministers make reports and the congress reviews whether the resolutions of its previous session have been carried out. There are no cases yet of serious challenge to a minister.[10] Nevertheless, the congress has not proved to be merely a rubber stamp. Debate over the forthcoming budget has been vigorous, with the delegates evidently authentically expressing the demands of their localities for more services and development projects. Qaddafi typically has had to intervene on the side of the experts and ministers in support of the allocation of development projects according to a rational economic plan and to prevent raids on the investment budget to finance the expansion of services. Nevertheless, the delegates have won increases in these allocations. The conflicting demands of the delegates have required formation of special committees to reduce and reconcile them, which, as Bleuchot points out, requires delegates to go beyond the simple recording of constituent demands (Bleuchot 1977: 495). On certain key issues Qaddafi has been challenged by the congress; it turned down a proposal to nationalize foreign trade and has objected to conscription. Qaddafi has, however, ultimately prevailed on each issue.

People's Power has revealed several notable defects. First, the system of imperative mandate appears simply to encourage localistic particularism at the expense of developing a view of the common interest. Second, numerous conflicts of authority have erupted between its different organs, especially between the Popular Committees and the Leadership Committees of the basic congresses and between civil servants and political activists inside the popular committees; this appears to be a symptom of a lack of clear responsibilities and division of labor as between administrators, per se and "popular supervision." The relation between elected leaders and the collective entities to which they are in principle accountable hasn't been up to the ideal. Some executive officers act alone in authoritarian manner, usurping the rights of the collectivity and accumulating petty personal power; others, hamstrung by excessive control, afraid of political criticism, or paralyzed by conflict, eschew responsibility and initiative. Moreover, in spite of these numerous structures of control, the problems of negligence, inertia, sabotage, and corruption remain preoccupations of the leadership. Finally, the problem of nonparticipation remains. Figures given by Bleuchot indicate absenteeism in basic congresses ranging from 30 to 50 percent. He suggests that nonparticipants include not only the apathetic but also those who, being outside the political line defined by the leader and, seeing no way to press their views, simply drop out of the system (Bleuchot and Monastiri 178–81).

In 1977–78, Qaddafi launched yet another wave of popular revolution, this time connected with the turn toward the socialization of the economy. Workers were urged to seize the businesses in which they worked and tenants the apartments in which they lived. "Revolutionary Committees" of militants committed to the new socialization measures, were set up in these various places charged with "self-managing" them. These changes seemed to signify the spread of the new political structure further and deeper into society. Moreover, these revolutionary committees have appeared, as well, inside the People's Power structure charged with "agitating the people to take revolutionary decisions" and acting as "watchdogs of the revolution." Qaddafi seems, thus, to have realized the need for an ideological "vanguard" to lead his revolution at the base as well as the center, but this so far, as not taken the classic form of a Leninist style party.

Although the process is not yet over, Qaddafi's institution-building experiments have made a definite difference for the development of the Libyan political system while yet falling short of the regime's ostensible hopes for them. They do seem to have contributed to the weakening of opposition, both traditional and nontraditional, to the leader's ability to control his oft recalcitrent bureaucracy, and to the enhancement of the regime's legitimacy and support. A good many people, hitherto politically inactive, seem to have been drawn into the political arena and to have acquired a sense of participation, for which Qaddafi has no doubt been given much credit. A wider segment of the population than formerly has been able to acquire local power and even to make its wishes known on national issues. Qaddafi's efforts have no doubt contributed to the politicization of the Libyan population and to making basic political resources and opportunities more widely available. The system probably does contribute something to keeping the leader in touch with opinion at the bases and, indeed, may perhaps be seen as a modernized version of traditional tribal consultation not incompatible with Libya's inherited political culture.

Nevertheless, as institutions of participation — as a system of accepted channels and procedures for making decisions and recruiting leaders, universally open to Libyans, the structures Qaddafi has built remain fragile and defective. They remain very much the creatures of the leader who can change the rules of participation at will and can hardly be held accountable in any formal way. They remain virtually closed to those who cannot accept the goals and norms of the system as he has defined them. As long as power remains so concentrated and personalized at the top, there is a danger, if not a likelihood, of the simultaneous bureaucratization of the formal input channels of the system, and the development of patron-client-like ties inside or outside the formal structures as the real system of access. In such a case, real access to the center of power would seriously contract. Moreover, while a system which insists on consensus may be appropriate for a small, patriarchal desert community, to insist on consensus in an increasingly differentiated society facing many alternatives inconceivable to the desert nomad may mean that the real issues are avoided and consensus merely imposed, with the consequent alienation and withdrawal of those outside the imposed line. There is evidence that this has happened: one of the biggest costs of Qaddafi's insistence on conformity with his personal ideological vision has been the repression and alienation of politically conscious middle-class intellectuals and, for them at least, more the stifling than the encouragement of participation. Ruth First has these intellectuals in mind when she claims that the biggest contradiction in the Libyan institution-building effort is the fact that, while it calls for participation, it nevertheless "suffocates any political thought or action not initiated by the state" (First, 1974: 1). Like many other authoritarian-populist regimes, the Libyan regime has made political resources more widely available and has legitimized the notion of mass participation, but it has made far less progress in institutionalizing the participation of its emergent mass citizenry.

RESOURCES

Analysis of the use of resources by elites deals with the dynamics of power: how it is concentrated, expanded, and expended. It can focus on intraelite dynamics — the struggle for power and policy in the micro-arena at the top — or on the efforts of a political elite to expand its power in the larger public arena. Of course, the two arenas need not be separate; indeed, what characterizes the Libyan case is precisely the breakdown of the division between them as the charismatic leader tries to mobilize support from below against elite and counterelite rivals; as such this discussion will consider both arenas. In so doing, it will divide the evolution of the political game in Libya into three distinguishable phases.

PHASE 1: *The Seizure, Expansion, and*
Consolidation of Power (1969–73)

In 1969 when the Free Officers carried out their coup, there was a near vacuum of political power in Libya in the sense that no one force or alliance of forces could any longer control the political arena and, moreover, that rising social forces unintegrated into the traditional system were on the verge of entering it. This situation presented considerable opportunities for the new officer-elite to create political power.

The first priority of the new elite as it seized power was to secure control over the state apparatus, especially the army, the coercive base of any regime. By the time of the power seizure, the Free Officers had a network in the army, but they were a minority (perhaps only 60–170 of the 600-man officer corps, although the movement also appears to have given itself roots in the ranks as well as the officer corps by including NCOs). The power seizure was made easier by the fact that other officer groups of higher rank, also planning or sympathetic to a coup, cooperated unwittingly with Qaddafi's forces, unaware that they were led by junior officers. Subsequently, nearly all middle-rank and senior officers (about 430) were purged, and Free Officers were promoted into the empty commanding positions (Breton 1969: 364). For a brief period Qaddafi did cooperate with some higher ranking officers, appointed Colonel Musa Ahmad as Interior Minister and Colonel Adan Hawaz as Defense Minister in the first cabinet; but when these Neguibs of Libya — possibly in connection with leftist-nationalist groups — showed signs of staking out independent positions, they were purged. It seems plausible to suggest that the elimination of all higher ranking officers decimated the representatives not only of the upper class but even of the educated middle class in the officer corps — including some who had been committed to various middle-class political movements — leaving as a rump those more recently recruited from lower-middle- and lower-class backgrounds similar to Qaddafi's and more likely to be receptive to his orientation. The control of the Free Officers over the officer corps has not been challenged since 1969.

Purges in themselves, however, are seldom a sufficient guarantee of control over either the military or the state; the first coup could, as elsewhere in the Arab world, have been simply a prelude to many more. Moreover, although when the new leaders took power no opposition group was strong enough—so long as they remained united—to overthrow them, the traditional elite remained strong enough to frustrate their desire to link up with the masses. The middle class could try to bargain its indispensability to an elite bent on modernization for a share of power on its own terms, and this the officers did not want to concede. To contain these challenges and consolidate their rule, the Free Officers had to legitimize their claim to a monopoly of power.

In fact, they seem, in the first couple of years, to have succeeded in winning wide popular acceptance and legitimacy (Leveau 87–88, Hudson 313). The mere act of removing a despised *ancient régime*, fallen into growing discredit because of its close links to the Western powers, its widespread corruption and incompetence, and its isolation of Libya from the Arab world generated some legitimacy resources for the new leaders among almost all parts of the population, excluding only the small traditional-turned-comprador elements which benefited from the regime. The new regimes' Arab nationalist and pro-Nasir stance and Nasir's personal patronage of the young officers also lent legitimacy. An important section of the mainstream educated middle class was Arab nationalist in orientation, regarded Nasir as its political hero, and deeply resented Libya's isolation from the Arab world. Even among the great notable families of Tripoli there was an Arab nationalist tradition which looked to Egypt. But, significantly, the biggest demonstrations of support for the coup came from the popular quarters of the city. This initial upwelling of support was consolidated and expanded by the regime's nationalist achievements in the early years—the evacuation of the foreign bases, the successful oil negotiations, the Arabization of the cities, and the expulsion of the Italian settlers. Libya's support for the Palestinians, defiance of the West, and new presence on the Arab stage symbolized to many Libyans that their country, so long a deferent dependent of the West, was beginning to determine its own fate. Qaddafi's religiosity and the particular Islamic twist which he gave to Libyan nationalism no doubt evoked an additional response among the deeply religious masses. Populist reforms —raising of minimum wages, rent controls, redistribution of colonial-held lands (around 100,000 hectares), popular housing schemes—demonstrated the regime's concern for the deprived. As in Nasirite Egypt, early nationalist successes and populist reforms seem to have created a generous fund of political capital for the new regime which could be invested or expended. As in Egypt, the most supportive parts of the population were the semiurbanized masses crowding into towns and the petty bourgeois employee class, both of which recognized themselves in the new rulers. The petty bourgeoisie, exposed to some modern education in Libyan schools were rebelling against their traditional fathers but they were far less cosmopolitan than the Western-educated bourgeoisie; as such, they saw in the Arab nationalism espoused by the new rulers a congenial way of escaping from tradition without abandoning their cultural identity (Breton 1969: 362). The uprooted urban masses were likewise looking for a new but familiar identity to replace their declining tribal loyalties. Much of this support base, however, remained amorphous, passive, and unorganized. In 1971–72, the organization of the ASU represented a first attempt to draw it into systematic participation, but, as has been seen, its effectiveness was limited.

Just as in Nasserite Egypt, the new regime soon also encountered opposition from two sides. The traditional tribal leaders were necessarily ambivalent in their attitude toward the new elite. To be sure, the ease with which the coup knocked off the apex of the tribal structure and the lack of resistance from the tribes or Senussi order indicate that the bonds between the monarchy and its tribal constituency had been severely eroded if not snapped. The Islamic orientation and tribal origin of at least some of the new rulers may have helped to neutralize tribal resistance (although Libya's terrain may also not have been favorable to resistance). Thus, the new rulers did not have to cope with the overt tribal enmity which modernizing revolutions in Yemen, Iraq, and Afghanistan have faced. But, if the apex of the tribal structure was destroyed, its local roots persisted. Outside the old Senussi center, Jaghjoub, the tribal leaders were not necessarily loyal to the old regime, but they did resent the efforts of the new leaders to penetrate their local bastions and reduce their influence over the rural-tribal population through appointment of modernizing officials to local government and the extension of the ASU organization. Fathaly and Palmer have shown that, four years after the revolution (1973), traditional tribal leadership continued to enjoy strong mass support; the masses remained highly particularistic, nonparticipant, mistrustful of those outside their own family, fatalistic, and of low achievement motivation—in short, hardly promising material for mobilization by a modernizing leadership; and that the actual effectiveness of government penetration was very modest, both in performance of modernizing tasks and in mobilization of mass participation in them. On the other hand, their data do also indicate the seeds of change. About half the typical community did not oppose the government's officials, and younger, better educated and more urbanized parts of the population were more receptive to the government. It seems plausible to suggest that in 1973 the rural masses of the peripheries remained to a great extent simply outside the political arena, but that their more modernized "vanguard" was just ready to be brought in (Fathaly, et al., 1977: 47–48).

If the regime encountered resistance from the most traditional part of the population, its relations with the most modern (or at least most educated) part—namely, the upper and middle classes—seem also from the start to have been ambivalent. These social strata did welcome the overthrow of the old regime and the nationalist victories of the new one. But on a number of counts they had strong reservations about Qaddafi's course. Some bourgeois families suffered from the populist reforms (e.g. rent reduction) and the decline of commercial activity in the first years after the coup. They could hardly have been enthusiastic about the regime's inclusion of national capital within the scope of sanctioned forces only on condition that it submit to heavy taxation to prevent its excessive growth and that it remain "nonexploitive"—a vague enough formula. Westernized, secular, and cosmopolitian, these classes found no attraction in Qaddafi's xenophobic nativism or his religious fundamentalism. Many had strong reservations about Pan-Arabism if it meant the loss of Libya's separate identity and control over its oil wealth. Those who were politically active in parties of the nationalist-left—the Ba'th, the ANM, and Marxist groups—were disappointed at the regime's unwillingness to share power with them or permit organized party life. Neither Qaddafi's fanatical anticommunism, his lukewarm "socialism," or prohibitions on the right to strike went down well with leftists or worker activists. The resignation of the first civilian cabinet under Suleiman Maghrebi, a radical politician and trade union organizer under the old regime, was an early sign of the deterioration of relations between the regime and the middle-class nationalist-left. There were early conflicts over the government's effort to assert control over the voluntary associations, especially the student union. The banning of all political parties and the restriction on all autonomous political activity outside the ASU meant a decision by the regime to expend valuable political capital to have its way in the organization of the political arena. The cost the regime would pay, as in Egypt, was the political apathy or hostility of the politically active parts of the educated middle class—in particular the intellectuals who, under other conditions, could have supplied the cadres for a revolutionary experiment.

In this period, however, the discontent of the middle classes was contained by a combination of cooptation and repression. An important part of the educated middle class, especially the technocrats, was ready to accept the regime's offer of income, careers, and a chance to participate in the modernization of the country. This is not to say that Qaddafi and the technocrats saw eye to eye on everything. Indeed, those technocrats who served the regime, while not actively opposing Qaddafi's views, did have their own opinions. As against his stress on the importance of moral activism and self-reliance in the development enterprise, they were more likely to look on development as a technical project, to advocate the importing of the most advanced technologies, and to downplay the role of the masses. As against his Pan-Arabism and tendency to put Libyan resources at the disposal of the Arab cause, they preferred an Algerian-style road to development, concentrating Libya's resources on its own modernization (Breton 1970: 238–40). But, in fact, there was a great deal of overlap in these differing positions — Qaddafi, for example, seems to share the technocrats' fascination with modern technology; even if a contradiction was occasionally perceived, Qaddafi, if he wished to modernize, could not dispense with the technocrats, and they, for their part, found satisfactions in working for a modernizing regime which paid well. As for those who chose opposition, divided among themselves and without mass bases, they appear to have been easily controlled by police measures. Thus, in the first stage, the new elite, having built substantial legitimacy, was able to control its opponents through a mix of utilitarian rewards and coercion.

PHASE 2: *Expending Political Power: Middle-Class Resistance and Intraelite Conflict (1973–75)*

This period was marked by setbacks to Qaddafi's policies and prestige; by rising resistance to his course, which for the first time appeared inside the RCC itself; and by vigorous efforts on Qaddafi's part to contain this resistance through the greater activation of his potential mass base. This conflict culminated in 1975 in the breakup of the inner elite core.

It was not long before the costs of suppression of middle-class political activity became apparent; it was easier to suppress such activity than to root out passivity or enforce enthusiastic performance in the service of regime goals. The tightening up of political control in 1971–72 — with the banning of political parties, creation of the ASU, and insistence by Qaddafi that the middle class participate through it — appears to have met with an apathetic response on the part of that class. The bureaucracy, a middle-class preserve, performed sluggishly; as early as 1971, Qaddafi was "resigning" in protest at bureaucratic inertia as well as the failure of the "people" to "accept their responsibilities" or "raise their level of thinking." Qaddafi's Pan-Arab policies also provoked disquiet; as Egyptians poured into Libya and plans for the merger with Egypt matured, "regionalist" sentiment grew, especially among bureaucrats who felt their positions and opportunities endangered by this new competition and were awakened to the danger that Libyan oil revenues would be soaked up by the bottomless Egyptian pit. In early 1973, opponents of union used the downing of the Libyan airliner by Israel as an occasion to launch anti-Egyptian demonstrations which embarrassed Qaddafi and directly challenged his policies and prestige (Bleuchot 1973: 380–82, 1975b: 446–47). It was at this juncture that Qaddafi launched his "Popular Revolution," by most accounts a counterattack aimed at purging his opponents, shaking up the bureaucracy from below, and enlarging and activating his own mass following on a more sustained basis. He may have calculated that, while at a disadvantage in the smaller political arena composed of elites and middle class, he would be able to prevail by expanding the scope of conflict through the mobilization of the lower-middle and lower classes into the political arena.

If the Popular Revolution allowed Qaddafi temporarily to regain the initiative, late 1973 and 1974 brought the collapse of his Pan-Arab policies. The project of union with Egypt failed, and friendship soon turned into rising emnity. There followed a similar fiasco with Tunisia. Qaddafi, left out of the October war and in disagreement with its political consequences, risked his legitimacy by his lack of enthusiasm for this first credible war by the Arabs against their main enemy. Qaddafi now seemed to be on bad terms with almost every Arab leader; the policies of the prophet of Arab unity seemed to produce exactly its opposite. It seems impossible that Qaddafi's prestige and legitimacy could have escaped serious tarnishing as a result of these setbacks, precisely because they were based so squarely on a vision of Pan-Arabism. Indeed, by late 1974, Qaddafi seemed to assume a distinctly lower profile, apparently withdrawing from active political leadership to engage in "ideological matters." The collapse of hopes for unity seemed to bolster the opposing "Technocratic-regionalist" trend, manifested, for example in the 1974 purging of the popular committees and cooptation into them of educated, middle-class elements (Bleuchot 1974: 321). But, before long, Qaddafi had resumed his activist posture. Externally, his Arab policy shifted from unionism to efforts to undermine the (many) Arab leaders who, he claimed, were betraying Arabism. Internally, Qaddafi's radical policies led to open clashes with students in the streets. The causes of growing student discontent were multiple. Qaddafi's puritanical, nativist cultural policies seemed to them an effort to repress personal freedom; the prohibitions on imported Western music and alcohol, on holding hands between the sexes, the forcible cutting of long hair, were all seen as encroachments by the state on legitimately private concerns. For Qaddafi, the students represented a conduit of Western cultural contagion which had to be cut. Moreover, they seemed to him to have little sense of obligation to the community. They avoided military service and work in the villages; they wanted, he charged, to remain students forever. If they would not voluntarily accept their obligations, Qaddafi would force them to (Bleuchot 1975b: 447) — hence, the first round of student disturbances and arrests in the spring of 1975. Thus, on all fronts Qaddafi seemed to be rather recklessly expending political capital, with little obvious return.

It is hard to know at what point policy disagreements inside the RCC turned into an irreparable cleavage. There is evidence that some RCC members regarded complete unity with Egypt with considerable reserve. The "reform" of the Popular Committees in 1974 may have been an effort by RCC members to curb Qaddafi's radical populist demagoguery. Their alarm seems to have grown as Qaddafi's Pan-Arabist policies, after the failure of union with Egypt, began to grow more erratic; resistance seems to have mounted to the diversion of funds to finance political adventures and subversion throughout the Arab world. Muhayshi, the leader of the anti-Qaddafi group, would later accuse Qaddafi of damaging the economy by interfering in economic and technical matters in which he had no competence. The final showdown between the two sides seems to have come over the allocation of funds when Muhayshi, then Planning Minister, objected to the channeling of funds he wanted for local development into Pan-Arab entanglements. The opposition to Qaddafi appears to have expressed the "technocratic-regionalist" views long associated with high officials and the middle class (Bleuchot 1975b: 447). Moreover, the cleavage in the RCC was at least partly along class lines, with Qaddafi's opponents largely of middle-class background and his supporters exclusively of lower-class origin.

In the course of the conflict, the collective leadership norms that confined conflict to the inner core, prohibiting an expansion of its scope, clearly broke down — either because Qaddafi had violated collective decision making, or his opponents decided to go outside it, or both. The evidence suggests that Muhayshi (perhaps with Beshir Hawadi) led an attempt to mobilize army units in support of a demand for Qaddafi's resignation, evidently relying heavily on personal links to officers from his home region. Other units may also have been involved, but it seems that the other members of the anti-Qaddafi faction, though sympathetic to Muhayshi, may not have actively participated in an attempt to rally army units.[11] If this is true, Muhayshi must certainly have been at a great disadvantage. Qaddafi, we know, had personally constructed much of the Free Officers organization, and his personal web of clients was likely to be far more extensive than Muhayshi's; moreover, as the visible and real leader of the revolution, Qaddafi possessed a personal legitimacy, however tarnished in 1975, with which the other Free Officers could not compete. It also appears that Qaddafi exercised, by strength of personality, such a hold over his followers that they were very reluctant to stand openly against him. (This interpretation is supported by their anxiousness to placate him and persuade him to withdraw his frequent "resignations.") Finally, it is important to note that Qaddafi had always remained close to his army base. He retained the post of Defense Minister, and in that capacity he was without doubt able to exercise direct control over promotions and dismissals (rewards and punishments) in the army. Four RCC members remained loyal to Qaddafi, including Prime Minister Jalloud — who probably presided over the font of patronage —, the second and third men in the army, Chief of Staff Abu Bakr Yunis and Assistant Chief of Staff Mustafa Kharubi, and the Interior Minister at the time, Khweldi Hameidi. Thus, Qaddafi's control over both rewards and the levers of coercion had remained relatively direct and effective. Significantly, he had evidently allowed no political officer to turn the army into a personal "fiefdom" comparable to that of Amer in Egypt. On the other hand, the opposition RCC members seem to have lacked comparable institutional bases. Only two held ministerial portfolios, Muhayshi as Planning Minister and Huni as Foreign Minister. Interestingly, Bashir Hawadi, most implicated after Muhayshi in the anti-Qaddafi conspiracy, was Secretary-General of the ASU at the time, but if he tried, he was unable to activate this organization — à la Ali Sabri in his conflict with Sadat — against Qaddafi, even though the ASU had been somewhat associated in 1974 with the middle class opposition. There is no evidence that the middle class as a whole was active in the conflict, either. Muhayshi, despite being Planning Minister, seems — if indeed he tried — to have failed to bring any of the government technocrats who presumably shared his "technocratic-regionalist" tendency into the conspiracy against Qaddafi. Thus, unlike Qaddafi, his opponents were unable or unwilling to try to mobilize more resources by expanding the scope of conflict, perhaps aware that Qaddafi could beat them at this game. Had the anti-Qaddafi faction acted in unison in the smaller military arena to rally their (presumed) clientage networks, their chances might have been better, but they seem not to have done so.

This case of elite conflict helps illustrate the workings of authoritarian populist political systems like the Libyan one: (1) In times of severe elite conflict, the formal universalistic rules supposed to govern decision making and conflict resolution, always fragile in any case, are likely to break down. (2) When this happens, the main resources which determine the outcome of conflicts are likely to be a) intraelite personal connections and b) control of strategic positions, insofar as these can be used to mobilize support in the military; force becomes the ultimate resort. (3) But, in contrast to traditional oligarchies, conflicts at the top in such systems are far less likely to be isolated from the wider public arena of participation. The wishes of large numbers of people can affect outcomes, but less through formal institutions of participation, like the ASU, than through a kind of informal reading by the elite actors involved of amorphous public sentiment — or more, accurately, of what the public will stand; it is in this way that the personal popular legitimacy of contestants can make a difference — i.e., can help shape the mobilization of military resources and the way and extent such resources can be brought to bear. It would be very difficult to show or measure in what ways Qaddafi's preponderant personal legitimacy was brought to bear in the 1975 conflict, but it seems unquestionable that it was a factor which the actors had to consider in their calculations.

Thus, by the end of 1975 Qaddafi appears to have expended a great deal of his previously earned political capital on efforts to impose political and cultural policies against the growing resistance not only of the middle class but of part of the top elite itself. It seemed unlikely that he could long go on expending power at such a rate without tapping new resources.

PHASE 3: *Political Institutionalization and Social*
Innovation: Investment or Dissipation of Power? (1975–)

The third stage has been marked by: Qaddafi's triumphant emergence from the interelite conflict, and the reestablishment of solidarity within the top elite; continuing efforts of Qaddafi to elaborate and adapt his ideological vision to new circumstances; new experiments with ways to mobilize and institutionalize participation among Qaddafi's supporters; and continuing resistance to Qaddafi's policies.

By the end of 1975, Qaddafi was forced to concede that the present generation of Arab leaders were not ready for Arab unity. But if unity was not within the realm of immediate possibility, what could Qaddafi's role be in inter-Arab politics and what would happen to his "mission"? Qaddafi did not give up his Pan-Arab mission, but, rather than seeking Arab unity per se, he seems to have come to see Libya's role as that of a catalyst for the radicalization of the Arab world, and as an obstacle to the trends moving toward capitulation to Israel and her Western imperialist backers. To these ends Qaddafi has employed Libyan financial resources and struck a close alliance with the U.S.S.R. to secure the military hardware needed to make a radical Pan-Arab bid credible. At the same time, he has turned his attention to the internal restructuring and modernization of Libya with a view, among other things, to strengthening his base and making it an attractive example for the rest of the Arab world. Although his efforts to restructure Libya continued to provoke resistance, the new stress on internal modernization did coincide with the Algerian-style state building preferred by the technocratic elites.

In 1976–77, Qaddafi unleashed now rounds of the popular revolution and began his second wave of institution building out of which emerged the People's Power structure. As a means of sustaining and enlarging his legitimacy and passive popular support, these efforts were probably worth the political capital and effort invested. But as a means of activating participation and generating the acceptance of responsibility and commitment desired by Qaddafi, their success was probably modest; the traditional political cultural barriers were too tenacious and the structures themselves too new and too flimsy.

In this same period, student resistance to the growing scope of Qaddafi's imprint on Libyan social life escalated into violent eruptions (including politically damaging invasions of Libyan diplomatic missions abroad). In response, Qaddafi took draconian measures, carrying out the first executions since the revolution (of officers involved in the Muhayshi affair and of students who had attacked ASU buildings). These actions shocked and hardened elements of middle-class opinion against him (Bleuchot 1977: 486–87).

In June 1977 came the mini-war with Egypt. From this conflict, a new realignment of opinion seems to have emerged in Libya. As Egypt's post-

1973 policies edged her toward accomodation with Israel and opened the door to an influx of American influence in the area, Sadat was seen more and more as the natural enemy of Arab nationalism. Thus, Qaddafi and his Pan-Arab supporters now found themselves on the same side with the "regionalist" anti-Egyptian current they had previously opposed. By standing up to Sadat, Qaddafi's stature seems to have been significantly enhanced in both Pan-Arab and regionalist circles. One observer, no friend of Qaddafi's, concluded that "Qaddafi's defiance enhanced his prestige and his popular support had probably never been greater" (Gera 534–37). Qaddafi's policy of expanding the army had proved its worth. Then, in late 1977, Sadat's trip to Jerusalem vindicated Qaddafi's emnity to the Egyptian leader and stiffened support for his determination to play an outward-oriented rejectionist role in the Arab world. Libya, after Jerusalem, could still play an historic role on the Arab stage.

In the next few years Qaddafi was fairly consistent in his support, financial and political, for the "Rejection Front," and his subsidies to Syria and the Palestinians no doubt helped to stiffen their resistance to any one-sided political settlement. Yet, apart from this credible contribution to the Arab cause, Qaddafi's foreign policy initiatives in the late 1970s seemed to become increasingly erratic, costly, and counterproductive. The seemingly indiscriminate attacks on friend and foe alike threatened Libya with international isolation. Qaddafi's attacks on the PLO leadership and the disasterous intervention in support of Idi Amin must have tarnished his image. His support for the efforts of Tunisian dissidents to overthrow Bourguiba has only incurred the emnity of a neighbouring state; whether his intervention in Chad will be more successful remains to be seen. Given that similar foreign policy adventures had previously resulted in a major intra-elite conflict, Qaddafi's course at the end of the decade seemed particularly incautious.[12]

Nevertheless, Qaddafi must have thought he had the political capital to invest—or dissipate—and his continuous ideological and political experimentation inside Libya did not abate. In 1977–78, he launched radical innovations on two fronts. The appearance of the *Green Book*, Part II, showed that Qaddafi was far from satisfied with the emerging socioeconomic system in Libya. He attacked in speeches the 40,000 Libyan import merchants whom he said consumed without producing. The bourgeoisie was accused of tax evasion. At the second General People's Congress, he proposed that external trade be nationalized to prevent waste on luxuries, but merchants were well enough represented at this session to deflect his proposal—a sign that Qaddafi was again risking the alienation of part of his own base. In the *Green Book*, his view of socialism now approached the Marxist view. Hiring of labor was considered exploitation, and private accumulation of wealth beyond personal needs, injustice. Commerce and real estate were "nonproductive" forms of enterprise. Evidently, the growing concentration of ownership, soaring prices, and exorbitant profits in these sectors had attracted the regime's increasing disfavor. Qaddafi seemed to be groping for a mixed form of economy which would greatly narrow the scope of private capitalism, replacing it with state, cooperative and self-managed forms of production. Accordingly, in 1978 he unleashed new waves of Popular Revolution in which workers seized the businesses of their employers and turned them into cooperatives, private apartment housing was distributed to tenants, and import business was nationalized.

These economic reforms have had costs. Naturally, they have faced opposition from those with something to lose, and the death penalty has been declared for economic crimes such as sabotage and embezzlement. Whatever the costs of private capitalism, it is not easy to replace as a motor of economic activity: consumer shortages, black marketeering, and inefficiency have resulted from the attempt. Qaddafi continues his feud with the bureaucrats who are still too inefficient and negligent to suit him, but to whom in many cases his socioeconomic policies now entrust the running of the economy. Other Qaddafi projects also seem to be in trouble: land redistribution and settlement programs are encountering resistance, and, despite massive investment, state agricultural projects are not doing well; ten years after the revolution, the leader's ambitious plan to reverse the decline of Libyan agriculture has yet to bear fruit.

Not satisfied with taking on the bourgeoisie, Qaddafi also became embroiled in controversy with the religious establishment. Certain religious leaders, probably with links to the merchant communities, attacked Qaddafi's new version of socialism as Marxist. But just as likely to outrage the traditional imams was Qaddafi's increasingly open attack on the traditional Islamic *Shari'a* and *hadith*, his insistence that the Quran alone represented the authentic Islam and that, moreover, he was qualified to interpret it. Such a role has never been attempted by an Islamic ruler except among the heterodox communities. It represents a mortal threat to the orthodox establishment, different and perhaps more dangerous than the secularizing of an Atatürk or a Bourguiba. As such, Qaddafi risked religious revolt at the very time when the middle class was being further alienated.

Still, it would be a mistake to think that—as he celebrated the 10th Anniversary of the Revolution in September 1979—Qaddafi and his regime were isolated. Although he has antagonized numerous elite groups— intellectuals, bureaucrats, the 'ulama, tribal chieftains, and the old bourgeois families—Qaddafi appears to have offset these losses through the mobilization of a broad mass base. Through his popular revolution and the new political structures which issued from it, he has drawn into the political arena on his side many heretofore politically inactive persons. His radical native populism appeals to their deepest instincts. His stock remains high with the majority who have benefited from his redistributive and populist policies. Generally, the takeover of business has been welcomed by the masses, especially the employees who now run their firms. "A House for Everybody," a program to provide every Libyan with decent lodging-whether the flat that one formerly rented or new accomodations built with interest free loans — is understandably very popular.

Moreover, Qaddafi's development policies, backed by massive oil revenues, are having a tangile effect on living standards. Tens of thousands of Libyans now attend school. The per capita income has increased from around $2,000 in 1970 to about $10,000 by 1980, one of the highest in the world. As non-Libyans flood in to take the lowest paying jobs, even lowly Libyans have many opportunities to move up in the social scale. Libya remains very much dependent on foreign technology and knowhow, but it is visibly acquiring the infrastructure of a modern society, and Libyans are learning how to run it.

For the many Libyans who have seen their living standards so greatly improve and who are perhaps secretly proud of the higher profile their small country now assumes in the Arab and international arenas, Colonel Qaddafi's ideological and foreign policy foibles are easily forgiven. For some, his assumption of the role of modern *mahdi* may even have an emotional appeal at a time when the Arab masses are increasingly disillusioned by the cynicism and worldliness of their leaders. This unique combination of resources — moral and material — in Qaddafi's hands is without doubt what permits him to continue to expend political capital on erratic messianism abroad, and iconoclasm, puritanic repression, and egalitarian leveling at home.

CIRCULATION OF ELITES

The conditions of political recruitment in Libya have been shaped by three basic factors:

1. The prerevolutionary distribution of social resources — wealth to some extent, but educational opportunities more so — helped determine who would enter the political elite on September 1, 1969 and thereafter. The expansion of education in the late 1950s and 1960s meant that some persons of very modest status, like Qaddafi, could get access to a high school education (and subsequently to the military academy). Had educational opportunity been more closely linked to wealth, the world would have missed the Qaddafi phenomenon. Nevertheless, the potential elite recruitment pool (as defined by access to high school education) was still tiny in 1969; only 8 percent of school-age children got to high school in the 1951–68 period (Fathaly et. al 1977: 14). The fact that Qaddafi and his colleagues did get such

an education indicates that they were either lucky or exceptionally bright or ambitious. The prerevolutionary distribution of social resources also determined that the sons of the middle class would go on to university and acquire the technical or administrative qualifications which would give them access to the bureaucracy and ultimately to general elite positions after 1969.

2. During the military coup-de'état, core elite positions in the political system were captured by new men who lacked many social resources but who had political organization and access to levers of the military bureaucracy. Participation in that *coup d'etat* probably remains a political resource today. The act of coup d'état could have opened an entirely new, semiinstitutionalized channel of top elite recruitment, but so far, at least, it has been a unique event and the new elite has been able to close off this route to power—to close the Pandora's box, in a sense. From the act of coup resulted a significant and unnatural cleavage between political power (elite status) and social (class) position which must perhaps be eventually redressed.

3. Subsequently, the regime has redistributed and expanded access to resources and defined new channels of mobility while closing off or contracting others. Wealth—except insofar as it still gives differential access to education, no longer appears translatable into significant political power. High tribal/family status has similarly been curbed as a usable resource. Access to educational resources has been expanded, greatly broadening the recruitment pool; if those getting high school or college education represent the widest potential elite recruitment pool, it had more than doubled in size by 1975, and by 1980 had at least tripled again.[13]

Upward from this base or pool of potential recruits reach two and possibly three kinds of career ladders to mobility. One leads through the university, then branches off, one route going through the state bureaucracy and public sector, the other into academia. Achievement and seniority presumably determines mobility within the middle rungs of these career routes, but access to the very top rungs of the ladder — top bureaucratic and cabinet positions—requires cooptation from above. It seems reasonable to think that, besides outstanding performance in one's career, other critical resources for the final jump are political loyalty (or a nonpolitical stance) and a personal connection (patronage). Such a connection might be established on the basis of family or kinship links, school or other kinds of friendships, or that chance by which potential upward movers come to the attention of those looking for competent or reliable subordinates. Leveau talks of Jalloud's "clientele" and it is plausible that he has presided over the distribution of patronage in the state apparatus, but Qaddafi and other RCC members and even civilian cabinet ministers undoubtedly also have exercised the right to recruit personnel (Leveau 95–6). One way of skipping rungs on this career ladder is to have known a member of the RCC, especially Qaddafi, before the revolution, perhaps in school or perhaps through participation in the civilian wing of his movement. There is simply no evidence as to the relative weight which is given to career achievement, political loyalty, and personal patronage as resources in recruitment, nor are such weights likely to be fixed.

It seems reasonable to suggest that a second career ladder runs through the military, especially the Free Officers organization; to date, however, it has only rarely given access to top decision-making positions — either to the core elite which has not expanded, or to the cabinet, which has remained largely civilian. We know little as to whether high military commands bring with them political influence — either with decision-makers at the top or in giving privileged access to middle-ranking bureaucrats; but the role high-ranking officers play in similar Arab authoritarian populist systems suggests that they probably do (the revolt of the eastern region military commander in 1980 indicates that such commands do have the power to mount "warlord"-like challenges to the center).

A third possible route to power might be service in mass organization structures — from the ASU to the Popular Committees and People's Power. At present, such service has led to subelite careers, but the ladder may reach up further. Do delegates to the General People's Congress exercise political influence on cabinet decisions or have special access to the bureaucracy? The former seems unlikely, but the latter less so. Will such service eventually open doors to cabinet positions or even to the core elite? So far it has not, and unless it does so in future, these organizations are not really likely to take root as institutions of political participation. In the case of this career route, both election from below and cooptation from above play a role.

As under the old regime, the very top elite positions — so far at least — remain closed, monopolized, but based not on heredity or religious criteria but on participation in the leadership of the revolution. But, below this level, access to elite positions is now more open; the new regime has expanded and more equally distributed the social resources needed for political recruitment and it has opened up more and better channels leading to greater upward mobility than hitherto obtained. It has, moreover, reinvigorated the leadership of the state, producing a core elite which has not been devoid of vision and political skills and which has deep roots in the masses, assisted by a general elite with technical and administrative skills.

Whether this leadership is the best that Libya could have had is another question. The lack of a *party* recruitment channel seems to be a major liability of the system — that is, a channel through which committed political cadres could be selected and socialized and eventually move into core elite positions. In its absence, the role of purely technical qualifications, on the one hand, and of personal connections, on the other, are likely to take on disproportionate bulk. Moreover, the recruitment system has notably failed to make use of the nontechnical intelligentsia which often combines the motivation and political vision needed to carry out real change in developing societies. The youth of the current elite means that it has time to correct these liabilities before a crisis of elite turnover must be faced. However this very youth may also create a crisis of circulation by frustrating the ambitions of the current generation of middle elites who can never realistically hope to enter the core elite, barring a violent seizure of power or voluntarily retirement at the top. This is one of the peculiar vulnerabilities of authoritarian populist systems, which lack an institutionalized mechanism for periodic elite turnover and which often produce a young core elite (although rarely as young as in Libya). Thus, the circulation of elites is blocked for the foreseeable future — unless the number of positions at the core should be expanded horizontally, or power diffused downward toward the middle elite through introduction of some interelite accountability mechanisms.

Is the new elite crystallizing into a new ruling class if such a process is defined to mean the use of political power accruing from elite functions to acquire privileged access to social resources for the elite and its children, thus closing the gap between political power and riches and slowing down mobility? Some such movement seems inevitable, but remains as yet embryonic. Mobility has not been blocked off. If Qaddafi's own life style is an obligatory example for other elite members, there may be some ideological constraints on the transformation of the elite into an ostentatiously consumptive stratum living very differently from the people. Sadat's Egypt may be the future of Libya, but it is not there yet.

CONCLUSIONS

At the top of the pyramid of power in Libya is a new elite of lower-middle-class background whose socialization experiences have produced in them an intense populist and Arab nationalist outlook which is modernizing but rejects both Western liberalism and Marxism-Leninism. The effort of this elite to find its own authentic "third way" has profoundly shaped politics in Libya. This elite is headed by a charismatic leader Mu'ammar Qaddafi, who, enjoying wide mass support, appears practically unchallengeable by other elites. While such unrestrained personal power is not untypical of the Middle Eastern state, few elites anywhere have so impressed a personal ideological vision and political style on the state as has Qaddafi. Libyans have felt the consequences of their leader's strengths and weaknesses far more directly and immediately than peoples living in less personalized political systems. Qaddafi's nationalist achievements, his drive to modernize, and his determination that all Libyans share in the benefits of modernization have been applauded by most of his countrymen; substantial numbers have resented his costly foreign policy adventures and the social and political instability issuing from his continual ideological innovation.

The desire of the Libyan revolutionaries to modernize has required them to reach an accomodation with educated technocrats and administrators who, up to now, have come from a higher social status than they. In their effort to impose a radical nativist-populist vision on the country, Qaddafi and his comrades have encountered resistance from these middle elites and from the middle class as a whole. Qaddafi has repressed this resistance and curbed the wealth of the Libyan bourgeoisie, but he has not destroyed it as a class. Indeed, under the new regime—at least for a period—it has found opportunities to diversify its resources through collaboration with or recruitment into the modernizing state apparatus. It, along with upwardly mobile elements of the petty bourgeoisie making careers in the state, may, in spite of the disapproval of the leader, be on the way to constituting a new "state bourgeoisie." The conflict between the egalitarian and nativist notions of Libya's revolutionary elite and the perhaps irrepressible appetites of those below them for the life style that Libya's wealth can buy them is likely to remain a basic cleavage in Libyan politics for the foreseeable future and, indeed, a source of potential instability. To help contain such opposition, consolidate the regime, and promote their goals, the new leaders have worked to mobilize a mass base, causing thereby a widening of the scope of conflict and participation. This alliance between a petit bourgeois political elite and a lower-class mass base meant to contain the power of the bourgeoisie is typical of radical populist systems.

In political structure, the new Libyan regime may be considered "authoritarian." Power is concentrated in the hands of a small elite, barely subject to formal mechanisms of accountability, and in good part resting on and exercized through control of the military and civil bureaucracies and the personal legitimacy of the leader. In contrast to liberal regimes, organized political opposition is not tolerated and inviolable legal norms are of modest effect as restraints on political action. The regime does try to use its power to effect social change, but in contrast to "totalitarian" regimes, it lacks the organizational weapon—an ideological vanguard party; hence it enjoys a lesser capacity to penetrate, mobilize, and transform society and remains more vulnerable to subversion from within by the residues of traditional political culture.

To say that the Libyan regime is "authoritarian" does not necessarily mean that it lacks popular support or that it is unresponsive to popular wishes, for the values of leaders and the need to build and sustain support have kept elites sensitive to mass demands. It does not even mean there is no mass participation in Libya. The Libyan leader has shown himself less content than other authoritarian modernizers to impose change exclusively from above through the bureaucracy, and has genuinely tried to encourage mass participation; hence his continuous experimentation with new forms of mass organization—punctuated, when these prove wanting, by calls to the masses to rise and reinvigorate them from below.

But participatory institutions are not built in a day, and those so far created in Libya are regarded too instrumentally by the leader and remain too much his creations to make and remake at will for the institutionalization of participation to have proceeded very far. Thus, at least by comparison to both constitutional and totalitarian political systems, the Libyan political system remains personalistic, the emanation of a charismatic leader, font of all ideology, policy, and legitimacy. The cost of this type of political sytem is that, given the constraints on autonomous group politics, political activity tends to remain individualistic, personalistic, or "anomic." The continuing power of the ideological-moral impulse radiating from the center, and the modernizing thrust given the system by a technocratic middle elite recruited on achievement grounds, prevent Libya from slipping back into a mere new form of traditional patrimonialism. But, insofar as the new political structures remain ineffective as channels of mass participation, some such slippage seems inevitable and, moreover, there is little to prevent a new state bourgeoisie from eventually emerging to claim a monopoly of political power. In that case, national populism, incapable of institutionalizing itself, would have proved to be a merely transitory phenomenon.

NOTES

1. Qaddafi thus differs from the Muslim Brotherhood which rejects Arabism as an obstacle to Pan-Islamism.

2. Certain other bits of evidence support this contention. The fact that the revolutionaries-to-be chose military careers rather than the university, at that time an upper and middle class preserve, suggests that as a group they were at most on the lower fringes of the middle class. Also, the fact that the revolutionary movement included NCO's and other nonofficers, suggests that there was no significant social gap between the Free Officers and lower-class soldiers. This contrasts with the case of the Egyptian Free Officers.

3. That they were no longer of lower-class financial status by the time of the power seizure is indicated by the fact that all members of the movement in the years before the coup were expected to buy personal automobiles in order to maximize their mobility.

4. Unless Abdul Ati al-Ubaydi, Prime Minister since 1977 should be considered among the core elite rather than as a mere technician of middle elite status.

5. It is worth noting that in their modest educational credentials the new Libyan elite does not differ significantly from the traditional elite it displaced. Not only the royal family, but eight of eleven prime ministers under the old regime, lacked higher education.

6. Moreover Bleuchot presents some evidence of disaffection in Misurta subsequent to Muhayshi's fall (Bleuchot and Monastiri 178: 178; Bleuchot, 1975).

7. Curiously, thanks to the work of Fathaly, Palmer, and Chackerian, we actually have better statistical data on (a sample of) the subelite than on the elites above it. Of the officials in their sample, one-third were college educated and, in self-perception 45% middle class, 21% upper-middle class and 25% lower class. See Fathaly, et. al., 1977, pp. 91–102.

8. This contrasts with the splendorous life led by Sadat on the Nile or even with that of elites in "socialist" Syria, where a black Mercedes is known as a "Ba'thmobile."

9. Bianco's reports on the trips taken by the leadership to the countryside to meet with their local constituencies suggest something of Qaddafi's leadership style. In these expeditions Qaddafi seems to take personal charge of even the smallest details — waking everybody up, making sure nobody is lost, and arranging for food and lodging. Bianco's accounts give insights into the sources and extent of Qaddafi's personal preeminence (Bianco 11–12, 14–15, 23–5).

10. In 1979, some ministers were removed by the congress, but this initiative is more likely to have come from Qaddafi than from below.

11. Only Muhayshi was later tried — in absentia — for his role in the coup.

12. In this period Qaddafi managed to antagonize most of Western Europe and make Libya look like an international thug by his campaign to silence by assassination overseas opponents. He quarreled with France, hitherto a sympathetic state, over unsuccessful interventions in Tunisia and Chad and the sacking of the French embassy in Tripoli. His policies toward Tunisia have been uniformly counterproductive. The intervention in Uganda ended in death and humiliation for the Libyan army, Qaddafi's most critical constituency. His choice of allies — not only Amin but "Emperor" Bokassa as well — seemed to fall on the worst international pariahs, dictators who could hardly be considered populist or progressive. Qaddafi has supported the Iranian revolution, but his implication in the Iman Sadr affair and his later statement condemning the holding of the American hostages have cost him friends in Tehran, a kindred revolutionary center. Yet America was hardly a friend, and Qaddafi had encouraged a similar attack on the U.S. Embassy in Libya. Even toward the U.S., the major backer of this chief enemies — Israel and Egypt's Sadat — his policy shows little consistency: threats of an oil boycott never carried out, continued extensive economic relations, occasional friendly overtures, and an incident such as the Billy Carter affair. These actions gave serious cause to wonder whether any coherent strategy or conception lay behind Qaddafi's foreign policy decisions.

13. Figures given by Fathaly et. al. 1977: 14, show that 12,000 persons were enrolled in high school or college in 1970. By 1975 this figure had increased to 29,000. Reports indicate that by 1980 more than 100,000 Libyans were receiving such education.

REFERENCES

Bianco, Mirella (1975) *Gadafi, Voice From the Desert*, London.

Bleuchot, Hevre (1975a) "Les Fondements de l'Ideologie du Colonel Mou'ammar el-Qaddafi," in *La Libye Nouvel, rupture et continuité.*

―――― (1972) "Libye: Chronique Politique," in *Annuaire de L'Afrique du Nord.*

―――― (1973) "Libye: Chronique Politique," in *Annuaire de L'Afrique du Nord.*

―――― (1974) "Libye: Chronique Politique," in *Annuaire de L'Afrique du Nord.*

―――― (1975b) "Libye: Chronique Politique," in *Annuaire de L'Afrique du Nord.*

―――― (1976) "Libye: Chronique Politique," in *Annuaire de L'Afrique du Nord.*

―――― (1977) "Libye: Chronique Politique," in *Annuaire de L'Afrique du Nord.*

Bleuchot, Hevre and Monastiri, T. (1978) "Libye: L'Evolution des Institutions Politiques, 1969–78," in *Annuaire de L'Afrique du Nord.*

Breton, H. (1970) "L'Ideologie Politique du Regime Republicain en Libye," in *Annuaire de L'Afrique du Nord.*

―――― (1969) "La Libye Republicaine," in *Annuaire de L'Afrique du Nord.*

Carvely, Andrew (1973) "International Relations and Political Purposes: Libya Comes Out into the World since 1969," *International Journal*, Autumn.

Fathaly, Omar; Palmer, Monte; Chackerian, Richard (1977), *Political Development and Bureaucracy in Libya*, Lexington, Mass.

Fathaly, Omar and Palmer, Monte (1980) *Political Development and Social Change in Libya*, Lexington, Mass.

First, Ruth (1974) *Libya: The Elusive Revolution*, London.

Gera, Gideon (1978) "Libya," in Colin Legum, ed., *Middle East Contemporary Survey*, New York.

Hudson, Michael (1977) *Arab Politics: The Search for Legitimacy*, New Haven.

Leveau, Remy (1975) "Le Système Politique," in Centre de Recherches et d'-Etudes sur les sociétés mediterranéennes, *La Libye Nouvelle, rupture et continuite.*

6

Egypt: Diffused Elite in a Bureaucratic Society

SHAHROUGH AKHAVI

The Egyptian elite may be discussed in terms of the following two dimensions: (1) a dimension focusing on distinctions among political, social, and economic elites: (2) a dimension stressing the distinction between the "ruling class" of core and general elites and the "second stratum." While it is not easy to maintain these distinctions in practice, the validity of their analytical separation ought to be clear.

The bases of differention among political, economic, and social elites are, respectively, power, status-honor, and wealth. The boundaries of the categories clearly overlap, and it is an empirical question to determine at what point, to what extent, and with what consequences political elites may behave as social elites, economic elites, political elites, and so on. Since 1952 the political elite has — at varying times — consisted of military officers, cabinet members, party leaders, administrative officials of high rank, and managers of public enterprises. The social elite has been comprised of the village headmen (*'umdahs*), the clergy, urban professionals, brotherhood and lodge chiefs, trade union bosses, *futuwwāt* (local urban strongmen), and village council chairmen. The economic elite has included middle landholders (the aristocracy having been destroyed as a social force in the early 1950s), construction contractors, private entrepreneurs and financiers, and middlemen agents or brokers, as shown in Figure 6.1.

The most common examples of boundary overlap among elite categories involve high-ranking army officers who were able to carve out virtual bureaucratic fiefdoms within state agencies (Sadat, 1977: 167–69). Although such interventions by army figures in economic institutions had been particularly marked in earlier periods, the practice evidently continues to some extent in the Sadat period — for example, ". . . in those sections of the bureaucracy and public sector responsible for reclaiming and farming reclaimed land" (Springborg: 1979: 63)

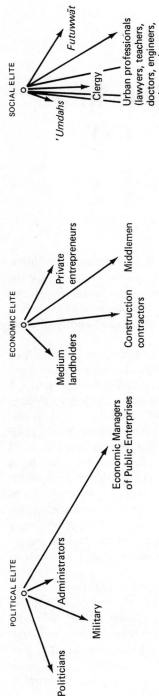
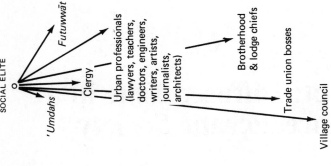

FIGURE 6.1   Schematic Representation of the Array of Elites in Egypt.

The distinction between the "ruling class" and the "second stratum" suggests itself in light of the recently increasing interest in the theories of the early 20th century political sociologists — especially Mosca — and of Marx by specialists of Middle East politics. The ruling class is that identifiable social force that is said to rule society in a virtually proprietary sense. The second stratum operates as a reservoir for the ruling class, which is both responsive to, and partially autonomous from, the former. These concepts are particularly apparent in the recent study by Binder (Binder, 1978: *passim*). It is more rewarding to study the relationships between decision makers and their social basis of support in society than to assume a monolithic model of rule according to which the political system may be analyzed in terms of the power position and class interests of a putative military caste (Cf. Rodinson, 1968, *passim*; Vatikiotis, 1961 and 1968, *passim*; Be'eri, 1966: *passim*; Hurewitz, 1969: 125 ff.; Abdel-Malek, 1968: *passim*; Halpern, 1963: *passim*).

A final preliminary point bears mentioning. The determination and location of elites is itself a problem. Analysts of the Egyptian elite(s) have either adopted a common-sense approach or relied on incumbency. Among those for whom common sense has served to identify elites should be mentioned those biographers (Lacouture, Stephens, Mansfield) who implicitly subscribe to a version of the "great man theory." The most thoroughgoing elite analysis of the Egyptian ruling political elite (Dekmejian, 1971) has specified that cabinet position is the determining factor of elite status. Binder's investigation focuses on officership in the National Union and Arab Socialist Union — the mass mobilization organizations of the 1960s and 70s. An additional method could be reputational, based on attribution by those "in the know" (Harik 1974). A reputational elite analysis would probably conclude, among other things, that 'Uthman Ahmad 'Uthman, a construction engineer and contractor, is a more politically influential figure than Deputy Prime Minister Fikri Makram 'Ubayd. Yet, determination by incumbency in office would suggest the primacy of 'Ubayd in view of his holding that title.*

DESCRIPTION

Unitl 1952, the most obvious trait of the Egyptian political and economic elites was their foreign origins. The line of foreign conquerors extends back 2,500 years from the Persians through the Macedonians, Arabs, Tulunid Turks, Ikhshid Turks, Fatimids, Ayyubid Kurds, Mamluks Ottoman Turks, French, and British. These foreigners basically desired

---

*Since these lines were written, 'Uthman was appointed Deputy PM for Food Security Affairs in February 1981.

to squeeze the utmost out of the *fallahin*, from whom they generally kept aloof. With the passage of time, the native population reasserted itself and would begin to occupy important positions in the state and to influence both policy and culture. This phenomenon may be clearly discerned under the later Ptolemies, during the last centuries of Byzantine rule, and under the Fatimids and Ayyubids. Each time, however, the newly emergent Egyptians were once more submerged by a fresh wave of conquerors and subjected to a new ruling class (the Romans, Arabs, Circassians and Turks). (Issawi, 1963: 110.)

The 1952 "revolution" in Egypt changed this picture dramatically. It swept into political power a group of junior officers who were themselves native sons. This factor, it has been argued, provided *ipso facto* legitimacy to the rule of the new leaders (Binder, 1965: 399).

How many persons comprise the present Egyptian political elite? This question is not easy to answer with assurance. Its size has grown since the less complex days of the early 1950s. Not only has the size increased, but the ruling elite no longer may merely be equated with the military, as frequently occurred in the 1950s and 60s in the writings of various scholars. Moreover, public administrators and high-ranking officials in the public sector of the economy should be considered as members of the political elite if, as will often be the case, they play political roles.

Growing differentiation in the political elite occurred relatively early in the republican period in response to the modernization policies of the regime. Such policies entailed the creation of a central planning apparatus and a Ministry of Industry, both of which were established in 1956. The overwhelming majority of positions created by economic planning and industrialization may be characterized as technocratic in nature. The incumbents in these positions therefore did not play manifestly political roles. However, it is easy to imagine that a number of decisions these technocrats would be called upon to make could have political consequences. Feasibility studies to determine the geographic location of factories, for example, could easily have an effect on existing patron-client relationships among individuals. Moreover, outstanding figures, such as Dr. 'Aziz Sidqi — a highly skilled economist — may with justification be considered members of the political elite (in his case in his capacity as Minister of Industry, and, later, Prime Minister).

These considerations lead to the estimate that, in the 1960s and 70s, the size of the political elite grew a good deal from the very small junta of 10 to 12 army officers who governed the country in the early- and mid-1950s. Reasonable estimates of the size of the *ruling* or core elite today would probably not exceed 50 to 60. This includes the President of the Republic, the Vice-President, some five Deputy Prime Ministers (who are simultaneously entrusted with ministerial portfolios), about 25 other cabinet officials, some four or five Counsellors to the President, about 25 governors of Egypt's governorates (provinces), the head of General Intelligence, and the Speaker of Parliament. It will be noted that the General Secretary of the majority party in Egypt, known as the National Democratic Party, is Vice President Husni al-Mubarak.

To answer the question of size of the political elite, we need to consider two other categories: the general or "strategic" elite (Perlmutter, 1974: 114 ff); and the "second stratum." The former refers to all those individuals, such as party leaders, members of parliament, public sector managers, industrialists financiers, military commanders, ambassadors, judges, undersecretaries in ministries, editors, and lawyers who collectively operate as a support system for the ruling elite. The second stratum differs from this group in the sense that it is the social pool from which the strategic and ruling elites derive. Data provided by Moore (1977: 262) on the numbers of Egyptian civilian officials in government and the public sector of the economy indicate that the strategic elite consists of about 21,500 individuals. This is suggested by Table 6.1, which contains Moore's data.

Table 6.1. Number of Egyptian Civilian Officials in Government and the Public Sector[2]

	1962–63	1966–67	1971–72	Percent Increase 1962–1972
Top officials (grade 1 and above	967	1,544	1,905	97
Grades 2 and 3	9,897	—	20,433	106

If we were to extrapolate these figures in order to arrive at data for 1981–82, we would have to number the top officials at 3,800 and the second and third grades at 40,000. While these figures are probably too high, the general trend toward a burgeoning in the number of general elites is unmistakable over the last two decades.

Binder, working with older data from the late 1950s and early 1960s, provides the following picture for the second stratum elite, reckoned as the members of the basic units and officers of the district bureaus of the Arab Socialist Union (ASU) — the now defunct mass mobilization organization:

Rural ASU basic unit committee members and district bureau
    officers: 28,000
Urban ASU basic unit committee members and district bureau
    officers: 2,000
(Binder, 1978: 44)

It will be readily seen that these are large numbers, indeed. It remains to be seen what influence the dissolution of the ASU will have on the size of the Egyptian political elite. The "multiparty" system instituted by President Sadat in 1978, and the holding of the first elections for the Consultative Assembly (termed Majlis al-Shura) in late September 1980 do not suggest a diffusion of power, however, to newcomers who might challenge the government. The infinitesimal number of votes captured by the opposition Liberal Socialists Party of Mustafa Kamil Murad; plus the fact that the latter party did not even field an election list in fourteen of Egypt's governorates; both of these factors lead one to be cautious about a supposed broadening of the base of politics.

Thus far, the description of the Egyptian political elite has concentrated on size. What may be said about the social background of and/or social base of support for the political elite? From the very beginning of the evolution of elite literature on Egypt, both "bourgeois" and Marxist sociologists and political scientists have been impressed by the political elite's ties to the moderately well-to-do rural strata (Binder, 1965: *passim*; Be'eri, 1966: 1–38: Be'eri, 1970: 492–96; Abdel-Malek, 1968, *passim*, and specifically at 45; Hussein, 1973: 95; Perlmutter, 1974: 113; Binder, 1978: *passim*). The suspicion of existing linkages between the post-1952 elite and the rural middle holders rarely permitted analysts holding such views to make any concrete causal statements about origins determining decisions on public policy. On the contrary, apart from the Marxist-influenced sociological writings, the tendency typically was to be cautious about such statements of deterministic causality (Dekmejian, 1971: 212). Observers have been on safer ground in suggesting that regime policies typically have not hurt the middle landowners *on the whole*.

The question of the origins of the Egyptian elite throws into relief the more recent emphasis on officers and civilians with engineering backgrounds. This is a point that was suspected by scholars working in the mid-1960s (Binder, 1965: 422) but reported with greater reliability by later studies (Dekmejian, 1971: 173 ff, 201, 204; Moore, 1978: *passim*; Akhavi, 1975: 91–95). Yet, Dekmejian's major finding that army officers with engineering backgrounds would figure more importantly in the Egyptian political elite is disconfirmed for the Egyptian cabinet through the decade of the 1970s. Although some 19 percent of the cabinet members in the 70s were trained as civilian engineers, only 8 percent turned out to be "military technocrats" (N = 172) [Dekmejian's term for officers with engineering training.][1] On the other hand, there has been a very marked increase among those who entered the Egyptian cabinet through academia. More specific data will be provided below.

It has been estimated that the increase in the salience of such professionals as engineers and academicians has been accompanied by the attenuation of the power of the army officers (Dekmejian, 1971: 217; Waterbury, 1976: 434–35; Akhavi, 1978: *passim*). Yet, even in the early 1970s certain scholars continued to stress the primary—if no longer exclusive —role of the military in shaping public policy (Be'eri, 1970: 101; Feit, 1973: 138 ff.; Perlmutter, 1973: 130–66).

A general rise in the proportion of academicians has been outlined, with a general assertion (cf. systematic analysis of their role within the elite structure) that individuals from Egyptian universities and institutes have been advanced into elite positions for their management and technological skills (Dekmejian, 1971: 200; Moore, 1974: 209). However, weaknesses in their own organizational base have precluded them from establishing institutional autonomy vis-à-vis the central government (Moore, 1974: 209–13; Springborg, 1978: 275–95). Instead, social forces such as the journalists or lawyers occasionally feel strong enough to raise criticisms of existing policies—as happened, for example, in the debates of the People's Assembly in December 1976.

STRUCTURE AND CIRCULATION OF THE EGYPTIAN ELITE

The new elites that emerged in republican Egypt have created institutional and noninstitutional structures to establish stronger links among themselves and with the population. In the nearly three decades of the republican period, the following institutional and noninstitutional structures have been created:

I. Institutional
1. Free Officers' Movement
2. Free Officers' Executive (Revolutionary Command Council)
3. Liberation Rally/National Union/Arab Socialist Union/National al Democratic Party
4. Cabinet Ministries, Public Agencies and Authorities and Public Organizations
5. *Mukhābarāt* (intelligence services)
6. Office of the Presidency of the Republic
7. National/People's Assembly
8. Consultative Assembly
9. Universities
10. Media
11. Trade Unions
12. Peasant Cooperatives
13. Professional Syndicates
14. Village Councils
15. Women's Societies
16. Sports Associations
17. Military Institutes and Clubs

II. Non-Institutional

    1. Extraordinary Meetings
    2. Crony groups
        a. Patronage Networks
        b. Social Circles and Groups
    3. Ad Hoc Committees
    4. Charismatic Movement

The tendency in the beginning to make the conspiratorial movement, and especially its Executive (later called the RCC) the repository of power seemed natural enough, given the origins of the new ruling elite. But, in a broader perspective, the process of building more differentiated institutional structures, both to accommodate and to radiate power and influence, has not ceased. The latest move, initiated in 1978, toward institutionalization in the political system consists in the idea of a multiparty system. The antecedents of this movement may be seen in the notion of the three tribunes (*manābir*) — in effect political groupings — earlier in the decade.

By the beginning of the 1980s, the multiparty system was an idea whose time appeared to have come only on paper. The National Democratic Party of President Sadat, which held its first party congress at the end of September 1980, won all the seats contested in the elections to the Consultative Assembly in the same month. And, although the lack of attention paid these elections by the press may possibly be attributed to the Iraqi-Iranian military conflict, it is remarkable how little effort seems to have been spent mobilizing the people behind the new institution.

In a word, in Egypt persists the abiding problem of detaching political structures and processes from the personalities in the government. The list of officials of the National Democratic party reads like a veritable "who's who" in the regime. Now, it may be that President Sadat did not wish for such a turn of events in inaugurating the idea of a multiparty system; yet, there is evidence to show that a paternalistic attitude continues to inform discussions — at least in public — about the political process in Egypt. Among the most favorite similes employed in the press today is that President Sadat is like the father of the Egyptian family. Thus, no political institutional structure, apart from the Presidency of the Republic, has gained widespread legitimacy among urban strata. It is probable, however, that the National People's Assembly has won relatively greater legitimacy outside Cairo than in the capital. Possibly, the same generalization may be said to have held with regard to the ASU.

Early regime experiments at creating a mobilization organization fell afoul of the distrust by President Nasser not only of his companions but of the very concept of delegation of authority (Lacouture, 1973: 143; Rodinson, 1968: 101; Little, 1967: 136). The creation of the first mobilization organization stemmed from the desire "merely . . . to block the formation of other parties" and to wage a battle against internal rivals on

Nasser's behalf (Binder, 1966: 218–19). The second experiment did not progress much further, but it did *seek* to establish rapport with the masses "in an attempt at unifying the Egyptian population behind a narrowly preserved regime" (Binder, 1966: 219).

In the 1960s, two organizations endeavored to institutionalize political participation at the national level: the National Union (created in 1956 and abolished in 1961); and the ASU. The National Union "was repeatedly characterized as a 'school,' one that was to become a liaison between the government and the people" (Dekmejian, 1971: 54–55). But the dearth of cadres, lack of a comprehensive program, and basic inattention to it by the ruling elite doomed it. Its successor in 1962 began in the same inauspicious circumstances, but particularly in 1965–67 its autonomy coherence and division of labor began to approach levels which the regime's ideology of democratic cooperative socialism seemed to require. Ultimately, however, the ASU became a battleground for the playing out of political rivalries among the leftist politician, 'Ali Sabri, the Defense Minister and Army chief, 'Abd al-Hakim 'Amir, and President Nasser himself. When Sabri, whom Nasser seconded to be Secretary General, bested 'Amir and began to ease him out of the bureaucratic fiefdom that he had established, Nasser purged Sabri. Thus, from 1969 the ASU lost its coherence and stability; by the time of its abolition in 1978, it was scarcely considered to be an effective institution among the citizens of urban Egypt.

In theory, the relationship of the mass mobilization organizations to the state administration has been similar to that of the League of Yugoslav Communists to the state organs: A paralleling of institutional structures of party and state was to exist. However, the regime in Egypt has always meant the state organs to supersede the party apparatus, in contrast to the situation in communist political systems. In particular, the supreme agencies of the party have consistently been staffed by the members of the ruling elite. In the ASU, the leading organs were the Supreme Executive Committee (a body with a membership of from 8 to 12 individuals); the Central Committee (150 to 200 persons); and the Secretariat (10 to 15 officials). These agencies were the control mechanisms for the government's desire to use the mobilization organizations as "a means to organize popular strength for the reconstruction of society on a sound new basis" (Vatikiotis, 1961: 83). The problem with such formulations, from the point of view of committed cadres, was the age-old question in Egypt: *quis custodiet custodes*?

The National Democratic Party (NDP), whose first party congress was held between September 29 and October 1, 1980, has chosen officers whose ties to the government are very close (see Table 6.2.). Of course, such close ties may be expected, since — according to the new system — the majority party controls the government. But in this case the absence of opposition parties (save in name only) makes the current circumstances similar to that existing in the 1960s.

TABLE 6.2. Officers Elected to the National Democratic Party (Egypt)

Name of Official	Party Position	Gov't. Position
1. Muhammad Anwar al-Sadat*	Chairman	President of Republic
2. Husni Mubarik*	Secretary General	Vice-President
3. Mustafa Khalil	Deputy Chairman, Member of Politburo	Former Prime Minister 1978–1980
4. Mansur Hasan	Deputy Secretary General, Member of Politburo	Minister of Culture and Information
5. Kamal al-Shadhli	Deputy Secretary General, Member of Politburo	----------------------------------
6. Muhammad Nabawi Isma'il*	Deputy Secretary General, Member of Politburo	Deputy Prime Minister and Minister of the Interior
7. Sufi Abu Talib	Member of Politburo	President of People's Assembly
8. Fu'ad Muhyi al-Din	Member of Politburo	Deputy Prime Minister
9. Fikri Makram 'Ubayd	Member of Politburo	Deputy Prime Minister
10. Kamal Hassan 'Ali*	Member of Politburo	Deputy Prime Minister and Minister of Foreign Affairs
11. Ahmad Badawi*	Member of Politburo	Minister of Defense
12. Mustafa Kamal Hilmi	Member of Politburo	Minister of Education
13. Amal 'Uthman	Member of Politburo	Minister of Social Affairs
14. Zakariya al-Barri	Member of Politburo	Minister of Awqaf
15. 'Abd al-Latif Bultiyah	Member of Politburo, Secretary of Cairo Governorate NDP	Former Minister Labor, 1970–71, 1975–77;
16. Albert Barsum Salamah	Member of Politburo	Former Minister for People's Assembly Affairs, 1973–76
17. Ibrahim Badran	Member of Politburo	Former Minister Health, 1977–1978
18. 'Ali Mansur	Member and Chairman of Politburo	Minister of State for Presidential Affairs

*Denotes individuals with military backgrounds

While the table is self-explanatory in terms of the structure (but not the configurations) of power, a few words may be added. The regime has separated the position of provincial governor from secretary of the NDP for the governorate. Although data for only 10 secretaries are available, in just one case is the Governor and Secretary the same individual (Kafr al-Shaykh). A second point worth considering is that the Defense Minister, Lt. General Ahmad Badawi, was coopted into the Politburo at the Party Congress. And, although President Sadat insisted in his closing speech to the Congress that "the army is the property of the people and not of the party," he did not hesitate to recruit the leading army officer into the Politburo of the NDP. Why this step should have been taken at the time, rather than two years ago, is not clear; it may be supposed that a direct channel of communication between army and party has been deemed necessary at a period of rapid inflation, very high prices for even staple commodities, and the stalled negotiations between Egypt and Israel on West Bank Palestinian autonomy.

The membership on the Politburo of the Ministers of Social Affairs, Education, *Awqaf*, as well as of the former Minister of Labor, can be explained presumably by the important role of the women's movement, youth, religion, and labor in the discussion of public policy in Egypt today. (Amal 'Uthman is a woman in what apparently has evolved as the token cabinet position for women in the regime.) The services of, Abd al-Latif Bultiyah, the former Minister of Labor, are all the more valuable to the government because of his long tenure as the leader of the General Confederation of Egyptian Trade Unions (technically a nongovernment position) in the late 1960s and early to mid-1970s. The significance of the addition of Albert Barsum Salamah lies in the unrest in Egypt among members of the Coptic community in spring, 1980. Salamah, an associate of the second Copt in the cabinet, Deputy Prime Minister Fikri Makram 'Ubayd, will presumably help to coordinate matters among the regime, the patriarchate and the Coptic community. The role of the former Minister of Health may be tied more to his former position as Vice-Chancellor of Cairo University than to his cabinet post. Student unrest has been an abiding issue in the 1970s.

Although it may be too soon to tell about the NDP's development in light of the models of party rule, previous efforts have suggested a sort of Egyptian corporatist model of representation and mobilization. The "chambers," as it were, in which were housed the five groupings (the army, the workers, the peasants, the national capitalists, and the professions) were all coordinated by the state apparatus. Whenever it seemed as though corporate autonomy might be realized on behalf of any of these groups, the regime either finessed such development or merely intervened directly to suppress it (Harik, 1973: 87). The regime has always faced the dilemma, under these circumstances, of needing to draw on the rural influentials for support — and there has been a strong bond between the latter and leaders in the five groupings; and, on the other hand, the denial of their hopes for effective political participation (Binder, 1978: 29–30).

At certain junctures dissensus will spill over, despite the regime's attempts to confine it. How else is one to interpret the vigorous and vital debate led by the lawyers in the press and the People's Assembly in the December 1976-January 1977 period? Rarely, as in the debates over the National Charter in the early 1960s, meaningful discussion has occurred in the Egyptian political system about the structure of power. But such debate has typically been the prerogative of luminaries whom it would be embarrassing for the regime to intimidate. In the 1970s, under the slogan of "the sovereignty of law" and the elimination of internment camps, debate has been cautiously encouraged over certain lines of internal policy. Yet, in a speech marking ten years of rule, for example, President Sadat virtually excluded the possibility of party leaders expressing deeply held contrasting views about existing policy by his sweeping declaration that "Egypt comes first, because it is above parties, individuals and leaders;" and declaring that "the ideology of nationalism must supersede all other ideologies, party differences and sloganeering" (*Al-Ahram*, October 2, 1980). Under such guidelines, it becomes difficult for sincerely committed individuals to know when they might be regarded to have overstepped the acceptable bounds of behaviour. The inescapable conclusion is that the model of rule has continued, in the 1970s, to follow the patterns outlined in the 1960s by Heaphy as a "non-political model for nation-building." In other words, the ruling elite is in the position of regulating, or administering, the society. As the same observer put it:

> the Governor is conceptualized as an organization man who serves as a point of communication between the central government and the local level. He is not seen as an instrumentality for political transactions, the specific outcomes of which cannot be controlled by a central government (Heaphy, 1966: 183).

It is not that the members of the elite do not themselves recognize this fact. Thus, a leading member of the social elite — Dr. 'Abd al-Malik 'Awdah, Dean of the Faculty of Economics and Political Science at Cairo University — put it this way in a recent seminar on "How Are We Going To Administer Egypt?"

> Are we going to convert Egypt from a state where policies and implementation are centralized into a decentralized state with respect to laying down policies and executing them? Or will we apply local administration at the level of implementation and leave public policy to the centralized state?
> The fundamental issue, when all is said, is one of political philosophy. In Egypt, which is a riverine society, the state is greater than the individual, contrary to the situation in non-hydraulic societies..." (*Al-Ahram*, October 3, 1980).

Yet, local political participation evidently has been significant in certain instances, and a caveat has been submitted in an important monograph on the political anthropology of a Nile Delta village against assuming too simple a monocratic model of domination and communication. Based on a study of the ASU at the turn of the decade of the 1970s, the author of this book perceived the party organization as an effective institution for the communication of needs, values and goals from the group up: "leaders are representative, power is diffused among various groups, concern with ideology is limited, and political mobilization is carried out with moderation" (Harik: 1974, 64–65).

Observations of this sort suggest that a significant discontinuity has existed in Egyptian politics between the role of the party organization at the national, provincial, and district levels, on the one hand, and the village at the other. Nonetheless, it has been argued more frequently by scholars of the Egyptian elites that the calculi of state bureaucrats are overriding in the overall modernization process. In this context, then, village level patterns of political participation must not be differentiated from urban level and national level patterns *in kind* but, at most, in degree. Harik himself has pointed to the domination of party by state elsewhere:

> Egyptian politics of radical reform have been implemented primarily by the bureaucracy . . . extensive changes in the culture and process of rural society have been achieved in Egypt by means of increased numbers of government civil servants, aided only to a secondary extent by political cadres (Harik, 1972: 288–89).

If the ASU generally had not distinguished itself in the effort to evolve political cadres with sufficient political influence to matter in the shaping of public policy, it was not for want of trying. The sources seem agreed that the ASU underwent a searching *samo-kritika* during the 1965 –1968 period. The unformalized promise by former President Nasser that a genuine "vanguard organization" (*al-jihāz al-ṭali'i*) would be created within the ASU raised the expectations of a number of activists and intellectuals. Yet, as the veteran leftist journalist in the 1960s, Ahmad Hamrush, put it: ". . . the Vanguard of Socialists did not fill the vacuum that caused Gamal Abdel Nasser sleepless nights" (Binder, 1978: 326). Lurking behind this ironic statement is the intellectuals' full knowledge that the regime would not authorize the active work of the vanguard organization. In 1968, for example, much was made of the fact that officials of the ASU would be elected, rather than appointed as before. This implied the possibility that the vanguard organization would have an important communication and aggregation role to play. Yet, the not unpredictable regime meddling in the electrons led the ASU to continue to be a virtual appenage of the state administration right up to its abolition in 1978 (*Middle East Record*, 1971: 535–47; Dekmejian, 1971: 326–71; Akhavi, 1971: *passim*).

Apart from party organizations, other formal institutions of intraelite communication and action include cabinet ministries, state agencies, and public organizations. One expects that significant patterns of bargaining and coalition-building take place within these structures for advantage, access, and support. An early study found the prevalence of "a highly personalized pattern of administration in which the interplay of religious, class and family interests was, and to a considerable extent still is, the most distinctive behaviour trait." (Sharp, 1957: 158)

No doubt the stark simplicity with which this conclusion is stated — if ever originally true — must be modified to account for change in the structure of the administrative system during the last two decades. As a result of expanding tasks, new functions, and the division of labor, the process of elite interaction within the bureaucracy has taken on new patterns alongside the traditional ones. In a recent paper, two scholars have investigated the relationship between changes in the ministerial elites and public policy outputs in the context of the budgetary process. They indicate a degree of movement away from the apparent hegemony of nepotistic or other ascriptive characteristics and toward a bureaucratic interests framework. Here, the authors stress the correlation between higher levels of bureaucrats' education and budgetary requests made on behalf of more "technocratic" objectives by agencies in which they are the incumbents (Dekmejian and El-Dahry, 1976: *passim*). This is, of course, not to say that higher levels of education among Egyptian elites explain the bureaucratic process in this society. Quite evidently, as in any other complex organization, the Egyptian bureaucracy is riven with cleavages, and these provide part of the structural framework. Among these divisions may be mentioned ideological, patron-client, and intra- and interoffice rivalries. The few glimpses that we have been afforded by the studies on intraelite processes indicate the salient role of corruption as sponsored deliberately by the ruling elite to maintain the allegiance of the strategic elites and their supporters among the approximately half million technocrats in the civil service and public sector.[2]

Such studies also point to the increasing spread of what Weber termed *Zweckrationalität* (rationality with respect to a goal in social action). This is the meaning behind the creation of such entities as the Ministry of Industry or the Petroleum Authority. Yet, the creation of such entities has not been in itself a move in the direction of rationality as defined in terms of a rational calculus means-ends perspective. Instead, such moves — especially if initiated, as they have been, under the aegis of centralization of authority — accommodate better the other meaning of rationalization: imposing clear lines of command from the top and organizing on the basis of a hierarchy of articulated lines of power. Such a pattern of *rationalization* has little to do with a rationality in social action in Weber's and Mannheim's sense. Historically, of course, bureaucratic rule has prevailed through the great departments of the state. The pattern of bureaucratic control has evolved piece-meal over the past century and now includes a tangled set of overlapping controls by the central ministries over a labyrinth of regions, provinces, legal municipalities (Cairo and Alexandria), police districts, communes and villages, almost none of which enjoys any real tax or budgetary autonomy. (Sharp, 1957: 158).

This assessment again requires modification, since significant advances have been made in creating channels for communication between local citizens and the government. But the stress on the lack of tax powers in the localities is apt. Political economists will rightly point to the historical trend tthat national income in Egypt has been generated over the centuries from within the Nile River valley. Now, however, the majority of Egypt's income derives from non-Nile River sources: petroleum exports and sales, tolls from the Suez Canal, tourism, and remittances by Egyptians residing abroad. This shift may portend changes in the relative autonomy of provincial, district, and village bodies to the extent that the slender ribbon of the Nile River valley no longer constitutes the country's "lifeline." According to this line of reasoning, rule from the ministries may be loosened as state leaders become aware that the country's future no longer hinges on the productivity of such a small area.

Sociological data on the Egyptian cabinet in the 1970s indicate some interesting patterns. The following tables provide information on age, education, and careers of 172 cabinet ministers (including President Sadat, who has sometimes served as Prime Minister) during the time period from October 1970 through June 1979. Some of these 172 served one term only; others moved into other cabinet positions; and yet others stayed on in one post for several terms. Over this ten-year period, Egypt had 16 governments; although occasionally a government lasted for a whole year, the mode has been two per year, with new cabinets usually introduced in March-April and October-November. Tables 6.3 through 6.7 present a profile of the members of the Egyptian cabinet.

Some important conclusions derive from these data. In the first place, the correlations between large turnover of cabinet members and policy changes may be discerned. The confrontation between Sadat and the "anti-state" and "anti-party" alignment in May 1971 has become a virtual legend in Egypt. It is not clear how such a powerful coalition could have been overcome by Sadat, against whom were ranged the leaders of the army, police, secret police, party, and aspects of the media. Withal, it was natural for him, upon victory, to purge the cabinet of real and presumed loyalists to the opposition group.

The January 1972 government, again, saw the departure of more than half the ministers. This may be partially related to continued purges of the state apparatus some months after the May "corrective revolution"; but it presumably also had something to do with the winter student-worker demonstrations. These addressed the government's domestic and

TABLE 6.3 Numbers and Continuity of Egyptian Cabinet Members

Month & Year	Oct. '70	Nov. '70	May '71	Sept. '71	Jan. '72	Mar. '73	Nov. '73	Apr. '74
Number	31	31	32	30	33	34	31	34
Carryovers	—	23	17	22	15	16	28	21
Month & Year	Sept. '74	Apr. '75	Mar. '76	Nov. '76	Oct. '77	May '78	Oct. '78	Jun. '79
Number	30	31	29	27	28	28	29	30
Carryovers	26	12	24	19	19	23	12	26

TABLE 6.4 Age of Egyptian Cabinet Members

Month & Year	Oct. '70	Nov. '70	May '71	Sept. '71	Jan. '72	Mar. '73	Nov. '73	Apr. '74
Mean Age	54.8	51.8	52.0	53.1	53.0	53.0	53.6	53.6
St'd Dev.	7.4	7.9	5.9	6.5	5.8	5.4	5.1	6.7
Month & Year	Sept. '74	Apr. '75	Mar. '76	Nov. '76	Oct. '77	May '78	Oct. '78	Jun. '79
Mean Age	53.7	54.9	56.2	54.2	53.9	55.2	54.9	54.3
St'd Dev.	7.2	5.6	5.3	6.5	5.3	5.3	6.5	7.3

TABLE 6.5 Education Specialization of Egyptian Cabinet Members

Education Specialization	Number	%
Economics and Social Science	25	14.5
Engineering (civilian)	33	19.2
Engineering (military)	14	8.1
Humanities	8	4.7
Law	34	19.8
Medicine	9	5.2
Military	25	14.5
Natural Science	16	9.3
Unknown	8	4.7
Totals	172	100.0

foreign policy—especially Sadat's failure to deliver on his promise that 1971 would be Egypt's "year of decision" in the conflict with Israel. This term was a reference to Sadat's unwillingness to continue renewing the cease-fire along the Suez Canal in the absence of Israel's withdrawal from Sinai.

The large-scale cabinet changes of March 1973 may be explained to some extent by Sadat's anti-Soviet moves (the expulsion of Soviet advisors in July 1972) and his preparations for the coming conflict with Israel in October 1973.[3] The April 1974 shifts amounted to changes in less than half the cabinet, it is true; however, a substantial minority of ministers left at this time. This was the period that Sadat launched the initiative known as the *infitāh* ("opening"), inviting extensive foreign investments and establishing a number of free economic zones to provide appropriate incentives. In April 1975, the cabinet lost more than 60 percent of its incumbents as a result of his intensification of *infitāh* and the probable objection to this on the part of a number of ministers whose departments' jurisdictions largely covered the public sector of the economy. One must remember that *infitāh* was accompanied by the undoing of several socialist measures adopted by the Nasser governments in the 1960s (Aulas, 1976: *passim*).

Another low point in continuity of the cabinet was reached in October 1978. This was, of course, a month after the signing of the Camp David Accords. Interestingly, Sadat's surprise trip to Israel in November 1977 did not lead in May 1978 to a major overhaul in that government. Perhaps it required the concrete fact of the peace treaty with Israel to cause extensive disaffection. (On the domestic causes, see below under *Elite Resources and Uses*.)

Although it has not been included in the table, data on the cabinet changes in the spring of 1980 indicate a large carryover.[4] Launching an offensive on the constitutional front, Sadat decreed the elections for the

TABLE 6.6 Level and Place of Education of Egyptian Cabinet Members

Year	Oct. '70	Nov. '70	May '71	Sept. '71	Jan. '72	Mar. '73	Nov. '73	Apr. '74
Level								
Secondary		0	1	1	1	1	1	1
B.A. & B.S.	6	6	10	9	7	10	9	9
M.A. & M.S.	3	3	3	3	2	1	2	2
Ph.D	9	8	10	6	17	14	13	17
M.D.	1	2	2	2	1	0	0	0
Military	12	8	6	7	3	9	8	6
Unknown	3	5	2	3	3	4	4	3
Place								
Egypt	22	25	26	24	21	25	21	25
Abroad	7	6	5	5	11	9	9	7
Unknown	2	0	1	1	1	1	1	2

Year	Sept. '74	Apr. '75	Mar. '76	Nov. '76	Oct. '77	May '78	Oct. '78	Jun. '79
Level								
Secondary	1	1	1	1	1	0	0	0
B.A. & B.S.	8	7	7	6	6	6	10	10
M.A. & M.S.	1	6	6	5	5	6	2	4
Ph.D.	14	10	10	11	11	11	13	14
M.D.	0	0	0	0	1	1	0	0
Military	4	4	4	5	3	3	3	3
Unknown	4	4	4	3	3	3	3	1
Place								
Egypt	20	19	19	18	20	20	25	27
Abroad	7	11	9	8	7	7	2	2
Unknown	3	1	1	1	1	1	2	1

Because certain individuals studied at both civilian and military institutions, the total in each case exceeds the number of incumbents in the cabinet.

TABLE 6.7.   Cabinet Recruitment According to Incumbent's Previous Occupation

Profession	Number	%
Academia	52	30.2
Business (private)	9	55.2
Courts/Law	12	7.0
Diplomatic Corps	11	6.4
Journalism	2	1.2
Labor	2	1.2
Ministerial Bureaucracy	55	32.0
Party/Parliament	4	2.3
Presidential Bureaucracy	7	4.1
Provincial Administration	7	4.1
Public Sector Bureaucracy	21	12.2
Unknown	4	2.3
Totals	186	108.2

Absolute figures and percentages total more than 172 and 100, respectively because in some cases individuals were deemed to be equally active in two occupational sectors.

Consultative Assembly (q.v., *supra*). He has apparently opted for the symbolism of Egypt in the 1923–1952 period, with its stress on ideas of liberal democracy. It remains unclear whether the Consultative Assembly is meant to parallel or supervene over the People's Assembly. In any case, it has been seen by some as a mechanism for the infusion of new elites into the political system and of preventing previous elites' entrenchment.

It is, evidently, not the case that low carryovers of cabinet ministers automatically entail their dismissal or disgrace. In fact, considerable numbers of previous cabinet members currently occupy responsible and frequently politically influential positions.[5] There is a good deal of what may be termed lateral movement among cabinet ministers, and one cannot tell from a formal title whether the new position means a demotion, a promotion, or no change in terms of power.

Another trend that emerges from this data is that the cabinet has not "grown younger" over the decade. It was speculated that as the Sadat period began — in fact, commencing with the March 30, 1968 Manifesto issued by President Nasser on the state of the nation — brilliant young technocrats increasingly would enter the governing ranks. In fact, the mean age slowly increased over time, and the oldest cabinets came in the mid- and late-1970s. Doubtless outstanding examples of highly skilled young individuals may be cited among Egyptian cabinet ministers. But these have been active throughout the post-1952 period; in addition, the young technocrats certainly have not dominated the ruling elite in the 1970s. The Egyptian cabinet's mean age throughout this period was 53.8.

By contrast, the mean age of the Algerian ruling elite during the same period was ten years less. On the other hand, the Egyptian cabinet ministers collectively have not been notably older than those in other countries (at least on an impressionistic basis). It cannot be said of them that they represent a tired old group of bureaucrats, as has frequently been stressed of the "aged" Soviet elite, for example.

Data on education background indicate the important role of civilian engineering and law in preparing the careers of the Egyptian ruling elite. Following these two fields, a strictly military training still counted for something in the overall pattern. Yet, as an aggregate figure, the information on purely military training backgrounds of incumbent ministers is misleading. Officials in this category had become rare in the mid- to late-1970s. In the cabinets of 1979 and 1980, in fact, only three individuals qualified: the Defense Minister, the Minister of the Interior, and the Minister of Foreign Affairs. These are usually considered the most sensitive and powerful portfolios, it is true. And if one notes that both the President of the Republic and the Vice-President also had strictly military educations, then it becomes clear that the proportional influence of the army officers remains strong indeed. Nevertheless, a military education as such does not indicate that the individuals in question automatically serve the corporate interests of the army. Only the defense minister is in perpetual contact with colleagues on the general staff, whereas the others have multiple and cross-cutting responsibilities in the cabinet, the parties, and committees of all kinds.[6]

The trends in level of education indicate a marked rise during the early- to mid-1970s of ministers coopted into the cabinet with Ph.D. degrees. This trend tapered somewhat in the April 1975–1978 May 1978 period but began to rise again at the end. A projection into the future suggests that about half the cabinet will continue to have earned Ph.Ds; that by the mid-1980s the mean age of cabinet members will be 56; and that approximately two-thirds of the ministers will have completed their university education in Egyptian institutions. With regard to this last datum, it is notable that, in the most recent period, cabinet officers were virtually exclusively trained in Egyptian universities. This bespeaks of the greater self-reliance emphasis by the Sadat regime in numerous public speeches by leading members of the ruling elite. It is also a function of the expansion of the Egyptian university system from four universities in the 1960s to about 25 today.

One final sociological finding from this data is the significant proportion (nearly a third) of ministers for whom academia proved a stepping stone to a ministerial position. The only other field rivaling academia in this respect has been the ministerial bureaucracy. In brief, vertical and horizontal recruitment into the cabinet appear to be equally important. It bears mentioning that service in the public sector of the economy appears to be less promising as an avenue to ministerial status than in the 1960s.

In summary, the Egyptian ruling elite seems to be a diffused elite, quite different from the pattern of a more coherent group of individuals united by corporate interests unique to them. The notion of praetorian solidarities binding a military elite together is simply not an accurate description of the Egyptian political system. A more useful conceptualization is one which stresses patron-client relationships, whereby cross-cutting loyalties and personalism become operating factors. More will be said about this below.

In regard to the Public Organizations of the economy as institutional vehicles for elite behavior, substantive power in decision making has not lain with their corporate broads but rather with the President, through the ministries to which the organizations have been attached. Because policy more often than not is handed down through the ministries, procedural issues tend to be those about which contention and bargaining take place. There has been discussion about the dismantling of the public organizations, but it would seem that for the time being they will be left to operate as before. The managerial leaders in these organizations tend to affiliate around two groups: the appointed members of the board of directors (designated by the President), and the elected members, chosen by the workers in the enterprise. Because of education-level differences, these two groups might be expected to conflict. However, it has been argued that the members of the board in the Public Organizations have exhibited greater mutual compatibility than incompatibility, tending to verify Homans' proposition that increased interaction correlates positively with degree of liking and cooperation (Farid, 1970: 15–19). On the other hand, it has been also reported that Egyptian industrial workers in general feel anger toward board members they have elected because these members become subservient to the appointed ones (El-Sayed, 1978: 48). Therefore, the compatibility may be a function of abandoning one's constituency, rather than deriving from meaningful and rational discussion of the issues.

Virtually no evidence exists about elite conflict and cooperation within the Public Organizations. Presidential appointment has tended to ensure dependency and acquiescence. The directors of private enterprises, which predominated prior to the July 1961 socialization measures, were not appointed to the boards of the Public Organizations. Yet, the regime wished to avail itself of the experience and skill of these individuals. Thus, many were retained in the capacity of managers of particular firms within the Organizations. This often led to situations in which general managers would be called into ongoing meetings of the board of directors of the Organizations in order to explain certain matters; and, having made their points, they were thereupon politely shown the door. Deprived thus of decision-making authority, such managers became demoralized, and many resigned without being replaced. A complicating factor, too, was the relatively better salaries in the public sector (Farid, 1970: 31–32).

In the Sadat period, a proliferation of private companies may be seen. Names such as Kafrawi, Madbuli and, of course, 'Uthman may be seen on advertising billboards in many parts of Cairo. But their activities appear restricted to housing and hotel construction. The Public Sector and Ministerial bureaucracies are integrated in such a way that they present fascinating grounds for research in patronage. The little that has been written about the behavior of officials in the Public Sector Organizations in the past has indicated such characteristics as careerism, lack of initiative, routinization, and strict adherence to the demands of the ruling elite (Berger, 1957: 148; Baker, 1978: 178ff). In the 1960s, the Higher Supervision Committee, headed by Nasser's closest crony, Marshal 'Amir, was able to enforce conformity among Public Sector elites. In the Sadat era, perhaps this role is being performed by 'Abd al-Qadir Hatim in his capacity as General Supervisor of the Specialized National Councils (*al-Ahram*, October 5, 1980).

Considerations of space forbid a discussion of the intelligence services as a vehicle for elite power and influence. But the difference between the Nasser and Sadat periods is as follows: "Nasser allowed the growth of an elaborate apparatus in his private office, the secret security services . . ." (Vatikiotis, 1978: 159). Some four different agencies conducted espionage on society and upon each other. Sadat has relied far more upon patronage and frequent changes in elite ranks to keep his rivals off balance.

Of the remaining institutional structures, a few words are in order concerning the professional syndicates. Sadat has seemingly made it a practice to honor each in turn in 1980, presenting awards and making public speeches to their members. A recent study of the lawyers' syndicate provides insight into its efforts to avert domination by the mass mobilization organization in the late 1960s and early 70s. In the confrontation, the ASU used such heavy-handed tactics that, after the purge of its leaders in May 1971, the new Secretary-General publicly attacked the previous leaders' meddling in syndicate elections. The Lawyers' Syndicate had "very damaging evidence" to divulge against the ASU, which "was forced into a holding action as its leaders tried to protect their reputations and ensure that no opponents could use the syndicates against them in the struggle for power" (Springborg, 1978: 293–94).

The engineering profession, headed by 'Uthman Ahmad 'Uthman, has been described as a new channel for an old elite. Technocratic in value orientation, its syndicate has worked hand in glove with the regime to promote the latter's policies. The sons of the old Egyptian elite, it has been argued, have entered the engineering ranks in large numbers and have found in the profession the wherewithal to perpetuate their own class interests (Moore, 1978: 2, et. seq.). An indication of the engineers' links with the regime is that seven cabinet ministers were awarded medals of recognition by President Sadat on "Engineer's Day," October 12, 1980 (*al-Ahram*, October 13, 1980).

As for informal structures available to elites in Egypt, the patron-client network is the most important. It has been suggested that in Egypt "the institutional framework is extensive and the ties between multiple sponsors and multiple clients diffuse and cross-cutting" (Moore, 1977: 258). Yet, the presence of horizontal linkages among intermediaries with roughly equal resources diffused throughout the system has to be stressed as well. The mechanism linking such individuals with one another is a *shillah*. "Bureaucrats who manage to beat the system cannot be considered personal retainers or 'clients' of their administrative superiors or any other single patron" (Moore, 1977: 261). The individuals cited in footnote 5 have no doubt managed to reach their postcabinet positions as a result of personal contacts. But these contacts are not necessarily with those who are their hierarchical superiors. Often, their postcabinet jobs carry the equivalent of ministerrial rank. Individuals who, early in their careers, begin the political climb to higher office apparently have to make their own choices at critical junctures as to when to hopscotch from one crony group to another. Thus, cabinet reshuffles do not necessarily lead to the demise of their political career but are frequently lateral moves to positions from which they may continue their careers.

Some details of the personal careers of typical beneficiaries of *shillah* connections have been published in the literature. First-order resources, such as wealth, have yielded in the Republican period (that is, since 1952) to "strategic personal contacts within administrative and political structures as the main basis for clientelism . . ." (Springborg, 1975: 94). It often happens that the favors extended to political climbers are "one-shot affairs" (Moore, 1977: 263). As a consequence, the *shillahs* are notably unstable. The welter of cross-cutting patron-client formations suggests a great deal of flux below the surface. Often, corruption becomes the lubricant facilitating political exchanges. A recent inquiry on corruption suggests that Nasser deliberaely encouraged the police and security apparatus in the mid- and late-1960s "to exploit their power for personal ends" in order to maintain his eroding authority (Waterbury, 1976: 435). Another scholar suggests that corruption "appears to be extensive, yet decentralized . . . paralleling the structure of the *shillah* . . ." (Moore, 1977: 271, 263). The reason for the *diffusion* of corruption appears to be the enormous size of the bureaucracy, rendering it difficult for one individual to control the process.

ELITE RESOURCES AND USES

In general, elites command a wide variety of resources. These include access, wealth, status-honor, knowledge, age, scientific or technical skills, information, piety, administrative rank, documentation, jobs, bureaucratic power, and allies. The tactics they can use include repression, mobilization, exclusion, temporization, dismissal, promotion, cooptation, conformity, innovation, and many others. It becomes clear that one cannot easily separate tactics and resources if they are classified as above. Mobilization is both a resource and a tactic to a member or members of an elite seeking to advance its interests.

Let us examine a case in the Sadat period in which the President wielded certain resources and employed particular tactics in an internal policy shift. In 1976, seeking to establish a tutorial democratic system Sadat sanctioned a "multiparty system" for Egypt. Accordingly, three tribunes, or platforms, were established within the old ASU—a center, left, and right. Things worked more or less according to plan at the start, although the left-wing party, headed by Khalid Muhyi al-Dinr, the *bête-noire* of all Egyptian regimes under Nasser and Sadat, proved highly critical despite having only a tiny parliamentary following. The serious problems arose when—as the left persisted in its attacks—certain important personalities in private business and the professions resurrected the old Wafd Party. This organization had been the dominant party of Egypt prior to 1952 and had been dissolved by the Free Officers in early 1953.

Stung by the criticisms of the left, Sadat made a public attack on "irresponsible elements" in Egyptian society in May 1978. He then decreed a national referendum which duly registered the approval of "98 percent" of the population of Sadat's principles of procedure. The next month, in what was probably its last action, the Central Committee of the ASU approved an ethical code of conduct that effectively rendered the left a pariah organization. Coordinate with these developments, Sadat entered the fray himself and ordered the merger of the New Wafd Party into the center tribune of the ASU, which led to the latter's final demise. There then followed a purge which, as has already been noted, led to the elimination of all but twelve cabinet members in October 1978.[7] Sadat's own political organization, the National Democratic party, was thus born as the product of the merger mentioned above. And, although pro forma efforts to create a loyal opposition party have taken place, the electoral results of September 1980 speak for themselves.

This case demonstrates several points: (1) Although the state machinery is too vast for one individual to manipulate at all moments, if President Sadat wishes to do something badly enough, he can employ the necessary resources. (2) In this case the resources included his administrative rank, his status-honor, information about the movements of his adversaries, job patronage, and bureaucratic power all together. Sadat also appears to have availed himself of all the tactics mentioned, although mobilization is a harder task for him than it apparently was for his predecessor. (3) The institutional structure is relatively fragile, since Sadat could not tolerate even what amounted to verbal sniping from the

National Progressive Union party (the left), with its two-member representation in the Parliament.

It is useful to consider resources and tactics within the following broad dichotomy in the public policy of regimes since 1952: (1) a great stress on *creating* social productivity in a context where it is perceived by the ruling elite to be badly lacking; and (2) strong emphasis on *distributing* social productively. These are the classic orientations of fascist and socialist public policy. As ideal types, they do not apply automatically to reality. But perhaps a simple matrix such as the following will assist in following and comprehending elite action in terms of resource use and tactics associated with them during the nearly 30 years of presidential rule in Egypt.

Creation of Social Productivity

	Strong	Weak
Strong	1956–1965	1952–1955
Weak	1973–1980	1967–1973

Distribution of Social Productivity

FIGURE 6.2   Simple Matrix Depicting Regime Performance With Respect to Resource Use

Because Sadat has led Egypt into a peace treaty with Israel, his political line in the period especially since 1977 has been social peace (*al-salām al-ijtimāi*), prosperity, and welfare services for all needing them. The themes of public campaigns suggest that distribution of benefits is central to public policy. In practice, however, economic policies seem geared to increasing productivity and output. Despite the slogan of social peace, *infitāh* has tended to increase class antagonism and lower-class resentment against the liberal bourgeoisie, state bureaucrats, and middlemen (Baker, 1978: 148). While the causes of low performance with respect to distribution of social productivity are complex, frequently the result of non-coordination between private and public sector, inadequate delegation of authority, red tape, and so forth, the result has been to widen the elite-mass gap. Much of the resources produced in the Sadat period have been channeled into construction of hotels and resorts. Whereas large amounts of foreign exchange have entered Egypt as a result of the tourist boom, the profits do not seem to be benefiting the large mass of the population directly. In the meanwhile, the income tax law has failed to provide the regime with the leverage to level income differences among social groups. A campaign is under way to revise the law, but the reality in the last ten years has been public finance administration under the terms of the existing law.[8] When this is added to Sadat's calls for "Egypt comes before everything," the picture closely resembles that of a rightist regime attempting to find the country's "place in the sun." Resources are apparently being utilized in the interests of a corporatist model of politics. Industrialization has classically been the method to create social productivity according to this model, with the rural sector generating the savings to finance it. In Egypt, too, the agricultural sector lags, and the country continues to be a net food importer in spite of its historical pattern of self-sufficiency and of exporting foodstuffs (especially grain).

Given the above and the structure of elite politics in Egypt, it comes as no surprise that foreign policy initiatives become a means for rationalizing slow progress domestically. Nasser's foreign policy successes were tied to his charismatic personality, a resource he utilized to advantage until the 1967 war. Strictly speaking, charismatic authority and followership reject careerist motivations, meting out of material largesse, and pecuniary aspirations. Yet, the process of institutionalization in Egypt witnessed the emergence of these qualities over time, not only in the last decade but in the Nasser period as well (Entelis, 1974: 463–64). As organizations such as the ASU, public sector corporations, cooperatives, and local administration evolved, Nasser's charisma (Dekmejian, 1971: 3–16) was supposed to interpenetrate and sustain them. However, if this were ever a likelihood in the first instance, it was consistently vitiated by the predilection of Nasser's "administrative staff" to behave as bureaucratic barons. For that matter, such "infeudation" was positively encouraged by Nasser as part of what has been termed by one scholar "planned corruption for the purpose of balancing the elites" (Waterbury, 1976: 436–45). With bureaucratic chiefs affiliating around one another and, vertically, with subordinates and superiors, it became increasingly difficult to serve the common interest of the public as the affiliations became ends in themselves. It will be conceded that the arrangement just described dissipates the image of a charismatic followership spontaneously submitting to a salvationist leader. Yet, despite these observations, the ideal type of the charismatic leader has since been affirmed, with suggestions that conscious focus on the psychodynamics of the charismatic leader will push us further along the path of understanding (Dekmejian, 1976: 158–72; Bowie, 1976: 148–57).

Charisma may have more explanatory value with regard to elite-mass relations than to intraelite politics. Its inapplicability to the latter may be illustrated by the conflict between the 'inseparables" of the Egyptian revolution: Nasser and 'Abd al-Hakim 'Amir. Possibly as early as the Suez war of 1956, and certainly by the early 1960 Nasser had come to doubt seriously the wisdom of permitting the Egyptian army to become a state within a state. In the attempt to confine the growing power of

'Amir, he promoted two resources which he hoped he could control and thus be able to regulate 'Amir's actions. These resources were: (1) a political vanguard organization within the ASU that would be staffed by committed ideologues and apparatchiks, and (2) the intelligence apparatus.

We know now that during the 1960s a certain duality of power existed between Nasser and 'Amir (Stephens, 1971: 359). The conflict with 'Amir began to take on serious proportions in the context of his failed role as Egypt's "High Commissioner" in Syria. 'Amir's ineptitude in handling the Syrian secession from the unity with Egypt in 1961 generated bitterness among rivals within the elite. At the heart of the animosity was 'Amirs apparent ability to remain Nasser's closest aide. His influence over Nasser remained strong enough to lead Nasser to shelve his project of separating the post of defense minister from that of commander of the armed forces. Fearing 'Amir would lead a military coup against him if he pressed the issue of professionalizing the military, Nasser went so far as to make 'Amir First Vice-President and eliminated the rivals from the Presidential Council, which was abolished. Ultimately, 'Amir's crony, Shams al-Din Badran, became Defense Minister. Therefore, the separation which Nasser finally accomplished between the two positions in fact did nothing to meet growing fears of empire building by 'Amir and his entourage (Sadat, 1977: 155 ff.)

Given this, Nasser actively encouraged the ASU "ideologues" to emerge and consolidate the regime's ideology. The utilization of ideology to expand political *power* meshes well with the frankly utilitarian orientation that the regime had toward it from the start. It has been observed that ideology occupies a "relatively unimportant place . . . in Egyptian politics," and that "the politico-military elite is culturally non-ideologically inclined and anti-intellectual" (Binder, 1965: 445). Other scholars have suggested that "practical ideology" (defined as that "legitimating particular political strategies or tactics in a logical and systematic way") does not flourish. (Moore, 1971: 106, 107). Content and consistency do not constitute the primary objectives of its formulators. Of greater importance are the manner in which ideology is presented, its uses, and the targets to whom the messages are directed (Kerr, 1965: 127–44; Kerr, 1963: 9–40; Binder, 1964: esp. 198–229; Rejwan, 1974, *passim*; Akhavi, 1975b: 190–211).

Now, the vehement attacks by the left ideologues against the "power centers" must be seen in the backdrop of Nasser's need to reign in the military leadership. Yet, complicating the situation was the fact that the left was itself splintered between the ASU leaders and the more authentic Marxist left, the latter of which articulated its views in the journal *al-Tali'ah*. Apparently, this fractionalization itself was deliberately encouraged by Nasser, who was ever on the alert against conspiratorial moves against him (Shamir, 1973: 310).

To add yet another astounding feature to these developments, Nasser had insisted that none other than 'Abd al-Hakim 'Amir should be positioned within the Marxist wing of the ASU vanguard organization as its *deus ex machina*! The rapid influx of radical leftists into the vanguard organization — itself designed to counterbalance the growing power of the army — posed a danger for Nasser. He could not afford to permit the crystallization of a genuine militant organization lest it eventually confront his own authoritarian rule. 'Amir was placed in the midst of the Marxists, and they were "require[d] that all business be transacted through him. 'Amir would not engage in ideological discussion with the leftist leadership in the vanguard and he did make some effort to keep them under surveillance" (Binder, 1978: 333).

The ideological weapon clearly represented a double-edged sword for Nasser, and he had to be careful not to be hurt by its use. He employed it to domesticate his rivals. The ASU vanguard organization was encouraged to elaborate a socialist ideology with the aim of counterbalancing the growing power of the army leadership. But Nasser never permitted the committed intellectuals on the left to take their ideology so seriously as to mobilize others independently. He utilized the power of appointment to promote rivalries within the left, as well as to break up the putative unity of the Marxist left itself. In making 'Amir decisive to the operations of the Marxist left, Nasser exhibited his extraordinary consistency in avoiding permanent commitments. He used ideology as a resource to supply himself with as much tactical power and autonomy as possible.

SOCIALIZATION FACTORS

The Military Academy, which began accepting Egyptian commoners in 1936, comprised a key socializing institution for the ruling elite in the early Republican period. But, as the army declined as a source for talent among the political elite, the significance of the Academy diminished. Egypt now has about 25 state universities, and, as has already been noted, the ruling elites in recent times have been graduates of these institutions in very large measure. While foreign education has, of course, not ceased to count for something in the overall scheme of things, it is less a factor than is commonly assumed.

Early on, the state's control over the educational system was anchored in Law 112 of 1959. This law

> prohibited any Egyptian student from accepting a scholarship from any foreign government, organization, or individual without the approval of the President of the Higher Committee for Student Missions ... so that today government authority regulates both students studying at government expense and at their own (Quabain, 1966: 184).

Domestically, too, the regime has practiced the centralization of authority in regard to the universities. The Ministry of Higher Education has substantive and virtually limitless discretionary authority to regulate the educational process. The Supreme Council of the Universities, an arm of the Ministry, has responsibility for the entire range of higher education matters, including the creation of new institutions, expansion of existing ones, admissions, curriculum, new programs, phasing out old programs or facilities, degree requirements, and faculty appointments, promotions, and terminations (Qubain, 1966: 72–73).

The chancellors of the universities of Egypt are appointed by presidential decree. Politics has mingled with education at the universities to the extent that the Chancellor of 'Ayn Shams University is the Chairman of the NDP's Program Committee; the Chancellors of Asyut and Zaqaziq Universities are NDP Secretaries-General of Asyut and Sharqiyah governorates, respectively; the Chancellors of Minya and Mansurah Universities have been elected to the Majlis al-Shura (the "upper house" of the legislature) as NDP deputies; and those of Cairo, Alexandria, and Asyut have been appointed to that body by presidential decree (doubtless also to affiliate with the NDP).[9]

Apart from wishing to control the educational process, regime intervention is based on the desire to train technocrats in far higher numbers than previously. In the earlier period, Egyptian universities "created a surplus of university graduates in such unproductive fields as law, commercial accounting, and liberal arts" (Kerr, 1965; 169). But deliberate sponsorship of fellowships in science and technology have characterized recent regime efforts (Be'eri, 1970: 431; Qubain, 1966: 188).

The question then presents itself: Given the shift in emphasis to science and technology, what impact has this had on the sources of university student attitudes, ideology, and inspirations? Certainly, student demonstrations have continued to be a factor in Egyptian politics in the Sadat period. Yet, it is difficult to assess these developments as constituting leftist or rightist protest. One normally thinks of the importance of Marxism to student attitudes. But one must be cautious in the absence of concrete data on affiliations. Marxism has not done well either within Egyptian society or among Egypt's elites. "The fact that most Arab countries recently celebrated the centenary of Lenin's birth with varying degrees of fanfare only underlines their relative impermeability to his teachings" (Moore, 1971: 106). The socializing institutions for Marxism are, of course, informal discussion groups and networks. Although the ASU vanguard and *al-Ahram* had been the locus of certain leftist activity in the past, it has been seen that by and large the elements there were "regime" (or safe) leftists. Famous Egyptian Marxists have not been barred from writing their views in publications in Egypt. But the point is that these people seldom had the opportunity to institutionalize their position. Isma'il Sabri 'Abdullah had had occasion to go further along this route than others when he was Minister of Planning in the earlier part of the Sadat period, but he was fired when *infitāh* was fully launched in 1975. The major socializing vehicle of Marxist thought has been the journal *al-Tali'ah*, but it is currently proscribed, and the leftist writers have been purged.

Of the other publications, occasional independent lines of thought emerge. Egyptian elites appear to read *al-Ahrām* and *al-Akhbār*. The formats are similar, although *Al-Ahrām* seems to carry more pedantic and social-scientific material. Sadat has permitted Mustafa Amin to write for his old paper, *al-Akhbār*, whereas he had been imprisoned for many years by Nasser under charges of espionage on behalf of the United States. Recently, he cautiously critized the short tenure of Egyptian cabinet ministers (the mean is 1.5 years), which he declared has resulted in inconsistency in policy, delays in implementation, lack of initiative, and public ignorance of their names and activities (*al-Akhbār*, October 17, 1980). This marks an implicit criticism of Sadat's practice of frequent cabinet turnover in order to reward supporters and check potential opposition to his policies. Sadat has recently sought to counter such verbal sniping by launching, in March 1981, a new newspaper, *Māyū*, which represents his personal views.

The heavy-handed attempts by the regime to socialize Egyptian elites according to its own vision has presented the intellectuals especially with a dilemma. While all seem to agree that the Sadat period has provided an opening up of the climate of discussion, the universities continue to be rewarded for technocratic achievement rather than for open debate and research on social values and change. Empirical research of a high order is going on in a number of newly established institutes within these universities, leading to ever increasing knowledge regarding income distribution, mobility of migrants, and the like. But it is difficult for other constituencies to have access to the findings of such research and therefore to discuss the implications of their findings. The conclusions of such reports are retained by a small circle of academics and government officials, and completed studies often are shelved owing to the sensitive nature of their conclusions. Consequently, while political and social thought are not forbidden, elites still seem to be socialized either not to engage in such thought or to "write for the desk drawer."

One factor that must be acknowledged despite the lack of data is the role of Islamic thought and movements. Early in the Sadat period, the press indicated a rise in the activities of the Muslim Brotherhood. In 1974 the government arrested members of the Islamic Liberation party, whom it charged with conspiracy to overthrow the government. In 1977, the so-called Repentence and Renunciation group carried out the assassination of the Minister of Awqaf. It has been estimated that between one-fifth to one-third of the Egyptian student population is influenced by organizations of the Islamic right (Büttner, 1979: 65–66). In 1980, the Interior Minister announced to the First Congress of the NDP that 25 members of the Islamic Liberation party had been arrested for plots against the government (*al-Ahram*, September 30, 1980). Sadat's promise to the Congress that he would not permit religion to mix in politics will doubtless be translated into ever closer supervision of students in the Islamic societies. The socialization patterns and content will once again be determined by edict from above. Partially in response to the need to regulate socialization of elites in terms of Islamic culture and beliefs, President Sadat has decreed the creation of a League of Arab and Islamic Peoples, to be established in Cairo, with himself as chairman of its founding committee.[10]

Socialization of Egyptian youth has been influenced by their study abroad. Within the Arab world, Ba'thist ideology no doubt has played a role of some importance. But just as there does not appear to be a "pure" Ba'thism, so Egyptians' socialization with respect to Ba'thism probably amounts to the influence upon them of an amalgam of leftist ideas that draws its content from diverse sources, such as Marx, Lenin, Mao, Gramsci, Munif al-Razzaz (the Jordanian Ba'thist), Lutfi al-Sayyid (the father of Egyptian liberal thought), Sati' al-Husri (the Syrian socialist), and Michel 'Aflaq (ideologist and cofounder of the Ba'th Party). The influence of rightist currents of thought from abroad center around the writings of the Syrian leader of that country's Muslim Brotherhood organization, Mustafa al-Siba'i. The activites of the Brotherhood in Egypt are probably loosely coordinated with its foreign branches, and it is likely that one of the characteristics that the regime finds troublesome is the urban focus of its activities, notwithstanding the statistically rural basis of its membership. Furthermore, it is a distinctly "middle class" movement whose members "had passed through varying degrees of Westernization and had already accepted some of its premises" (Mitchell, 1969: *passim*, and at 329, 331).

Perhaps something needs to be said about the rural middle-holders as an agency of socialization. Although a social stratum is not normally considered an institution (as opposed to family, mosque, or school, for example), the values of the middle land owners have supported the Egyptian political elite throughout the last three decades. The People's Assembly has consistently reflected this connection. "The parliamentary elite is to a substantial degree traditional, historically established, rural-agrarian in origin . . ." (Binder, 1978: 160). At certain junctures, the regime has had to back away from its overidentification with the rural middle holders.

> . . . the profound structural changes in the economic and political system during 1961–1962 unleashed important conflicts of interest between the regime and the new rural elite, which became much more clearly exposed during the second half of the sixties . . . the regime's assessment

of the situation during 1965–1966 resulted in a change in policy designed to encourage the small peasantry . . . to assume a new political role in the countryside and to be trained to become a competing elite (Abdel-Fadel, 1975: 121–22).

Perhaps this tendency might have continued, but the reality in the 1970s (the Sadat period) has apparently been a restoration of the old emphasis on support for the more well-to-do peasantry. The 1975 amendment to the land law is a case in point. According to its provisions, (1) rents were increased by 25 percent; (2) the grace period for being in arrears in rental payments was drastically reduced from 36 to 2 months; (3) civil courts replaced the village committees in matters of rent disputes, thereby depriving the poorer peasantry of a forum in which their views had been sympathetically aired; (4) the rental could now again be in kind, reversing the provisions of the original law of 1952 and probably facilitating extortion (Aulas, 1976: 89–90).

It would be interesting to look at the social basis of the current People's Assembly and Consultative Assembly to determine whether the previous pattern holds. The argument, it will be noted, is not that the deputies themselves are rural middle holders, but that they come from families characterized as such. Whereas occupationally they may be expected to be quite diverse, their rural origins would tend to reinforce values and methods identified with that social force: paternalism, antisecularism, opposition to rapid social mobility changes, and so forth.

CONCLUSIONS

Egypt is a bureaucratic society in which the political elite is diffused both structurally and in terms of values. No monolithic force regulates the public policy of the country. The President of the Republic in the last decade has consciously relied on retraditionalization as a means of development, but this does not mean that rule and power can be analyzed in any reductionist or simplistic manner. This may seem surprising in a system as centralized as Egypt. But while in a centralized system the state may dominate public life, this in itself tells us little about the nature of incumbents in state positions, their values, their resources, or their interrelationships.

The description, structure, circulation, resources, and socialization of the Egyptian political elite have been examined in the foregoing pages. Perhaps the following themes may be mentioned by virtue of a summary: (1) civilianization of the elite; (2) rationalization of work methods; and 3) stratification between elite and society.

It will not do to call the Egyptian system praetorian. The evidence shows that the military has no played the role in politics that this term connotes. Moreoever, the formulators of this concept have insisted that praetorian societies lack social cohesion; it is a patent absurdity to attribute lack of cohesion to Egypt. Even at the time when Egypt was supposed to be a "praetorian society par excellence" (1965–1967), only some 5–7 percent of the state's employees had military backgrounds (Moore, 1978: 17–18). The trend toward civil rule in the Sadat period is unmistakable, and the consequences seem to be improved mobility opportunities for those in the free professions over army/police in terms of jobs and incomes.

The technocrats appear to have been receiving the largest share of political influence and wealth in Egypt during the last decade. Rationalization of work methods is a hallmark of this group. But the other meaning of rationalization continues to apply in Egyptian politics. Thus, one continues to hear and read about leaders urging logical, means/ends decision making while these same leaders practice the routines of hierarchalization and control. Of the technocrats as a whole, perhaps the most conspicuously successful group in the last ten years has been the contractors, for whom the 1981–1985 Development Plan has allocated 45 percent of total investments (*al-Ahram*, October 17, 1980).

Egyptian society continues to be a highly stratified society, with wealth continuing to play an important role in separating elites from nonelites in the last decade. This wealth is based on gains in the industrial, financial, and construction sectors. Education, skills, and access through clientage loom large as resources, command of which gives their retainers sizable advantage in the competition for authority and influence. It will be noted that ability in itself is insufficient to reach the automatic-tenure, pension-guaranteed positions in the civil service.

Despite reassurances to the contrary, Egypt appears to be moving increasingly away from the model of a planned economy. One of the most telling symptoms of this is the change that has occurred in the salary structure for officials in the public and private sectors of the economy. Whereas a decade ago the public sector paid higher salaries, the private sector now pays either competitive or higher salaries. This does not necessarily mean a decline in the relative power of the bureaucratic state, however, for its impact has consistently been overwhelming, even during periods of capitalist development. In the final analysis, Egypt's future development will depend on the ability of its political elite to moderate the influence of the state apparatus on public life. The particular configurations of elite actions, however, will depend on internal and external forces that are not altogether clear at this point, despite what we now know about the subject.

NOTES

1. This information is based on data gathered by Moushira El-Geziri, a graduate student in political science at the American University in Cairo. Interestingly, cabinet officers with nontechnical military backgrounds in the 1970s comprise 14 percent of the total, again contrary to expectations that they would be less represented than the officer-engineers. A fuller picture of the cabinet in the Sadat period is presented below.

2. The table is based on Moore, 1977: 262. He lists 137,814 employed in "specialized jobs" and 288,044 in "technical jobs" in 1971–72. If one allows for growth in the work force, the figure of 500,000 does not seem improbable in calculating the size of the "support system," as it were, for the strategic elites in the 1980s.

3. In his book, *Red Star Over the Nile* (Princeton: Princeton University Press, 1977), Alvin Z. Rubinstein suggests that February-March 1973 was a critical turning point in Sadat's decision to launch the October war of 1973.

4. More than two-thirds of the ministers were retained in the new spring 1980 cabinet.

5. The following is a randomly gathered list of cabinet member circulation into noncabinet posts: (17.4% of Number)

Cabinet Member	Cabinet Post And Years	Post-Cabinet Position [1980]
1. Dr. Mustafa Khalil	PM, 1978–1979	Deputy Chairman, NDP
2. Dr. Muhammad Kamil Laylah	Higher Education, 1973	Chancellor, 'Ayn Shams University
3. 'Uthman Ahmad 'Uthman	Housing and Reconstruction, 1974–1975	Chairman, NDP Committee on Popular Growth (*tanmiyah sha'biyah*); Leader Engineer's Syndicate
4. Albert Barsum Salamah	State for People's Assembly Affairs, 1973–1976	Deputy Secretary-General, NDP
5. 'Abd al-Latif Bultiyah	Labor, 1970–1971, 1975–1977	Secretary-General, NDP Cairo Governorate
6. 'Abd al-'Aziz 'Isa	Justice, 1973–1975	Full Member, Majlis al-Shura (Appointed)
7. Zakariya Tawfiq 'Abd al-Fattah	Foreign Trade, 1975–1978	Governor, Suez Canal Bank
8. Dr. Mahmud Amin 'Abd al-Hafiz	Tourism, 1973, 1978–1979	Governor of Gizah
9. Nasif Tahun	Supply, 1978–1979	Chairman, Agency for the Construction and Development of Egyptian Villages
10. 'Abd al-Qadir Hatim	Deputy PM for Information, 1971–1974	Assistant (*musā'id*) to the President of the Republic
11. Engineer Tawfiq Kararah	Land Reclamation, 1978–1979	Governor of Daqahliyah
12. Dr. Muhammad 'Abd al-Rahman Baysar	*Awqaf*, 1978–1979	Chancellor of al-Azhar University
13. Dr. Na'im Abu Talib	Transport, 1977–1978	Governor of Alexandria
14. Muhammad Hamdi 'Ashur	Local Administration, 1970	Full Member, Majlis al-Shura

15. 'Abd al-'Aziz Hijazi	PM and Deputy PM, 1970–1975	Leader of the Businessmen's Syndicate
16. Sayyid Mar'i	Agriculture, 1970–1971	Assistant to the President of the Republic
17. Mamduh Salim	Interior, Deputy PM, PM, 1971–1978	Assistant to the President of the Republic
18. Kamal Henry Abadir	Communications, 1970–1971	MP in People's Assembly and Chairman of its Committee on National Security and Defense
19. Muhibb Stinu	Tourism, 1977–1978	Chairman, Housing Committee, People's Assembly
20. Ahmad 'Ali Kamal	Irrigation, 1974–1975	Chairman, Organization for Reclamation and Irrigation of Pyramids Desert Region; Member, Board of Directors, Al-Ahram Bank
21. Ibrahim Najib	Tourism, 1971–1972, 1974–1976	Engineering Consultant, Arab Contractors Corporation ('Uthman Ahmad 'Uthman's company)
22. Hafiz Badawi	Social Affairs, 1970	Chairman, Legislation Committee, People's Assembly
23. Shams al-Din Wakil	Higher Education, 1972	Chairman, Executive Council UNESCO
24. 'Abd al-Halim Mahmud	Awqaf, 1972	Full Member, Majlis al-Shura
25. Muhammad Hamid Mahmud	Local Administration, 1974–1978	Chairman, Committee on Arab Affairs, People's Assembly
26. Sulayman 'Abd al-Hayy	Transportation, 1971, 1972	Chairman, Supreme Consultative Committee for Construction
27. Dr. Ibrahim Badran	Health, 1977–1978	Director, Academy of Scientific and Technological Research; Vice-Chancellor, 'Ayn Shams University
28. 'Abd al-Mun'im al-Sawi	Information, 1977–1978	Full Member Majlis al-Shura (Appointed)
29. Muhammad Mitwalli Sha'rawi	Awqaf, 1976–1978	Full Member, Majlis al-Shura (Appointed)
30. Dr. Mahmud Mahfuz	Health, 1972–1975	Full Member, Majlis al-Shura (Appointed)

6. A linear regression trend analysis suggests the continued decline in numbers of such individuals in the future. (It is, of course, impossible to say what effect the current conflict between Iraq and Iran might have on President Sadat's perception of Egyptian security needs. The progress — or lack thereof — of peace negotiations between Israel and Egypt will perhaps also have a bearing on the cooptation of military figures into the cabinet in the future.)

Supporting the notion of a marked decline in influence of military officers is the percentage of provincial governors with army backgrounds. Of the 27 governors (incuding the Gaza District), seven are army officers in 1980. The governorates are Northern Sinai, Southern Sinai, Gaza District, Matruh, Red Sea, Suhaj, and Minya. Security considerations can readily justify the appointment of generals to the first five on this list. By comparison with earlier periods, the proportion of governors who were officers sometimes went as high as 80 percent (Akhavi, 1975b: 89–90).

7. This and the previous paragraph are based on an article by my good colleague, Friedemann Buttner, (1979, esp. 58–60).

8. In reality, the existing law was introduced in 1939, and it has been amended 87 times. According to the Director of the Information Section of the Taxation Department of the Ministry of Economics, only 30–35 percent of the people paid taxes during the last several years. "We do not need a new law but the consolidation of the existing one," he told *al-Ahram* in an interview published by the paper on October 17, 1980.

9. This information has been culled from issues of *al-Ahram* newspaper during September and October 1980.

10. He first mooted the idea before the first Congress of the NDP in the context of an attack against mixing religion and politics. He made it official about a week later. See *al-Ahram*, October 9, 1980.

REFERENCES

General Reference

Arab Report and Record
Cahiers d'Orient Contemporaine
Europa Yearbook
Facts on File
Keesing's Contemporary Archives
The Middle East and North Africa
The Middle East Record. Tel Aviv and New York. Jerusalem University Press
    and Wiley. 5 Vols., 1961, 1967, 1968, 1969–1970.
U.S. Department of State, Embassy in Cairo. *Directory of UAR Personnages.*
    1964, 1965, 1966.
Who's Who in the Arab World

Journal Titles, Middle Eastern Studies

L'Afrique et l'Asie Modernes
American Journal of Arabic Studies
American Universities Field Staff Reports
The American Zionist
Arab Economist
Arab Report and Record
Arab World
ARAMCO World Magazine
Asian and African Studies: Journal of the Israel Oriental Society
British Society for Middle Eastern Studies: Bulletin
Bulletin of the School of Oriental and African Studies
Cahiers de l'Orient Contemporaine

Central Bank of Egypt Economic Review
Commentary
Contemporary Jewry: A Journal of Sociological Inquiry
Der Islam
Die Welt des Islams
L'Egypte Contemporaine
International Journal of Middle East Studies
Iranian Studies
Israel Magazine
Jerusalem Journal of International Relations
Jerusalem Quarterly
Jeune Afrique
Jewish Journal of Sociology
Jewish Observer and Middle East Review
Journal of Arabic Literature
Journal of Energy and Development
Journal of the Middle East
Journal of Modern African Studies
Journal of Palestine Studies
Journal of South Asian and Middle Eastern Studies
Journal of the Royal Central Asian Society
Maghreb Review
Maghreb-Machrek
Mideast Observer
Middle East
Middle East Economic Digest
Middle East Economic Survey
Middle East Forum
Middle East International
Middle East Journal
Middle East Monitor
Middle East Record
Middle East Report
Middle East Review
Middle East Research and Information Project (MERIP) Reports
Middle East Studies Association Bulletin
Middle Eastern Affairs (1950–1963)
Middle Eastern Studies
Midstream
The Mizan Newsletter: A Review of Soviet Writing on the Middle East
    (1959–1971)
Le Monde Diplomatique
Muslim World
National Bank of Egypt Economic Bulletin
Near East Report
New Middle East (1968–1973)
New Outlook
Orient (1957–1969)
Orient: German Journal for Politics and Economics of the Middle East

Oriente Moderno
Quarterly Index Islamicus
Record of the Arab World
Revue des Etudes Islamiques
Revue Egyptienne de Droit International

Books

Abdel-Fadil, Mahmud (1975) *Development, Income-Distribution and Social Change in Rural Egypt (1952–1970)*. Cambridge: Cambridge University Press.

Abdel-Malek, Anouar (1968) *Egypt: Military Society*. Tr. C.L. Markmann New York: Random House.

Abul-Fath, Ahmed (1962) *L'Affaire Nasser*. Paris: Plon.

Ahmad, Jamal Mohammad (1960) *The Intellectual Origins of Egyptian Nationalism*. New York: Oxford University Press.

Baker, Raymond William (1978) *Egypt's Uncertain Revolution Under Nasser and Sadat*. Cambridge, Mass.: Harvard University.

Be'eri, Eliezer (1970) *Army Officers in Arab Politics and Society*. New York: Praeger.

Berger, Morroe (1957) *Bureaucracy and Social Change in Modern Egypt*. Princeton: Princeton.

_____ (1970) *Islam in Egypt Today*. Princeton: Princeton University Press.

_____ (1960) *Military Elites and Social Change in Egypt Since Napoleon*. Princeton, N.J.: Center for International Studies, Princeton University.

Binder, Leonard (1964) *The Ideological Revolution in the Middle East*. New York: John Wiley.

_____ (1978) *In A Moment of Enthusiasm: Power and the Second Stratum in Egypt*. Chicago: University at Chicago Press.

De kmejian, R.H. (1971) *Egypt Under Nasir*. Albany: SUNY.

_____ (1975) *Patterns of Political Leadership: Lebanon, Israel, Egypt*. Albany, N.Y.: State University of New York.

Estier, Claude (1965) *L'Égypte en révolution*. Paris: Juillard.

Farid, Saleh (1970) *Top Management in Egypt: Its Structure, Quality and Problems*. Santa Monica: Rand Corporation.

Halpern, Manfred (1963) *The Politics of Social Change in the Middle East and North Africa*. Princeton: Princeton University Press.

Harik, Ilya (1974) *The Political Mobilization of Peasants*. Bloomington, Indiana: Indiana University Press.

Heikal, Mohamed (1973) *The Cairo Documents*. New York: Doubleday.

_____ (1975) *The Road to Ramadan*. New York: Readers Digest Press.

Hurewitz, Jacob C. (1969) *Middle East Politics: The Military Dimension*. New York: Praeger.

Hussein, Mahmoud (1973) *Class and Class Conflict in Egypt, 1945–1970*. New York: Monthly Review Press, 1973.

Issawi, Charles (1963) *Egypt in Revolution*. London: Oxford University Press.

Kerr, Malcolm H. (1971) *The Arab Cold War*. 3rd ed., New York: Oxford University Press.

Khadduri, Majid (1973) *Arab Contemporaries*. Baltimore, Md.: Johns Hopkins University Press.

―――― (1970) *Political Trends in the Arab World*. Baltimore, Md.: Johns Hopkins University Press.

Lacouture, Jean and Simone (1958) *Egypt in Transition*. London: Metheuen.

Lacouture, Jean (1973) *Nassser*. New York: Alfred Knopf. Tr. Daniel Hofstadter.

Little, Tom (1967) *Egypt*. New York: Praeger.

Mabro, Robert (1974) *The Egyptian Economy, 1952–1972*. London: Oxford University Press.

Mansfield, Peter (1969) *Nasser*. London: Metheuen.

Mayfield, James B. (1971) *Rural Politics in Nasser's Egypt: A Quest for Legitimacy*. Austin, Texas: University of Texas Press.

Mitchell, Richard P. (1969) *The Society of Muslim Brothers*. London: Oxford University Press.

Moore, Clement Henry (1981) *Images of Development*. Cambridge, Mass.: MIT.

Naguib, Mohammed (1955) *Egypt's Destiny*. Garden City, N.Y.: Doubleday.

Nasser, Gamel Abdel (1954) *The Philosophy of the Revolution*. Washington, D.C.: Public Affairs Press.

Nyrop, Richard F., et. al. (1976) *Area Handbook for Egypt.*, 3rd ed., Washington, D.C.: United States Government Printing Office.

O'Brien, Patrick (1967) *The Revolution in Egypt's Economy: From Private Enterprise to Socialism*. London: Oxford University Press.

Perlmutter, Amos (1974) *Egypt: Praetorian State*. New Brunswick, N.J.: Transaction.

―――― (1977) *The Military and Politics in Modern Times*. New Haven, Conn.: Yale University Press

Qubain, Fahim I (1966) *Education and Science in the Arab World*. Baltimore, Maryland: Johns Hopkins University Press.

Rejwan, Nissim (1974) *Nasserist Ideology: Its Exponents and Critics*. New York: Wiley.

Riad, Hassan (1964) *L'Égypte nasserienne*. Paris: Editons de Menuit.

Sadat, Anwar (1957) *Revolt on the Nile*. London: Allen Wingate.

―――― (1977) *In Search of Identity*. New York: Harper.

Safran, Nadav (1961) *Egypt in Search of Political Community*. Cambridge, Mass., Harvard University Press.

St. John, Robert (1960) *The Boss*. New York: McGraw-Hill.

Sayed, Salah el- (1978) *Workers' Participation in Management* (Cairo: AUC Press.

Stephens, Robert (1971) *Nasser*. London: Penguin.

Vatikiotis, P.J., ed. (1968) *Egypt Since the Revolution*. New York: Praeger.

Vatikiotis, P.J. (1961) *The Egyptian Army in Politics*. Bloomington, Ind.: Indiana University Press.

―――― (1969) *The Modern History of Egypt*. London: Weidenfeld & Nicolson.

―――― (1978) *Nasser and His Generation*. London: Croom, Helm.

Vaucher, Georges (1959, 1960) *Gamal Abdel Nasser et son équipe*. Paris: Rene Juillard.

Waterbury, John (1979) *Egypt: Burdens of the Past, Options for the Future*. Bloomington, Indiana: Indiana University Press.

Wheelock, Keith (1960) *Nasser's New Egypt*. New York: Praeger.
Wilber, Donald N. (1969) *United Arab Republic: Its People, Its Society, Its Culture*. New Haven, Conn.: HRAF Press.
Wynn, Wilton (1959) *Nasser of Egypt: The Search for Dignity*. Cambridge, Mass.: Arlington Books.

Articles

Akhavi, Shahrough (1975a) "Egypt: Neo-Patrimonial Elite," in *Political Elites and Political Development in the Middle East*. ed. Frank Tachau. Cambridge, Mass.: Schenkman Publishers. pp. 69–114.
Akhavi, Shahrough (1975b) "Egypt's Socialism and Marxist Thought: Some Preliminary Observations on Social Theory and Metaphysics," *Comparative Studies in Society and History*, XVII, 2 (April), pp. 190–211.
_____ (1971) "Political Participation in a Military Society: The ASU in Egypt," paper delivered at 5th Conference of the Middle East Studies Association, Denver, Colorado (11–13, Nov.).
_____ (1978) "Radicalism and the Military: The Egyptian Army as a Contingent Factor," Typescript. SUNY Conversations in the Discipline Symposium Paper. (April 20–22) Fredonia, New York.
Aulas, Marie-Christine (1976) "Sadat's Egypt," *New Left Review*, No. 98. (July-August), pp. 84–95.
Awad, Louis (1968) "Cultural and Intellectual Developments in Egypt Since 1952," in *Egypt Since the Revolution*. ed. P.J. Vatikiotis. New York: Praeger, pp. 143–61.
Badeau, John S. (1955) "The Role in Search of a Hero: A Brief Study of the Egyptian Revolution," *Middle East Journal*, IX, 4 (Fall), pp. 373–84.
Be'eri, Eliezer (1966) "Social Class and Family Background of the Egyptian Army Officer Class," *Asian and African Studies*, 2, pp. 1–38.
Binder, Leonard (1965) "Egypt: The Integrative Revolution," in *Political Culture and Political Development*, ed. Lucian Pye and Sidney Verba. Princeton, N.J.: Princeton University Press, pp. 396–449.
_____ (1966) "Political Recruitment and Political Participation in Egypt," in *Political Participation and Political Development*, ed. by Joseph La Palombara and Myron Weiner. Princeton, N.J.: Princeton University Press, pp. 217–40.
Bowie, Leland (1976) "Charisma, Weber and Nasir," *Middle East Journal*, XXX, 2 (Spring), pp. 141–57.
Buttner, Friedemann (1979) "Political Stability without Stable Institutions: The Retraditionalization of Egypt's Polity," *Orient: Deutsche Zeitschrift für Politik und Wirtschaft* XX, 1: 53–67.
Cowen, David (1968) "Literary Trends in Egypt Since 1952," in *Egypt Since the Revolution*, ed. P.J. Vatikiotis. New York: Praeger, pp. 162–77.
Crabbs, Jack Jr. (1975) "Politics, History and Culture in Nasser's Egypt," *International Journal of Middle East Studies*, Vol. VI., No. 4 (October), pp. 386–420.
Crecelius, Daniel (1966) "Al-Azhar in the Revolution," *Middle East Journal*, XX, 1 (Winter), pp. 31–49.

Crecelius, Daniel (1971) "Non-Ideological Responses of the Egyptian Ulama to Modernization," in *Scholars, Saints and Sufis*, ed. Nikki Keddie. Berkeley: University of California, pp. 167–209.

Dekmejian, R.H. (1976) "Marx, Weber and the Egyptian Revolution," *Middle East Journal*, XXX, (Spring), pp. 158–172.

Dekmejian, R.H. and Kamal El-Dahry (1976) "Elites and Public Policy: The Egyptian Budgetary Process," paper presented to 10th Conference of the Middle East Studies Association, Los Angeles, California, (10–13 November).

Entelis, John P. (1974) "Nasser's Egypt: The Failure of Charismatic Leadership," *Orbis*, XVIII, 2 (Summer), pp. 451–464.

Feit, Edward (1973) "Egypt: Modern Military-Administrative Rule in an Ancient State, 1952–1970," in Feit, *The Armed Bureaucrats*. Boston: Houghton Mifflin, pp. 132–63.

Halpern, Manfred (1969) "Egypt and the New Middle Class: Reaffirmations and New Explorations," *Comparative Studies in Society and History*, XI, 4 (October), pp. 97–108.

_____ (1962) "Middle Eastern Armies and the New Middle Class," in *The Role of the Military in Underdeveloped Countries*. Princeton, N.J.: Princeton University Press, pp. 277–315.

_____ (1970) "The Problem of Becoming Conscious of a Salaried New Middle Class," *Comparative Studies in Society and History*, Vol. XVII, No. 1 (January), pp. 27–30.

Harik, Ilya (1971) "Opinion Leaders and the Mass Media in Rural Egypt: A Reconsideration of the Two-Step Flow of Communications Hypothesis," *APSR*, LXV, 3 (September), pp. 731–40.

_____ (1972) "Mobilization Policy and Political Change in Rural Egypt," in *Rural Politics and Social Change in the Middle East*. ed. Richard Antoun and Ilya Harik. Bloomington, Indiana: Indiana University Press, pp. 287–334.

Harik, Ilya (1973) "The Single Party as a Subordinate Movement," *World Politics*, XXVI, 1 (October), pp. 80–105.

Heaphy, James (1965) "The Organization of Egypt," *World Politics*. Vol. XVIII, No. 2 (January), pp. 177–93.

Humphreys, R. Steven (1979) "Islam and Political Values in Saudi Arabia, Egypt and Syria," Middle East Journal, XXXIII (Winter), pp. 1–19.

Kerr, Malcolm H. (1963) "Arab Radical Notions of Democracy," St. Antony's Paper's #16 (Middle Eastern Studies #3), London: Chatto & Windus, pp. 9–40.

_____ (1965) "Egypt," in *Education and Political Development*, ed. James S. Coleman. Princeton: Princeton University Press, pp. 169–94.

_____ (1962) "The Emergence of a Socialist Ideology in Egypt," *Middle East Journal*, XVI (Autumn), pp. 127–144.

_____ (1975) "The Failure of Nasserism as a Belief System," in *The Economics and Politics of the Middle East*, ed. A. Becker, et. al., New York: American Elsevier, pp. 41–54.

Kirk, George (1963) "The Role of the Military in Society and Government in Egypt," in *The Military in the Middle East: Problems in Society and Government*. Columbus, Ohio: Ohio State University Press, pp. 71–88.

Khadduri, Majid (1953) "The Role of the Military in Middle East Politics," *American Political Science Review*, XXXXVIII, 2 (June), pp. 511–24.

McCann-Erikson Advertising Company, Ltd. (1977) "McCann-Erickson/Egypt/ Decision Makers," London. Summary report.

Moore, Clement Henry (1974) "Authoritarian Politics in Unincorporated Society: the Case of Nasser's Egypt," *Comparative Politics*, VI, 2 (January), pp. 193–218.

_____ (1971) "On Theory and Practice Among the Arabs," *World Politics*, XXIV (October), pp. 106–26.

Moore, Clement Henry. (1978) "The Reproduction of a Bourgeoisie." Paper delivered to The MIT-Cairo University Faculty Seminar, MIT, Cambridge, Mass. (May)

O'Kane, Joseph P. (1972) "Islam in the New Egyptian Constitution," *Middle East Journal*, XXVI, 2 (Spring), pp. 137–48.

Perlmutter, Amos (1970) "The Arab Military Elite," *World Politics*, XXII, 2 (January), pp. 269–300.

_____ (1967) "Egypt and the Myth of the New Middle Class: A Comparative Analysis," *Comparative Studies in Society and History*, X, 1 (October), pp. 46–65.

_____ (1970) "The Myth of the Myth of the New Middle Class: Some Lessons in Social and Political Theory," *Comparative Studies in Society and History*. Vol. XII, no. 1 (January), pp. 14–26.

Reid, Donald M. (1974a) "The National Bar Association and Egyptian Politics, 1912–1952," *International Journal of African Historical Studies*, VII, 4, pp. 608–46.

_____ (1974b) "The Rise of Professions and Professional Organization in Modern Egypt," *Comparative Studies in Society and History*, Vol. XVI, no. 1 (January), pp. 24–57.

Rodinson, Maxime (1968) "The Political System," in *Egypt Since the Revolution*, ed. P.J. Vatikiotis. New York: Praeger.

Semaan, Khalil I.H. (1968) "A New Source for the Biography of Jamal Abdal-Nasir," *Muslim World*, 58, 3 (July), pp. 242–52.

Shamir, Shimon (1973) "The Marxists in Egypt: The Licensed Infiltration Doctrine in Practice," in *The USSR and the Middle East*, ed. Michael Confino and Shimon Shamir. New York: Wiley, pp. 293–319.

Sharp, Walter (1957) "Bureaucracy and Politics — Egyptian Model," in *Toward the Comparative Study of Public Administration*, ed. William J. Siffin. Bloomington, Indiana: Indiana University Press, pp. 145–78.

Springborg, Robert (1975) "Patterns of Association in the Egyptian Political Elite," in *political Elites in the Middle East*, ed. George Lenczowski. Washington, D.C.: American Enterprise Institute for Public Policy Research, pp. 83–107.

_____ (1979) "Patrimonialism and Policy Making in Egypt," *Middle Eastern Studies*, XV, 1 (January).

_____ (1978) "Professional Syndicates in Egyptian Politics, 1952–1970," *International Journal of Middle East Studies*, IX, 3, (August), pp. 275–95.

Szyliowicz, Joseph (1973) "The Arab Republic of Egypt," in Szyliowicz, *Education and Modernization in the Middle East*. Ithaca, New York: Cornell University Press, pp. 253–324.

Vatikiotis, P.J. (1961) "Dilemmas of Political Leadership in the Arab Middle East: The Cast of the U·A·R·," *American Political Science Review*, LV, 1 (March), pp. 103–11.

‾‾‾‾‾‾ (1968) "Some Political Consequences of the 1952 Revolution in Egypt," in *political and Social Change in Modern Egypt*. London: Oxford, pp. 362–387.

Waterbury, John (1976) "Corruption, Political Stability and Development: Some Comparative Evidence from Egypt and Morocco," *Government and Opposition*, XI, 4 (Autumn), pp. 426–445.

Zartman, I. William (1974) "The Study of Elite Circulation," *Comparative Politics*, 7, 3 (April), pp. 465–88.

‾‾‾‾‾‾ (1963) "The United Arab Republic (Egypt)," in *Government and Politics in North Africa*. New York: Praeger, pp. 102–124.

Newspapers

al-Ahram (Cairo)
Christian Science Monitor
The Daily Star (*Beirut*)
Daily Telegraph (*London*)
The Egyptian Gazette
Le Figaro (*Paris*)
France-Soir (Paris)
Frankfurter Allgemeine Zeitung
The Guardian (*Manchester*)
The Jerusalem Post
Le Jour (*Beirut*)
Le Monde
Neue Zürcher Zeitung
The New York Times
La Nouvelle Observateur (*Paris*)
The Observer (*Loondon*)
L'Orient (*Beirut*)
The Times (*London*)
Washington Post
Die Welt

Index